Publication of / de

THE SUPREME COURT OF CANADA / LA SOCIÉTÉ HISTORIQUE DE
HISTORICAL SOCIETY / LA COUR SUPREME DU CANADA

Edited by / Sous la direction de

DeLloyd J. Guth

Volume I for 1991

Published by / Publié par

Carleton University Press
Ottawa, Canada
1991

CHIEF JUSTICE WILLIAM JOHNSTONE RITCHIE

RESPONSIBLE GOVERNMENT AND JUDICIAL REVIEW

Gordon Bale

Carleton University Press,
Ottawa, Canada
1991

©Carleton University Press Inc. 1991

ISBN 0-88629-134-8

Printed and bound in Canada

Carleton Library Series 165

Canadian Cataloguing in Publication Data
  Bale, Gordon
    Chief Justice William Johnstone Ritchie

  (The Carleton Library ; 165)
  Includes bibliographical references.
  ISBN 0-88629-134-8

    1. Ritchie, W.J. (William Johnstone), Sir, 1813-1892.
  2. Canada. Supreme Court—Biography. 3. Judges—
  Canada—Biography. I. Title. II. Series.

  KE8248.R48B34 1991   347.71'03534   C90-090436-4

Distributed by: Oxford University Press Canada,
                70 Wynford Drive,
                Don Mills, Ontario,
                Canada. M3C 1J9
                (416) 441-2941

Cover design: Aerographics Ottawa

Acknowledgements

Carleton University Press gratefully acknowledges the support
extended to its publishing programme by the Canada Council
and the Ontario Arts Council.

The Supreme Court of Canada Historical Society gratefully
acknowledges the grant in aid of publication for this volume,
made by the Minister of Justice and the Attorney General of
Canada.

Table of Contents

Foreword

This first volume from the Supreme Court of Canada Historical Society offers new beginnings at the end of my own career. As in ancient times, an inauguration allows one "to take omens", in this instance to declare that this Society will make the Court's past more accessible to present and future Canadians.

In 1875, Canada saw the birth of its Supreme Court, as a general court of appeal for the entire Dominion. But throughout its first seventy-five years, the Supreme Court was not truly supreme because its judgments could be appealed to the Judicial Committee of the Privy Council. Indeed, judgments in the provinces could be appealed directly to the Privy Council, without reference to the Supreme Court of Canada. Whatever history the Court made was within the shadow cast from Council chambers in Downing Street, London. Back in Ottawa, the Court's history likewise was not seen as a subject worthy of independent study by lawyers and historians.

The situation changed gradually but dramatically after World War II. Canadian appeals to London ended after 1949. In 1975, the Court acquired control over its own docket through the introduction of the requirement that leave be granted by the Court, for almost all appeals. Then, in 1982, the repatriation of the Constitution included the Charter of Rights and Freedoms, significantly enhancing the importance of the Court. This gave recognition to principles that transcend ordinary parliamentary legislation and that the courts, ultimately the Supreme Court of Canada, must interpret and apply in specific cases. At about this same time, the Court's first formal history appeared, sponsored by The Osgoode Society and written by Professors Snell and Vaughan.

Some have called this recent era the Court's coming of age. If that metaphor is accepted, it suggests that the Court's potential has been present since birth, in 1875. That is precisely what Professor Gordon Bale's important book now documents. It is singularly appropriate that the Society's first volume should introduce us to the Court's origins and to its most distinguished first member. William Johnstone Ritchie, masterfully presented by Professor Bale, was a politician who promoted the concept that government must be responsible to its electorate and a judge who introduced to Canada the principle that legislatures, provincial and federal, are subject to judicial review.

Professor Bale's biography proves again that the study of such constitutional issues cannot be severed from historical origins, social contexts, and — perhaps most importantly — the persons who shaped them. The world and century that was Chief Justice Ritchie's come alive again, thanks to this rich narrative of anecdotes, personalities and events. These have been skillfully researched to reveal a thriving legal culture in the Maritimes: the student apprentice of law, the struggling practitioner, the reforming politician, and then the dedicated trial and appellate judge. Ritchie brought a wealth of jurisprudential experience to Ottawa in 1875 and, when named the Court's second Chief Justice in 1879, proved to be just the sort of able administrator that the new Court needed.

This book and this Society arrive at a most timely point in our country's history. Read in the context of the Charter, the book shows a consistent strand from before 1875 through 1982 to 1991. Parliament, Charter, and Court now combine as the highest expression of national sovereignty and of Canada's commitment to the rule of law.

The Supreme Court of Canada Historical Society now exists to inspire public awareness of our country's unique English and French legal heritages, specifically in appellate jurisdictions. I am delighted to welcome the Society, to wish its membership well, and to encourage its commitment to excellence in legal and judicial history.

Brian Dickson
Chief Justice of Canada (1984-1990)
Ottawa
December 1990

Introduction

This volume admirably fulfills the first aim of The Supreme Court of Canada Historical Society, which is "to promote public knowledge of the history of the Supreme Court of Canada and related appellate courts." Professor Gordon Bale's pen portrait of William Johnstone Ritchie places before the reader the many contexts making up Canada's nineteenth-century court-based and legislated laws. Through Ritchie's words and actions we see how he studied law in the 1830s and how he practiced it in a Maritime town of the 1840s. At mid-century, we are plunged with Ritchie into the flow of a colony's political system, one that is channelled by patronage and privilege and that prefers accountability to *outremer* Westminster bureaucrats in the Colonial Office rather than to its own citizenry.

With formal politics out of his system, we next witness Ritchie's world from the trial bench, settling disputes involving both the mundane and the mighty. With the emergence of Canada in the turbulent 1860s, we catch glimpses of how this one judge judged, and even those rare occasions when he did not judge. For the ten years after 1865, Ritchie's world of law expands again, as chief justice in a colony that becomes a province in the Confederation of 1867. When he moves west eight years later to Canada's frontier capital, he leaves forever the old, local law practised in his younger, more settled days in New Brunswick. As a founding member of the Supreme Court of Canada, Ritchie is expected to fashion new law for the new nation, primarily out of the old law of England. But by the last decade of the nineteenth century it is clear that that is too large a charge for a Court that avoids novelty and lacks finality in its judgments. In 1892, Ritchie must bequeath a nascent Supreme Court to his country that remains accountable to another *outremer* Westminster bureaucracy, the Judicial Committee of the Privy Council.

Almost a century after his death, the story of Ritchie's life looms large enough to be a constitutional biography of young Canada itself. The issues that still confound debates over federal-provincial distribution of powers, and over the law-declaring roles of parliaments and judiciaries, faced Ritchie in New Brunswick and Ottawa. Gordon Bale gives us two basic constitutional documents in his book's Appendices, hitherto not readily available. They elegantly set out opposing arguments on final accountability for law-making in a parliamentary democracy.

Judge Steadman in 1868 championed a legislative supremacy that would soon be identified with A.V. Dicey in England, leaving review only to the next electorate. Judge Ritchie in 1870 urged that courts render "uniform judgments on the constitutionality and construction of all Dominion and Provincial statutes." Legislatures could always enact new statutes in response to such judgments. But the potential for sequential majoritarian excesses by legislatures would be checked. As Professor Bale shows, our legislatures had faced, debated and courageously resolved the matter, in Canada's Parliament and in the likes of New Brunswick's House of Assembly. By 1875, Ritchie's view prevailed. Canada had created a delicate constitutional balance whereby electorates, legislatures, their cabinets, and the judiciary had an interconnected accountability. Ritchie's story, as told by Gordon Bale, vitally reconstructs that formative era in Canadian law.

This book immeasurably helps the Society to initiate another of its objectives, "to encourage research into all aspects of the Court and related appellate courts in Canada, including the Judicial Committee of the Privy Council." Gordon Bale here sets a standard for research, analysis, argument and writing which the Society's subsequent annual volumes will find difficult to surpass. Despite a paucity of personal evidence surviving for Ritchie, Bale pieces together a most persuasive institutional biography. The Society remains in his debt for giving the greater part of four years to this project.

During that same time the Society itself has had its slow birth. A one-time grant from the Ministry of Justice, Ottawa, has provided $5,000 for start-up expenses and a $7,500 subvention for publication of this first volume. The Society gratefully acknowledges this support and hastens to add its commitment to be henceforth financially self-sufficient. The Dean and Faculty of

Law at the University of British Columbia have continued to give generous secretarial and communications support for the Society's development, as well as every encouragement to my efforts.

The Society began to exist informally when its founding Directors met at the Court in Ottawa on 8 June 1987, at the request of its present Executive Editor and with Chief Justice Brian Dickson's strong encouragement. The original idea grew out of conversations between James C. MacPherson, then the Courts's Executive Legal Officer, and myself. Among the members of that Court, the late Justice Julien Chouinard extended his gentle enthusiasm in ways that the Society now thankfully recognises, by dedicating this first volume to his memory.

Incorporated in Canada under Letters Patent dated 24 June 1988, this Society is dedicated "to foster understanding of the Court's contemporary role in the Canadian judicial system." To do so, Canadian courts and citizens urgently need routine reminding that their present makes no sense without their past, be it the last week or the last century. This Society defines itself for just that national mnemonic mission. It will actively encourage records management and archival policies within the Court, encourage the aims and research objectives of the Court's Library, and seek public and private support for all matters touching the Court's heritage. In pursuit of its general goal for public judicial education, this Society remains critically independent of the Court itself, answerable to its membership by way of its Board of Directors.

DeLloyd J. Guth,
Executive Editor
February 1991

Preface

This book began in 1987 with my short biographical sketch of William Johnstone Ritchie for the *Dictionary of Canadian Biography*. The editors invited me to assess his work on the Supreme Court of Canada, from 1875 until his death in 1892, while a Maritime co-author was to tackle the first 62 years of his life. Unfortunately Ritchie left no diaries, memoirs, or other private papers and exceedingly few of his letters survive. Discouraged by the lack of primary materials, my collaborator withdrew. However by then Ritchie's story had taken on a new life for me and I decided to persevere. With the able research assistance of Bruce Mellett, at that time a second year law student, we pieced together Ritchie's years in the Maritimes from scatterings of primary evidence.

The project might have ended there but for the happy coincidence of the birth of the Supreme Court of Canada Historical Society whose executive editor, Dr. DeLloyd J. Guth, (Faculty of Law, University of British Columbia), took a major interest in this biography and offered much encouragement and valuable advice. I am greatly indebted to him. Special thanks also are due to Professor David G. Bell (Faculty of Law, University of New Brunswick) who has generously and unstintingly made available to me any Ritchie material which he uncovered in the course of his own research. He and Dr. Guth took time and trouble to comment extensively on two earlier versions of the work. Professor J. Murray Beck, Mr. Gordon Fairweather, Q.C. and the Honourable William F. Ryan also very kindly read the manuscript and offered many helpful suggestions.

One of the great incidental benefits of this research has been the opportunity to meet Charles S.A. Ritchie (the brother of the late Mr. Justice Roland Ritchie) and his wife Sylvia (the granddaughter of the Chief Justice). They have graciously received me on a number of occasions and have given generously of their time and their family recollections. Other family members who have kindly responded to requests for information are Major General Roger Rowley, Mr. Justice David Ritchie Chipman of the Supreme Court of Nova Scotia, Appeal Division and Mr. James H. Smellie (Osler, Hoskin & Harcourt). Almost a century has passed since the death of the Chief Justice, during which time much has been lost within the family memory.

Any biography is a composite memoir, reconstructed out of the subject's contemporary evidence and the author's mental encounters with it. In helping me along this way, I have become indebted to Professor Wilbur F. Bowker, Q.C., Ms. Lorna Hutchinson, Professor Ann G. Condon, Dr. Franklin O. Leger, Q.C., Mrs. Percy Jones, Mr. and Mrs. Charles Murray and Mr. Richard A. Wagner. I am grateful to the staff of the National Archives of Canada, Public Archives of Nova Scotia, the New Brunswick Archives, Saint John Museum and Queen's University Archives for their assistance.

My thanks extend to Angela Reda who painstakingly typed the manuscript, met deadlines by working overtime and remained cheerful even after several revisions. I owe special thanks to Norman Siebrasse, a diligent research assistant, who contributed many thoughtful insights. A Queen's University Advisory Research Committee Grant permitted me to secure his assistance.

Finally but of paramount importance is the contribution made by my wife, Maureen. In addition to reading every chapter and making many helpful suggestions, she participated actively in accumulating material about Ritchie. Appendix 3, The Ritchie Lawyers and Judges, embodies some of her genealogical research on the Ritchie family. Most of all, I thank her for her constancy and encouragement.

Gordon Bale
Kingston, Ontario
March 1991

CHAPTER 1
Maritime Roots

If "what's bred in the bone will come out in the flesh," then law has been the backbone of the Ritchie family.[1] Thomas Ritchie, who was called to the bar in about 1798,[2] was the progenitor of a family whose record as lawyers and judges is unparalleled in Canadian history, with the possible exception of the Taschereau family. Five sons, eleven grandsons, five great-grandsons and three great-great-grandsons[3] followed Thomas Ritchie into the legal profession, and no fewer than six of this group went to the bench in Canada, including three of Thomas Ritchie's sons.[4]

One of Thomas's sons was Sir William Johnstone Ritchie[5] who, as one of the original puisne judges and as the second chief justice of the Supreme Court of Canada, achieved the most prominent position of all Ritchie lawyers. Called to the bar in the same year Victoria ascended the British throne (1837), and knighted on her sixty-second birthday, he died in the fifty-fifth year of her reign, an erstwhile representative of the Victorian values of classic, nineteenth-century liberalism. In his adopted colony of New Brunswick, he staunchly advocated responsible government and supported economic progress and development. As a judge, he became the father of judicial review in Canada, based on his decision in *R. v. Chandler*.[6] As a lawyer and judge, he kept the Ritchie family's hand firmly on the tiller of Maritime jurisprudence for six decades. At his death in 1892, he had seen the Supreme Court of Canada through its infancy, giving it stable, nurturing leadership.

William Johnstone Ritchie's grandfather was John Ritchie, who in 1770 emigrated from Glasgow, Scotland, on board the *Glasco* bound for Boston, Massachusetts Colony.[7] His father's death and the urgings of his uncle Andrew Ritchie, who had emigrated earlier, probably prompted the move. John and his wife Janet moved into the home of his uncle, who also set him up in business. However, by 1775 John, now a widower with an infant son, had moved to Annapolis Royal, Nova Scotia, where he soon married

Alicia Maria LeCain, the daughter of Francis Barclay LeCain. William Johnstone's father, Thomas, was John Ritchie's second son, born to Alicia on 21 September 1777.

John Ritchie's industry, together with his marriage into a well-established Annapolis family, helped him achieve social prominence. Because of this he was among several men who asked the government in Halifax for aid to resist a possible attack by American revolutionaries, and on 22 May 1779 he became captain of a company of light infantry. In 1781 two rebel schooners surprised the town and all able-bodied men were captured. John became a hostage and was later released in exchange for an American held prisoner in Halifax. The ignominy of this event caused John to resign his commission. However, his public standing remained unaffected and in a by-election in 1783 he entered the House of Assembly, only to be defeated in a general election in 1785. Subsequently, on 22 April 1786, he became a lay justice of the Inferior Court of Common Pleas. During this period generally John Ritchie's shipping business flourished and he accommodated his family in a comfortable lifestyle. Unfortunately, he lost several ships at sea and died suddenly on 20 July 1790, aged forty-five years, leaving his widow and four children in straitened circumstances. But Alicia LeCain Ritchie, strong-willed and competent, raised her children well with the support of the LeCain and Andrew Ritchie families.

Thomas Ritchie, thirteen years old when his father died, received his education locally — an education enhanced by contact with the many well-educated and cultivated Loyalists who had settled in Annapolis Royal. Thomas Barclay, a renowned lawyer who studied under the first chief justice of the Supreme Court of the United States, John Jay, took Thomas Ritchie into his office. After Thomas received his call to the bar he continued in association with Barclay until the latter was appointed British consul general at New York in 1799. Ritchie succeeded to Barclay's lucrative practice at the age of twenty-two, and handled it with great energy and ability.

In 1806 Thomas Ritchie turned his attention to public affairs in Annapolis County and was elected to the House of Assembly where he sat, unopposed, for eighteen years. In 1808 he proposed a bill to regulate Negro servitude. A measure of questionable wisdom that would have compensated slave owners, it failed to be enacted. An active member of the Assembly, he received recognition

"The Grange"

Adams-Ritchie House

as one of the four men who guided its deliberations in the 1820s. On 10 March 1824 he became a justice of the Inferior Court of Common Pleas.

On 30 June 1807 Thomas Ritchie married Elizabeth Wildman Johnston, daughter of William Martin Johnston, a physician practising in Jamaica. They initially lived in what is now known as the Adams-Ritchie house on St. George Street.[8] In about 1810 Ritchie erected a mansion called "The Grange" between two stretches of water, the Annapolis River and Allen Creek.[9] It had three storeys, containing eleven bedrooms and a basement with kitchen, servants' hall and dairy. Fine oak and elm trees grew around the house which was surrounded by a high hawthorne hedge. There was also a terraced garden, "the like of which was not known elsewhere in the Province,"[10] which remained open to visitors on Sunday.

After moving into "The Grange," Thomas Ritchie retained the Adams-Ritchie house and continued to conduct his law practice from there. He displayed maritime enterprise as well. During the War of 1812-14 with the United States, he and two other residents of Annapolis Royal bought and fitted the schooners *Matilda* and *Broke*. The *Matilda*, a fifty-ton vessel commanded by Captain John Burkett and carrying forty armed men, outdid all Nova Scotia privateers in 1813 by capturing twelve prize vessels.[11] The booty from this activity enabled Thomas Ritchie to improve and beautify "The Grange."

William Johnstone Ritchie was born at "The Grange" on 28 October 1813, the third son of Thomas Ritchie. His mother's family seems to have played a significant role in his upbringing. Her brother, J.W. Johnston, later premier of Nova Scotia, studied law with Thomas Ritchie just prior to William's birth. More significantly her mother, Elizabeth Lichtenstein Johnston, had been a prominent figure in the Thomas Ritchie household, having taken up residence there during William's early childhood. According to Mary Ritchie, in a family biography:

> I think there was an incompatibility of temper between Mrs. Johnstone and Thomas Ritchie, which probably she alone felt. She was a woman of great character and deeply and evangelically religious. The line between the "godly and the ungodly" was clear cut in her mind, and I fear Thomas and his mother seemed to her on the wrong side of the line. From the pictures and the stories of him, Thomas Ritchie was a downright, perhaps a domineering man, and it may be, not always sensitive to the feelings of others. ...

> [Mrs. Johnstone] was a much travelled, widely read woman, and she brought an intellectual and religious influence into the young Ritchie's [sic] lives, to which they owed a great deal in the future.[12]

The maternal grandmother's influence became more important with the death of William's mother in 1819. Eliza Ritchie left a family of five boys and two girls. Thomas Ritchie would remarry twice and have two more children from his third marriage.

Against this crowded background little is known about the young William Ritchie's early years. Some sixty years later, however, some inhabitants of Annapolis remembered him as a "rollicking, rosy-cheeked, bright-eyed boy, full of fun and animal spirits."[13] No doubt memories glow with age and fame, but there is no reason to think that a carefree boyhood could not grow out of a busy, dour, professional family.

He received his education at the Pictou Academy under Thomas McCulloch, a Presbyterian minister and the founder of the academy. This academy was incorporated by an act of the Nova Scotia legislature in 1816.[14] Prior to that time King's College at Windsor was the only institution for higher education in Nova Scotia. King's College was controlled by the Church of England, and so the founders of Pictou Academy intended their school especially for dissenters. Pictou Academy's incorporation bill as introduced and passed by the Assembly contained no religious tests. In order to avoid arousing the antagonism of supporters of King's College, the trustees did not seek the right to confer degrees, though it was intended "to impart the education usual in colleges."[15] However, the Council, dominated by leaders of the Church of England, took alarm at creating an institution which might "form a rallying point for dissenters against the Church."[16] As a result, the bill passed by the Council required all trustees, masters or teachers to be "members of the Church of England, as by Law Established" or to profess "the Presbyterian Religion, as the same is declared in the Westminister Confession of Faith."[17] There was an express proviso that no religious tests should extend to the scholars or the pupils of the academy. It was not until 1832 that Pictou Academy became non-sectarian, with the total abolition of all religious tests for both trustees and teachers. The 1832 act stated that the academy "shall not be confined to persons called Presbyterian"[18] and no theological lectures were to be delivered. When William Ritchie enrolled there, the school's function was to educate young men most of whom were Presbyterians and some of whom became Presbyterian clergymen. Although there was no attempt made by Pictou Academy to exclude members of the Church of England, it was not expected that Pictou would appeal to them. Why then did the son of a prominent and well-to-do Church of England family choose to attend Pictou Academy? King's College in Windsor was closer to Annapolis Royal but an education at Pictou was less expensive. Thomas Chandler Haliburton, a graduate of King's College who later became a judge and noted author, estimated that it cost a young man £120 a year to attend King's College, where students lived within the college walls on the plan of an Oxford college, but only £20 to board in a home at Pictou.[19] However, John Ritchie, William's eldest brother, did not attend college but was educated at home by tutors employed by his father, which must surely have been the most expensive alternative. Thomas Ritchie was clearly willing to spend money to provide his sons with a good education, making it seem unlikely that expense alone determined the selection of Pictou Academy.

Another possibility was that the Ritchie family opposed the high church orientation of King's College and that of Bishop John Inglis. It is clear that later in life William Ritchie was strongly low church. The Ritchie family might have allied itself with Thomas Chandler Haliburton who was then practising law in Annapolis Royal. Haliburton, although a member of the Church of England, bitterly opposed the "war cry of church and state" being raised against Pictou Academy because it was thought to "militate against the interests of the Established Church and of King's College at Windsor." He said: "I will never consent that this seminary of education for Dissenters, shall be crushed to gratify the bigotry of a few individuals of this town [Halifax], who have originated, fostered, and supported, all the opposition to Pictou Academy."[20] William Ritchie's attendance at Pictou may have been the father's tangible support for this beleaguered college. It may also have represented the religious sentiments of William's maternal grandmother.

It is possible that Ritchie selected Pictou Academy for the prosaic reason that it provided a superior education to that of King's College. Dr. McCulloch, the life and soul of the academy, did much of the teaching, including Greek and Hebrew, logic, moral philosophy and natural philosophy.[21] He was noted as "an inspiring teacher... capable of giving sound instruction in every branch of the curriculum."[22] A pioneer instructor of natural science, he assembled a Museum of Natural History with a collection of native birds that no less an authority than Audubon pronounced "to be the finest or among the finest he had ever seen." The academy had a library "deemed respectable at the time" and also a chemical laboratory, the first in the lower colonies.[23]

The academy continued to be a storm centre of controversies between the Assembly and the Council in Nova Scotia. It has been said that "in the story of the evolution of responsible government in Nova Scotia the name of Pictou Academy will always have a special significance."[24] The ferment and controversy have been graphically recounted by Joseph Howe, a father of responsible government in Nova Scotia:

> Into Pictou! that seat of disaffection and bad government — that abode of patriots and den of radicalism — that nook where the spirit of party sits, nursing her wrath to keep it warm, during ten months of the year, in order to disturb the Legislature all the other two. Into Pictou, that cradle of liberty — from whence, after strangling the serpents that would have crushed her, she is to walk abroad over the four quarters of the globe, regenerating and disenthralling mankind. Into Pictou, where it is a mortal offence to one man to take a pinch out of another's mull — and where, as the Yankees have it, it is impossible to live upon the fence; or in fact to live at all, without "going the whole Hog" with one of the parties into which its society is divided. The Lord only knows whether we may ever live to come out, but here we go merrily in — we may be burned by the Antiburghers, or eaten without salt by the Highlanders.[25]

William Ritchie graduated from Pictou Academy in about 1831 with a classical liberal education, but the air of political debate surrounding Pictou could not help but develop his political awareness. It at least seems to have contributed to a jaundiced view of the preferential treatment accorded to Anglican colleges, for later, as a member of the New Brunswick Assembly, he voted to cut the subsidy of a similar King's College in New Brunswick.

Notes to Chapter 1

1. Robertson Davies, *What's Bred in the Bone* (Toronto: Macmillan, 1985). An English proverb from 1290 says: "What's Bred in the Bone will not Out of the Flesh." Simon Darcourt, the biographer in Davies's novel, wished to find "what was bred in the bone of old Francis. Because what's bred in the bone will come out in the flesh, and we should never forget it" (p. 21).

2. Evidence is conflicting about the date of Thomas Ritchie's call to the bar. Some authors indicate 1795 and others 1798. I have chosen 1798 as he would then be twenty-one years of age.

3. Charles St. C. Stayner, "John William Ritchie: One of the Fathers of Confederation," *N.S. Historical Society Collections* 36(1968), pp. 276-77, n.14. This count was made in 1968 and the author by consulting family members has updated it to 1990.

4. The three sons of Thomas Ritchie who became judges are:

   John William Ritchie appointed to the Supreme Court of Nova Scotia in 1870 and judge in equity, 1873-1882.

   William Johnstone Ritchie appointed to the Supreme Court of New Brunswick in 1855, chief justice of New Brunswick, 1865, puisne judge of the Supreme Court of Canada, 1875, chief justice of the Supreme Court of Canada, 1879-1892.

   Joseph Norman Ritchie appointed to the Supreme Court of Nova Scotia, 1885-1904.

   A grandson, a great-grandson and a great-great-grandson were appointed to the bench. They are James Johnston Ritchie, a judge of the Supreme Court of Nova Scotia in 1912 and a judge in equity, 1915-1925; Roland Almon Ritchie, a judge of the Supreme Court of Canada, 1959-1984; and David Ritchie Chipman who is currently a judge of the Supreme Court of Nova Scotia. A simplified family tree found in Appendix 3 traces the growth of this family and its connection with the legal profession.

5. There is some question about the correct spelling of Sir William Johnstone Ritchie's middle name. While most works relating to the Ritchie family, except Stayner, spell it Johnstone, other sources, including James G. Snell and Frederick Vaughan's *The Supreme Court of Canada*, and Ritchie's 1843 marriage certificate list the name Johnston, no "e". The "Johnston" spelling is also used in N. Omer Coté, ed., *Political Appointments, Parliaments and The Judicial Bench: 1867 to 1895* (Ottawa: Thorburn & Co., 1896), pp. 300, 367 and 432.

Ritchie's gravestone seems the last, and most appropriate word on the issue. I have followed its spelling. C.S.A. Ritchie, in a letter dated 5 August 1988, informed me that "the name was originally spelled without an 'e'. At what time and for what reason the 'e' was added remains lost in the mists of time."

6. (1869), 12 N.B.R. 556.

7. The early history of the family has been compiled from: Stayner, "John William Ritchie: One of the Fathers of Confederation"; Mary C. Ritchie, "The Beginnings of a Canadian Family," *N.S. Historical Society Collections* 24(1938); W.A. Calnek and A.W. Savary, *History of the County of Annapolis* (Toronto: William Briggs, 1897); L.G. Power, "Our First President: The Honourable John William Ritchie," *N.S. Historical Society Collections* (1918) 19; Allan C. Dunlop, "Thomas Ritchie", Vol. 8: *Dictionary of Canadian Biography* (Toronto: University of Toronto Press, 1985) at 751-753.

8. This splendid building had been totally encased within a larger structure and when restoration began this far more significant building was found hidden away inside the facade. It is described as "New England Colonial and it is one and a half storey made of wood construction with a medium pitched gable roof. This symmetrical four bay facade has a centered transom and sidelighted doorway." N.S. Dept. of Culture, Recreation & Fitness, Inventory Site Form 05, 222 St. George Street, Annapolis Royal.

9. "The Grange" no longer exists. It became the Annapolis Academy in 1878 but subsequently proving impractical as a school, it was moved to a corner of the grounds and in 1938 burned. The plaque erected on the site of the Grange reads "Home of Judge Thomas Ritchie Born 1777 — Died 1852 Later used as The Annapolis Royal Academy. Here was established a family distinguished for its service to the legal profession in Nova Scotia through five generations to this day. One son, Sir William Johnstone Ritchie became Chief Justice of the Supreme Court of Canada." Charles S.A. Ritchie, Canadian Ambassador to the United States and a great grandson of Judge Thomas Ritchie unveiled the plaque in August 1962. Roland Almon Ritchie, a judge of the Supreme Court of Canada, with his brother C.S.A. Ritchie were special guests of the Annapolis Royal Historical Association.

10. C.I. Perkins, *The Romance of Old Annapolis Royal* (Annapolis Royal: Historical Association of Annapolis Royal, 1985) p. 33.

11. Thomas Ritchie's privateering activity is not mentioned in any of the family histories. However, it is recorded in the Markham Papers, Digby Biog. Notes, sh. 78, New Brunswick Museum and in Faye Kert's "The Fortunes of War: Privateering in Atlantic Canada in the War of 1812" (M.A. thesis History, Carleton University, 1986).

12. Mary Ritchie, "Beginnings," pp. 140-41.

13. "An Annapolis Boy," *Halifax Daily Reporter and Times*, 30 January 1879, p. 3.

14. An Act for Founding, Establishing and Maintaining, An Academy at Pictou, in this Province, S.N.S. 1816, c.29.

15. George Patterson, *A History of the County of Pictou Nova Scotia* (Montreal: Dawson Bros., 1877), p. 327.

16. Ibid., p. 326.

17. S.N.S. 1816, c.29, s.2.

18. An Act to Regulate and Support the Pictou Academy, S.N.S. 1832, c.5, s.10.

19. Patterson, *County of Pictou*, p. 325.

20. Ibid., p. 339.

21. Ibid, p. 330. For a list of studies of Thomas McCulloch see B. Anne Wood, "Thomas McCulloch's Use of Science in Promoting a Liberal Education" *Acadiensis* (Autumn 1987) p. 56, note 1.

22. Archibald MacMechan, "*Nova Scotia: General History 1775-1867*" in Adam Shortt and Arthur G. Doughty, *Canada and Its Provinces* (Toronto: T.A. Constable for Publishers' Association of Canada, 1913), vol. 13, p. 264.

23. Patterson, *County of Pictou*, pp. 346, 342.

24. Claude J. Kedy, "Pictou Academy: from its founding to the present — an important narrative in the History of Education in the Province of Nova Scotia" (M.A. thesis, Mount Allison University, 1933), p. 95.

25. Joseph Howe, *Western and Eastern Rambles: Travel Sketches of Nova Scotia*, ed. by M.G. Parks (Toronto: University of Toronto Press, 1973), p. 146.

CHAPTER 2

Ritchie Chooses The Law And Saint John

After graduating from Pictou Academy, William chose to study law in Halifax with his elder brother, John William Ritchie, who later became solicitor general of Nova Scotia (1864-67) and represented that colony at the London conference that framed the British North America Act.[1] This brother, called to the first Senate of Canada, was appointed a judge of the Supreme Court of Nova Scotia in 1870, and in 1873 became a judge in equity. Robert Laird Borden, in his memoirs, compared the two Ritchie brothers:

> John W. Ritchie was one of the ablest judges then, or at any time, on the Nova Scotia Bench. My partner, Wallace Graham, who had held many briefs in the Supreme Court of Canada and who had practised for more than ten years before Mr. Justice Ritchie told me that, in his opinion, the latter, in point of ability, was perhaps the superior of his distinguished brother, Sir William Ritchie.[2]

Details of William Ritchie's legal education remain unclear but its broad outlines can be reconstructed. In 1832 and 1833, almost contemporaneous with the commencement of Ritchie's legal studies, Beamish Murdoch wrote and Joseph Howe published the *Epitome of the Laws of Nova Scotia*.[3] Murdoch's four-volume work, only partly modelled on Blackstone's *Commentaries*, and drawing on Kent's *Commentaries on American Law*, probably assisted Ritchie in his legal studies, and also provided a glimpse into early legal education in colonial Canada. He wrote:

> The Student of Law, in Nova Scotia, if possessed of a degree from a College, must serve 4 years in the office of an Attorney, after which, if otherwise qualified, he is fully admitted to the Bar. If he has not obtained a degree, he must serve 5 years clerkship, after which he is admissible as an Attorney, and within one year after as a Barrister. — He must be of the age of 21 years, and must pass examination before a Judge and two Barristers,

before he can obtain either admission; and indeed he will not be permitted to commence his study regularly, until proper enquiries have been made as to his education and habits. Students generally begin to serve their time from 16 to 18 years of age, and are admitted to the Bar at 22 or later. Many in the Colonies who are destined to the profession, have cause to regret, that they are first hurried from school to an office, and again hurried into practice by the force of circumstances, without having enjoyed the opportunity of sufficient time to mature their reading, so as to give them ease and satisfaction in their progress at the bar.[4]

Murdoch suggested that a law student should attend "Superior Courts when legal arguments, or very important trials take place" but he warned that "his duties in the office should always be held paramount to any curiosity that may lead him away from it."[5] The author believed that much error then prevailed in the vain attempt to commit to memory large numbers of decisions and the substance of heavy tomes.

Instead he recommended "a thorough knowledge of the foundations and first principles of law, a general acquaintance with the best treatises," and a diligent study of cases that attracted his attention to be the basis for a sound legal education. He contended that "by tracing the reason and the connection of every case and position he meets with, to their sources, in first principles of reason and justice, he must be better qualified ... to prepare an opinion — an argument, and eventually a decision, than he would be if his memory had been burthened with the heterogeneous contents of very many folios."[6] Murdoch believed success in the legal profession required that a portion of some reputable lawbook should be read every day. It is significant that all his suggested treatises were English; but as most, if not all, were republished in the United States with American annotations, it is difficult to say how much American law might have been absorbed by the early Nova Scotian law student. The only indigenous American text which Murdoch recommended was Hoffman's *Legal Study*, which he described as "an American work of reputation" that should "be read carefully by every student." Murdoch also recommended that students read Blackstone's *Commentaries* on three occasions: once with a law dictionary in hand, secondly in conjunction with reading the major legislation of the colony relevant to the *Commentaries*, and thirdly alongside texts of the leading case judgments referred to in it.

William, as previously noted, articled with his older brother John who was admitted as an attorney on 25 January 1831 and as a barrister on 24 January 1832. This older brother had articled to his uncle, James William Johnston, at a time when Johnston's reputation already stood high at the bar and before he became deeply distracted by politics. Johnston was described as "the ablest and the most successful criminal pleader that this Province or perhaps British America has produced. Possessed of a keen and subtle intellect, and an instinctive acuteness, great power of concentration, vast stores of legal lore, and a fiery and impetuous eloquence, he seldom failed in bringing off his client in some way."[7]

That might suggest that the older brother had received a good grounding in the law but, in spite of this, John related that for ten years after his call "he had had almost no practice." It was at the very beginning of this ten-year period in 1832 that William commenced his articles. Both brothers thus had abundant leisure time to dedicate to a systematic study of the law. A biographer related that John was "wiser than most young lawyers" and during this period continued a "patient and thorough study of the law," which admirably prepared him to assume a "place amongst the leaders of the profession."[8] The same must undoubtedly be true about the studiously inclined younger brother. Probably both brothers availed themselves of the library in the Nova Scotia Barristers' Society, or borrowed books from their uncle's library. Thus, with little practical experience after an articling term of five years, William became an attorney on 2 May 1836. As he was not a graduate of a university or college authorized to confer degrees, he was not called as a barrister until one year later on 2 May 1837. We do not know whether the admittance examination was stringent or simply a formality, but statute did prescribe that it be conducted by "one of the Judges and two of the Senior Barristers" of the Nova Scotia Supreme Court. They were to be appointed "in such a way as the Court shall deem proper," and it was the judge who had to be satisfied that the student was duly qualified.[9]

Thomas Ritchie was irreconcilably disappointed that John and William, "the two best fitted to fill the position that he had built up, left his dearly loved Annapolis." Why William Ritchie did not return when this was his father's wish, and when the local saying had it that "Annapolis belongs to the Devil, the Church and Judge Ritchie,"[10] we will never know. But in 1837 William Ritchie went to Saint John, where, after residence for one year, he was admitted to the New Brunswick bar.

Ritchie might have selected Saint John because at the time New Brunswick represented a "fairer field for his abilities" than his native Nova Scotia.[11] Saint John, the third-largest city in British North America from the mid 1830s until the mid 1840s, was surpassed only by Montreal and Quebec City. Muddy York had a population of 5,505 in 1832 and 9,765 in 1835, according to the first census after it became the city of Toronto, while Saint John had a population of 12,073 in 1834.[12] Until the mid 1860s the population of Saint John exceeded that of Halifax.

In 1836 there were ninety-four barristers and attornies in Nova Scotia and of these thirty-six practised in Halifax, while as late as 1839 there were only thirty practising in Saint John.[13] Moreover, in the late 1850s, it was cheaper and much easier to go from Annapolis, his home, to Saint John than to Halifax. The Royal Western stage coaches ran three times a week between Halifax and Annapolis, took two days and cost £2.5s. The *Maid of the Mist* steamboat plied three times a week from Annapolis to Saint John, taking one day to make the crossing at a cost of $2.00 in summer and $2.50 in the winter. Thus the decision to locate in Saint John may have been made on purely economic grounds.

Economic considerations became more pressing with John Ritchie's marriage on 15 November 1836 to Amelia Rebecca Almon, the second daughter of Dr. William Johnston Almon who later became a senator. As John Ritchie had practically no clients and now had a wife accustomed to a high standard of comfort, there was no doubt pressure on William Ritchie to set up practice elsewhere. Also a third brother, James Johnston Ritchie, had recently arrived in Halifax. He had commenced his study of law at Annapolis with his brother-in-law, Charles McColla, but completed his articles with James William Johnston, the uncle with whom John had earlier articled. James was called to the bar in 1838. Obviously the extended Ritchie-Johnston clan now had more than enough lawyers for its own competitive good.

At about this time John Ritchie became a candidate in the 1836 general election for the two-member county of Annapolis constituency. Although party divisions were undefined, there was no doubt that John Ritchie and W.H. Roach favoured the existing oligarchical rule of merchants and professional men, including the disposition of patronage, and strongly opposed reform. Roach, a typical country assemblyman, had dipped deeply into the patronage barrel. In 1833 he introduced a flour inspection bill which saddled "the province with an unnecessary office costing more than £500 a year"[14] and then assumed the office created by his bill. He was also a magistrate and an acting commissioner of Bridewell, a prison which a grand jury found Roach to have operated as if it was his own property. Both John Ritchie and W.H. Roach were soundly defeated, although John Ritchie headed the poll in the town of Annapolis. He credited the Acadians with his defeat but another interpretation was that Joseph Howe's strategy and tactics enabled the supporters of reform to win a majority of seats.

This election distracted William from his legal studies and was probably not a pleasant experience. We know that ten years later his politics were diametrically opposed to the strong Tory views of John and the rest of the family. Roach was exactly the kind of petty and corrupt politician against whom William would later fulminate. It might be that such a rejection of his family's political views started in his youth.

While at Pictou Academy, Jotham Blanchard, a fellow graduate, had begun publishing in Pictou the *Colonial Patriot*, a newspaper dedicated to reform principles, including responsible government. If Ritchie had been so influenced, he might have decided that some separation from his Tory family was desirable. William did have an uncle, Andrew Stirling Ritchie, brother of William's father Thomas, who had been a merchant in Saint John and who had represented the city and county of Saint John in the New Brunswick Assembly from 1821 to 1827, but he had returned to Annapolis before William crossed the Bay of Fundy. Thus, Saint John, not totally new territory for the Ritchie clan, might have offered William the scope needed to establish his independence, especially in politics.

After crossing the Bay of Fundy, William Ritchie's rise was not rapid and, in later years, he recounted that after opening his modest office in Saint John, he sat for six months without a single client. After one year, he had only one case. His professional earnings in the second year of his practice amounted to only £5, but gradually people came to rely on him for judgment and prompt, careful attention to their interests. It is said that "he built up the most extensive and lucrative practice, probably, that anyone has enjoyed in the City of St. John."[15]

Notes to Chapter 2

1. Joseph Wilson Lawrence, *The Judges of New Brunswick and their Times* (Fredericton: Acadiensis Press, 1985). This edition is a reprint of a series which appeared in *Acadiensis*, 1905-1907. The relevant chapter is 19, "Sir William Johnstone Ritchie," by W.O. Raymond.

2. Henry Borden, ed., *Robert Laird Borden: His Memoirs* (Toronto: Macmillan, 1938), p. 23.

3. Beamish Murdoch, *Epitome of the Laws of Nova Scotia* (Halifax: Joseph Howe, 1832, 1833).

4. Ibid., I: 7.

5. Ibid., pp. 10, 11.

6. Ibid., pp. 4, 5.

7. Charles Stayner, "John William Ritchie," p. 200.

8. Ibid., pp. 200-201.

9. An Act for the better regulation of Barristers, Advocates, Attorneys, Solicitors and Proctors, practising in the Courts of this Province, S.N.S. 1836, c.89, s.4.

10. Mary Ritchie, "Beginning," pp. 151, 146.

11. Ibid. Lawrence, *Judges of New Brunswick*, p. 484.

12. Census of Canada 1870-71, vols. 1 and 4.

13. *Belcher's Farmer's Almanack* (Halifax: C.H. Belcher, 1837), pp. 20-30; *New Brunswick Almanack* (Saint John: Henry Chubb, 1840), pp. 20-22.

14. J. Murray Beck, *Joseph Howe* (Montreal: McGill-Queen's University Press, 1982), I: 115.

15. Lawrence, *Judges of New Brunswick*, p. 484.

CHAPTER 3

Matters of Honour and Heart

William Ritchie thoroughly identified himself with each client's case and conveyed the impression that the facts, law and equity lay with his client. This quality contributed not a little to his success as a pleader in the courts.[1] Such forceful advocacy led to his being challenged to a duel on 19 August 1845 by Edward L. Jarvis. Ritchie had acted as counsel in a suit against Jarvis's father in which the son gave evidence. Jarvis complained that Ritchie, in his address to the Master of the Rolls, had unduly attacked the credibility of his testimony and had "insinuated in studied language" that he, Jarvis, had fraudulent designs upon the property of Ritchie's client. Ritchie expressed surprise that Jarvis had permitted five months to elapse since the trial, and said "in the whole conduct of that case, I endeavoured to act, and feel that I did act, as an independent and honourable counsel should do, and that I made no comments whatever on the evidence or the law but such as the evidence, the just development of the rights of my client and the ends of justice warranted." In concluding his letter, he denied using the privilege of his profession to insult Jarvis and stated:

> I trust I have a better understanding of the duties of my profession, and a keener sense of honorable feeling and conduct, than to prostitute my professional privileges so unworthily. With such feelings, you may at the same time rest assured I shall never allow myself to be overawed or deterred from fearlessly doing my duty to my clients, please or displease whom it may.[2]

This letter did not satisfy Jarvis, who demanded that Ritchie should withdraw the offensive charge which had been made in court against Jarvis's veracity. After further correspondence Ritchie declined to accept a letter challenging him to a duel and said that, on receiving the first letter, he consulted "three members of high standing in the profession" and, on their advice, sent the letter he did. After receipt of the second letter, he consulted the

17

solicitor general and "his opinion was that my first letter was sufficient, and that I ought not to take any further notice of the matter." Jarvis published the correspondence, stating that it was solely for unprofessional and ungentlemanly conduct that he reproached Ritchie.

Ritchie's decision neither to apologize nor to fight a duel, taken with concurrence of his legal peers in 1845, marked a significant and salutary change in the attitude towards gentlemanly conduct. Less than a quarter-century had elapsed since New Brunswick's most celebrated duel, fought on Maryland Hill, four miles from Fredericton, between two lawyers. That affair of honour arose out of words uttered by George Wetmore in an assessment of damages case before a jury, in which George F. Street had acted for the other litigant. Street informed Wetmore that his conduct was improper and unprofessional and Wetmore sent Street a formal challenge. In the duel, which occurred on 2 October 1821, Street killed Wetmore, the son of the attorney general. A "hue and cry" was proclaimed, for perhaps only the second time in New Brunswick history, requiring all citizens "to make fresh pursuit and Hue and Cry after" Street and the two seconds.[3] The three escaped to Maine but later returned to stand trial for murder. The three accused had certainly committed or participated in a homicide, but as the duel had been fairly fought, Judge John Saunders charged the jury in such a way that the jurors realized that their duty was to acquit.

That duel had not prevented the advancement of George Street. In 1835 he was appointed solicitor general and in this capacity advised Ritchie to take no further notice of the duel challenge. Later in 1845 he was appointed to the Supreme Court of New Brunswick and, when he died in 1855, William Ritchie was appointed to fill the vacancy.

Meanwhile, Ritchie's legal career had advanced to the point where he could consider beginning a family. He had met a beautiful young woman, Martha Strang, one of five daughters of the late John Strang who had been a leading shipping merchant in St. Andrews when that port had extensive trade with Britain and the West Indies. They decided to be married in Scotland — a surprising location for their marriage as both bride and groom and most of their immediate family resided in New Brunswick or Nova Scotia.

But Martha Strang had strong family ties with Glasgow through two of her sisters. One was the wife of Robert Rankin, the

The Acadia
(Cunard Collection, University of Liverpool Archives)

other of John Pollok, Jr. and both husbands were partners in the important commercial firm of Rankin & Co. The sisters of the bride might therefore have arranged the Scottish marriage. For Ritchie, the marriage was an opportunity to return to the country of birth of his paternal grandfather.

On 25 August 1843, Ritchie boarded the *Acadia* in Halifax bound for Liverpool. The *Acadia*, a mixed steam and sailing vessel with three masts and a red funnel, had been built by John Wood on the Clyde in Scotland. Its bow carried a full length figure-head of a kilted Highlander in recognition of disbanded Highland soldiers who had been among Nova Scotia's first British settlers. A "side lever" engine, producing 425 nominal horsepower and consuming 38 tons of coal per day powered its twin wooden side paddle wheels. Samuel Cunard, a fellow Nova Scotian by birth, had commenced scheduled sailings across the Atlantic in 1840. He sailed on the maiden voyage of the *Britannia*, a sister ship of the *Acadia*, and reached Boston fourteen days after leaving Liverpool. The service was so well received that Cunard received no less than 1873 invitations to dinner from hospitable Bostonians.[4] However, on 2 July 1843, about a month prior to Ritchie's departure, the *Columbia*, another sister ship of the *Acadia* struck a reef near Cape Sable, Nova Scotia and sank. This took the bloom off the new service but fortunately the coasting steamer *Margaret* rescued all the *Columbia's* passengers, crew and the mails. The fate of the *Columbia* may have caused Ritchie to question the wisdom of crossing the Atlantic to be married but he remained undeterred.

The marriage took place on 21 September 1843 in St. Paul's Episcopal Chapel in Rothesay, the Isle of Bute. This small wooden chapel stood near the ruins of Rothesay Castle, the coastal house of the Scottish royal family from the middle of the fourteenth century and burned in the late seventeenth century. Behind Rothesay to the southeast stood Canada Hill, affording a panoramic view of the Firth of Clyde. It derived its name from the many people who climbed to its summit to wave farewell to departing relatives and friends bound for Canada. When the name, Canada Hill, came into currency remains uncertain. Some contend that it occurred at the time of the Highland clearances but Bute was an island of mixed farming and was unaffected by these clearances. The exodus from Bute occurred later when steam power robbed the island's textile mills of the advantage previously derived from its water power. In any case, the hill had probably acquired its name by 1843 and Ritchie and his bride probably hiked to its top and gloried in its striking panorama as well as their own happiness.

Why William Ritchie and Martha Strang chose to be married in a primitive chapel on the Isle of Bute rather than in Glasgow cannot be determined. Rothesay, an attractive village built around the sweep of a magnificent bay and noted for its gardens and palm trees, had long been a favourite holiday retreat for Glaswegians. In the 1840s steamboats made it easily accessible from Glasgow in three and a half hours and by the Glasgow and Greenock Railway and steamboat in two and a half hours.

In October 1843 Ritchie, his bride and his mother-in-law, Mrs. Strang, returned to Halifax in another Cunard ship, the *Hibernia*. She too was a side-wheeler which carried sail. In the 1840s the fare from Liverpool to Halifax was £42 which included food, wines and spirits. However, the east bound fare from Halifax was only £25, the same as the sailing packet fare. Because of the prevailing winds the westbound Cunarders left the sailing ship far behind but on an eastern crossing they had only a small advantage.[5] The Ritchie entourage arrived back in Saint John on 18 October, completing the last leg of the trip from Windsor, Nova Scotia across the Bay of Fundy in the wooden steamer *Herald*. Eight years later the *Herald* was wrecked on the Quaco Ledges of Nova Scotia. But Ritchie's first marriage was not destined to survive as long.

On 12 August 1844 a son, William Pollok, was born, followed on 4 December 1846 by a daughter, Martha Margaret Strang. But a blissful family life was not to be; Martha, Ritchie's wife, died on 20 May 1847, only a few months after the birth of their daughter. Ritchie, now a widower at thirty-three, with an infant daughter and a son of less than three years, went to live with his sister-in-law, Margaret Pollok, and her husband John Pollok, Jr. They lived in "a somewhat pretentious house" on Prince William Street, a fashionable part of Saint John.[6]

Some evidence suggests that the Pollok-Ritchie household may not have been entirely happy and harmonious. Pollok, made a partner in Rankin & Co. in 1838, was described as a man of brilliant parts. However, the history of that firm revealed that after the guiding hand of Robert Rankin was removed, Pollok could not "carry corn." His habits became irregular, often going to the office late and returning home early. His brother James died about 1847 of consumption, and about 1849 "sinister rumours were afloat about Mr. John Pollok's habits" which necessitated frequent visits to Saint John by senior partners of the firm. Pollok remained a partner but he died in 1852 at the age of about thirty-eight. His wife died in the same year at Bromborough Hall in Britain, "a grief stricken, heart-broken woman." If Margaret Pollok did become the surrogate mother for Ritchie's children, young William and Martha lost a second mother in their early years.

Ritchie remained a widower for several more years but did not continue to live on Prince William Street in the Pollok house. It probably belonged to Rankin and Co., because Francis Ferguson of that firm soon took up residence there. Ritchie moved into what was known as the Old Commissariat House. Ritchie had acquired this property under very favourable circumstances. In 1843 Oliver Goldsmith, a Commissariat officer, told Ritchie that he had received orders from the imperial government to obtain tenders for the Commissariat building and he suggested that Ritchie should tender for it. Ritchie did so, and to his astonishment his was the only one. Consequently, on 28 May 1844, he obtained the whole property, including a house and stone barn for £500. He initially rented it to Dr. Simon Fitch, a doctor who was just setting up his practice. Some years later and following a renovation, Ritchie and his cousin Lewis John Almon lived in it.

It is not known how Ritchie became a friend of Oliver Goldsmith, who was nineteen years his senior. Goldsmith, born in St. Andrews, New Brunswick, of Loyalist parents, was a grandnephew of Oliver Goldsmith, the great English poet. The young Oliver became Canada's first native-born English-speaking poet. His pastoral poem, *The Rising Village*, has been described as "the first poetic representation of the experiences by which the Loyalists triumphed over home-sickness and material obstacles and came to love and have faith in Canada, the home of their adoption."[7] Although a conscious imitation of his great-uncle's poem *The Deserted Village*, the Canadian counterpart had some aesthetic merit and was an important social document. Ritchie may have had literary interests that accounted for this friendship and later friendships with two Ottawa poets, Archibald Lampman and Duncan Campbell Scott.

On Oliver Goldsmith's transfer to Hong Kong, Ritchie and five other prominent Saint John citizens on 23 April 1844 presented addresses congratulating Goldsmith on his appointment and wished him well. However, even today the city of Saint John

The Ritchie Building, Saint John

possesses a tangible physical reminder of the Goldsmith-Ritchie friendship in the form of the Ritchie Building. This building still stands on the southwest corners of Princess and Germain streets on the same land which Goldsmith informed Ritchie the British government wished to sell. In 1853 Ritchie had the Old Commissariat House torn down, and by February 1854 he had expended some £5,000 on a new building. Lewis John Almon remarked that before Ritchie left to sit in the Assembly in 1854: "after he [Ritchie] was in Fredericton a week or so he would feel rather foolish to get word that his building was burned down and there was no insurance on it."[8] Consequently, Ritchie instructed Almon to take out insurance on the unfinished building. Ritchie proceeded to Fredericton, sat in the Assembly and within a few days received news that his building had indeed burned to the ground. He returned to Saint John to begin rebuilding and the result was a "chaste and handsome building." But it, too, was destroyed in the great fire of 20 June 1877, which devasted much of Saint John. Ritchie again rebuilt and the existing three-storey brick building at 46-54 Princess Street is the outcome. This handsome structure in its early days provided prestigious offices for many Saint John lawyers among these was Robert Rankin Ritchie, Ritchie's first son by his second marriage. Notman's photography studio occupied the upper floor for a number of years.

Ritchie established his reputation as a commercial lawyer but he occasionally entered the criminal courts — sometimes to take on unpopular cases, as for example, in the McGovern case. On 6 September 1847, James Briggs Jr. and his brother William attended a temperance meeting in the town of Portland, now part of Saint John, and while returning home along Main Street two shots rang out. James died instantly from a bullet in the back of his head and his brother suffered a wound to his arm. Dennis McGovern, a "low-sized man" in his twenties was arrested the day after the murder. A pedlar by trade, McGovern had recently arrived from Ireland with his wife and child. The father of the murder victim was a prominent and successful shipowner and shipbuilder. The Rev. William Harrison, rector of St. Luke's Anglican Church, in his funeral eulogy noted that death had "deprived our respected neighbours of an affectionate and much beloved son — their children of a kind and devoted brother — our Sabbath school of a promising teacher and you, my young friends, (the Sons of Temperance) of a devoted member of your society." Temperance groups from Saint John and Portland marched in the largest funeral procession ever witnessed in the city.[9]

The trial of Dennis McGovern and an accomplice, Edward McDermott, commenced in January 1848. Whoever acted as defence counsel for McGovern and McDermott courted the displeasure of the commercial and Protestant élite of Saint John. Nevertheless, Ritchie, R.L. Hazen and I.G. Campbell defended the accused before Justice James Carter, with William Wright and J.H. Gray acting for the crown. According to the evidence the murder took place on a dark, foggy night on a street without gas lighting. McGovern ran away after the shooting. Nobody testified that he fired the shots, nor did evidence tie him to possession of a gun. The jury returned a verdict of not guilty.

Ritchie did not deserve credit for a forensic triumph in obtaining the acquittal because the crown's case consisted only of circumstantial evidence. However, undertaking the defence required courage. Ethnic tensions in Saint John mounted throughout the 1840s. On 4 November 1840 Irish labourers brutally attacked Dr. George Peters, one of the city's leading physicians and scion of a distinguished Loyalist family. In June the following year an unruly mob attacked a city alderman. Arsonists also plagued the city. Ritchie and another lawyer, Moses Perley, took the lead in drawing up a petition to the legislature seeking an appointed stipendiary police magistrate and a police force responsible to the provincial executive. Further rioting occurred in 1842 and again in 1843. On 7 March 1844 a band of ribbonmen (Irish Catholics) attempted to barricade roads at York Point and were confronted by a group of Portland Orangemen led by Squire Manks. A mêlée developed in which Manks fired on the ribbonmen, wounding a Catholic youth. An outraged mob of Catholics surrounded Manks's house in Portland and only with great difficulty did the Mayor Donaldson and a force of constables succeed in arresting Manks.

On Christmas Eve 1844 a mob severely wounded two watchmen and the next evening two hundred men armed with clubs seized Portland Bridge at York Point in an attempt to intercept several opponents. The blockade continued throughout the week and the mayor and magistrates finally had to call out the 33rd Regiment who cleared the area using fixed bayonets. On St. Patrick's Day in 1845, rival factions gathered in Portland and a riot developed between mobs armed with muskets. After a bloody encounter resulting in at least two serious casualties, the mayor arrived with the military. These riots led to a flurry of proposals for policing Saint John. In the Legislative Assembly, Ritchie and Isaac Woodward attacked the existing city court and police system. Ritchie promised the mayor that if the city surrendered its police court authority to a stipendiary magistrate, the city could determine the other terms of the police bill. The proposal had appeal but the legislature ultimately failed to deal with it. But when ethnic violence broke out afresh, resulting in the death of a Saint John Catholic on 12 July 1847 and two months later the killing of James Briggs Jr., the lieutenant-governor-in-council moved decisively. In November 1847 Jacob Allan, one of the parish's four magistrates, organized an efficient ten-member police force.

On 12 July 1849 "the most frightening and widespread breakdown of order in the city's history" occurred.[10] Hundreds of Orangemen, with drums beating and banners flying, paraded behind "King Billy," a certain Mr. Joseph Caram, mounted on a white horse. Provocatively the marchers moved into the crowded Irish Catholic district of York Point and encountered a low-hanging arch of green boughs stretched across the street. As the Orangemen dipped their banners under the arch, the York Pointers pelted the marchers with stones and brickbats. The Orangemen fired warning shots and the procession continued without any serious injury. Mayor R.D. Wilmot rushed to York Point and urged the crowd to remove the green arch but the Irish Catholics refused because it symbolized their resistance to Protestant persecution. The mayor, seeking help to avert a riot, discovered that members of the new police force could not be found. At Indiantown, the Orangemen, reinforced by scores of upriver arrivals, regrouped and armed themselves with pistols, muskets and swords and marched back to York Point. Smarting from the humiliation of the green arch, their leaders launched an assault upon it. While tearing the green boughs apart, gunshot rang out. Who shot first remains unknown, but the brutal confrontation that followed claimed at least a dozen lives and an equal number of wounded. Most of the victims were Irish Catholics. Charges were laid but it was impossible to obtain convictions.[11] Parades of Orangemen were suspended until 1876 and the New Brunswick legislature refused to incorporate the Orange Order until 1875.

The tumultuous 1840s shattered the original Loyalists' dream of creating in New Brunswick a stable and civilized society that would be "the envy of the American states."[12] The Irish potato famine caused a deluge of immigrants and in a three-year period from 1845 to 1847, some thirty-two thousand Irish immigrants poured into Saint John. More than 90 per cent were Catholics and although a great many moved on, a substantial number remained, transforming a city that had previously been overwhelmingly Protestant. The immigrants were poor and many were undernourished and seriously ill. Hundreds perished on Partridge Island, the Saint John quarantine station, but typhus, smallpox and cholera still spread throughout the colony. Britain's recent embrace of free trade caused New Brunswick's timber industry to lose its tariff advantage over the Baltic states and plunged the colony into a deep depression. Public assistance for the poor Irish immigrants, a sensitive issue at any time, caused greater resentment because of the bleak economic situation.

It is against this broad picture that one must assess Ritchie's decision to defend Dennis McGovern, a poor Roman Catholic immigrant, against the charge of murdering James Briggs Jr., the son of a wealthy Anglican shipbuilder. It was a decision that illustrated Ritchie's deep dedication to the principle of fair play.

Ritchie did not devote all his energies to the law but gave strong support to agencies for general public improvement such as the Saint John Mechanics' Institute. The Institute provided a good library and lectures for the self-improvement of its members and for thirty years after its founding in 1838 remained at the centre of the educational and social life of Saint John. Ritchie became vice-president in 1846 and president from 1848 to 1852. In 1851 Ritchie, described as a "public spirited citizen, active in all that related to the prosperity and advancement of the city," organized an extensive exhibition which included science, crafts, arts and music. The Institute had a special building erected and the proceeds from the exhibition more than covered its cost. A scientific exhibit included the "Bude" light, an intense white light formed by the introduction of a jet of oxygen into the centre of an oil or gas flame. At the exhibition's close on 18 September 1851, Ritchie as president entertained the directors of the Mechanics' Institute and a group of about forty gentlemen at an exhibition banquet at his delightful retreat, the "Crow's Nest." Ritchie had purchased the land on this hill north of the city in an uncultivated state and had transformed it into a charming garden, with a spacious greenhouse and here hosted the banquet. After a convivial evening which included drinking of the customary toasts and:

> as dewy eve merged into sable night, the company broke up, delighted alike with the courteous urbanity and cordial hospitality of the host, the beauty of the spot, and the unalloyed pleasure of an evening such as it seldom falls to the lot of ordinary mortals to enjoy.[13]

Harmony, however, did not always prevail in Ritchie's relationships. Shortly after moving to Saint John, he started attending Trinity Anglican Church and held a pew when Dr. Benjamin Gray was the rector. He heartily approved of Gray's low church, evangelical principles and those of Dr. John W.D. Gray, who succeeded his father as rector in 1840. On 4 May 1845 John Medley, a product of the Oxford or Tractarian movement which emphasized the Catholic element in the Anglican church, became the first bishop of the diocese of Fredericton.[14] The evangelical party to which Ritchie staunchly adhered distrusted Bishop Medley and this feeling became more intense "as accounts came of terrible secessions to the Church of Rome, on the part of the most prominent of those concerned in the Oxford movement."[15] John Newman, who would later become a cardinal in the Roman Catholic church, numbered among the most illustrious. The evangelical party denounced the introduction of high church liturgy as the "entering wedge," the "step by step system" which would lead the Anglican church to Rome. Ritchie disapproved of Medley's Tractarian principles and opposed the bishop's decision to build a cathedral in Fredericton. Ritchie formed a committee and, acting as its head

> in a manner to give great pain to Mr. Gray [Dr. John W.D. Gray] who was present, he condemned the bishop's conduct in decid- ing on Fredericton as hasty, ill judged and impolitic, [and] said, "he would see his error too late, when the walls were crumbling to decay and a dozen people in the forsaken edifice", and much to that purpose, his lordship [Bishop Medley] reasoned cooly on the matter, but was much agitated... from his changing color.[16]

Even Ritchie's use of the scriptural invocation against building a house upon sand did not prevent Bishop Medley from erecting his Gothic cathedral modelled upon St. Mary's, Snettesham, on the grassy flat land beside the Saint John River in Fredericton.[17]

Ritchie must have possessed an enormous reservoir of energy for he was also president of the Saint John Agricultural Society, a body dedicated to the introduction of scientific methods of agri- culture. In addition to his active participation in the European and North American Railway, he was a director of the Saint John Gas Company, the Saint John Suspension Bridge Company and a trustee of the Saint John Savings Bank. He was also one of the original incorporators of the Saint John Phoenix Fire Insurance Company.

Despite development of his large and lucrative practice, and his extensive community and commercial endeavours, Ritchie also took an interest in politics. As George E. Fenety, a journalist and keen observer of the political scene noted: "Mr. Ritchie was brought up in an ultra Tory camp, yet he had sufficient independence of character, when he crossed the Bay and had made himself conver- sant with the political situation in this Province, to cast in his lot with the advocates of reform."[18] Entering politics as a liberal involved "risk and ... social ostracism" and "exposed him to very severe criticism among those who believed that a member of the old families should stand fast by ancient Conservative traditions."[19] New Brunswick had been separated from Nova Scotia in 1784 at the behest of the Loyalists who, fleeing from the revolution in the Thirteen Colonies to the south, flooded into the Saint John River valley. Naturally the values which they cherished were traditional ones and this came to be reflected in the law of the new colony.

The first session of New Brunswick's General Assembly had met in 1786 and at its conclusion, Solicitor General Ward Chipman prepared a statement to accompany the despatch of the newly enacted statutes for their usual overview in London. He stated that the restoration of Charles II (1660) had been decided as the date for the reception of English statute law and explained that this date was chosen because "the Colonies were not of sufficient importance before this period to become an object of attention to the Parliament of Great Britain, and after it so many acts are found expressly noticing and binding the plantations [i.e. colonies] that a presumption arose [that] they were not intended [to apply to the colonies] unless named, or words of universal import made use of." Chipman continued his explanation of the selection of 1660 as the reception date saying "by admitting all the statutes of a general tendency which were passed before the restoration as a force amongst us, the stability of the Province will be guarded from a spirit of innovation."[20]

In 1795 the House of Assembly had passed a declaratory bill to advance the reception date from 1660 to 1750. But the Executive Council killed the bill and entered on it the notation "rejected instantly," even though the reception date of English law was 1758 in Nova Scotia and 1792 in Upper Canada. "New Brunswick's governing elite," writes David G. Bell, "was so truly reactionary that every political dispute was transformed in their minds into a challenge to establish constitutional order" which was to be fought "with unflinching tenacity." Bell also writes:

> The creation of the almost purely Loyalist colony of New Brunswick, in which they received their patronage appointments, was their grand opportunity not merely to recoup their personal fortunes but also to vindicate those political principles for which they had sacrificed everything. The New Brunswick experiment was their chance to prove to themselves and to their new republican neighbors that a British colony, managed on wholesome authoritarian principles, would flourish and become the envy of the American states. To this end the men appointed to rule the new colony set out to make New Brunswick's political constitution "the most Gentlemanlike one on earth."[21]

By 1837 when Ritchie arrived in Saint John, New Brunswick society was no longer as wedded to traditional values but it was still not a fertile field for advanced liberal ideas. However, in taking up the reform banner and becoming a staunch advocate of responsible government in New Brunswick, Ritchie would expose himself to some risks.

Notes to Chapter 3

1. Lawrence, *Judges of New Brunswick*, p. 489.

2. Edward L. Jarvis, "Correspondence" (Saint John, 25 August 1845) Webster Collection PK 73, New Brunswick Museum. This source consists of the collected letters between Jarvis and Ritchie, printed by Jarvis in defence of his honour. William Hunter Odell was the last New Brunswicker to fight a duel and Bishop John Medley excommunicated him in 1848.

3. *Manners, Morals and Mayhem: A Look at the First 200 Years of Law and Society in New Brunswick* (Fredericton: Public Legal Information Services, 1985), pp. 21-24.

4. Henry Fry, *The History of North Atlantic Steam Navigation* (London: Sampson Law, Marston & Co., 1896), p. 62. In 1839 Cunard was awarded a contract to carry mail across the Atlantic and a clause required that the ships be suitable for equipping as warships and be at the disposal of the Admiralty in time of war. However, in 1849 the *Acadia* was sold to the German Federated States and converted into a warship named the *Erzherzog Johann*, renamed the *Germania* in 1853 and scrapped in 1858.

5. C.R. Vernon Gibbs, *British Passenger Liners of the Five Oceans*, (London: Putnam, 1963), pp. 174-76.

6. John Rankin, *A History of Our Firm* (Liverpool: Henry Young & Son, 1921) 2nd ed. revised, p. 88.

7. *The Autobiography of Oliver Goldsmith*, ed. by Wilfrid E. Myatt (Toronto: Ryerson Press, 1943), p. xvi, quoting Dr. V.B. Rhodenizer.

8. George Stewart, *The Story of the Great Fire in St. John N.B.* (Toronto: Belford Bros., 1877), p. 134.

9. George W. Schuyler, *Saint John: Scenes from a Popular History* (Halifax: Petheric Press, 1984), p. 43.

10. T.W. Acheson, *Saint John: The Making of a Colonial Urban Community* (Toronto: University of Toronto Press, 1985), p. 227.

11. W.S. MacNutt, *New Brunswick, A History: 1784-1867* (Toronto: Macmillan, 1963), p. 348.

12. Ann Gorman Condon, *The Envy of the American States: The Loyalist Dream for New Brunswick* (Fredericton: New Ireland Press, 1984).

13. *New Brunswick Courier*, 20 Sept. 1851, p. 2.

14. Robert L. Watson *Christ Church Cathedral, Fredericton: A History* (Fredericton, 1984), p. 8.

15. William Quintard Ketchum, *The Life and Work of the Most Reverend John Medley D.D.* (Saint John: J & A McMillan, 1893), p. 65.

16. Letter dated Carleton, July 11, 1845, written by Janet Kinnear to her sister Mrs. M. Lethem in London, England, New Brunswick Museum, Mrs. J.M. Robinson, — Collector, F 1, sh 73.

17. Watson, *Christ Church Cathedral*, pp. 7-8.

18. George E. Fenety quoted in Lawrence, *Judges of New Brunswick*, p. 486.

19. *The Daily Telegraph* (Saint John) 26 Sept. 1892.

20. David G. Bell, "A Note on the Reception of English Statutes in New Brunswick," *University of New Brunswick Law Journal* 28 (1979), pp. 197-98. The New Brunswick Supreme Court Appeal Division has confirmed this 1660 date of reception in *Scott* v. *Scott* (1970), 15 D.L.R. (2d) p. 374.

21. David G. Bell, "The Reception Question and the Constitutional Crisis of the 1790's in New Brunswick," *University of New Brunswick Law Journal* 29 (1980), pp. 17-72.

CHAPTER 4

Ritchie and Responsible Government

William Ritchie's involvement in New Brunswick politics came in the middle of a protracted period of transition to responsible government. He emerged as a staunch and true advocate of progressive principles, but to appreciate his role some understanding is required of what a politician of the time called "the present indescribable system of Government."[1]

Details of the system were never static, but for the early part of the nineteenth century a relatively small and exclusive group wielded considerable power. To a significant degree "the political life of the colony [was] dominated by a small, comparatively homogenous and extremely self-conscious elite, which exercised a commanding influence in the two houses of the legislature and in the executive council."[2] Much of the power of these leading men of the colony centred on positions in the Executive Council, which advised the lieutenant-governor on domestic matters, notably appointments to the judiciary and other high public offices, their major source of patronage. "Advised" must be emphasized, because many battles turned on the extent to which the lieutenant-governor was obliged to accept the advice of his council. There was no doubt that orders from the Colonial Office in London could override any machinations of the councillors. Reformers railed against this as the despatch system of government. Appointments made by the lieutenant-governor were generally for life or, what amounted to the same thing, during good behaviour. This élite made themselves self-perpetuating because "on a vacancy in their number by death or removal, they had it much in their own hands to nominate the person to fill it."[3] The Executive Council was doubly irresponsible: it was not electively responsible to the people, nor was it collectively answerable in fact to the Colonial Office, hundreds of miles across the Atlantic. Lieutenant-governors came and went, but the local oligarchy acted as if under an eternal, divine mandate.

Similar situations prevailed in all the provinces, exacerbated by the competing cultures in Lower Canada. The 1837 rebellions prompted the appointment of Lord Durham in 1838 to inquire into the government of the British North American provinces. To rectify the problems Durham proposed "to concede the responsibility of the Colonial administration...to the people themselves." This change he suggested "would amount simply to this, that the Crown would henceforth consult the wishes of the people in the choice of its servants," with "an assurance that the government of the Colony should henceforth be carried on in conformity with the views of the majority in the Assembly," in regard to internal domestic matters.[4]

To a large extent this was achieved painlessly in New Brunswick. In 1835 a delegation from the House of Assembly induced the liberal-minded new colonial secretary, Lord Glenelg, to pledge to "democratize" the Executive Council. This pledge involved no procedural changes to guarantee the House of Assembly a voice in the appointment of the executive; it simply meant that the lieutenant-governor would be more sensitive to the wishes of the Assembly in exercising his prerogative. This technique of constitutional change minimized opposition, but added to the 'indescribability' of the system. Lieutenant-Governor Harvey, when he arrived in 1837, did appoint an Executive Council which the Assembly found acceptable. Lord Durham felt that as a result of these changes "the constitutional practice had been, in fact, fully carried into effect in this Province: the Government had been taken out of the hands of those who could not obtain the assent of the majority of the Assembly, and placed in the hands of those who possessed its confidence."[5]

But this proved entirely too sanguine. Durham himself had envisaged a system close to the British practice, in which no money vote should be proposed without the previous consent of the crown, most officers of the government would be responsible to the legislature, administration would be by competent heads of departments, and good municipal institutions would be established.[6] All of these conditions were lacking in New Brunswick.

In particular, the elected House of Assembly was not free of its own large measure of irresponsibility. It already controlled almost half of the provincial revenues and gained almost complete control of the provincial purse in 1837, with the passing of the civil list bill. The same delegation which had induced the Colonial

Office to democratize the executive had secured agreement to this bill. By it the Assembly gained control of crown lands and of revenues arising from them, in exchange for a permanent civil list of £14,000 to provide for salaries of public officials and some other expenses considered essential. But there was no party discipline or other method to restrain log-rolling and promote a wider view of the good of the province.

> There was no restriction by the Government upon the expenditures; but every member had access to the public chest, in his own way, for the benefit of his constituents, without regard to system, calculation, or economy. The Budget was framed ... in a hap-hazard way, every member, no matter how outré his ideas of trade, having an equal voice in its preparation. There was no Board of Works at this time. The public moneys were expended on roads, bridges, etc., in accordance with the wants or wishes of the inhabitants of particular districts, affording large jobs sometimes to favourites and active supporters of candidates for the Assembly .... It was not then, as now, contrary to law for a member to hold a plurality of offices under the Government .... In some instances a half dozen offices were held by one member; and such members furnished a strong body-guard to support their employers, and to aid in perpetuating a system so favourable to the money spenders, and oppressive to the tax payers.[7]

Nor were there municipal incorporations (apart from Saint John) to dilute the power of the Assembly by providing an alternative source for local improvements.

This set the stage for a three-way battle over reform between those satisfied with the old patronage system, the local reformers, and the Colonial Office. The unchecked profligacy of the Assembly led to financial chaos. In 1842 "warrants for payment by the provincial treasurer were being hawked by money-lenders at large discounts" and "in many localities business dealings had been reduced to barter."[8] Colebrooke, the recently arrived lieutenant-governor, considered the financial situation to be desperate and committed New Brunswick to reform. But bills sponsored by Colebrooke, to surrender initiation of money grants to the executive and to establish municipal corporations as alternative sources for public works, were defeated. Why should members introduce any changes which would infringe upon their power? Executive councillors who enjoyed the confidence of the majority subscribed to the same view. No wonder a conservative member later said that "the passing of the Civil List Bill conferred on the people of this Province all the Responsible Government, which he would ever advocate, or which the Province could require."[9] In frustration, Colebrooke finally dissolved the House.

The election of 1842 was fought on the theme of responsible government, with Colebrooke's policies drawing the lines. Ritchie, in his first foray into politics, ran in the county of Saint John and was described as "a young Liberal of great determination, just beginning to show fire."[10] He "would pledge himself to support the Initiation of Money Votes by the Executive, in order that the means of extravagance should be put an end to. He would also go for a loan to pay off the Provincial Debt."[11] The loan would be contingent upon surrender of the initiation of money grants to the executive, as the only means of improving the colony's credit rating.

Although reformers such as Ritchie were close to the lieutenant-governor on financial matters, a political chasm prevented them from working effectively together. The liberals opposed extensive exercise of the royal prerogative, viewing it as an infringement of local self-government. As well, they consistently attempted to reduce the salaries of appointed officials, considering these to be wasteful patronage, while the Colonial Office saw these as the bond of sacred trust with the appointees. Such conflicts would emerge more fully in the future, and for the time being the electorate returned Ritchie to his law practice. The liberal defeat made it clear that New Brunswick voters were in no mood for a change. Only the most established of the reformers remained in the Assembly in 1843.

During the remainder of its session the House demonstrated its traditional bent. A constitutional crisis of sorts did take place when Colebrooke exercised his prerogative to appoint his son-in-law, Alfred Reade, to replace the deceased provincial secretary, against the advice of the Executive Council. Selection of an overseas appointee united conservatives and reformers. A large majority carried an address, which simultaneously approved the principles of responsible government while upholding the right of the lieutenant-governor to exercise the royal prerogative. In the end the Colonial Office disallowed Reade's appointment, and Colebrooke was obliged to select a provincial secretary enjoying the confidence of the Assembly after four council members resigned in protest against Reade's appointment. The status of the royal prerogative remained unclear, but the Executive Council was made effectively more responsible to the Assembly.

In 1847 Ritchie did win election to the House for the county of Saint John. In one of his first speeches he showed his under-standing of the necessity for thoroughgoing reform to achieve workable, responsible government. He believed that "one of the first principles of Responsible Government was the practical ben-efit of the country" and "he would rather see the Constitution stripped of its Executive branch" than that it should exist "merely to exercise the Government patronage." He also stressed:

> that there would never be a proper Government in this Province until such an Executive should be constructed as would com-mand the confidence, not only of that House, but of the country at large; and to an Executive of this description he would yield up the initiation of the money grants; and he had seen nothing since to induce him to alter his opinion.[12]

Responsible government, he said, "like faith without works, availed but little so long as it was not acted upon." Ritchie would not be placated by colonial self-government so long as it remained an irresponsible patronage machine.

The reformers, with a minority in the House, pressed their position by means of debate and resolutions against the govern-ment, whenever the opportunity presented itself. As well as attack-ing the government on the issue of the composition of the Executive Council, and over the initiation of money grants, Ritchie condemned the road appropriations systems, the most significant source of local patronage, as "wrong in principle, and rotten in both theory and practice."[13] He also criticized the government for not taking the lead in reforming the Post Office; a small point, but illustrative of the reform pressure which the liberals were putting on the government. One government member deemed the leading reformers, Lemuel A. Wilmot and Ritchie to be "as rabid a set of men as ever any Government had to deal with."[14]

The constitutional question was again raised sharply in the 1848 session when the despatch of Earl Grey, the colonial secretary, was debated. It had been addressed to the lieutenant-governor of Nova Scotia but with instructions that it apply in all colonies. It recommended adoption in the colonies of the British practice of departmental government, in which the chief public officers, in particular the attorney general, the provincial secretary and the solicitor general, would be members of a politically appointed cabinet and therefore would change with the government. Ritchie echoed liberal sentiment in saying that "this despatch would be hailed with delight throughout the length and breadth of the land." His resolution regarding it reiterated his position that the substance of responsible government must accompany the form. It read in part "that the circumstances of this Province present no obstacle to the immediate adoption of that system of Parliamentary Government which has long prevailed in the Mother Country, and which is a necessary part of Representative Institutions."[15]

In the debate the members of the government claimed that responsible government had already arrived, while the opposition said that "it was requisite...that as soon as a Government could not command a majority of supporters in the House, they should give way to others."[16] The three positions named in the despatch were open, and the liberals believed that with Earl Grey's despatch the tide had turned in their favour. They claimed entitlement to half the seats on the council, despite the fact that they were still a minority in the Assembly, and warned the conservatives to yield these up or be defeated at the next election. The government invited only Lemuel A. Wilmot and Charles Fisher, two leading members of the opposition. The rest of their party were bitterly disappointed when they accepted. The two leading reformers were now pledged to defend the government and not attack it. Most predicted that the two would be powerless to effect real change from within, as proved to be the case.

While this event severely weakened the opposition, the liberals out of government did not give up hope. "The opposition in the House, now led by Mr. Ritchie, set up an incessant fusilade, on account of the apathy of the Government in not backing up their professions."[17] Their efforts the following year and a half were not in vain, and in the elections of 1850, a "Reform House" was elected for the first time. Charles Fisher, however, lost his seat, and Lemuel A. Wilmot was appointed to the bench, leaving no prominent liberals in the government. Moreover, Wilmot's appointment had been made by the lieutenant-governor against the advice of his council, who had wanted no appointment to be made and the number of judges to be reduced. Ritchie wasted no time in seizing this opportunity to test the mettle of the new House. Immediately after the opening speech of the lieutenant-governor, he moved a vote of no confidence, based largely on this unconstitutional appointment.[18] The final vote, fifteen for and twenty-two against, "took the country by surprise;"[19] but perhaps it should not have been surprising that the members would want to speak in favour of reform before actually voting for it.

The 1851 session was nonetheless an active one. One petition introduced by Ritchie prayed that newspapers be mailed free of postage, in line with Ritchie's emphasis that practice should be in line with the rhetoric of responsible government. In constitutional matters Ritchie did not relent. Late in the session he initiated debate on the state of the colony and moved a series of resolutions condemning the government. One resolution protested the unconstitutional manner of James Carter's elevation to chief justice and Lemuel A. Wilmot's appointment to the bench. Ritchie said that while for some time it had been acknowledged that they enjoyed responsible government, "only a year or two pass away and Lord Grey inflicts the principle on the province that he is to say who shall be Chief Justice, who Puisne Judge."[20] Earlier in the session the Assembly had asked that all correspondence with the Colonial Office concerning the appointment be laid before it. Lieutenant-Governor Sir Edmund Head had produced the correspondence, carefully censored; "the scissors was applied just when they came ... to the most interesting portion, and seven asterisks is all they find."[21] Ritchie strongly protested and insisted that "the people's Representatives ... had a right to any despatches when the majority demanded them." Another of his resolutions asked whether "they should tamely submit to the dictation of the Colonial Minister, when he told them they must not arrange the salaries of their local ministers."[22] He complained "that the government had not introduced a measure of retrenchment in the salaries, beginning with the salary of the Lieutenant Governor." The tone and the substance of these resolutions revealed why the lieutenant-governor and the reformers were often at loggerheads, despite their agreement on the initiation of money bills. In the end, the vote on the principal resolutions was nineteen for and twenty-one against.[23] It represented the highest strength of the opposition to date and party feeling seemed to have coalesced. Ritchie would later claim that it was during this session that for the first time in New Brunswick a member voted against his personal predilections and along party lines.[24]

In the recess following this session one of the most important events of Ritchie's political career occurred. Two leading liberals from Saint John, R.D. Wilmot and John H. Gray, defected and joined the government. The remaining Saint John's liberals were thunderstruck. Ritchie's surprise at this turn of events turned to political dismay.[25] The reform star had been rising, and it seemed only a matter of time before a liberal government with the ability to make fundamental changes would come to power. Now the cohesiveness of the liberals weakened, individual self-interest triumphed, and the continuation of the old system seemed assured.

R.D. Wilmot was appointed not only to the Executive Council but also surveyor general. This post was remunerated, and so Wilmot had to return to his constituency for re-election. Ritchie, Charles Simonds and S. Leonard Tilley, all members from Saint John, determined to turn this election into a matter of principle, and swore to resign if the Saint John electorate preferred R.D. Wilmot over their candidate, Allan M'Lean.[26] In announcing his candidacy M'Lean announced that "my sole object in soliciting your suffrages is to give you an opportunity of expressing your opinions of the recent appointments in the only constitutional way available."[27] At this time it was said that "W.J. Ritchie, Esq., is by many considered to be the leading member of the opposition; at present he is doubtless the most active."[28] He campaigned vigorously for M'Lean, denouncing the corruption of the government, and pressing for a mandate for change. The final result was M'Lean 623 votes, Wilmot 896. The three resigned their seats in accordance with their pledge, and "for the next three years the government, with virtually no opposition to face, was all-powerful in the legislature."[29]

It might seem that Ritchie's vow was a mistake and a setback for the opposition. But it effectively turned the election into a vote on reform politics and would have been a significant victory had the result gone the other way. Ritchie must be admired for keeping to his promise when the election went against his candidate. Further, credence should be given to Ritchie's statement that "I feel that I cannot, after the opinion thus expressed by my Constituents, longer retain my position as one of the representatives of the City and County of Saint John, with honour to myself or usefulness to the County."[30] He felt the vote was a judgment on him as much as on M'Lean, and he could not remain in office without the confidence of his constituents. He might have felt it pointless to force reform on people who did not want it, and it was certainly thankless.

In the end, the resignations might not have been a mistake. It is true that for the next three years "conservatism ruled, and the historic method of doing business at the local level remained almost completely unaffected."[31] But this dose of the bad old ways might have been the purgative that was needed. The newspapers were critical of the following session, as was the lieutenant-governor who made public his "sense of the danger and difficulty likely to arise from this growth of legislation of a partial and private character."[32] The citizens of the province appeared equally unimpressed and sixteen new members were returned to the House in the elections of 1854. On 28 October a motion of want of confidence in the government passed easily, twenty-seven to twelve, and "shortly after, for the first time in New Brunswick history, a government resigned because of an adverse vote in the house of assembly."[33] Responsible government had arrived in New Brunswick, and in November Ritchie took his place in it as a member of the new Executive Council.

The new administration moved to fulfil its reform pledges. An election bill soon introduced the secret ballot to the province and extended the franchise. Ritchie was a strong supporter of this measure, and during debate spoke for two and a half hours on its virtues. And in 1856, despite continued resistance by individual members unwilling to yield their power, a resolution was passed giving control of financial initiation to the government.

Ritchie was a reformer from the beginning to the end of his political career. It is perhaps not surprising that Ritchie, as an outsider in New Brunswick, would be opposed to the entrenched patronage system. But his attachment to reform principles during periods of unpopularity, as well as his firm refusal to compromise them in order to retain his seat, redounded to his credit. William Johnstone Ritchie repeatedly, courageously, grounded personal and political choices in moral and legal principles.

Notes to Chapter 4

1. J.A. Street, member for Northumberland, quoted in *Saint John Morning News*, 28 Feb. 1848, p. 3.

2. P.A. Buckner, *The Transition to Responsible Government: British Policy in British North America*, 1815-1850 (Westport Conn: Greenwood Press, 1985), p. 306.

3. Beamish Murdoch, *History of Nova Scotia or Acadie* (Halifax: J. Barnes, 1865-67), quoted in George E. Fenety, *Political Notes and Observations; or a Glance at the Leading measures that have been Introduced and Discussed in the House of Assembly of New Brunswick* (Fredericton: S.R. Miller, 1867), I: ix.

4. *Lord Durham's Report*, ed. Gerald M. Craig (Toronto: McClelland and Stewart, 1963), p. 143.

5. Ibid., pp. 106-107.

6. Note that Buckner, *Transition*, pp. 257-59, states that there is ongoing debate about Lord Durham's vision. Durham never used the imprecise term "responsible government" in his report.

7. Fenety, *Political Notes*, p. 30.

8. W.S. MacNutt, *New Brunswick, A History: 1784-1867* (Toronto: Macmillan, 1963), p. 284.

9. Charles Simonds, member for the County of Saint John, quoted in Fenety, *Political Notes*, p. 118.

10. Ibid., p. 40.

11. *Saint John Morning News*, 28 Dec. 1842, p. 2, also ibid., p. 36.

12. Fenety, *Political Notes*, pp. 210, 243.

13. Ibid., p. 270.

14. Ibid., p. 246.

15. Ibid., pp. 272-74.

16. Ibid., p. 274.

17. Ibid., p. 291.

18. See *Journals of the House of Assembly of New Brunswick*, 6 Feb. 1851, p. 13.

19. Fenety, *Political Notes*, p. 370.

20. *Saint John Morning News*, 23 Apr. 1851, p. 2.

21. Ibid. For the censored despatches, see *Journals of the House*, 3 March 1851, pp. 139-53.

22. *Saint John Morning News*, 23 Apr. 1851, p. 2.

23. Fenety , *Political Notes*, pp. 399, 404.

24. *Saint John Morning News*, 17 Oct. 1851, p. 3.

25. See Fenety, *Political Notes*, pp. 413-19 for a description of this incident.

26. W.H. Needham, the remaining member from Saint John, was also a liberal, and supported M'Lean. It is not clear whether he promised to resign his seat if Wilmot should win, but in the event, he did not resign.

27. *New Brunswick Courier*, 4 Oct. 1851, p. 2.

28. *Saint John Morning News*, 3 Oct. 1851, p. 2, letter to the editor.

29. MacNutt, *New Brunswick*, p. 345.

30. *New Brunswick Courier*, 25 Oct. 1851, p. 2.

31. MacNutt, *New Brunswick*, p. 346.

32. From a despatch of Sir Edmund Head to the colonial secretary, dated 6 May 1853, which was laid before the House of Assembly on 14 Feb. 1854. *Journal of the House of Assembly of N.B.*, 1854, p. 36.

33. MacNutt, *New Brunswick*, p. 356.

CHAPTER 5

Victorian Liberal and his 'Just Reward'

Opponents of the newly ascendant Liberals soon named them "the Smashers," but their program was one of reform, not revolution. The speeches of Ritchie, who was widely held to be one of the few Liberals who actually understood the meaning of responsible government, displayed the pragmatic, incremental approach of the common-lawyer. His advocacy of reform was based not on abstract rights of man, but on the belief that reform was needed to insure the prosperity of the colony. While he held true to principles, they were concretely based in experience and self-reliance.

Extension of the franchise illustrated well the incremental approach of the party as a whole and of Ritchie in particular. The bill, introduced by the Liberal government in the 1855 session, extended the franchise from the traditional qualification of male persons holding £25 of real estate, to include male persons holding £100 in combined real and personal property, or with an annual salary of £100. This was aimed directly at the rising urban middle classes. In rural areas most men owned at least some real estate, and it appears that the assessment was sufficiently lax that the requirement of a £25 value was almost a formality.[1] On the other hand, merchants, salaried clerks and mechanics of the towns would often have only a leasehold, and so would not be entitled to a vote. The principle which Ritchie considered to be "the basis of the elective franchise" was that "every man who paid a tax has a right to have a voice in the affairs of that country which exercised the control of taxing him." He continued to say that "the present bill contains the happy medium between the owners of real estate and universal suffrage, inasmuch as every man having a stake, an interest in the country, will have the undoubted right of exercising the elective franchise."[2] The reform Ritchie advocated was to help increase the prosperity of the colony, not to vindicate abstract rights, and his view respecting the franchise was in the mainstream of the party, not with the most progressive wing of those advocating universal suffrage.[3]

Property held a central place in Ritchie's views on political economy as illustrated in his remarks on a bill to reduce the fees of the registrars of deeds and wills. The bill, he said, was a very important one, as "there was not in his opinion an official institution in the country of equal importance as that of the Register of Deeds and Wills. It lay at the root, the foundation of every other institution in the country....[T]he Registry office is the protection of the right of the country."[4] Time confirmed Ritchie in his opinions, and almost twenty years later, when he was chief justice of the province, his addresses to grand juries were a distillation of the view that the law and polity existed to aid the peaceful accumulation of wealth in the traditional order. On the subject of organizing sailors in the ports he said:

> The harbour is as essential to us as breath that passes through the nostrils is to man's life. Take away or destroy the harbour, and what would be done? All are interested in preserving order and peace at the port, — that vessels are not deterred from coming here, — all are interested in seeing that no man nor body of men interfere with others in their respective callings.

On the subject of labour organizing Ritchie commented that:

> He had read in the newspapers that large numbers of workmen had gone on persons' property with a view to persuading and inducing others to side with them. What he wished to call attention to is that men must be very cautious in any undertaking such as that. The law protects all — in the street, in the house, while performing their avocations and attending to their duties, official or private. If not so protected, would any men of sense live in the country? What would be wealth if there was no protection, — what security for life and property? Fair and legitimate protection must be given the property and industries of the country. Thank God we do not live in a country recognizing communistic principles, where people believe that property is a crime; that we do live in a country that encourages the accumulation of property; that to those who come every facility for acquiring wealth is afforded.

The role of the law was to preserve the peace, which meant, to Ritchie, preserving property rights: "The owners of property, interfered with, will protect themselves. Bodies of men may start off with good and peaceable intentions, but in controversy blood gets up and so conflicts might result."[5]

While noting that the court had nothing to say of the social or political aspect of labour combination, Ritchie said "it was the Court's duty to deal with it so far as it affected the rights of the citizens." In this regard he said: "Every man has a right to put a value on his labour, to work for whom he pleases. So also has the employer a right to say who he shall employ. No laborer has a right to say who shall not work for a certain employer. He can only speak for himself."[6]

This was to Ritchie not only a matter of property, but of freedom:

> No man or body of men has a right to say that other men must work a certain number of hours, that they shall receive a certain pay; they have no right to interfere with others' property and labour. What a dreadful state of thraldom it would be other wise? That men cannot do as they please; that they are to be restricted and tied down by others. What sort of feeling would it be to tell children — to educate them to it — that no matter what were their qualifications, what were their abilities, what their will, they must do as others; whether they were worth ten shillings, and another man one dollar they must take the lower. What a dreadful thing this would be, what a millstone about their necks. Men of spirit properly say earn what you can....In conclusion, he considered that there should be but one feeling that every man, from the humble to the highest, should possess equal rights; should have the freedom to dispose as he liked of his time and his property.[7]

Even when faced with what he saw as a threat to the social order, Ritchie was not undiscerning. He made it clear that he felt that the sailors involved were "more sinned against than sinning," and that "it was the bounden duty of the police ... not to lay hold of the unfortunate sailor, but to arrest those who incite them and who assist them." And while the concept of equal rights has undergone considerable change since Ritchie's time, we should not dismiss Ritchie's caution that "it was not for him to say who was right or wrong in the matter" as a mere facade of judicial neutrality. Ritchie's appointment to the bench had come in large measure because of his prominence as an elected politician. Certainly judicial neutrality was much easier to maintain when the laws and his predilections reinforced one another. While the law allowed labourers to combine, Ritchie remarked that "we may have our own opinion of the propriety of a strike among laborers, more especially where the severity of the past winter, and the present depressed state of trade are considered." There was no need to doubt his sincerity when he said that "the question for the Court to ask is, has anyone been intimidated,"[8] because the laws against intimidation of workers allowed sufficient scope for disapproval of such activity.

Pragmatism tempered Ritchie's economic views. *Laissez-faire* liberal theory and practical concerns clashed over the question of repeal of the usury laws, which restricted legal interest to six percent. Ritchie came down against disruptive change. The speech of the member introducing the bill was full of economic theory, with references to "the natural course of capital," supply and demand and the theoretical equivalence of money and butter, backed up by extensive quotations from economic treatises. Ritchie retorted that "it might be all very well to talk about theory, but in a matter of this importance they were bound to consider the practical effect which the passage of a Bill like this would produce in this country." He was not afraid of theory; while declining to enter into a prolonged debate, he noted that it was easy to repeal usury laws in England, where capital was so available that it had been years since money was worth as much as the legal interest rates. The situation was quite different in New Brunswick, where there was no great surplus of capital, and most of that was tied up in mortgages. Ritchie prophesied that if the bill were passed into law "the immediate effect would be that those now holding mortgages on real estate ... would call at once on the indebted party for their money, and if they could not redeem the mortgage they would proceed to foreclose .... They might depend on it that if the Bill passed, it would throw the whole country into confusion." The hard-nosed *laissez-faire* position would have it that some discomfort is necessary in allowing capital to find its most productive use, and that in the long-run the increased productivity would be to the benefit of all. Balancing the theory of long-run prosperity against what he saw as the certainty of short term disaster, Ritchie opted not to trust to theory.

Nor was he above throwing some populist swipes at capitalists along the way, saying: "He would implore the House in the name of every poor man in the country to take heed that they did, by passing this Bill, bind them hand and foot and cast them helpless at the foot of bankers and money brokers." If Ritchie would have the public beware of capitalists, he didn't spare his own profession either. While opposed to the reduction of the fees of the registrars of deeds and wills, he strongly favoured another provision of the bill which would prohibit any practising lawyer from holding the office, saying: "In England they would no more trust a lawyer to go among title deeds than they would a wolf among their sheep."

Ritchie emphasized that the fees of registrars should not be reduced below "what would secure an efficient administration of justice in the Country." This sentiment was echoed in his defence of a salary of £600 for the head of a proposed Board of Works, when he said that amount "was not more than sufficient to induce a respectable man to come to Fredericton to reside and give up his business, when at any moment he could be turned out by a vote of that House."[9] It seems more plausible to take Ritchie's professed concern with the efficient working of government at face value, than to suspect him of trading favours with lawyers and politicians with the view to sustaining the salaries and prestige of his class. With respect to the judiciary, where we might expect to see prospective nest-feathering, Ritchie was a long standing advocate of judicial salary reduction,[10] and he also introduced a bill for reducing the costs of action in the Supreme Court by abolishing the fees of the judges.[11] Ritchie also presented a petition to allow grand juries to elect their own foremen, rather than having him selected by the court.[12] A bill to this effect passed soon afterwards. These measures indicated a real concern for egalitarian principles and accessible justice, as opposed to support for the prestige and power of the courts.

In advocating law reform Ritchie knew how to appeal to the profession as well as to the larger public. In a grand jury address he urged the members of the bar to cooperate with the spirit of a recently enacted change in court procedure by shortening as much as possible the time occupied in examination and cross-examination of witnesses. He warned them that "a persistence in the attempts to prolong and postpone the trial of causes must eventually result in loss to themselves by impoverishing their clients — 'Killing the goose that lays the golden eggs.'"[13]

The motives behind another law reform bill were made quite clear by Ritchie when he introduced it in the 1855 sitting. A dispute between a "large and wealthy house in London" and a party in Saint John had been referred to arbitration, and the arbitrators, "three most respectable inhabitants of Saint John," had found that not only were the claims of the London house unfounded, but that there was a balance of £1,000 owing to the defendant in Saint John. At this point Ritchie had become involved. As he was proceeding to England on other business, he undertook to determine how the award against the London house might be recovered. In England he was advised that the claim would almost certainly succeed, but that a deposit of £500 would be required before an action could be commenced. He had no authority to leave such a deposit, and returned to New Brunswick to advise his client of the situation. There he found that his client had fallen into financial difficulty, largely as a result of the non-fulfilment of the contract by the London party, and would not be able to make any such deposit. This unfairness in transatlantic dealings Ritchie thought "extremely hard" but he concluded there was no help for it. Then came a final straw when the same solicitors he had dealt with in England sent out a process to be served on a party in New Brunswick "requiring that party to appear and answer within 40 days, in the Court at Westminster, otherwise judgment would be entered up against him by default."[14] Surprised, Ritchie investigated and found that indeed such a service was authorized.[15]

> Now the effect of this would be to compel all parties that made contracts in England to appear and answer for an alleged breach of the contract in the English Court within a specified term. Hon. members who had listened to what he had already advanced respecting the cost of entering an action in the Court of England, would at once see the position of a merchant or ship builder in this country who made a contract in England. It would in nine cases out of ten place the contractor entirely in the hands of the English house with which the contract had been made. How was a Ship builder or a Deal merchant to obey the process by leaving his business in this country and proceed to England to answer within 40 days to an allegation of a breach of contract; and if he could get there in time, how was he to meet the enormous expense of a defence in the Superior Courts of Westminster. After maturely considering the matter, he saw no means to escape from the operation of the Act of the Imperial parliament, and he cast about in his own mind what could be done by Legislation in this country to place its inhabitants on a footing with their fellow subjects in England. The only result at which he could arrive was embodied in [the bill he was presenting]. He would at once say that the Act was simply retaliatory. It would not prevent the service of summons on inhabitants of this Province, but it would if it became law, enable the inhabitants of this Province to bring a person living in England to answer in the Courts of this Province, in the same way as they were obliged to appear and answer in England.[16]

The response to Ritchie's speech was outrage, shock, and a measure of disbelief that the imperial Parliament would pass such an act. While the removal of tariffs which favoured timber from the colonies had a severe impact on the economy of the province and prompted cries that the colonies were being abandoned, the high-handed legislative disregard for the interests of the colonies such as Ritchie described no doubt also played their part in engendering a growing disenchantment with the mother country.

Ritchie's incrementalism by no means amounted to paralysis. As well as extending the franchise, the election bill brought in by the Liberals introduced the secret ballot, and Ritchie's support of this innovation was unstinting. Again Ritchie displayed a preference for practicality over theory, but this time the experience argued for change. He chided a member of the House who

> after consulting all the books and authors bearing on the case, had yet to be convinced of its being such an admirable and perfect system. He [Ritchie] was well aware that his hon. colleague was a reading man, and had read a great deal on the subject, but in his (Hon. Mr. R's) opinion one practical working of the ballot box was worth more, and to any unprejudiced mind, would be more convincing of its efficiency and beneficial results than all the books and authors his hon. colleague had consulted.[17]

In further support of the ballot, Ritchie cited the testimony of an American acquaintance to the effect that if the people of New Brunswick just tried the ballot, they would never relinquish it, and commented that "this testimony was worth as much, and he thought far more consideration, than all his hon. colleague had gleaned from his books." In a similar vein he said the ballot's "admirable working in St. John has made more converts to the principle than a year's talking," and supported this with a story about a friend who had blessed the ballot for allowing him to vote according to his own wishes without wounding the feelings of a friend.

Ritchie also railed against the fraud encouraged by the existing system, and what he termed "that abominable incubus — scrutiny." Personal experience with both these aspects of the electoral system no doubt fuelled his desire for reform. On the first count of the ballot in Ritchie's own election that term, he had been returned by only one vote, and it seemed that at least one, and possibly two of his voters had cast their ballots two or three times. Fortunately for Ritchie, the ballots cast for his opponent were not entirely regular either, and after the scrutiny Ritchie's lead had increased from one vote to half a dozen.[18] But the story persisted that Ritchie had been elected by only one vote, and that cast by himself.

Ritchie was active in promoting economic development as well as political reform. For example, in an 1847 House of Assembly discussion on the administration of crown lands, Ritchie came out strongly in favour of inducements to immigration and settlement. He proposed that the *bona fide* settler should receive fifty acres of land and be entitled in a few years to purchase up to one hundred more. Settlement by "natives of the old country (who) were hardy pioneers ... deserved encouragement."[19]

Ritchie's respect for practicality over doctrine which made him a progressive incrementalist in economic matters also surfaced in his religious attitudes. While a devout low church Anglican he embodied a liberal tolerance for the religious views of his fellows. In his first term he presented a bill to aid in establishment of a Methodist day school,[20] and he voted in favour of a controversial bill to allow "modern Calvinist" ministers to perform marriages.[21] The clearest expression of religious views came in his remarks during the debate on a bill to incorporate the Saint John Protestant Orphan Asylum. The act of incorporation explicitly set out a number of theological points on which the several Protestant denominations concerned could agree, and it stated that orphans would be provided with a Protestant education along these lines. Ritchie said that:

> [h]e could not consent that children should be bound down by such peculiar doctrinal views. To give any body of men such power over children, and ask to force a creed over them by Legislation, was certainly the most singular proceeding he had ever known .... [W]hen benevolent persons caught up those orphans without regard to sect or colour to provide for them, he did not think it right to give them legislative power to bring them up according to their peculiar notions. — He could not recollect all the theological propositions laid down, but they read very well to him as they caught his ear. However, his doctrine is, let every man worship God according to the dictates of his conscience.[22]

Ritchie's temperate attitude to problems of law and morality was also displayed in his later address to the grand jury on the matter of infanticide. "While there is generally a feeling of horror among our citizens on learning of such a case," he said, "the circumstances are mostly always of such a nature as to bring pity from nearly everybody for the unfortunate." Such sympathy was sometimes given practical expression, as the accused in the case had escaped, and Ritchie in his address hinted at "carelessness, neglect or connivance" on the part of the police. He continued with the predictable remark that "the law must be upheld," but noted that "in the case of infanticide it was well that discretionary power had been left for those having to adjudicate upon the fate of the person charged,"[23] and his harshest words were reserved for those involved in the escape. He was not unwilling to extend sympathy to a lawbreaker, but he was firm that this must be done in accordance with law and not outside of it.

This Assembly member, who extolled so many of the classic ideas of nineteenth century liberalism, was also actively involved in the struggle to build railways in the province. Indeed, the railway was the greatest symbol of progress in North America in the 1800s, and by mid-century had come to preoccupy the minds of the New Brunswick populace and its legislators. As P.B. Waite has put it: "Patronage and railways, these were the issues that divided New Brunswick, not Liberal and Conservative."[24]

There were three main railway proposals in New Brunswick. One scheme, the Intercolonial, would be built through the northern part of the province to link Nova Scotia with Canada. Another was the St. Andrews and Quebec railway. The third plan was the Saint John-Shediac line, which would eventually join with American roads at Portland, Maine. While the proposals did not have to be mutually exclusive, the colony divided at least three ways over the plans. Ritchie, representing Saint John interests, strongly advocated the Shediac route and had promoted legislative support for railways since 1847.[25] Despite the high cost, he

> was as willing to go as far as anyone in extending the right hand of encouragement, for the purpose of getting the Province aroused from its lethargy, and new life and vigour infused into its industrial interests ... he was willing to stake his political character on the success of the experiment.[26]

Certainly nothing increased his political stock more than advancing Saint John's railway interests. By pressing the government for action in 1849 on the European and North American Railroad, as the Shediac-Saint John line became known, Ritchie was labelled in Saint John as the man "who was to lead us out of darkness into business life."[27]

Promoters of the northern route to Quebec defended their route on the basis that it ran entirely through British territory, consequently sponsors of the southern route relied upon the spirit of international friendship. They maintained that "the spirit of peace has at last prevailed — national animosities, sectional and political hostility have disappeared between the English races, since the establishment of the boundaries of Maine and Oregon and the contests of war have been succeeded by a noble and generous rivalry for the promotion of the arts of peace."[28] At a conference held at Portland in July 1850 to discuss the proposed railway, flags were intertwined and peaceful and cooperative sentiments extolled.

In 1851 the New Brunswick legislature finally incorporated the European and North American Railway Company and Ritchie's name was among the list of the seventy-three original subscribers for shares in the company that read like a who's who of New Brunswick society. The grandiose title was not a totally pompous name. Its promoters thought that much of the trade to and from Europe, and to and from North America, could be diverted through Saint John because, once linked with Halifax, the sea voyage to Europe would be shortened by several days, compared with that from New York and other United States' ports. The preamble of the Act of Incorporation read in part as follows:

> Whereas it is contemplated, under concurrent Charters, to construct a continuous line of Railway from Bangor, in the State of Maine, through the Provinces of New Brunswick and Nova Scotia, to Halifax, or some other Port on the Eastern Coast of Nova Scotia, under the name of "The European and North American Railway Company," thereby affording an uninterrupted route of land communication to all parts of North America, from some Atlantic Port in the most direct line of emigration, traffic, and travel between the Old and the New World.[29]

But the advent of steam and iron ships would largely nullify the advantage of such a rail link to a seaport that was marginally closer to Europe. Steam and steel, which blighted the rosy prospects of the lumbering and shipbuilding industries of New Brunswick in the later half of the nineteenth century, had the same deleterious impact on the E.& N.A. Nevertheless, this railway would eventually become part of the Intercolonial which linked the four original provinces of Canada and then in 1919 became part of the Canadian National Railway.

Competing interests defeated this first attempt to spur acceptance of the European and North American proposal. The response from a disappointed Saint John was loud and resulted in the formation of the Saint John Railway League. Ritchie was a prominent member, advocating construction of the Shediac line in particular and railways in general. Later, in April 1849, Ritchie again moved for guarantees for the European and North American line. Fenety reported that "public indignation" over the previous Assembly refusal "produced a wonderful effect upon the nerves of honourable members," and the motion passed. As a result, "some who had not been known to smile in twenty years, looked the picture of happiness and contentment on this occasion."[30] Unfortunately for Ritchie and other railway supporters, the Executive Council overturned the House initiative.

During his absence from the legislature, Ritchie's legal career had not stood still. Before the 1854 election, Ritchie had been offered the honour of being appointed a Queen's Counsel. According to W.O. Raymond, Ritchie would only accept if it "should leave him entirely untrammelled as regards his political views." Sir Edmund Head wrote to the colonial secretary that:

> Mr. Ritchie is politically opposed to the existing council. Your Grace will therefore understand that this gentleman's appointment, if made by Her Most Gracious Majesty, is to be considered as offered and accepted without reference to party or political consideration of any kind. His professional claims are amply sufficient to justify my recommendation.[31]

His most significant client during this period was the European and North American for which he had lobbied so strenuously in the House and which was incorporated in 1851. As E.& N.A. solicitor, Ritchie helped draft the contract between the railway company and British contractors, Peto, Brassey, Betts and Jackson, which was signed on 29 September 1852. On 14 September 1853 Lady Head, the wife of the lieutenant-governor, turned the first sod "amidst the vociferous cheers of the surrounding crowd."[32] A day of celebration ended with a great display of fireworks for the public and with a ball for dignitaries and guests. Ritchie, although a widower at this time, probably attended the ball, which was marred by tragedy. The structure built for the orchestra collapsed at the conclusion of the dance, killing three and injuring many.

Railway construction commenced on 16 September 1853 and Ritchie continued as the corporation's lawyer after returning to the Assembly in the 1854 elections. By 1855 the agreement between the E.& N.A. and the builders broke down, primarily under the pressure of financing problems. Ritchie again crossed the Atlantic, this time as solicitor for the railway, and attempted to secure further financing. He arrived back in Saint John in June 1855 and one newspaper wrote: "We heartily trust that the common report is true, and that he has been unsuccessful. If so, a more sane plan for the construction of Railroads in this Province, may shortly be initiated, we trust under the management of the government."[33] However, after Ritchie's initial reconnaissance to England, John Robertson, representing the railway and Charles Fisher, the government, obtained a loan of £800,000 from Baring Brothers in London. The railway was completed on 5 August 1860.[34]

The most important measure of the first year of the Liberal government was the prohibition bill. Ritchie's remarks in debate demonstrated both a traditional liberal tolerance and respect for private morality. While Ritchie's speech acknowledged the "great good" temperance institutions had done, he clearly felt that persuasion was the best tactic in the battle against liquor.

> Hundreds of families in the province were indebted to [the Sons of Temperance] for saving some one of each family by moral suasion and the example they set. He regretted they considered it necessary to adopt coercive measures .... [T]hese coercive laws were not in accordance with the spirit of the people, and therefore could never be carried out, and if any hon. member thought a law could not be carried out, but would remain a dead letter on the statute book, he should be censured for saying so. If the bill before the committee should become law, it was impossible it could be practically carried into effect unless a large majority of the people earnestly desired it; and he believed there was a majority of the people against it. If ever there was a measure that ought to be submitted to the people, for their approval or rejection, this was one, and he would now offer the hon. mover of the bill that if he would insert a clause to that effect, he (hon. Mr. Ritchie) would support the bill, and then, if the majority of the people approved of it, he would do his best, both by precept and example, towards carrying it into effect. He was willing to yield to the wishes of the majority, but at present he felt confident that a majority of the people were opposed to the measure; and if that opinion was correct, the measure was impracticable, because the people would consider it an improper and unconstitutional interference with their rights, and they would believe they were right in evading the law; it would lead to smuggling, perjury, and illicit distillation, from one end of the country to the other, with all the civil consequences attendant thereon, and

the very fact that one law on the statute book would be disregarded and contemned [sic], people would gradually lose their wholesome respect for the laws of the land that was so conducive to good order.[35]

While Ritchie claimed he would support the bill if it enjoyed wide support, his references to "coercion" and "unconstitutional interference with ... rights" indicated that this may have been an argumentative tactic concealing a more fundamental opposition. Whatever the basis of Ritchie's opposition, he was one of the government members to vote against the bill.[36] He had said that "[s]hould the bill pass he would be glad to find that his judgment was wrong,"[37] but his predictions were as accurate as if made in hindsight. The chaos and lawlessness created by the bill was such that in May of 1856, not five months after enforcement commenced, Lieutenant-Governor Manners-Sutton dissolved the House and called for new elections. This was a constitutional gamble by which Manners-Sutton, relying on the unpopularity of the prohibition bill, hoped to rid himself of a government he disliked without provoking a public outcry over his high-handed tactics. The gamble paid off: the prohibitionists were defeated, the Liberals lost their majority, and the new government quickly repealed the prohibition laws. The change of government was only temporary, and with this divisive issue out of the way, the Liberals recovered their strength and were returned in general elections only a year later.

Ritchie did not stand in either the election which removed the Liberals from power, or the one which returned them: on 17 August 1855, he was appointed a puisne judge of the Supreme Court of New Brunswick, to fill the vacancy created by the death of George Frederick Street.[38] New Brunswick historian Stewart MacNutt said that Ritchie's "promising political career was blighted by the early acceptance of a judgeship."[39] Ritchie chose a judicial career as the higher calling.

In the volatile atmosphere of New Brunswick politics, Ritchie's appointment to the Supreme Court was accompanied by both praise and protest. Liberal supporters noted that the new judge had, as a barrister, "gained an eminence rarely attained, while his long and diligent struggle for the establishment of Liberal principles in this Province must have an important influence in securing a just reward for such meritorious service." There was confidence that Ritchie would fill his new position admirably, and at the same

Martha and William Ritchie
Portrait by unknown artist c. 1854
(New Brunswick Museum, Saint John)

time regret that his influence in a political capacity would be lost: "His ability to discharge the important duties of the high office to which he has been appointed, is acknowledged by everybody, and the only regret among his friends is, that his talents and influence will not in future be available in conducting the political affairs of the Province."[40]

Other observers were less charitable. A Fredericton paper asked what accomplishments Ritchie could show to justify his appointment.

> Where is the one great measure he has introduced that marks the statesman, or even the politician of ordinary capacity? Where are his measures of judicial reform that stamp him as a great lawyer? You will seek for them in vain. He frittered away his first four years in Parliament railing at high salaries, and threatening again and again, in childish bravado, to remove the seat of Government to St. John.[41]

Opponents of the promotion alleged that it was the result of dubious political dealings between Ritchie and Attorney General Charles Fisher. Fisher, who was also rumoured as a candidate for the judgeship, had needed Ritchie's support to claim leadership of the new government in 1854.[42] One paper maintained that "Mr. Fisher is merely nominally the leader of the government, and he owes his elevation to the accident that Mr. Ritchie dared not return to his constituents" and that the government was "essentially a Ritchie Government."[43] Another paper thought that if Charles Fisher claimed the perquisites of the office of attorney general, the right to the first judicial vacancy, Ritchie would succeed him and "Mr. Ritchie can get returned; I don't think he will have serious opposition in St. John; and the Government can go on in spite of all its enemies, and he can 'lead' it."[44] Ritchie's appointment removed Fisher's chief political competitor within the government, but it also promoted an ally for the cause of government by law, not by men, to the colony's highest court.

Another significant change in Ritchie's status occurred less than nine months after his appointment to the bench. On 6 May 1856 he married Grace Vernon Nicholson, a daughter of the late Thomas L. Nicholson of Saint John and a stepdaughter of Admiral William Fitz-William Owen. The evening wedding took place at the residence of Admiral Owen in Saint John. The second Mrs. Ritchie, only nineteen at the time of her marriage, acquired a ready-made family — young William was now eleven and his

The "little lake" now called Ritchie Lake

sister Martha about two years younger. This second marriage, when Ritchie was already forty-two would produce twelve more children, seven sons and five daughters. Grace became a life-long companion for her husband.

In 1851, prior to his second marriage, Ritchie purchased for £1,000 a large tract of land adjacent to a little lake about eleven miles from Saint John. After completion of the European and North American Railway from Saint John to Hampton in 1859, passing within about a hundred yards of the lake, and the erection of a station, Ritchie and his family moved into the new house. Ritchie's family at this time consisted of Grace, the two children by his first marriage and two by his second.

The railway named this area Quispamsis from Maliseet *Quispem Sis* meaning "little lake." The Ritchie home was about a quarter of a mile down a lane and surrounded by woods. The two-and-half storey frame house, with its large verandah covered with grape vines, was surrounded by a fine rose garden and a number of lilac trees. To the rear was a barn and a good-sized apple orchard and at the side a carriage house. Rolling lawns descended to the lake where Ritchie kept a number of boats. Ritchie also had some horses and a bridal path was developed around the lake.[45] He gave his estate the name of Kawatcoose. The Ritchies would live there until their move to Ottawa and Grace would give birth to seven more children while residing there.

Notes to Chapter 5

1. *Debates of the House of Assembly of New Brunswick for 1855*, p. 51.

2. Ibid., pp. 62-63.

3. James Steadman, who as a judge later opposed Ritchie's views on judicial review, apparently believed the right to vote was an inherent right belonging to man by nature (see ibid., p. 73).

4. Ibid., p. 57.

5. *Saint John Daily News*, 14 May 1874, p. 2 "Circuit Court."

6. Ibid., 12 May 1875, p. 9 "Circuit Court."

7. Ibid., 14 May 1874, p. 2.

8. Ibid., 12 May 1875, p. 9.

9. *Debates, 1855*, pp. 34, 57, 126.

10. Ritchie voted in favour of the bill for the reduction of judicial salaries; see *Journals of the House*, 25 Apr. 1850.

11. Introduced by Ritchie on 31 Mar. 1851, and taken by Ritchie to the Legislative Council on 5 Apr. 1851 after having passed the House. See the *Journals of the House* for those dates, and Fenety, *Political Notes*, p. 396.

12. *Journals of the House*, 27 Mar. 1851, p. 238.

13. *Morning Freeman*, 15 May 1873, p. 2, "Circuit Court."

14. *Debates, 1855*, p. 48.

15. By 15 & 16 Vic. (U.K.) c.76, ss.18 & 19.

16. *Debates, 1855*, p. 48.

17. Ibid., p. 63.

18. Ibid., pp. 69, 73.

19. Fenety, *Political Notes*, p. 201.

20. Introduced by Ritchie 20 Feb. 1850, passed 28 Feb. 1850, taken to Council by Ritchie 1 Mar. 1850. See *Journals of the House* for those dates.

21. 22 Feb. 1850. The House was evenly divided on the question.

22. *Debates, 1855*, p. 45.

23. *Saint John Daily News*, 12 May 1875, p. 9 "Circuit Court."

24. P.B. Waite, *The Life and Times of Confederation: 1864-1867*, 2nd ed. (Toronto: University of Toronto Press, 1962), p. 233.

25. One cause for which he consistently agitated was removal of the seat of government in the colony from Fredericton to Saint John. Such a proposal had for many years divided the colony, and the uncertainty prevented construction of permanent and appropriate government buildings "compatible with the dignity and wealth of the Province." In a March 1848 attempt the resolution was soundly defeated in the Assembly by twenty-six to eight (see Fenety, *Political Notes*, pp. 280-81).

26. Ibid., pp. 223-24.

27. Ibid, p. 291.

28. G.P. deT. Glazebrook, *A History of Transportation in Canada* (Toronto: McClelland & Stewart, 1964), 1:149.

29. An Act to incorporate the European and North American Railway Company, S.N.B. 1851, c.1.

30. Fenety, *Political Notes*, p. 327.

31. Lawrence, *Judges of New Brunswick*, p. 490.

32. *Saint John Courier*, 17 Sept. 1853.

33. *New Brunswick Reporter*, 29 June 1855, p. 2

34. MacNutt, *New Brunswick*, pp. 379-80. For a critical view of Ritchie's role with the E. & N.A., see "The Great Bubble Railway," *Head Quarters*, (Fredericton) 18 July 1855, p. 2.

35. *Debates, 1855*, p. 109. Ritchie's reference to a law remaining "a dead letter on the statute book" is probably a reference to an earlier prohibition law which had been repealed after having proved practically unenforceable.

36. James Hannay, *History of New Brunswick*: (Saint John: J.A. Bowes, 1909), II:173.

37. *Debates, 1855*, p. 109.

38. Lawrence, *Judges of New Brunswick*, p. 494.

39. W.S. MacNutt, "The Coming of Responsible Government to New Brunswick," *Canadian Historical Review* 33 (1952), p. 121.

40. *Saint John Morning News*, 20 Aug. 1855, p. 2.

41. *Head Quarters*, 22 Aug. 1855, p. 2.

42. Ibid., 5 Sept. 1855, p. 2.

43. Ibid., 8 Aug. 1855, p. 2.

44. *New Brunswick Reporter*, 10 Aug. 1855, p. 2.

45. For the description of Kawatcoose, I am indebted to Mrs. Eleanor M. Jones of Quispamsis. Gordon Fairweather, in a letter dated 27 September 1989, stated "Ritchie Lake is now surrounded by houses and Quispamsis is the fastest-growing municipality in New Brunswick — a dubious distinction given the proliferation of shopping malls and traffic. Chief Justice Ritchie would, as I do, seek a remoter summer retreat."

CHAPTER 6

Puisne Judge and Principled Dissenter

Early in William Ritchie's judicial career on the New Brunswick Supreme Court, the case of *Beardsley* v. *Copeland* (1857) offered a splendid opportunity to define his jurisprudential character. The plaintiff, engaged in lumbering, employed the defendant to go to the Fredericton boom and to see that all the timber with Beardsley's mark was properly rafted. Copeland agreed to devote the whole of his time for the benefit of his employer. However, the plaintiff discovered that the defendant had worked eighty-one days for another boom company, so he sued for the money that Copeland had received from that other boom company. This was an action of an equitable nature and lay, in general, when a defendant received money which in equity ought to be paid to the plaintiff.

Ritchie instructed the jury that if the defendant had agreed to devote all his time exclusively to the plaintiff's business, the wages he had earned from the other boom company would belong to his employer and could be recovered. The jury gave a verdict for the defendant, which meant that Copeland could retain the wages paid by the other boom company, in addition to the wages he had been paid by Beardsley. The plaintiff appealed to the full Supreme Court on grounds that the verdict was contrary to both the law and the evidence.

In a decision rendered by Chief Justice Carter, the majority of the court, with only Ritchie dissenting, held that the plaintiff might have sued to recover damages based on breach of contract but that no action lay in tort (i.e., a personal wrong or injury independent of the breach of contract), against the defendant. The law in 1990 recognizes concurrent remedies in both contract and tort, but not so in this majority decision. Ritchie's dissenting decision was not simply based on the defendant having done something wrong (a tort) but also on the basis that he had received wages to which he was not entitled under terms of his contract with the plaintiff. Ritchie's decision fits the modern law in recognizing a fiduciary duty in an employee and thereby giving wide scope to the concept of restitution. The majority, however, was concerned that "if this action will lie, is it not somewhat unaccountable that there should be no similar case reported?"[1]

Ritchie based his decision on general principles of law and on reason, justice and equity, which he contended favoured the plaintiff's right to the additional wages paid the defendant. The lack of any precedential cases certainly invited such arguments. Ritchie insisted upon the highest standard of integrity from the employee and firm adherence to principles rather than a slavish or narrow approach to law. He stated:

> I cannot avoid the conclusion that the defendant, having agreed to serve the plaintiff for a certain time, having entered on such service and professed to continue therein, and having received his wages and board for the entire period, is now estopped from saying his labour or time, or the proceeds thereof during that period, was his own; and having wrongfully disposed of what rightfully belonged to the plaintiff, and received the proceeds thereof, he cannot either in law or justice retain the money so received; but that the plaintiff waiving any *tort* or the damage, may recover the money actually realised by the defendant, in an action of *indebitatus* assumpsit, as money had and received to his use.[2]

The case revealed a certain tenacity and independence of mind, perhaps bordering on intellectual arrogance, that set the more creative judge apart from merely competent colleagues. He was the most junior judge on the court and unable to sway any member to his perception. Nevertheless, he wrote an elaborate dissent of some seventeen pages. It was well-crafted but never succeeded in combatting the problem perceived by the majority, that the plaintiff would receive a large compensation for a nominal injury. The plaintiff did not allege that the defendant had neglected his duty to look after his logs, but only that the defendant breached his contract by concurrently rendering services to another boom company.

Ritchie's decision could be interpreted as pro-employer and rendered by a person who in legal practice had acted more often for employers than for employees. But it did seem that his search for the absolute principle might just as easily have cut the other way to have favoured the employee rather than the employer.

Ritchie might have been faulted for a failure to recognize that by insisting on principle, the fruits of the hard work and initiative on the part of the employee were unfairly transferred to the first employer, who had done nothing to earn them other than sign the original contract. Judges, it is said, write most freely in dissent, for they know that their decision will not affect the litigants. Ritchie might have felt more liberty in evolving a restitutionary remedy because it would not be applied to the particular defendant. But, of course, at trial he was prepared to deprive the employee of the additional remuneration.

In another early case, *The Queen* v. *Dennis* (1857), Ritchie convicted a prisoner for an offence committed after the day on which the circuit court was adjourned. However, Ritchie decided to reserve the question of whether he had jurisdiction to try such an offence for the full court. Ritchie thought he had jurisdiction, but when the liberty of the subject was in issue, he controlled any tendency he had towards intellectual arrogance and decided to defer to the full court. Chief Justice Carter affirmed the conviction and stated that "although the reason for the adjournment might be the unfinished state of the civil business, ... the criminal jurisdiction is not confined and restricted to the trial of indictments previously found, nor to offences committed before the adjournment."[3]

The case of *Simpson* v. *Read* (1858) brought home the profound difference between the society of the 1850s and that of the 1990s. A father brought an action of trespass against the defendant, Read, for seducing his daughter, who was under age. The father had hired out his daughter as a servant by the month and received her wages. When she became pregnant she returned to her father's house and he supported her during the pregnancy. At trial Ritchie held that the father might be considered to have a constructive right to his daughter's services and, having been deprived of her wages, he was entitled to £30 in damages. On an appeal to the full court, the judges regretted that "the law does not provide some redress for a parent who has sustained so great an injury as this plaintiff has, but it does not do so"[4] and quashed the verdict for the plaintiff. Chief Justice Carter held that the loss of service was the gist of the action and therefore the relationship of master and servant had to exist to permit recovery. Had she been living at home, the loss of service would have been presumed but not where the parent parted with the right to her services.

The distinction seemed artificial. Ritchie reaffirmed his view that the father's right to receive his daughter's wages might be regarded as a constructive right to her services. However, he deferred saying "but my learned brethren being so clear on the point, I shall not allow my doubts to delay the decision."[5] Ritchie did venture the opinion that the evidence adduced at trial led him to conclude that the daughter herself was not without a remedy, for she could sue for breach of promise of marriage. The case appears shocking today, recognizing what is virtually the father's property right in his child; but in the context of the time, Ritchie's trial decision expanded existing law by allowing compensation for damage. He would not throw up his hands and recite that "the law may not be just but it is the law!"

The differences allowable in the 1850s were also exemplified by the state of the criminal law. Had the daughter been raped rather than seduced, the penalty would have been death, as a mandatory and not simply a maximum sentence. One must doubt whether a mandatory death sentence really promoted the interests of women, as male juries were exceedingly reluctant to convict.

In *Allison* v. *The President of the Central Bank* (1859) the plaintiff was the agent of Fairbanks Company of Halifax, owner of several bank notes issued by the Central Bank and payable to the bearer. The plaintiff, as agent, demanded payment and when refused, sued on the notes. At the trial Ritchie had found for the plaintiff. On appeal to the full court the bank contended that a mere agent with no interest in the note could not sue. All members of the court agreed that this defence could not prevail. Ritchie thought that such a defence would introduce a dangerous doctrine into mercantile law and

> would hamper exceedingly the law relating to bills of exchange, which, when payable to bearer, or indorsed in blank, are transferable by mere delivery, and may be sued upon by any person who has the lawful possession of them. The principle is much stronger in the case of Bank notes, which are intended to be circulated as money. I think that where the *bona fide* holder of a Bank note presents it for payment, the Bank is bound to pay it, whether he has a beneficial interest in it or not, and if payment is refused, he can bring an action.[6]

This exemplified the sort of functional common sense, informed by the needs of commerce, which Ritchie adopted in applying the law. He had a keen, simple sense of debt and credit in human relations.

In *Myers* v. *Smith* (1858), a tenant brought an action of replevin, to recover goods taken by the landlord, Smith, when Myers had not paid his rent. The law allowed the landlord to distrain or seize property of the tenant. However, this landlord had forcibly broken the outer door of the house in order to seize the property and this, the tenant argued, made the distress illegal.

At trial, Justice Parker ruled that Myers was neither entitled to recover his property without paying the rent due nor entitled to recover damages against the landlord for breaking the outer door. Parker regarded the breaking of the door to be simply an irregularity. The full court upheld this decision with only Ritchie dissenting.

Ritchie thought that the tenant should succeed in his action, because Smith's wrongful taking should not create any benefit arising out of his illegal act. Ritchie again took a firm moral stand, against wrongdoing by the landlord, but he recognized the need for the law to attain a proper balance between the rights of the landlord and of the tenant. He realized that the right to distrain for rent placed the landlord in a more advantageous position than other creditors. After concluding that because the outer doors were locked the landlord was not entitled to distrain, Ritchie stated:

> Can he [the landlord] then act in direct defiance of the law; break and enter, and distrain, and ask a court of law to sustain any part of such conduct? I can really see no hardship whatever on the landlord. He has without this great security. The law gives him large powers for the recovery of his rent, unknown in the collection of other debts; but it by no means says, because rent happens to be due, that at all hazards and under all circumstances he may take the law into his own hands.[7]

Ritchie, therefore, unlike the majority, would not accept that breaking into the house occupied by the tenant was simply an irregularity, excused by a statute which said that "any irregularity in conducting a distress where rent is due, shall not make the distrainor a trespasser." He vigorously rejected this classification of the landlord's conduct, stating that "I cannot look upon the matter alleged in this case, as a mere irregularity in conducting the distress, but as an illegality from the first, rendering the distress not merely irregular, but absolutely illegal and void."[8] Ritchie's decision seemed more reasonable in its balancing of the two interests in conflict than that of the majority. His decision would tend to deter landlords from resorting to self-help in situations likely to lead to breaches of the peace. A person's home was still his castle, even if rented and even when he was behind in his rent.

Ritchie continued to be an uneasy colleague. In *Kinnear* v. *Ferguson* (1859), the plaintiff sued to recover the amount of two promissory notes drawn by the defendant. Ferguson had provided Kinnear with timber as security for the payment of the notes, but the timber was not to be sold without giving fourteen days notice to the defendant. Kinnear sold the timber but his notice to the defendant was defective. Ferguson contended that he should be given credit, not just for the sale price received by Kinnear, but because the sale was improper he should be given credit for the highest value of the timber. At trial, Ritchie directed the jury that the plaintiff was chargeable with the highest market value of the timber on the day of sale. Kinnear appealed to the full court on the ground of misdirection.

The judgment of the full court, delivered by Chief Justice Carter, held that the payment was the amount actually received by the plaintiff, not the highest value of the timber on the day of sale. The defendant had to either adopt the sale or repudiate it altogether. He might have sued for improper conversion or for a breach of agreement by the plaintiff, but any such damages suffered by the defendant were not available as a set off to the plaintiff's claim on the promissory notes. The full court held that Ritchie had misdirected the jury and ordered a new trial. Ritchie acknowledged "having doubts about the case" and reluctantly concurred in the judgment of the chief justice but "with great hesitation."[9]

He had been basically a commercial lawyer, but on the bench he rendered thoughtful and detailed judgments on a whole range of non-commercial subjects. As a trial judge, he would have no choice, but when sitting as a member of the full court he still chose to write long careful judgments in many areas. For instance, in *Bennett* v. *Jones* (1859) the issue related to family law: basically, whether a husband who had wrongfully turned his wife out of his house could terminate his legal liability for her support by offering to take her back. The wife's brother brought an action against the husband to recover for fifty-six weeks board and lodging which the brother had furnished to his sister. The trial judge had directed the jury that the husband, having compelled his wife to leave without cause, did not relieve himself from liability to a third person who supplied the wife with necessaries after the offer to take her back was made. The husband appealed on the ground of misdirection.

Ritchie wrote the leading judgment, insisting that for there to be a continuing agency there must be a continuing necessity. To hold the agency to be irrevocable would be to frustrate the public policy of encouraging reunion of spouses living apart. Ritchie's decision would restrict and confine the wife's agency of necessity, a serious matter when wives generally had little or no opportunity to enter the work force. However, Ritchie's decision was sympathetic to the interests and vulnerability of wives. In concluding his judgment, he stated:

> The result then of my present judgment is, that the learned Judge should have submitted to the jury the question whether the defendant did or did not make his wife a *bona fide* request to return, receive support, and live with him; and if so, whether she refused on any well founded belief that indignities or cruelties would be renewed upon her return? And they should have been told that if she did, she was justified in remaining away. But if the offer was clear, distinct, positive, and *bona fide*, and she had no reasonable grounds for believing she would be subjected to further ill treatment, she was bound to return, and if she did not, the right to pledge her husband's credit ceased.[10]

Ritchie's decision ordering a new trial was concurred in by two of the other three judges including the trial judge, Justice Parker, whose decision was overruled. Parker said, "It will be more satisfactory that the case should go to another trial, and the facts be left more openly to the jury."[11]

The master of the rolls, N. Parker, dissented and his decision would have provided greater autonomy to the wife. He noted that "the course of English jurisprudence has been to build up a system in which the separate rights of the wife are distinctly recognized and upheld." This would not be today's assessment of the law in 1859! However, he indicated that the husband desired her return to save his own pocket and stated:

> Now, the question is, not whether, as a christian wife, she ought not to forget and forgive, but whether she is legally bound, under these circumstances, either to return or starve. Her consent was necessary to their union: has not the act of her husband restored to her the right of exercising her own judgment as to a reunion?[12]

Ritchie certainly did not allow that much autonomy to a married woman.

71

The dissenting judge contended that because the common law courts did not at this time possess jurisdiction to order restitution of conjugal rights, the agency of necessity in a wife wrongly forced from her husband's home must continue, except in the case of great misconduct on her part. He recognized that terminating the agency of necessity meant most wives would have no choice but to return to their husbands. Both Ritchie's majority judgment and the dissent were sensitive to the great dependency of wives upon husbands, because women generally lacked any economic power. Given such realities, the greatest evil would have been to deny the wife sustenance, by leaving her outside everyone's legal liability for support.

In The *Queen* v. *Dowling* (1862) the issue was whether the City of Fredericton had been authorized by its city charter to impose tolls for the anchorage of vessels by virtue of section 54, which empowered the city "to regulate the anchorage, lading and unlading of vessels arriving at the City." Ritchie joined all members of the court in quashing a conviction for failing to pay the anchorage tolls. He stated: "The power to impose a tax which may affect the shipping of a great river, should be given in clear and unambiguous language; and not by mere implication. I think the words of the Act will not bear the construction contended for."[13] The judgment represented the usual application of the principle that regulations and rules made under an act of the legislature had to be clearly authorized by the legislation. The principle that ambiguity in taxation legislation should be resolved in favour of the taxpayer also assisted the taxpayer.

This case cast light on the subsequent decision in *The Queen* v. *The Assessor of Rates for the City of Fredericton* (1864). The issue was whether the City of Fredericton could levy a tax on the salary of the lieutenant-governor, Arthur Hamilton Gordon, under its charter. Section 59 of the charter authorized the city to levy a tax "upon the income of the inhabitants of the City, derived from any trade, profession or calling within the Province." While in the previous case the court unanimously held the anchorage fee invalid, the court in the case of the lieutenant-governor split three to two in holding that his salary was not subject to tax.

Ritchie was one of two dissenting judges who held the lieutenant-governor was subject to tax. He was not over-awed by persons in high authority. It also revealed his strong democratic convictions when he held that all holders of public offices should contribute "their fair proportion towards the necessary public expenditure of the City, the benefits derivable from which, they enjoy in common with the rest of the inhabitants." His reasons for judgment illustrated that Ritchie had a modern, functional approach to the interpretation of statutes:

> I think it more reasonable to conclude that the Legislature contemplated the raising of a revenue on the incomes of tradesmen, professional men, and those of a similar and higher vocation, rather than on those of a similar or lower degree, descending as it would to the humblest laborer, and others of that class; it being scarcely reasonable to suppose that it was intended to tax incomes from such occupations or callings, and leave the salaries of all officials, high and low, to escape scot-free, as it appears to me would be the necessary result of the construction contended for.[14]

He would not permit rules of construction to dictate results which he regarded as unjust. He stated:

> But it has been argued, that as this Act imposes a tax, it should receive the strictest and most limited construction. No doubt it is a good rule of construction, that where a charge is to be imposed on the subject, it ought to be done in clear and unambiguous language; but it must be borne in mind, that in this case, as the larger incomes of the numerous office-holders, inhabitants of the City are released, a greater burthen is cast on the smaller incomes and taxable property of the other inhabitants, whereby not only a greater, but, an unequal burthen is in effect imposed on them. This I think, ought not to be done by denying a word its known, and natural signification, unless it is quite clear that the intention was, in this particular case, not to give it that meaning.[15]

Ritchie thus put into proper perspective the rule that an act imposing a tax should be strictly construed in favour of the taxpayer. He made the rule subservient to the overriding principle that taxing statutes, in common with all statutes, must be construed to achieve their object and purpose.

This anticipated the modern approach to the interpretation of all statutes. They are to be liberally construed in order to achieve their objective. Driedger, after quoting the rule that if there is any ambiguity in a taxing statute it must be interpreted in favour of the taxpayer, commented as follows: "But one might ask, why must it be? It may well be that a construction against the taxpayer might better carry out the intention and object of the Act."[16] Ritchie's dissenting decision did just that and in so doing anticipated the modern rule enunciated by Justice Dickson (as he then was), that

> fiscal legislation does not stand in a category by itself .... The correct approach, applicable to statutory construction generally, is to construe the legislation with reasonable regard to its object and purpose and to give it such interpretation as best ensures the attainment of such object and purpose.[17]

Ritchie's decision might also be regarded as courageous for, although substantial progress had been made towards responsible government, the lieutenant-governor still retained some influence over judicial appointments and advancement.

Notes to Chapter 6

1. (1857), 8 N.B.R. 458 at p. 462.

2. Ibid., p. 482.

3. (1857), 8 N.B.R 423 at p. 425.

4. (1858), 9 N.B.R. 52 at p. 53.

5. Ibid., p. 54.

6. (1859), 9 N.B.R. 270 at p. 272.

7. (1858), 9 N.B.R. 207 at p. 214.

8. Ibid., p. 215.

9. (1859), 9 N.B.R. 391 at p. 393.

10. (1859), 9 N.B.R. 397 at p. 406.

11. Ibid., pp. 406-7.

12. Ibid, pp. 409-10.

13. (1862), 10 N.B.R. 378 at p. 379.

14. (1864), 11 N.B.R. 1 at p. 5.

15. Ibid., p. 6.

16. Elmer A. Driedger, *The Construction of Statutes*, 2d ed. (Toronto: Butterworths, 1983), p. 206.

17. *Covert* v. *Minister of Finance (N.S.)* [1980] 2 S.C.R. 774 at p. 807. Dickson's decision was a dissent but there is no indication that the majority disapproved of this approach to the interpretation of taxing statutes. By insisting on the importance of substance over form, the majority decision rendered by Justice Martland exemplified even more clearly what Dickson stated to be the correct approach to the interpretation of fiscal legislation.

CHAPTER 7

The Hea Affair

Ritchie clearly did not think that going to the bench meant joining a cloister. Five years as a judge had not blunted his interest in public affairs, particularly those that touched life-long commitments, especially to public education.

The University of New Brunswick, established in 1859 as a secular institution, was the successor to King's College in Fredericton, which had come under bitter attack for the Anglican restrictions in its charter, and for a strictly classical curriculum inappropriate for a developing province. Justice Ritchie gave "the most practical evidence of...confidence"[1] in this reformed institution by enrolling his eldest son William in the first session. This confidence was not blind, however, and father and son were instrumental in bringing about the dismissal of the first president of the university, Dr. Joseph Hea, after a tenure of less than a year.

Beginning in September of 1860, when he took charge, Hea's position was a difficult one.[2] The act which established the new University provided that its president could not be a clergyman, which meant that the former principal of King's College, the Reverend Dr. Edwin Jacob, could not continue as president. Dr. Jacob had received an earlier disappointment. He thought he should be the first bishop of the new diocese of New Brunswick and enjoyed considerable low church support, but in 1844 the Archbishop of Canterbury appointed John Medley. Dr. Jacob was also disinclined to accept his demotion to mere professor, and for more than a month he refused to relinquish his quarters in the Arts Building to the new president.

This initial tension was exacerbated by Dr. Hea's determination to make his mark on the administration of the institution, particularly with regard to "the control and restraint of students out of lecture hours." As might be imagined, this project was not welcomed by the students, and Dr. Hea complained that "I was met among the Students by the spirit I expected, a bad one." The president's disciplinary tactics were not calculated to change this attitude: "Mild means were ineffectual," he said, and "sternness and severity of manner were required to enforce attention." So, on one occasion he was forced to point out that "there is such a thing as the toe of a boot, and an application of that kind would accelerate the progress of an offender over the terrace," although he claimed he was "not stating that [he] *would* apply it, but as an abstract proposition." Referring to another incident, Dr. Hea was adamant that, contrary to the contention of the student involved, he did not use the expression "toe of my boot" at all: he stated firmly that, "I said I would take him by the neck and throw him out of the college." He did not state whether this was meant as an abstract proposition or not. In any case, there was certainly nothing abstract about the toe of his boot, nor his shoulder, when one evening during study hours the president went to check up on one of the students. After knocking and failing to receive prompt admission, Dr. Hea applied both boot and shoulder to the door, hoping, he explained, "to force the door before there was time to conceal anything."[3]

While Dr. Hea considered his general habit in dealing with students to be one of extreme courtesy, with resort to severity only when milder measures failed, the students were of the opinion that his conduct ranged from "undignified and improper" through "arbitrary and tyrannical" all the way to "rude," "violent ... and passionate."[4] On one occasion when young William Ritchie had misunderstood an order of Dr. Hea's to report to the library, Ritchie said that "he appeared so violent, I was prepared to receive a blow."[5] Another student reported that "on the evening of [Dr. Hea's] kicking at the door, he did not appear like a rational being," and further that he had been slow to answer the door because he thought the knock was that of another student, but "when he heard the kick at the door, he knew it was Dr. Hea. No one else in the College would have been guilty of such a thing." What the president described as a severe reprimand, the student reported as being delivered "in a violent passion, and in so inarticulate a manner, that I could not understand him."[6]

The conflict between the students and the president on these and many other matters was brought to a head by the young William Ritchie when Dr. Hea directed the students to tidy their rooms in preparation for a visit by a number of Fredericton gentlemen who were to be shown the college. When Hea came to inspect he was not satisfied with the state of Ritchie's room, and told him to improve the situation. Ritchie's reply was that "all his private property was in its proper place, as he had put everything as he was accustomed to do, at that time of day, and [he] suggested that perhaps the beds had not been made." Dr. Hea did not appreciate Ritchie's suggestion, and stated that "he did not mean the servant-work, but that he referred to books and things lying about the table."[7] Ritchie asked pointedly whether the visitors were coming to see him, or his private property, and further asked Dr. Hea to postpone the visit, intending to consult his father as to the legality of the president ordering the students to open their rooms to visitors. Dr. Hea told him that there were some dozen visitors, too many to ask to postpone the visit. Sarcastically Hea offered to give Ritchie their names so that he could go to town and tell them the visit was to be postponed. Ritchie replied ingenuously that "I will have much pleasure in doing so." By this time Dr. Hea felt that he had suffered "a great deal of insolence and rudeness" from Ritchie. "At last," said Dr. Hea, "as a test of obedience, I ordered him to perform a certain act" — namely to put down a book of matches which Ritchie had taken from a shelf. "He was very insolent, but at length complied, under my threat, 'Disobey me at your peril, if you dare!'" Ritchie complied, saying "I believe it is the best course to obey you at the present."

The next day Dr. Hea imposed a punishment of two hundred lines of Virgil on Ritchie, and ordered him not to leave the college until it was done. Ritchie nonetheless went to Fredericton and "took some advice upon the subject," perhaps from his father. This inference is strengthened by the studied correctness of Ritchie's response; he wrote out the punishment, and submitted it attached to a written protest, which read as follows:

> Mr. Ritchie writes the following imposition, being reluctant to do anything which may be construed into insubordination, or resistance to legitimate authority: but he solemnly protests against the justice of the President's conduct, in inflicting punishment where no offence was committed; and he solemnly denies the right of the President to inflict punishment without calling a Board of Discipline, in compliance with the Statutes.[8]

It might be more accurate to say that Mr. Ritchie did not wish to do anything which would amount to outright rebellion, but his manner, which he described as studiously polite, made his true opinion of Dr. Hea quite clear. Hea reciprocated the feeling, and when Ritchie delivered the punishment, the president tore up the protest without reading it.

Not surprisingly, the other students took Ritchie's part in the matter, and eighteen of a student body of about twenty went so far as to deliver to the president a signed memorandum supporting Ritchie's protest. Of more consequence, at least so far as the president was concerned, a number of them also wrote to their parents requesting that they be removed from the university. As a result eight parents, including Judge Ritchie, presented to the lieutenant-governor, J.H.T. Manners-Sutton, in his capacity as Visitor of the university, a petition seeking the removal of the president. On 2 March 1861, the Visitor whose own son was a student at the university informed the president that charges had been brought against him and that he would conduct an inquiry to be held in the university library.

Both parties were represented by counsel. The first meeting was a brief one, at which the Visitor directed the prosecution to prepare a list of charges more detailed than the general ones in the originating petition. As well as the complaints of the illegality of the order that the students should admit visitors to their rooms, and the injustice of Ritchie's subsequent punishment, the twenty-six charges included allegations that Hea had listened at the door of students' rooms, that he used violent language and gestures, that he told a profane story about a Methodist parson, and that he inquired too closely into the religious and social status of students. Hea claimed that the allegations that he had made threatening gestures and delivered reprimands in tones that roused the entire residence were exaggerated; he admitted to being stern and severe at times, but never more than the insolence, lack of application, and occasional "very gross personal discourtesy" on the part of the students warranted. He claimed that the students played cards and cooked in their rooms against his orders, and were given to drawing caricatures and writing lampoons directed against him.

The young Ritchie, who was then seventeen, was the first to testify and gave his evidence in a "clear, distinct, and candid manner," which showed the same assertive poise which he had displayed in his earlier dealings with Dr. Hea. Counsel for Hea at one point "tried to convince the witness, that at his age he was not competent to judge as to what was gentlemanly conduct." The reporter noted that "the witness however was of a different opinion." In the end it appears that the lieutenant-governor shared Ritchie's opinion, as on the two charges which turned on the word of Ritchie and another student against the president, the Visitor found the facts to be as Ritchie had stated them. He also found that Ritchie properly objected to showing his room at Hea's request, as the rooms "must be regarded ... as private apartments set apart for, and belonging during the period of occupation, exclusively to the students who occupy them, although liable to be entered at any time by the proper authorities, for the purpose of maintaining discipline and order." As well, the Visitor found, again, as Ritchie had contended, that the president was not empowered to set such an imposition as he had done without calling a board of discipline.

While Ritchie won his points on the merits, the Visitor noted, with some understatement, that Ritchie's behaviour had "combined with studied politeness in words, a manner which was not calculated to restore the equanimity of the President, or consistent with the relations which ought to exist between a student and the President of the university." This censure was tempered by the comment that Ritchie was then "smarting under a sense of what he regarded, and in my judgment had reason to regard, as a double injustice." (Regarding cooking in the rooms, especially of stolen poultry, which Dr. Hea had said he was most anxious to stop, the Visitor found that there had been no cooking except a few vegetables, two squirrels, and a woodpecker, which were cooked "for anatomical purposes." It appears that Ritchie had been tempted to taste the squirrel, but there is no evidence it became a habit.[9]) Ritchie's sensibilities were injured not only by his own treatment at the hands of Dr. Hea but also by the president's behaviour in accusing the ex-principal, Dr. Jacob, of drunkenness in the presence of the students, and reading to them a letter addressed to Dr. Jacob on this matter. The Visitor found that this was calculated to diminish the students' respect for Dr. Jacob, but that such impropriety also prejudiced Hea's own authority. The latter was true in Ritchie's case; he commented that "I felt quite disgusted" by Dr. Hea's conduct.

The young Ritchie's proud refusal to suffer injustice, and his scrupulous regard for legality in his protests, seemed to reflect the influence of his father, who apparently advised him in his initial resistance to Hea's punishment, and who was one of the parents to petition for Hea's removal. Justice Ritchie's concern for strict fairness in the proceedings is also shown by an addendum to the petition for the removal of Dr. Hea submitted to the Visitor, which was signed by Ritchie and four of the other complaining parents. It read:

> We the undersigned having read the foregoing to our sons, some of them think that the conversation mentioned in the Thirteenth Section may have been introduced by one of their number and not by Dr. Hea. We, therefore, feel bound to mention this, though we do not think it alters the principle involved. At the same time we are informed that the President has, upon several occasions, introduced and encouraged among the students of different denominations, discussions upon controversial questions in religious matters, which we consider still more highly objectionable.[10]

Legal resistance to illegal abuse of power proved effective in the end: the Visitor's final conclusion was that although the evidence did not support all of the twenty-six charges, it showed that the president

> although not deficient in zeal or industry has in the performance of his duties been wanting to a marked degree in that even courtesy of demeanour and language, that habitual self-control and command of temper, which are at least as necessary as zeal and industry to secure to any officer of the University the respect of the Students, and which are absolutely essential to enable the President to maintain harmony and discipline in the University.

The Senate of the University of New Brunswick considered the charges and the Visitor's judgment in May and concurred with the judgment. Dr. Hea tendered his resignation effective 1 July 1861. His eleven-month presidency is remembered in a history of the University of New Brunswick with the comment that "with one unfortunate exception, and that for a period of only a few months, the Presidency was in the hands of extremely able men."[11] Dr. Hea subsequently moved to Toronto and became an adjuster for the Toronto Insurance Company.

In 1863 young William enrolled in the Harvard Law School, together with his first cousin, Thomas Ritchie, from Halifax. The faculty at that period consisted of only three professors, and the law library boasted only thirteen thousand volumes. The school had no entrance examination and did not require any prior course of study, but a non-college graduate had to be "at least nineteen years of age, and produce testimonials of good moral character."[12]

Both the Ritchie boys graduated with LL.B degrees in 1865. It would be interesting to know whether the Judge and his brother John W. Ritchie, by sending their sons to Harvard, manifested a dissatisfaction with the kind of legal education they themselves had received or whether they simply thought that their sons should receive every possible educational advantage.

Young William became an attorney in New Brunswick on 9 June 1866 and received his call to the bar three years later. On 15 November 1870, he married Joanna Robinson Hazen, the daughter of Joanna and Robert Fraser Hazen, the residuary heir of the Chipman dynasty. Only four months after his wedding, on 26 March 1871, at the age of twenty-six, William committed suicide in Malta. Isaac Allen Jack, a friend and fellow student at the University of New Brunswick, recorded tersely in his journal the following day that "a Telegram from Malta announces the death of poor Will Ritchie."[13] Justice Ritchie's involvement in the Hea affair and his sending young William to Harvard indicated his firm commitment to his family, and the death of a son whose temperament seemed so like his father's must have been a great blow.

Notes to Chapter 7

1. From the petition requesting the removal of Dr. Hea as president of the University of New Brunswick presented to His Excellency, the Honourable J.H.T Manners-Sutton, Lieutenant-Governor of New Brunswick, in his capacity as Visitor of the University, reported in the Saint John *Colonial Empire*, 27 Mar. 1861.

2. See Dr. Hea's testimony, reported in 15 Mar. 1861. The *Royal Gazette* reports Dr. Hea's appointment on 25 July 1860.

3. Proceedings of the Visitor's Court at the University of New Brunswick, testimony of Dr. Hea, reported in the Saint John *Colonial Empire*, 15 Mar. 1861.

4. From the allegations against Dr. Hea submitted to the Visitor of the University, reported by *Colonial Empire*, 28 Mar. 1861.

5. Proceedings of the Visitor's Court, testimony of William Pollok Ritchie, reported in ibid., 14 Mar. 1861.

6. Proceedings of the Visitor's Court, testimony of Robert Matthew, reported in ibid., 14 Mar. 1861.

7. Report of the Visitor, reported in ibid., 28 Mar. 1861.

8. Ibid., 14 Mar. 1861.

9. Testimony of Allen Jack, reported in ibid., 15 Mar. 1861.

10. Reported in ibid., 28 Mar. 1861.

11. A.W. Trueman, *Canada's University of New Brunswick: Its History and Its Development,*(New York: Newcomen Society in North America, 1952), p. 17.

12. *A Catalogue of the Law School of the University at Cambridge, for the Academical Year 1863-64* (Cambridge: Sever & Francis, 1864) p. 17.

13. Journal of Isaac Allen Jack, 27 Mar. 1871, A 20, New Brunswick Museum.

CHAPTER 8

Propelled into the American Civil War

Ritchie's work as a judge drew him into the *Chesapeake* affair, pushing him briefly onto the international stage. In 1863, while the American Civil War raged destructively, a conspiracy was hatched in Saint John. The leading participants were Vernon Locke alias John Parker, John C. Braine and H.A. Parr.[1] They proposed to seize the *Chesapeake*, a six-hundred-ton steamer that plied between New York City and Portland, Maine, and convert her into a Confederate privateer to prey on Northern shipping. On 5 December 1863, sixteen "passengers" had booked passage in New York on the *Chesapeake* for Portland. Two days later, when the ship was twenty miles off Cape Cod, the sixteen overpowered the watch, shot and killed the second engineer, wounded the chief engineer and the first mate, seized and handcuffed the crew and put Captain Willets in irons. Braine took command of the *Chesapeake* and she steamed north along the coast of Maine. When the ship neared Saint John, a pilot boat came alongside and Captain John Parker boarded and assumed command of the *Chesapeake*. Parker transferred Captain Willets and all but five of his crew to the pilot boat, which returned to Saint John. On 9 December, news of the capture of the *Chesapeake* on the high seas raced through the city. Captain Willet telegraphed the owners and soon the United States secretary of the navy ordered all available vessels to steam north and recapture the *Chesapeake*.

Parker had failed to obtain an adequate supply of coal to fill the depleting bunkers of the *Chesapeake* at Saint John, and later a storm on the Bay of Fundy forced the steamer to take refuge at Shelburne, Nova Scotia. The cargo of the *Chesapeake* was sold for sacrifice prices along the south shore of Nova Scotia in order to buy coal. On the morning of 17 December 1863, while the Nova Scotian schooner *Investigator* was supplying the *Chesapeake* with coal in Sambro Harbour, the United States gunboat *Ella and Annie* steamed into the harbour and recaptured the *Chesapeake*, but not before her new crew had fled ashore. After securing the *Chesapeake* the Americans boarded and searched the *Investigator*, finding on board John Wade, one of the original captors of the *Chesapeake*. Lieutenant Nichols, who commanded the *Ella and Annie*, made Wade a prisoner and was about to tow the *Chesapeake* to Boston. However, another United States gunboat, the *Decotah*, commanded by Captain Clary, an officer senior to and wiser than Nichols, arrived on the scene. Clary realized that the seizure of a vessel in a British colonial port, and the boarding of a Nova Scotian vessel, was a serious breach of British territorial rights. Consequently Clary ordered Nichols to proceed with the *Chesapeake* to Halifax. Lieutenant-Governor Doyle ordered that none of the ships involved were to leave Halifax until a full investigation had been made. John Wade was to be turned over to the high sheriff of Halifax, but while Wade was being transferred a scuffle developed, instigated by Dr. W.J. Almon. In the confusion, Wade escaped in a small boat manned by two crack oarsmen.

The rest of the *Chesapeake* captors had also scattered. The scene then reverted to Saint John, where some of the original captors reappeared. The United States consul in Saint John requested the arrest of the men named in the deposition of Captain Willets and Daniel Henderson of the *Chesapeake*. Lieutenant-Governor Gordon issued a warrant under an imperial statute which implemented the Webster-Ashburton Treaty of 1842. But delay in issuing this warrant permitted many of the wanted men to escape and only three were arrested: David Collins, James McKinney and Linus Seely. They appeared before Police Magistrate H. T. Gilbert and the hearings lasted from the beginning of January until 24 February 1864.

The police magistrate held that he had jurisdiction in the case of piracy and that there was no authority for any "letters of marque" identifying the vessel as *Retribution*, a private armed vessel in the Confederate service to be endorsed over to John Parker, the alias assumed by Vernon Locke. Thus, Locke had no authority to create officers for the Confederate service within New Brunswick. The magistrate also held that the jurisdiction of the lieutenant-governor was not a subject upon which he could adjudicate. He issued a warrant of commitment confining the prisoners to the Saint John gaol, pending their extradition. The magistrate's ruling was appealed to the Supreme Court, and on

10 March 1864, Justice Ritchie quashed the warrant of commitment. He found a number of grounds for discharging the warrant
and ordered the prisoners to be freed.[2]

The United States had not made a proper requisition under
the extradition treaty, alleging the act of piracy. The offence was
not committed in the United States but on the high seas and the
offenders had never, after committing the offence, entered the
United States. Ritchie also held that the police magistrate did not
have jurisdiction over the offence of piracy and should have
referred the matter to the judge of the Court of Vice-Admiralty.
Ritchie agreed with the magistrate that there was a *prima facie* case
of piracy. As neutrals, the prisoners had not established that in
seizing the *Chesapeake* they were acting under the legitimate
authority of a belligerent government, so the seizure became an
act of legitimate warfare and not an act of piracy.

Ritchie's decision, against the potentially troublesome background of the affair, was hailed by some observers as the best
solution to a difficult problem. Had the extradition warrant been
upheld, the United States would have found itself in the uncomfortable position of having to prosecute up to eleven British subjects on piracy charges. Conversely, had Ritchie appeared
sympathetic to the pirates and recognized their belligerent status,
he ran the risk of inflaming American opinion. While he ultimately
released the group, the judge made clear his reservations about
their conduct:

> ... I cannot refrain from expressing my deep regret that any
> inhabitants of New Brunswick, being British subjects, should
> have been seduced from their clear duty to their sovereign, and
> have availed themselves of the hospitality of a friendly power
> by going into its territory and obtaining a passage from one of
> its ports, on board one of its ships, and, by a stratagem possibly
> justified by the wages of war in a belligerent, have risen against
> an unarmed crew peaceably engaged in their lawful calling, and
> dispoiled them of the property under their charge, and that too
> with an amount of violence resulting in the death of one of the
> crew, which, under the evidence in this case, would not seem to
> have been necessary for the accomplishment of the end sought
> to be attained — an example, I may be permitted to add, I
> earnestly trust will not be followed by any of Her Majesty's loyal
> subjects in this province.[3]

The New York *World* credited Ritchie with having saved the
United States government from "a serious and embarrassing

dilemma."[4] MacNutt claims that the captives' release also kept the population of Saint John satisfied. There was a large measure of sympathy for the prisoners, as most of the Maritimes harboured significant pockets of Southern support.[5] Justice Ritchie in concluding his decision stated that he was not affected by such considerations:

> ... whomsoever it may please or displease must be to me, judicially, a matter of indifference. The only duty I have to discharge is to my sovereign, to the people of this Province, and to my own conscience. That duty is, faithfully, to the best of my humble abilities, impartially, to declare the Law as I honestly believe it to be, wholly regardless of circumstances.[6]

Ritchie's decision was praised by the *Morning Freeman* as "able and elaborate" and the crowd in the courtroom were reported to have greeted the decision with applause.[7] If this did occur, Ritchie probably would have strongly disapproved. The *Morning Telegraph* declared that the discharge of the men was universally approved.[8] Ritchie might have felt that he was in a somewhat difficult position and that his impartiality could be impugned. His eldest brother J.W. Ritchie, acted for the Confederate States in relation to the *Chesapeake* affair in Halifax.[9] Dr. W.J. Almon, who was largely responsible for John Wade's escaping, had three daughters and one son, each of whom married a sibling of Justice Ritchie. The implication of Justice Ritchie's decision was that, although the men could not be extradited to the United States, they could be charged and tried for piracy in New Brunswick. However, the discharged men immediately left Saint John and thus escaped re-arrest on the charge of piracy. In Halifax, adjudication of the ownership of the *Chesapeake* came before Justice Stewart of the Vice-Admiralty Court in Halifax, and on 15 February 1864 he decided that the seizure was not an act of war and ordered her returned to her lawful owners.

The act planned in New Brunswick, and the violation of British territorial waters by the American warships, threatened to sour relations between the United States, Great Britain and its maritime colonies. It was an especially volatile and dangerous time for British North America. In 1861 the *Trent* affair had flared into a diplomatic crisis that came close to precipating war between Britain and the United States with British North America the battleground. Captain Charles Wilkes, commanding the Union frigate *San Jacinto*, stopped the *Trent*, a British merchant ship, on the high seas and seized two emissaries from the southern Confederacy. This violation of the right of freedom of the seas caused a storm of protest in Britain and the issuing of an ultimatum demanding their release together with an apology. The Union released the two emissaries but offered no apology. Nevertheless this proved sufficient and war was narrowly averted. There had been rumours prior to the *Chesapeake* of Confederate plots being planned from north of the border. In addition, the colonies were very concerned about grumblings in the United States Congress about repudiating the trade reciprocity treaty. Some Yankees looked north and saw a disagreeable trading partner: "The colonies on our border, who are directly benefited by this treaty, have displayed the same feeling of hostility toward us that pervades the mother country."[10]

The surrender of the *Chesapeake* and the captured prisoners to the authorities in Halifax, together with assurances from United States secretary of state, William Seward, that the actions of the Union warships were not authorized by Washington, calmed the situation. The smooth diplomatic work of Seward and Britain's ambassador to Washington, Lord Lyons, is credited with the fact that the *Chesapeake* affair is virtually forgotten today. However, some credit should also be accorded to two able judicial decisions — one rendered in Halifax by Justice Stewart that restored the *Chesapeake* to its rightful owner and the other in Saint John by Justice Ritchie, which denied the availability of extradition but nevertheless implied that there was a *prima facie* case of piracy in New Brunswick.

Notes to Chapter 8

1. The account of the *Chesapeake* affair has been taken from Gertrude E. Gunn, "New Brunswick Opinion on the American Civil War" (MA thesis, University of New Brunswick, 1956), pp. 130-46. See also Robin W. Winks, *Canada and the United States: The Civil War Years* (Montreal: Harvest House, 1960), pp. 244-63; George Cox, "Sidelights on the Chesapeake Affair, 1863-64" *Collections of the Nova Scotia Historical Society* 29(1951), pp. 124-37, and R.H. McDonald, "Second Chesapeake Affair 1863-64," *Dalhousie Review* 54 (1974-75), pp. 674-84.

2. The proceedings and judgment have been published in *"The Chesapeake": The Case of David Collins, et al before His Honor, Mr. Justice Ritchie with His Decision* (Saint John: J. & A. McMillan, 1864).

3. Ibid., p. 48.

4. New York, *World*, 12 Mar. 1864.

5. MacNutt, *New Brunswick*, p. 399.

6. "The Chesapeake" Proceedings, p. 52.

7. *Saint John Morning Freeman*, 12 Mar. 1864.

8. *Saint John Morning Telegraph*, 12 Mar. 1864.

9. J.R. Holcombe, a Southern barrister, presented Solicitor General J.W. Ritchie with a "service of plate" from the Confederate states "for the professional services he had gratuitously rendered in the case of the *Chesapeake*." *Halifax British Colonist*, 8 Sept. 1864, p. 2.

10. Brian Jenkins, *Britain and the War for the Union* (Montreal: McGill-Queen's University Press, 1980), II:347.

CHAPTER 9

Politics and the Next Chief Justice

In September 1865 Sir James Carter resigned as chief justice of the New Brunswick Supreme Court. The timing of this resignation was orchestrated by the lieutenant-governor, Arthur Hamilton Gordon, to create a vacancy on the bench which could be offered to Albert James Smith, leader of the anti-confederation government, thereby neutralizing his opposition to colonial confederation. Smith, however, refused the appointment and recommended Robert Parker, who reputedly obtained Smith's support for having declared that "he would rather vote for a hedgehog than for a supporter of Confederation."[1] Robert Parker was appointed chief justice on 22 September 1865 and John C. Allen, the attorney general, moved to the vacant seat on the court. Robert Parker was then sixty-nine years of age and had almost thirty-one years of service on the bench of the New Brunswick Supreme Court. Had he been in robust health he might have blocked Ritchie's advancement to chief justice for many years. However, two months later Parker died.

Lieutenant-Governor Gordon had difficulty accepting responsible government, for he asked Robert L. Hazen if he would accept appointment to the bench. This Hazen declined and the lieutenant-governor then asked "if he would accept the Chief Justiceship if it were offered to him." Hazen replied that "he would give an answer when the offer was made."[2] The opportunity never occurred because Albert J. Smith, who headed the government, was a strong personal friend of Ritchie's and he then urged that Ritchie succeed Chief Justice Parker. Had Lieutenant-Governor Gordon not been compelled to recognize that in the matter of judicial appointments it was his duty to accept the advice of his ministers, Robert L. Hazen might have become chief justice on the death of Robert Parker. In 1851 Ritchie had strongly criticized the lieutenant-governor for failing to follow the advice of the Executive Council in making judicial appointments. Now, fourteen years later, he would benefit from his earlier efforts, which helped to establish that although appointments to office were vested in the lieutenant-governor he should only act on the advice of his ministers.

On 30 November 1865, William Johnstone Ritchie was elevated to the position of chief justice of the New Brunswick Supreme Court. As with his appointment to the bench a decade earlier, he found himself in the middle of a political row, played out to the fullest by the era's highly partisan press. What made the promotion so highly charged was the fact that he had been elevated over the head of the longer serving and still popular Lemuel A. Wilmot. To those opposing the anti-confederation government of Albert J. Smith, the passing over of Wilmot was an insult to "the senior judge on the Bench and one of the ablest men the Province has ever produced. Such an act can be characterized as nothing more nor less than an outrage."[3]

The situation was complicated by political and religious considerations, ripe for exploitation by the press. Allegedly the Roman Catholic Timothy Anglin, founder and editor of the *Saint John Freeman*, a paper established to give the Irish a voice, had influenced the decision to appoint the Anglican Ritchie over the Methodist Wilmot who was well known for his strong anti-Catholic views. One paper proclaimed that Wilmot had been "sacrificed at the shrine of politico-religious bigotry and hate, and every politician concerned in the immolation must answer for it."[4] Also relevant was the question posed by one correspondent: "Why, then, was Judge Ritchie perferred [sic], and Judge Wilmot slighted? Plainly, because the former was known to be opposed to Confederation, and the latter to be in favor of it."[5]

Wilmot had occasionally used the Bench as a forum for his pro-confederation views. Those who supported Ritchie as chief justice claimed that the government could not overlook:

> Judge Wilmot's conduct during the agitation of the Confederation question, when he converted the Bench of Justice into a political platform, from which he delivered harangues that elicited cheers and hisses from the audience and shocked the sense of propriety of the whole people.[6]

Despite Wilmot's behaviour, however, the opposition maintained that the appointment of Ritchie over the senior judge meant that "the bench has been prostituted, the ermine dragged in the mire, [and] the bar insulted."[7]

Another paper, the *Colonial Farmer*, contended that the appointment of Ritchie in preference to Wilmot was "so subversive of every principle of honor, justice and right, as should call forth an expression of opinion from every press in the Province. A greater insult could not have been offered to Judge Wilmot, nor a greater outrage perpetrated upon the Province." The paper conceded that Wilmot had voted by open ballot in the York election in favour of the pro-confederation candidate, but it said he merely supported "the well-known policy of the British Government" and "he confined himself to voting, and an expression of opinion, neither canvassing or influencing any one at the election." Ritchie, however, the paper contended,

> if what is said be true, done [sic] both, and even more, for it is publicly asserted that he contributed largely to the funds at the general as well as the election in York, and some go so far as to assert that the money advanced on those occasions was the price agreed upon for the office of Chief Justice. We cannot vouch for the truth of these statements, but presume there must be at least some foundation for the reports.[8]

The paper branded Ritchie's appointment "unjust and iniquitous" and predicted that Lemuel A. Wilmot's "memory will be cherished in the hearts of the people, ages after the present political Chief Justice shall have been entirely forgotten."

L.A. Wilmot, although the senior judge of the bench, had never dedicated himself to the law and consequently was not a notable judge. He publicly expressed strong anti-Catholic and anti-French Canadian opinion. As a judge he received a reprimand for a speech he made about a priest who flogged a boy for reading the Bible.[9]

The lieutenant-governor, who was by this time a strong proponent of confederation, in his letter to the colonial secretary announcing the appointment of Ritchie as chief justice, said:

> Ritchie is very decidedly the ablest lawyer now on the Bench, and will, I have no doubt, discharge the duties of his high office in a perfectly satisfactory manner. His appointment has my entire concurrence and approval, and I am satisfied that in selecting him for the post a sound discretion has been exercised.[10]

Had it not been a good appointment, it is unlikely that the lieutenant-governor would have readily concurred. Nevertheless, when the New Brunswick Barristers' Society met on 9 February 1866 an attempt to adopt a congratulatory address to Chief Justice Ritchie failed. The *Colonial Farmer* noted that leading members of the bar deprecated and condemned "the principle of political appointments" which this appointment was "considered to be" and their opinion must have been gratifying to Wilmot and "must be regarded as a rebuke to the government" and "very unpleasant to the Chief Justice."[11] The bar probably divided on the issue of departing from the precedent of appointing the senior judge to the chief justiceship. Some attempted to equate an anti-confederation stand with being anti-British because Britain now favoured union of British North America. The *New Brunswick Reporter* took this position when it said "as long as Judge Wilmot's politics agree with those of the British Government he can expect no favor, no justice from the present Government of our Province."[12]

The inflammatory opinions surrounding the appointment appeared to have more to do with the snubbing of a popular, long-standing figure in the colony than dissatisfaction with Ritchie's judicial ability. One observer's comments seemed to put the appointment properly into its political context:

> It is a standing joke against him [Ritchie] to this day that he obtained a seat in the Assembly and the subsequent office of Judge by one vote, and that his own; and now that he has reached the very height of his ambition, it cannot be a very consoling thought to him that he — a junior judge — has been promoted over the head of Judge Wilmot, many years his senior on the Bench. This however, is not his fault, and there can be no doubt that he will perform the duties of his office with dignity and ability. His record as a Puisne Judge is a sufficient guarantee for that.[13]

The government simultaneously appointed John W. Weldon to the puisne judgeship created by the elevation of Ritchie. This appointment also drew sharp criticism. John Boyd, an ardent proponent of confederation and subsequently a Canadian senator, said in a letter to the editor:

> On the morning of Mr. Weldon's appointment we met, and he put out his hand to me; I took it and said: —"Mr. Weldon, you have worked well for your party, and you have got your reward. I believe it is customary to congratulate persons on receiving such appointments, but I can congratulate no man who receives an appointment at the expense of my country." Knowing that Mr. Weldon was not eminent in the legal profession, I concluded his advancement was the reward of his services against the consolidation and unity of British North America, and therefore at the expense of the country. In saying this I merely said what Mr. Weldon's pretended friends said behind his back, except

some Anti-Confederates who questioned the value of his political services, compared with their own.[14]

The *New Brunswick Reporter*, although unenthusiastic about Weldon's appointment, took a more philosophical outlook:

> It is a law of nature that nothing ever goes to loss. Bad wine makes very tolerable vinegar; spoiled hay is converted into good manure; and so a middling lawyer often drops down into a very respectable Judge.[15]

Notes to Chapter 9

1. MacNutt, *New Brunswick*, p. 437.

2. Lawrence, *Judges of New Brunswick*, p. 399.

3. *Saint John Morning News*, 1 Dec. 1865, p. 2.

4. *Saint John Morning Journal*, 1 Dec. 1865.

5. Ibid., 8 December 1865, p. 2.

6. *Saint John Morning Freeman*, 2 Dec. 1865 p. 2.

7. *Saint John Morning Journal*, 1 Dec. 1865, p. 2.

8. *Colonial Farmer* (Fredericton), 4 Dec. 1865.

9. C.M. Wallace, "Lemuel Allan Wilmot," *Dictionary of Canadian Biography*, vol. 10, p. 713.

10. Quoted in Lawrence, *Judges of New Brunswick*, p. 494.

11. *Colonial Farmer*, 19 Feb. 1866.

12. *New Brunswick Reporter*, 8 Dec. 1865, p. 2.

13. *St. Croix Courier*, quoted in the *Saint John Morning News*, 6 Dec. 1865, p. 2.

14. *Saint John Morning News*, 8 Dec. 1865, p. 2.

15. *New Brunswick Reporter*, 8 Dec. 1865, p. 2, quoting Lever on the appointment of a judge.

CHAPTER 10

Judicial Review and Confederation

Confederation resulted from the Charlottetown, Quebec and London conferences of 1864-67 and was embodied in an imperial statute, the British North America Act of 1867.[1] The delegation of powers to Canada's parliament and to the provincial legislatures, largely contained in sections 91 and 92 of the B.N.A. Act, lay at its heart and defined the constitutional nature of the new country. In time it came to be regarded as axiomatic that the judiciary was the umpire to determine whether a statute enacted either by Parliament or a provincial legislature was within the powers assigned to it by the constitution.[2] However, the B.N.A. Act did not provide expressly for judicial review, and section 90 in conjunction with sections 55 and 56, which together provide for federal disallowance of provincial enactments, form the basis for an entirely different mechanism for regulating the division of legislative powers.

In this alternative approach, Parliament would use disallowance to restrain the provincial legislatures within their proper sphere. Parliament itself would be restrained by the imperial power of disallowance, or by its good judgment and regional pressures on federal members of Parliament. This would imply a stronger role for the federal government, while according greater respect to the notion of parliamentary supremacy. Both approaches are internally consistent, and neither the B.N.A. Act itself, nor the speeches of the framers in the debates leading up to its enactment, is conclusive as to which method was to be preferred.

Did the Fathers of Confederation intend judicial review of legislation? The sparse notes of the Quebec conference are inconclusive. George Brown would have "let the Courts of each Province decide what is local and what is general Government jurisdiction, with appeal to the Appeal or Superior Court." However, Jonathan McCully, a firm believer in parliamentary supremacy, complained that Brown would "land us in the position of the United States by referring matters of conflict of jurisdiction to

Courts" and thereby "set them over the General Legislature."[3] Robert B. Dickey proposed "a Supreme Court of Appeal to decide any conflict between general and state rights,"[4] but did not indicate whether he believed the existing courts could carry out this function.

William A. Henry, who would later become a colleague of Ritchie's on the Supreme Court of Canada, stated at the Quebec conference that the general legislature should have broad general powers excluding those given to the local legislature and "Anything beyond that is hampering the case with difficulties." The difficulties anticipated in this prescient opinion surfaced in the Privy Council's treatment of the powers enumerated in section 91 as specific grants to the federal Parliament, rather than as mere examples of the peace, order and good government power. While this indicated his support for a strong central government, Henry clearly indicated his belief that a federal constitution would entail judicial review, stating: "Hereafter we shall be bound by an Imperial Act, and our judges will have to say what is constitutional under it as regards general or local legislation." However, this remark seemed to be based on an analogy with the American system, as Henry prefaced his remark by saying "In the United States there is no power to settle constitutionality of an Act."[5] He must have meant that under the American Constitution only the judiciary had power to hold an act unconstitutional and that there was no power similar to the power of reservation and disallowance in the United States. But during the following day of debate the Quebec conference adopted two resolutions relating to the power of reservation and disallowance which read:

> 50. Any Bill of the General Parliament may be reserved in the usual manner for Her Majesty's Assent, and any Bill of the Local Legislatures may in like manner be reserved for the consideration of the Governor-General.

> 51. Any Bill passed by the General Parliament shall be subject to disallowance by Her Majesty within two years, as in the case of Bills passed by the Legislatures of the said Provinces hitherto, and in like manner any Bill passed by a Local legislature shall be subject to disallowance by the Governor-General within one year after the passing thereof.[6]

These resolutions weakened Henry's analogy with the American system, and made his earlier approval of judicial review less significant.

The debates in the 1865 Parliament of the Province of Canada are scarcely more edifying on the question of whether the federal power of disallowance was intended to dispense with judicial review or to supplement it. The debates do reveal the importance attached to the power of disallowance, which in itself implied a strong federal government that could obviate the need for judicial review. As Alexander Mackenzie said:

> The veto power is necessary in order that the General Government may have a control over the proceedings of the local legislatures to a certain extent. The want of this power was the great source of weakness in the United States, and it is a want that will be remedied by an amendment in their Constitution very soon. So long as each state considered itself sovereign, whose acts and laws could not be called in question, it was quite clear that the central authority was destitute of power to compel obedience to general laws. If each province were able to enact such laws as it pleased, everybody would be at the mercy of the local legislatures, and the General Legislature would become of little importance....The Central Parliament and Government must, of necessity, exercise the supreme power, and the local governments will have the exercise of power corresponding to the duties they have to perform.[7]

John Scoble also stressed the importance of the power of disallowance, and implied that he perceived no need for judicial review, when he stated:

> A careful analysis of the scheme convinces me that the powers conferred on the General or Central Government secures it all the attributes of sovereignty, and the *veto* power which its executive will possess, and to which all local legislation will be subject, *will prevent a conflict of laws and jurisdictions in all matters of importance,* so that I believe in its working it will be found, if not in form yet in fact and practically, a legislative union.[8]

John Rose indicated his belief in the centrality of the power of disallowance when he said, "this power of veto, this controlling power on the part of the Central Government is the best protection and safeguard of the system."[9] Rose did not say that the disallowance power was the only safeguard of the federal system but, if he did envisage judicial review as a safeguard of the system at all, he ranked it below disallowance; Rose said that without the power of disallowance, he would have found it difficult to vote for confederation.

However, the existence of the power of disallowance did not imply that there was no place at all for judicial review. Some saw disallowance as a means of preventing unjust local laws, while judicial review would be used to police the division of powers. George Brown saw disallowance in this light, and said, "By vesting the appointment of the lieutenant governors in the General Government and giving a veto for all local measures, we have secured that no injustice shall be done without appeal in local legislation."[10] Paul Denis thought that the power of disallowance "must of necessity exist somewhere in order that the minority may be protected from any injustice which the majority might attempt to do them."[11] George Etienne Cartier thought that the power of disallowance would be "exercised in case of unjust or unwise legislation."[12] Cartier did not mention unconstitutional laws in regard to disallowance and from this it might be inferred that he considered this to be a function for the judiciary. This inference was strengthened by Cartier's exchange with A.A. Dorion, but considerable doubt remained.

> *Hon. Mr. Dorion* — We shall be — I speak as a Lower Canadian — we shall be at its mercy, because it may exercise its right of veto on all the legislation of the local parliaments, and there again we shall have no remedy. In case of difference between the Federal power and the local governments, what authority will intervene for its settlement?
>
> *Hon. Atty. Gen. Cartier* — It will be the Imperial Government.
>
> *Hon. Mr. Dorion* — In effect there will be no other authority than that of the Imperial Government, and we know too well the value assigned to the complaints of Lower Canadians by the Imperial Government.
>
> *Hon. Atty. Gen. Cartier* — The delegates understood the matter better than that. Neither the Imperial Government nor the General Government will interfere, but the courts of justice will decide all questions in relation to which there may be differences between the two powers.
>
> *A Voice* — The Commissioners' courts. (Hear, hear.)
>
> *Hon. Mr. Dorion* — Undoubtedly. One magistrate will decide that a law passed by the Federal Legislature is not law, whilst another will decide that it is law, and thus the difference, instead of being between the legislatures, will be between the several courts of justice.
>
> *Hon. Atty. Gen. Cartier* — Should the General Legislature pass a law beyond the limits of its functions, it will be null and void *pleno jure*.
>
> *Hon. Mr. Dorion* — Yes, I understand that, and it is doubtless to decide questions of this kind that it is proposed to establish Federal courts.
>
> *Hon. Atty. Gen. Cartier* — No, No! They will be established

solely to apply and adjudicate upon the Federal laws.

Hon. Mr. Dorion — In Great Britain, Parliament is all-powerful, every one admits it—and I would like to know whether it is proposed to give to the Federal Parliament the omnipotence enjoyed by the Imperial Parliament. Without that, the system proposed to be established is no longer a political monarchical system, but rather a vast municipality. If all the courts of justice are to have the right of deciding as to the legality of the laws, the Federal Parliament will not be able to make them without a justice of the peace or commissioner of small causes setting them aside, under the pretext that they are not within the jurisdiction of the central power, as is now done in the case of a *procès-verbal* of road work. That is not the monarchical system; it is the republican system. In England, as it is here at the present moment the Legislature is all-powerful, and I believe that was the principle which it was sought to adopt. If the differences between the Federal and the Local parliaments are not to be submitted to the decision of a Supreme Federal Court, I do not see who can possibly decide them.[13]

An early constitutional writer, W.H.P. Clement relied on a shortened version of the above exchange to claim that "Throughout the debates, it was clearly recognized that the exercise by the Dominion Government of the power of disallowance, was to be exercised in the support of federal unity, — e.g. to preserve the minorities in different parts of the confederated provinces, from oppression at the hands of the majorities.... [I]t was not intended to obviate the necessity for resort to the courts."[14] This claim was questionable: what the exchange makes most apparent is the confusion regarding the role of judicial review. As B.L. Strayer remarked almost one hundred years later:

Cartier's remarks as quoted are reasonably unedifying. He first casually explains that the Imperial Government will decide disputes over jurisdiction. When this proves objectionable to his compatriot, he suggests that the court will decide "differences". He then is forced to say it will not be the federal courts, the creatures of Parliament, which will decide.[15]

Whatever Cartier's views, Dorion certainly seemed to believe that the establishment of a "political monarchical" system similar to that of Great Britain implied that the central Parliament not be subject to judicial review.

The Parliament of the United Province of Canada in its 1865 debates on confederation certainly directed far more attention to the power of disallowance than to judicial review. Yet again, the significance to be attached to this is uncertain. The power to dis-allow any provincial statute conferred on the governor general, and therefore effectively upon the federal cabinet, was an extremely controversial feature of the resolutions, "born of the spirit of compromise that permeated the deliberations of the Fathers of Confederation"[16] at the Quebec conference in 1864. It was heartily approved by those who had hoped for a legislative union but who had to settle for a federal union and vehemently condemned by those who sought a true federal union. For instance, Mr. J.B.E. Dorion said: "I am opposed to the scheme of Confederation, because by means of the right of veto vested in the Governor by the 51st resolution, local legislation will be nothing but a farce."[17] Philip H. Moore wanted to provide a means of overriding the federal power of disallowance because "Exercising it in an arbitrary manner, as the Federal power is privileged to do, it must from the very nature of things create dissatisfaction and difficulty between the two governments."[18] The power of disal-lowance was one of the provisions which caused James G. Currie to say the union was "neither federal nor legislative, but a mongrel between both."[19]

One member clearly believed that judicial review was implied by a federal system: Joseph Cauchon said judicial tribunals were "charged by the very nature of their functions to decide whether such a law of the Federal Parliament or of the local legislatures does or does not affect the Constitution."[20] However, even more clearly than Henry, he relied on a comparison with the American system. He noted that judicial review was established there, and asked "Why then should the case be otherwise so far as we are concerned?"[21] The power of disallowance, and the fact that a Supreme Court was not established by the Canadian constitution, provide two answers to his rhetorical question.

In general, though, as no immediate changes in the judicial structure were being proposed, the opportunity for debate was correspondingly reduced. The existing court system continued but with the power to appoint and pay all provincial superior court judges transferred to the general government. The general Parlia-ment was to have the power "to establish a General Court of Appeal for the Federated Provinces."[22] Resolution 32 provided that "All Courts, Judges and officers of the several Provinces shall aid, assist and obey the General Government in the exercise of its rights and powers, and for such purposes shall be held to be

Courts, Judges and officers of the General Government."[23] The most straightforward inference from resolution 32 was that the courts should prevent the provincial legislatures from poaching upon the federal domain, without interfering with the federal Parliament. However, one could also argue that once the general government exceeded its rights and powers, the duty of the judges to obey ceased and judicial review of federal legislation became permissible.

John A. Macdonald, who better than anyone should have been able to clarify the relationship between the veto power and judicial review, inferred that there would be no need for judicial review:

> We have given the General Legislature all the great subjects of legislation. We have conferred on them, not only specifically and in detail, all the powers which are incident to sovereignty, but we have expressly declared that all subjects of general interest not distinctly and exclusively conferred upon the local governments and local legislatures, shall be conferred upon the General Government and Legislature. We have thus avoided that great source of weakness which has been the cause of the disruption of the United States. We have avoided all conflict of jurisdiction and authority.[24]

Macdonald did, however, anticipate a limited form of review, but not explicitly judicial review and only in case of actual repugnancy between laws. This amount of review, Macdonald felt, was explicitly provided for in section 45 of the Quebec Resolutions. In his own words:

> There are numerous subjects which belong, of right, both to the Local and the General Parliaments. In all these cases it is provided, in order to prevent a conflict of authority, that where there is concurrent jurisdiction in the General and Local Parliaments, the same rule should apply as now applies in cases where there is concurrent jurisdiction in the Imperial and in the Provincial Parliaments, and that when the legislation of the one is adverse to or contradictory to the legislation of the other, in all such cases the action of the General Parliament must overrule, *ex necessitate,* the action of the Local legislature.[25]

The B.N.A. Act did not incorporate section 45 of the Quebec Resolutions, and section 95, which granted concurrent legislative power over agriculture and immigration, became its nearest equivalent. That section stipulated that provincial law should have effect in the province "as long and as far only as it is not repugnant to any Act of the Parliament of Canada." The B.N.A. Act did not specify what agency would determine any inconsistency. Strayer has noted that Macdonald might have expected the courts to determine this but he believed it more likely that Macdonald anticipated "a role for the Canadian Parliament similar to that of the Imperial Parliament," as the Quebec Resolutions and the B.N.A. Act placed "the federal cabinet in the position that the Imperial cabinet had formerly occupied with respect to the power of disallowance of provincial legislation."[26] That certainly would have extended the spirit of full parliamentary supremacy to the federal Parliament, with the courts intervening only in cases of contradiction between laws.

Gérard V. La Forest (justice of the Supreme Court of Canada since 1985), in his 1955 study of the power of disallowance and reservation, did not address the issue of whether the veto power was intended to eliminate the need for judicial review. He did note that "The Imperial authorities were quick to voice their approbation of the principle of strong central government for the proposed federation"[27] and quoted a dispatch of 3 December 1864 in which Edward Cardwell, the secretary of state for the colonies, acknowledging receipt of the Quebec Resolutions, said:

> They [Her Majesty's Government] are glad to observe that, although large powers of Legislation are intended to be vested in local bodies, yet the principle of central control has been steadily kept in view. The importance of this principle cannot be over-rated. Its maintenance is essential to the practical efficiency of the system and to its harmonious operation, both in the General Government and in the governments of the several Provinces.

Subsequently, in the House of Commons at Westminster the two possible remedies for invalid legislation, the power of disallowance and judicial review, were both mentioned. The parliamentary under-secretary of the Colonial Office, C.B. Adderley, said "he did not think that any serious conflict of the kind anticipated by the honourable member could take place so long as the supreme power was vested in the Governor General to veto Acts." Edward Cardwell, the former colonial secretary, said that in relation to possibly invalid federal laws "the question would first be raised in the Colonial law Courts; and would ultimately be decided by the Privy Council at home." Cardwell indicated that he thought a defect of the B.N.A. Act was that it did not create but merely empowered the federal Parliament to establish a

Supreme Court. He noted that "the present state of feeling in the North American Provinces" made it difficult to remedy this defect.[28]

Debates leading up to the enactment of the B.N.A. Act indicated that some favoured disallowance and others judicial review, and the act itself, with its soothing ambiguity, reflected this difference of opinion. During the debates some of the most trenchant criticisms of this ambiguity were made by Christopher Dunkin. He remarked caustically that the new constitution followed the British system, in that it was "not meant to be in fact the half of what it passes for in theory." He excoriated proponents of the proposed act for the two-faced nature of the reassurances they offered: "We are told to take for granted that no clashing of interest or feeling need be feared; that the Federal union offered us in name will be a legislative union in reality. Yet, whoever dislikes the notion of a legislative union is assured it will be nothing of the sort .... To be sure there is the grand power of disallowance by the Federal Government, which we are told, in one and the same breath, is to be possessed by it, but never exercised."[29] In light of these political pressures, it was no wonder that the B.N.A. Act itself provided no sure guidance as to the role of judicial review in policing the division of powers.

After confederation, doubt continued to exist about the role the courts would play in restraining provincial legislatures and the Parliament from encroaching on the legislative powers assigned to each other. Sir John A. Macdonald, in the early days, appeared to have assumed "that the proper and perhaps the only control on invalid provincial legislation would be the power of disallowance resting with the governor general."[30] In a report on the use of disallowance prepared in his capacity as minister of justice, Macdonald said:

> Under the present constitution of Canada, the general government will be called upon to consider the propriety of allowance or disallowance of provincial Acts much more frequently than Her Majesty's Government has been with respect to colonial enactments. In deciding whether an Act of a provincial legislature should be allowed or sanctioned, the government must not only consider whether it affects the interest of the whole Dominion or not; but also, whether it be unconstitutional, whether it exceeds the jurisdiction conferred on local legislatures, and in cases where the jurisdiction is concurrent, whether it clashes with the legislation of the general Parliament.

Macdonald recommended that the minister of justice

> make a separate report, or separate reports, on those acts which he might consider:
> 1. As being altogether illegal or unconstitutional;
> 2. As illegal or unconstitutional in part;
> 3. In cases of concurrent jurisdiction, as clashing with the legislation of the general parliament;
> 4. As effecting the interests of the Dominion generally:
>
> And that in such report or reports he gives his reasons for his opinions.[31]

Macdonald clearly envisaged a political process for policing the division of powers: "where a measure is considered only partially defective, or where objectionable, as being prejudicial to the general interests of the Dominion, or as clashing with its legislation, communication should be had with the provincial government with respect to such measure, and that, in such case, the Act should not be disallowed, if the general interest permit such a course, until the local government has an opportunity of considering and discussing the objections taken, and the local legislatures have also an opportunity of remedying the defects found to exist."

Prior to the introduction of the first bill to establish the Supreme Court of Canada, the governor general on 11 March 1869 wrote to the Earl of Grenville, secretary of state for the colonies inquiring "whether it would be expedient to establish a tribunal with powers analogous to those of the Supreme Court of the United States, for the decision of all questions of constitutional law and conflict of jurisdiction." He noted that section 101 of the B.N.A. Act empowered the Dominion Parliament to establish a general court of appeal but that Imperial legislation might be "required to enable the Dominion Parliament to establish a Court with original jurisdiction over such subjects." The Earl of Grenville replied in a despatch dated 8 May 1869 that he saw "no reason for the establishment of such a tribunal" and thought that any constitutional questions "could be entertained and decided by the Local Courts, subject to an appeal to the Judicial Committee of the Privy Council, and it does not appear in what respect this mode of determination is likely to be inadequate or unsatisfactory."[32] The Earl of Grenville thus had no doubt that Canadian courts should engage in judicial review under the supervision of the Judicial Committee of the Privy Council.

Macdonald, on 21 May 1869 introduced Bill 80 to establish a Supreme Court and it clearly envisaged that the court would only have the power to declare an act of a provincial legislature to be *ultra vires*, not an act of Parliament. In section 53(1) the Supreme Court was to have exclusive original jurisdiction "in all cases in which the constitutionality of any Act of the Legislature of any Province of the Dominion shall come in question." Section 50 also provided that the federal cabinet might direct a special case be laid before the Supreme Court for its opinion as to the constitutionality of any act of a provincial legislature.

The inference from the 1869 bill was that Macdonald clearly envisaged a one-sided and restricted concept of judicial review, as only provincial legislation could be impugned and then only by the Supreme Court of Canada and not by provincial trial or appellate courts. The fact that he proposed granting exclusive jurisdiction to engage in judicial review to the Supreme Court also seemed to imply that he did not believe that the lower courts inherently possessed such a power. In any case, judicial review was to be merely a supplement to the federal government's power of disallowance. Macdonald indicated that Bill 80 was introduced for discussion, not final enactment, and after second reading it was not proceeded with.

On 18 March 1870 Macdonald introduced Bill 48 to establish a Supreme Court of Canada. It differed from the 1869 bill in that it did not confer exclusive and original jurisdiction on the Supreme Court to determine the constitutionality of a provincial statute. But section 47 of the 1870 bill, like section 50 of the 1869 bill, explicitly mentioned only a provincial act being referred to the court for a constitutional opinion, not an act of Parliament. This bill also was not proceeded with because many members of Macdonald's caucus from Quebec had misgivings about the creation of a Supreme Court. They feared that, as a majority of the judges would be common lawyers, the court might fail to interpret Quebec's civil code properly.

The uncertainty amongst politicians was reflected in the judiciary in New Brunswick which divided on the issue of judicial review. Judge James Steadman, a county court judge, declined in 1868 to take jurisdiction to determine whether a post-confederation amendment to the Insolvent Debtors Act[33] was void because it exceeded the power of the New Brunswick legislature. Soon after, in the case of *R. v. Chandler*,[34] Ritchie came to the opposite conclusion when confronted with the question of the propriety of the judiciary assuming the role of reviewing duly enacted legislation. This occurred in 1869, very early in the life of the newly confederated constitution, and was the first time in Canada that a provincial superior court faced a constitutional challenge to a formally valid statute enacted after confederation. By this time, Ritchie had been a judge of the New Brunswick Supreme Court for thirteen years and chief justice of that court for three years. While he had not personally taken an active part in events leading up to confederation he had been strongly opposed to it,[35] despite the fact that his eldest brother, John William Ritchie, was one of the Fathers of Confederation.[36]

The case centred on Horace L. Hazelton, an American citizen from Boston, who had come to New Brunswick in 1866 as secretary-treasurer of a mining company. He had opened several mines, and had invested some $40,000 of his own money to do so, but in addition had expended $25,000 of funds that he held as trustee of an American estate. The mining company failed and he could not recover any money. Lawson Valentine became the administrator of the estate and obtained a judgment for $25,000 against Hazelton. Having learned of the judgment against him, Hazelton then in Boston, returned to Saint John so that his bail bond could be discharged. Unable to pay his debt, he was committed to gaol in Saint John and Valentine attached all his property in Massachusetts. Hazelton applied to the court of Massachusetts to come under the bankruptcy legislation but the courts declined to accept jurisdiction because he was confined in New Brunswick.

After almost a year in gaol, Hazleton applied for his discharge to James W. Chandler, a county court judge, pursuant to the same 1868 amendment to the Insolvent Confined Debtors Act which Judge Steadman had faced. This amendment did not abolish imprisonment for debt entirely, but rather provided that a confined debtor could make an application for discharge to a county court judge, who was given the duty to discharge the debtor if it appeared the debtor had no property and had not made a fraudulent conveyance or given any undue preference since the commencement of the suit against him. In *Chandler*, Chief Justice Ritchie issued a writ of prohibition to restrain James W. Chandler from releasing Hazelton under the authority of the amending statute, on the grounds that the 1868 amendment was beyond the powers of the provincial legislature.

Counsel for the creditor advanced what is today a familiar argument, namely that the B.N.A. Act clearly assigned bankruptcy and insolvency to the federal Parliament and the New Brunswick statute enacted after confederation was clearly an insolvency act. He concluded therefore that the court had a duty "to impose its authority," to strike down the provincial statute, inferring that this judicial authority implicitly flowed from the B.N.A. Act.[37]

Counsel for the imprisoned debtor challenged this, arguing that the statute was valid because it had been assented to by the lieutenant-governor and the governor general had been advised not to disallow the act. Therefore, according to counsel, the act "must have force of law until disallowed by some higher authority or repealed."[38] The higher authority presumably was not the judiciary but the federal Parliament, which might legislate with reference to section 91(21) on bankruptcy and insolvency, and to the extent of any inconsistency render the provincial statute inoperative. This argument, based on the idea of parliamentary supremacy, challenged the authority of the court to determine whether a statute was *ultra vires* a provincial legislature, and thus forced Ritchie to confront the contradiction in a constitution which engrafted a system of limited government onto a parliamentary system, which had for two centuries recognized the omnicompetence of Parliament.

Hazelton's counsel insisted that *R. v. Kerr* (1838), a New Brunswick Supreme Court decision, had held that the court had no jurisdiction to hold a provincial statute invalid if the lieutenant-governor had given his consent. In that case a New Brunswick act limited the height of wooden structures in Saint John, and Kerr was prosecuted for erecting a building exceeding that limit. He had argued that a colonial legislature had no power to infringe property rights by setting limits to the height of buildings without paying compensation. Chief Justice Chipman had held:

> The propriety and necessity of such enactments are within the competency of the legislature alone to determine. It is a thing unheard of, under British institutions, for a judicial tribunal to question the validity and binding force of any such law when duly enacted. While the law remains on the statute book the Courts are absolutely bound to give effect to it.[39]

Chipman also noted that colonial legislation might be disallowed by the British Crown even when its own representative in the colony had given his consent. This power afforded "a remedy for any improper colonial legislation". Ritchie distinguished *Kerr* easily on the ground that it involved an asserted repugnancy with English common law, and noted that Chipman had qualified his statement as applying to "at least a law not objectionable on account of its repugnancy to an Act of Parliament relating to the colonies."[40] Ritchie was thus clearly relying on the repugnancy doctrine, saying: "Where an Act of the British Parliament conflicts with our own the latter must give way."[41] He found a clear repugnancy and held that the statute was *ultra vires* on the grounds that:

> [t]he Imperial Statute says that the Parliament of Canada shall exclusively legislate on bankruptcy and insolvency .... The subordinate legislative body of this Province, in defiance of this statute, has undertaken to legislate on this subject .... Their right to do so is now contested, and under these circumstances can there be any doubt as to what we are bound to do? We think not. We must recognize the undoubted legislative control of the British Parliament, and give full force and effect to the statute of the Supreme Legislature, and ignore the Act of the subordinate, when, as in this case, they are repugnant and in conflict .... The constitution of the Dominion and Provinces is now, to a great extent, a written one, and where under the terms of the Union Act the power to legislate is granted to be exercised exclusively by one body, the subject so exclusively assigned is as completely taken from the others, as if they had been expressly forbidden to act on it; and if they do legislate beyond their powers, or in defiance of the restrictions placed on them, their enactments are no more binding than rules or regulations promulgated by any other unauthorized body.[42]

This view of the effect of the B.N.A. Act was challenged by Steadman, the county court judge who had earlier declined to take jurisdiction to deal with the same issue. In a lengthy paper setting out his reasons, he contended that before confederation the courts were subordinate to the legislature and their function was to interpret and administer the laws.[43] The courts did not possess, according to Steadman, any negative jurisdiction to declare a law invalid. It was the prerogative powers of reservation and disallowance, together with imperial legislation, which prevented colonial legislation from clashing with imperial interests. Steadman did not believe that the B.N.A. Act either expressly or by implication conferred on the judiciary "a negative jurisdiction to determine what laws passed by either of the legislative bodies of the Dominion shall or shall not be of binding force." He conceded that powers exclusively given to one body were prohibited to another body, but he maintained that without express jurisdiction conferred on the courts "it is not within their province to determine a question involving the constitutional exercise of that authority."

Steadman had a firm belief in the supremacy of the legislature and did not believe that even a federal constitution eroded that principle. He maintained that if the B.N.A. Act had envisaged that the judiciary were to determine the validity of statute law, "it would have been considered a matter of sufficient importance to have been made a subject of special enactment" because it involved "a principle so entirely adverse to the theory of all British institutions."[44]

Steadman insisted that the B.N.A. Act was not the supreme law, in the sense that the constitution of the United States was the supreme law, and stated:

> it is not the supreme law in the sense that it controls through any inherent authority in the judiciary, all Statute Law of the Dominion Parliament and Provincial Legislatures. It could not be such without taking from the Constitution the principle which affirms the supremacy of the legislative authority.[45]

Supremacy of Parliament was one of the fundamental principles of the British constitution, and if the preamble did not have the effect of introducing it into the Canadian system, it was difficult to know what significance to attribute to it. This was made clear by Dicey, who in early editions of his book on constitutional law stated "The preamble of the British North America Act, 1867, asserts with *official mendacity* that the Provinces of the present Dominion have expressed their desire to be united into one Dominion 'with a constitution similar in principle to that of the United Kingdom.'"[46] Dicey then asserted that "if preambles were intended to express the truth" one should read United States for the United Kingdom because "no one can study the provisions of the British North America Act, 1867, without seeing that its authors had the American constitution constantly before their eyes, and that if Canada were an independent country it would be a Confederacy governed under a constitution very similar to that of the United States." He noted that the power of the Canadian federal government and Parliament greatly exceeded that of the federal government in the United States and this was most noticeable "in the authority given to the Dominion Government to disallow Provincial Acts." The power of disallowance, Dicey conceded, might have been "given with a view to obviate altogether

111

the necessity for invoking the law Courts as interpreters of the Constitution," but he concluded that in both the United States and Canada "the Courts inevitably become the interpreters of the Constitution."[47]

This analysis and the "inevitability" of judicial review which Dicey perceived were based on an assumption of the legitimacy of judicial review, because the Judicial Committee of the Privy Council, which he called "the true Supreme Court of the Dominion," had by that time rendered decisions about the respective powers of the federal Parliament and provincial legislatures. If Dicey had written before these decisions it seemed likely that rather than attribute "mendacity" to the preamble, he would have applied more conventional canons of interpretation and argued in favour of parliamentary or legislative supremacy and against judicial review of legislation. The power of reservation and disallowance, by providing alternative means of enforcing the constitutional allocation of power, would have allowed a consistent interpretation of the document as a whole, without necessitating judicial review.[48]

Steadman did not rely only on principle in his defence of legislative supremacy, but pointed also to the B.N.A. Act itself. He noted that there was no express conferral on the courts of a power of review, but that the B.N.A. Act preserved the sovereign's negative power over laws passed by the Canadian Parliament, while transferring to the governor general similar power over laws passed by the provincial legislatures. These federal powers of reservation and disallowance he inferred to be the exclusive mode of preventing the usurpation of legislative power. Steadman maintained that "It is a clear principle, that jurisdiction cannot be taken by one Court where it is expressly conferred upon another and higher tribunal." He argued that the legislatures must be superior to the courts, as they possessed the power to create the judiciary. This meant that not only would judicial review be wrong, it would also be unenforceable, because the province had the power "to abolish entirely any court, and to constitute any other court in its stead with such jurisdiction as it may choose to confer."[49] This argument was clearly based on the B.N.A. Act, particularly section 129, which not only provided that existing laws were continued until subsequently "repealed, abolished or altered" by the appropriate body, either Parliament or the provincial legislature, but also that all courts of civil and criminal jurisdiction were sustained subject to the same condition. This section, in conjunction with section 92(14), giving the provinces power relating to the administration of justice in the province, including the constitution, maintenance and organization of provincial courts, both of civil and criminal jurisdiction, strongly supported Steadman's view that the judiciary was a tribunal inferior to the legislature.

Of course, had Ritchie faced this argument, he might have responded, like the modern authority, Professor W.R. Lederman, with an argument for the independence of the judiciary based on sections 96 to 101 of the B.N.A. Act.[50] The point here is not to enter into the contentious question of which interpretation was "correct," but rather to suggest that these apparently conflicting provisions of the B.N.A. Act were just that: internal contradictions resulting from conflicting views on the nature of the desired union, left ambiguous in the document itself.

In fact, Ritchie did not make any argument as to the inherent powers of the judiciary, nor did he address most of Steadman's arguments. This was probably because they were not known to him. While Ritchie would likely have known that Steadman, in 1868, had declined to take jurisdiction to determine whether the 1868 New Brunswick amendment to the Insolvent Confined Debtors law was unconstitutional, it was unlikely that he would have known the details of Steadman's arguments. Steadman was a county court judge and his reasons for judgment, even if not rendered orally, would not have been reported. Only in 1873 were two hundred copies of Steadman's opinion, together with his observations upon two subsequent cases, printed for the use of members of the House of Assembly. (See Appendix 1, p. 311)

Ritchie, had he been faced with Steadman's arguments, would probably have considered them irrelevant. He would have acknowledged the supremacy of Parliament — the imperial Parliament. This was the source from which he believed his power to engage in judicial review derived, not from inherent powers of the court, nor from any of the provisions of the B.N.A. Act. Ritchie felt he was simply applying the law which had been duly enacted by the highest authority. Steadman thought that judicial review was *not* legitimate as "Jurisdiction in the judiciary to declare a law void can only be sustained on the theory that the British North America Act has reduced the respective legislatures of the dominion to the character and capacity of ordinary municipal governments,"[51] a theory which he rejected. Ritchie, however, noted that

"Imperial Parliament has intervened, and by virtue of its supreme legislative power, has taken from the subordinate legislative body of this Province the plenary power to make law."[52] In his view the B.N.A. Act had not "reduced" the status of the legislatures, as they had always been limited in their powers.

Ritchie's position found support in section 2 of the Colonial Laws Validity Act: "Any Colonial Law, which is, or shall be in any respect repugnant to the Provisions of any Act of Parliament extending to the Colony to which such Law may relate...shall, to the Extent of such Repugnancy, but not otherwise, be and remain absolutely void and inoperative."[53]

Steadman considered the act, but contended that it operated to make the repugnant colonial law void only in England and did not allow the colonial courts to declare colonial legislation void for repugnancy. This position was clearly mistaken. However, as a matter of practice, Steadman was quite correct that "The prerogative power vested in the Sovereign, has always been found sufficient to restrain the colonial legislatures within proper limits, and to prevent unnecessary conflict with the laws of Parliament."[54] In practice, there was no instance in any of the federating provinces "where the Courts before Confederation assumed jurisdiction to declare the *Sovereign will* and to disallow a law enacted by the Legislature"[55] even though the colonial legislatures did not possess full sovereignty. Steadman's view seemed to have been prevalent, as Joseph Doutre, writing in 1880, said:

> Previous to "The British North America Act, 1867", the Provincial Courts did not consider they possessed the power of inquiring and deciding whether the laws of their respective Legislatures were constitutional or not. Occasional attempts were made to test the validity of statutes, but they were ineffectual in their results.[56]

While judicial review for repugnancy to the laws of England was technically available, Britain was not in the habit of using judicial review as a tool for controlling the constitution of the colonies.[57]

Further, the Colonial Laws Validity Act had been enacted largely in response to the enthusiasm of Justice Benjamin Boothby in South Australia, for striking down local legislation as repugnant to a variety of English statutes as well as to what he deemed English constitutional principles and common law. The act was emancipatory, not restrictive, and gave a narrow definition of repugnancy, which preserved imperial authority while allowing otherwise free rein to local legislators.[58] The act was an expression of the imperial policy of allowing the colonies with responsible government to enjoy the greatest possible freedom in legislating on matters which did not affect imperial interests.[59] This policy, moreover, was well known in the colonies. Macdonald considered that "of late years Her Majesty's Government has not, as a general rule, interfered with the legislation of colonies having representative institutions and responsible government, except in cases specially mentioned in the instructions to the governors, or in matter of imperial and not merely local interest."[60]

The division of powers in Canada was clearly a matter of exclusively local concern; indeed, the B.N.A. Act was an imperial statute in form only, having been determined in Canada and enacted by the imperial Parliament without any significant change.[61] The imperial practice of enacting constitutional amendments only on the request of the colony or dominion concerned emphasized this, and as early as 1861 the local nature of a constitution was recognized by the British secretary of state, the Duke of Newcastle. "In a response to a request from the Governor of South Australia that he be given an Instruction requiring him to reserve or disallow all local acts intended to alter the Constitution Act, Newcastle was unsympathetic. Constitution Acts, in his view, were no more than 'Colonial Laws ... making provision for matters in which the colonists are exclusively interested' and 'alterable by the usual methods of legislation.'"[62]

These considerations were reflected in section 5 of the Colonial Laws Validity Act which restricted the application of section 2 by providing that "every Representative Legislature shall, in respect to the Colony under its Jurisdiction, have, and be deemed at all Times to have had, full Power to make Laws respecting the Constitution, Powers and Procedure of such Legislature." Thus it could be argued that the statute did permit a change in the distribution of powers through the concerted action of the federal Parliament and the provincial legislatures. Perhaps the decisive factor in determining the appropriate application of the Colonial Laws Validity Act to the B.N.A. Act was the federal nature of the Canadian constitution. However, this underlined the novelty of Ritchie's position; the application of the Colonial Laws Validity Act could not be obvious in the entirely new context of a federal constitution, especially when it apparently did not apply to the constitution of a colony with a unitary form of government, which was the closest available comparison.

While soon accepted practice would admit only one interpretation of the Colonial Laws Validity Act, such interpretation was not obvious in the context of the time. Given this, it appeared that while Ritchie relied on the doctrine of repugnancy, he did not rely on the Colonial Laws Validity Act itself. Nowhere did he refer specifically to it, and while he must have been aware of it, it seemed unlikely that Ritchie would not have made some argument respecting section 5 if the act had been referred to in argument.

In fact, we know Ritchie had the American example firmly in mind, for in the *Chandler* case he made a detailed comparison of the Canadian and American distribution of the insolvency and bankruptcy powers. Ritchie likely relied implicitly on the American example to support an inherent power of the judiciary to interpret a written constitution, justifying it in the Canadian context with an offhand reference to the repugnancy doctrine, and without acknowledging that the judiciary was not specifically entrenched in the constitution, as was the Supreme Court of the United States.

Rather than questioning the court's authority to strike down a provincial statute for being repugnant to the B.N.A. Act, we might question the court's jurisdiction to interpret the B.N.A. Act. To the argument that because the governor general, on the advice of the federal minister of justice, had not disallowed the provincial statute, it must be held valid, Ritchie responded: "you surely do not contend that the assent of the Governor General would make an Act law, where there was no right to legislate." He then went on to lecture on the need for legislative bodies of the Dominion to appreciate fully the great change in the constitution of the country brought about by the B.N.A. Act and the need to respect the limitations it imposed on provincial legislative power. He urged:

> Nothing can be gained by exceeding the limits fixed, but much inconvenience and loss must result to individuals, and the public interest be jeopardized; for in all usurped jurisdictions the usurpation can operate, only to lower in public estimation the legislative or judicial body, by which jurisdiction not rightly belonging to it is grasped.[63]

Steadman responded directly to this argument, saying:

It is urged that the consent of the Queen in the one case and of
the Governor General in the other, cannot extend the powers of
legislation or render valid a law not within the authority conferred by the British North America Act. It is not to be supposed
that the exercise of the negative authority, in its assent or dissent,
has the effect of extending or limiting the legislative jurisdiction.
*The office and purpose of the negative power is to determine what is
within the powers conferred.* And the Act having placed this jurisdiction in the Sovereign and Governor General, the question
involved in the proposition does not arise. By the assent the law
is declared and affirmed to be within the authority, and no other
tribunal is created by the Act or invested with jurisdiction to
question the correctness of that decision. It is wholly a question
of legislative authority, and having been once determined by the
jurisdiction specially named for that purpose, and always aided
by high legal authority, *why raise it again?*[64]

Thus Steadman would claim that repugnancy doctrine was itself
irrelevant, since, as a matter of law, judicial opinion could not be
determinative of whether a provincial act encroached on a federal
field. Ritchie believed that because in "our [the court's] opinion"[65]
the impugned provincial statute dealt with matters directly within
the forbidden class of insolvency, therefore it did. Steadman held
that by its own terms the B.N.A. Act made the governor general's
opinion determinative of such questions. If he did not disallow
the bill, thereby indicating that in his opinion it was within the
power of the local legislature to pass, it was therefore, by definition, within the provincial sphere. If the provincial legislature
passed an act, thereby indicating that it believed the act to be
within its competence, and the federal cabinet, enjoying the confidence of Parliament, indicated its agreement with this view by
not disallowing the act, then the matter was settled by the appropriate authorities, and repugnancy was impossible.

Steadman would have claimed that a judicial body usurped
jurisdiction in undertaking review of legislation in defiance of the
constitutional principle of parliamentary and legislative supremacy. Ritchie, on the other hand, no doubt meant to imply that
judicial usurpation occurred when a court acted in accordance
with jurisdiction conferred on it by the legislature, in those circumstances in which the legislature lacked competence under the
B.N.A. Act to enact such legislation. He claimed that the governor
general had no power "to extend the authority of the Local Legislature or enable it to override the Imperial Statute."[66] This simply

assumed that the opinion of the court, that is, of Ritchie himself, must be "correct," without exploring reasons why he should be empowered to make that determination.

Arguments that a legislative body should not exceed its authority, and that such a body cannot make valid law where it had no right to legislate were unexceptionable, but in large part they begged the important question of who should have the power to determine the limits of legislative authority. The claim that the B.N.A. Act had wrought a fundamental change in the constitution of the country was a conclusory one which was no better supported by the document itself than the opposite conclusion arrived at by Steadman.

Paul C. Weiler has more recently contended that judicial review of legislation came to be "exercised in Canada immediately after Confederation and encountered so little inquiry or debate that it must have been tacitly assumed by everyone to be proper."[67] This was not the case in New Brunswick. The *Chandler* case raised a storm of controversy. Ritchie's holding not only challenged the supremacy of the legislature, but it caused Hazelton, a sixty-year-old man, to languish in jail for two years. This came to the attention of George Edwin King, the attorney general, and in March 1870, in response to Ritchie's decision of the previous summer, he introduced a bill entitled "A Bill relating to Imprisonment for Debt" which would limit imprisonment in a civil suit to twelve months. King conceded that it was not a very bold enactment but it had the advantage that it could be passed by both branches of the legislature. He maintained that "when society exacted of a man that he should remain one year confined in gaol, he should be fairly entitled to his discharge, having fully atoned for any mistake he may have made in conducting his affairs."[68] He noted that the new federal bankruptcy legislation had the effect of reserving imprisonment for debt to the poor man, because the law applied only to traders and thus excluded most persons from its benefits, and even a trader could not go into bankruptcy unless he owed $500. King indicated that although his bill had a general and provincial effect, it would have a particular effect in the case of Mr. Hazelton. After outlining the predicament in which the unfortunate Hazelton found himself, King indicated that passing the bill would be an act of mercy and charity for "[t]he only chance of escape for that man lies in this legislative body, or the grave to which he, as well as all of us, are hastening."

S.R. Thomson, the lawyer who represented the creditor, Valentine, read of the introduction of the bill and wrote to the Speaker of the House of Assembly complaining that the legislation was retrospective and *ultra vires*.

> Apart from the impropriety of affecting the rights of any one by an *ex post facto* law, this Bill is, as I humbly conceive, *in pari materia* with the Act formerly passed by the Legislature since the "British North America Act, 1867," and which upon my application to the Supreme Court was by that court declared to be, under that Act of the Imperial Parliament, *ultra vires* the legislature of this Province.
>
> I hope that the House will pause before it passes the proposed law, and thereby save my client the trouble and expense of a second application to the Court.[69]

William H. Needham, a member of the Assembly, thought that Thomson's letter was a "sort of threat" and in his opinion the act was valid because they were "simply legislating on civil rights."[70] Needham had concurrently introduced a more ambitious bill which would have abolished imprisonment for debt.

Thomson acted on his threat to prevent the legislature from releasing Hazelton and on 10 March 1870, less than a week after King's bill passed the House and before it had been enacted as law, obtained an injunction issued out of the Supreme Court in Equity by Justice J.W. Weldon, forbidding the sheriff or gaoler from releasing Hazelton upon penalty of one thousand pounds. The injunction stated that the sheriff and gaoler were not to discharge Hazelton out of their custody "by virtue of any such Act or Acts or for any other reason whatsoever" and the custody of Hazelton was to continue "until orders shall be made to the contrary."[71]

Needham was outraged: "The idea of an inferior tribunal daring to issue an injunction against an Act of the legislature," he said, "was preposterous." On 12 March 1870 he introduced a bill for "the protection and indemnification of all persons for carrying out the Acts of the Legislature." Andrew Rainsford Wetmore, the Premier of New Brunswick, said that the injunction was "a most extraordinary aggression on the part of the Judges of the Supreme Court—that a Judge by putting his name to a paper could prevent the operation of any Act passed by this Legislature."[72] King, who would later become premier and subsequently a puisne judge of the Supreme Court of Canada, thought the issuing of this injunction to be "a most extraordinary and alarming extension of judicial power." He said the duty of a judge had generally been thought to lie in the interpretation of existing law but "to extend their power to issue an injunction to a man not to act under a law passed or to be passed, was an assumption of power of such an alarming nature that this Legislature would not hesitate for one moment to put its foot on it and stamp it down."[73] On 16 March 1870, Needham's indemnification bill received its first and second readings and, to make it clear to the courts whose authority was superior, he introduced a bill "to declare void the injunction issued by Justice Weldon, one of the Judges in Equity, in the matter of Horace L. Hazelton," and a separate bill "to declare void the judgment of the Supreme Court in the case of the Queen against James W. Chandler."[74] Both these bills received their second reading on 17 March 1870.

The introduction of these bills demonstrated the attitude of the province's leading politicians towards judicial review, and their views were made more explicit in the debate which took place when Needham moved that the House go into committee on his indemnification bill before it received its final reading. Needham again indicated that the injunction issued by Justice Weldon gave rise to the bill but he also noted that county court judges, one of whom must have been James Steadman, had discharged debtors under the 1868 amendment respecting insolvent debtors and then the Supreme Court had held the act *ultra vires*. Needham thought it possible that these county court judges and sheriffs who had discharged confined debtors might be liable to creditors even though they had acted under the law enacted by the legislature in discharging them. The bill originally introduced by King to counter Ritchie's holding in *Chandler*, which would restrict the length of imprisonment in a civil matter, had passed the Legislative Council and only awaited the assent of the lieutenant-governor to become law.[75] "The moment that Bill becomes law," Needham said, "we are placed in this anomalous position, that the law commands the prison doors to be thrown open ... and a Judge issues an injunction to keep that prison door locked." He continued:

> It is a grave matter whether we have power to pass such a law or not. If we have not power it is time we knew it. If we are powerless in reference to the rights settled on us by the Charter of 1867, it is time we acknowledged our imbecility and petitioned Her Majesty to abolish our Legislature.[76]

A.R. Wetmore agreed with Needham and added that he had read Chief Justice Ritchie's decision in *Chandler* with great care and thought the House might have been right in passing the 1868 amendment and that "the judgment of the Supreme Court, if the question had been brought up on appeal, would not have been sustained." The Speaker of the House, however, urged that the indemnification bill should not be passed. "Though he held the rights and liberties of this House as sacred as any other man," the Speaker said "he did not see the necessity for bringing on a contest between this House and other judicial powers and bodies, while they are exercising a power they think they have a right to exercise." In reply Needham quoted from Chief Justice Chipman that "it was a thing unheard of in British institutions for a Judicial tribunal to question a law when duly enacted." He asked the rhetorical question "Has the Supreme Court, under the change in our Constitution, any more power than before?" to which he replied:

> If they had he would like to see it pointed out; but has the House of Assembly any more power over the Supreme Court than they had before? Hear it ye men of New Brunswick. They have! for we can annihilate them by a word of our breath as easy as we can a County Court. If they would turn to the 129th section of the British North American [*sic*] Act of 1867 they would find it.[77]

Here again was the argument used by Steadman that section 129 was a clear indication of legislative supremacy. The legislature did appear to be supreme in that it had the power to "annihilate" the courts.

Needham "then read from the Journals of the House of Assembly of Nova Scotia to show that the decision whether the Acts of the Local Legislatures were constitutional, rested with the Privy Council of the Dominion."[78] This reference, to the memorandum prepared by Sir John A. Macdonald dated 8 June 1868, related to the power of disallowance possessed by the federal cabinet over acts of the provincial legislature, which was printed in an appendix by the Nova Scotia legislature. Needham also made essentially the same argument that Steadman had previously made against judicial review:

> Though [a provincial law] might be a direct violation of the North America Act, yet the Judges of the Supreme Court have not the power to decide upon its constitutionality. ... [This] will be proved by examining the North America Act, Sections 90, 55

and 56, that when a Bill passed this Legislature, the moment it received assent of the Lieutenant Governor it became law, and remains so until annulled ... subject only to the approval of the Governor General and the Privy Council of Canada.... It is a fallacy to say that because we have a written charter the judges of the Supreme Court have a right to take upon themselves the power to decide upon the constitutionality of law, when in that charter it is placed directly in the hands of the Governor General and Privy Council [Canadian cabinet].[79]

Needham asked rhetorically: "Was the Supreme Court the head of the country? They have no power to decide upon the constitutionality of our laws," and he concluded with a passionate appeal to democratic values:

Hon. members need not tell him that because he was a lawyer he was setting up his opinion above the Judges of the Supreme Court. Though he had to bow to them in Court, he was their master here, and they had to bow to him. He stood on higher ground than they did because he helped to make the laws, but they were but expounders of them. While he knew they acted conscientiously, he did the same, and he was not prepared to yield to them when they declared an Act of ours unconstitutional which had been passed under the authority of our Charter and had received the sanction of the Governor General, who alone has the power to determine whether it was constitutional and legal. He would ask the members to stand up in defence of the people's rights. They had now a chance to talk about the people's rights, and they could do it honestly and in truth. The case was the Supreme Court *versus* the people. He was on the side of the people, and the members of the House should assert their rights.[80]

Some members of the House expressed a reluctance to man the barricades and defend the people against judicial aggression. J.L. Moore counselled caution and said "When we undertake to legislate in reference to any matter and it is proved to be not within our jurisdiction, then it becomes a grave question whether it would be considered an act of the Legislature at all." Moore implored the Assembly "as guardians not only of the People's rights, but of the character of this Legislature, not to pass this act without giving it more consideration than it had yet received."[81]

However, the majority of the House were closer to Needham than to Moore. The attorney general advocated passing the indemnification bill in order to guard the independence of the Legislative Assembly. He thought the injunction issued by Justice Weldon was "extraordinary" and in a completely different category than the judgment of Chief Justice Ritchie saying:

> Whatever difference of opinion there might exist as to the judgment of the Supreme Court in the case of the Queen against Chandler, whether it was based upon a proper consideration of law or not, no one would for a moment suppose that the injunction granted by the Judge of the Supreme Court, brought before the House, stands in the same position.[82]

King indicated that the bill to allow any person to be freed from jail after a confinement of two years in any civil suit did not refer to solvency or insolvency. If the legislature could not pass that bill, King insisted, it could not pass an act abolishing imprisonment for debt. But King maintained that the B.N.A. Act conferred power to pass law relating to private rights and "[t]he lawyer that would say he had no power to pass that Act [abolishing imprisonment for debt], and that it was interfering with insolvency, would utter an opinion that would be entitled to no credit whatever." While King may have implied that the bill he had introduced to reverse the effect of Ritchie's judgment was distinguishable from that which Ritchie had found *ultra vires*, this must have been largely an attempt to forestall another finding of unconstitutionality. The original bill had used "the debtor" as a short form of the words "any person confined in gaol or on the limits in any civil suit," and section 4 of King's bill had provided that release from imprisonment would not prevent any other civil proceeding against "the debtor." The substantive difference between the bills was that the former provided for release of the debtor only after an inquiry by a judge, whereas in the latter release was automatic. If the former act was unconstitutional, the latter was clearly a colourable attempt to evade the constitutional restriction.

While King was diplomatic in defence of his new bill, he did not hide his disapproval of the courts: "having tasted blood in the case of Queen against Chandler, the spirit of the Court was aroused, and one of the Judges [Weldon] took it upon himself to make a dead set, not only against our past legislation, but anything we may think fit to pass." King adopted the words of Ritchie in *Chandler* that a body usurping power lost esteem but turned the words against the court.

The response of King to the mounting conflict between the New Brunswick legislature and the courts was of great significance, as it revealed the opinion of a well educated and thoughtful lawyer to the issue of judicial review of legislation immediately after confederation. King said:

> We have no Court of Appeal established now, and under the laws of the country there is no existing body who have the right to decide upon the constitutionality of [an Act]. Suppose a man is released under the Act passed the other day, the Judges decide it is unconstitutional and the Court claims indemnity, but where is the constituted authority to decide the question? Why should you ask us to stultify ourselves when the law constitutes no authority upon the matter?... It is a wicked thing to trample upon the Judiciary, because we are here to-day and may pass what we think is right, but other people may come to-morrow, and once open the flood-gates and breakdown the spirit of the Judiciary and evils would flow in upon you, from which there would be no escape. But there may be a question whether any body that is under the control of a legislative body and that receives from the legislative body no distinct functions to decide upon its Acts, should ... have the power to decide upon the acts of the legislative body which gives it life and breath.[83]

When asked what was the paramount authority in the country, King replied: "The three estates of the realm and not the Supreme Court." The three, in a provincial context, must have been the two branches of the legislature, the House of Assembly and the Legislative Council,[84] and the lieutenant-governor. These three estates, he said "vitalize the institutions of the country, and among them the Supreme Court."

George King, who had received his education at both Mount Allison College in Sackville, New Brunswick, and at Wesleyan University in Connecticut, was alert to the ways in which the Supreme Court of the United States differed from Canadian courts. He said:

> In the United States a Supreme Court is provided for in the very instrument that gives force to any of their acts of legislation, which instrument is the fundamental constitution of the United States, on which the government itself is built, and that same instrument gives sanction to the co-ordinate body — the Supreme Court of the United States, and they all exist together in a co-ordinate and concurrent life, but here there is nothing of the sort. Here it is a body you bring into life, and you have the power to put an end to it, and is it wise to allow that body to decide upon the validity of your acts in a mere matter of Government, for if a Supreme Court has power to decide upon the matter, so has a County Court or Magistrate's Court. Is it wise and consistent with the best interests of the country that the

Courts of the country should, by virtue of their existence, have power to determine upon these matters and control our actions. I think it is a serious question whether they have or not. We know a Court of Appeal is about being established, which will have the power of determining the constitutionality of Acts of the Provincial Legislature. The Dominion Parliament have the power to give this power if they give it expressly. Then our Acts can come under the control of law through the operation of that Court so established, but until that court shall be established, I do not think it is wise for the Courts to exercise these rights, because it leads to a continual conflict with the judicial power. They have the right to call them in question, but not the right to stultify them, as they would if they placed burdens upon those who act under our laws. We should consider these matters calmly, and take the best advice we can get, but unfortunately we do not have the presence of the Judges here to tell us whether an Act is proper or not, and have not the benefit of their good judgment in the matter, therefore we have to act upon the best light we can get, and to guard our own independence we should protect and indemnify any person acting under any Act of this Assembly.[85]

King thus was of the opinion that the judiciary did not have any inherent power to hold a statute to be *ultra vires* because it conflicted with the division of powers in the B.N.A. Act but that this power might be conferred upon the courts by the legislature.

The desire to assert legislative supremacy prevailed, and King's indemnification bill passed the House of Assembly by twenty-five votes to three. Needham then withdrew his bill to declare void the injunction Chief Justice Ritchie had issued in *Chandler*, saying that the object sought would be achieved without it.

On 7 April 1870 Horace Hazelton was finally released from the Saint John gaol, two years and two weeks after his incarceration on 21 February 1868. Isaac Allen Jack recorded in his journal that "Osgood came down with all the necessary papers today the act for that purpose having rec'd the Gov. Genl's [Lt.Gov.] assent and Hazelton is at last free. I called and saw him at Osgood's and was told there was quite a convocation at the gaol when he left." On the following day, Hazelton left by train for the United States and Jack recorded in his journal that "I am truly delighted he is off but he got off only by means of the most damnable legislation ever perpetrated in this province —perhaps any part of the empire."[86] Why Jack regarded the legislation freeing Hazelton as damnable was unclear. It might have been because the legislature exercised its purported supremacy over the courts. An Act relating to Imprisonment for Debt did possess an unusual feature — it was to "remain in force for one year after the passing of this Act, and no longer." This sunset provision might have been introduced in anticipation that imprisonment for civil debt would soon be abolished; but this was not done in New Brunswick until 1874.

The imprisonment of Horace Hazelton had given rise to more extended debate about the propriety of judicial review of legislation than had previously taken place in Canada. The debate in the New Brunswick House of Assembly in 1870 indicated that most legislators, including several thoughtful lawyers, did not accept the proposition enunciated by Ritchie in *Chandler* that it was the duty of the courts to police the division of powers set out in the B.N.A. Act.

Doubts about the propriety of judicial review persisted in New Brunswick. At the opening of the legislature on 27 February 1873, the lieutenant-governor said that he was happy to inform them that the Common Schools Act of 1871, impeached as unconstitutional, had been sustained unanimously by the Supreme Court of New Brunswick. In the debate on the address, Michael Adams stated that he did not believe that the provincial Supreme Court had any right to determine the constitutionality of the school law and that it was impolitic for the government to approve or assent to such a doctrine. John James Fraser thought there was merit in the opinion of Adams but was not fully prepared to concede the point, believing it to be a debatable question. A Fredericton newspaper which fully subscribed to Adams' position stated:

> No one doubts that the Legislature could abolish the present Supreme Court and set up an entirely new Court in its stead, or that the Legislature now controls every officer through whom the Court executes its decrees. What real authority has the Court as opposed to the Legislature? Is it not almost mockery that such a body should set itself above the Legislature? Is it not almost criminal negligence in the Government and legislature to submit to such an imposition?

The newpaper concluded with a warning to the government and the legislature that they should take care "lest they bequeath to their successors a weakened and impaired Constitution."[87]

O. McInerney in the Legislative Council also objected to the inclusion of the section expressing satisfaction that the Common Schools Act had been sustained because he did not think the

Supreme Court had such power. On 22 March 1873 the provincial secretary made a motion ordering the printing of the paper prepared by Judge Steadman, arguing that the judiciary lacked the power to determine the validity of acts passed by the provincial legislature. This was the last significant volley fired in the conflict between the legislature and the courts in New Brunswick over the propriety of judicial review. Ritchie's view, that it was the duty of the court to engage in judicial review, prevailed, but opponents of judicial review had fought a spirited campaign in New Brunswick.

An early reference to Ritchie's decision in *Chandler* came from Sir John A. Macdonald. As previously noted, Macdonald initially saw the federal power of disallowance as the sole mechanism to keep the legislatures in their proper sphere. However, his opinion soon began to change. In a report to the federal cabinet and the governor general concerning provincial legislation dated 12 July 1869, he expressed the view that a section of an Ontario statute was *ultra vires* because it was legislation in regard to criminal law, and then remarked that the provision was so just that he was "unwilling to object to it, and leaves the objection to be taken before the courts."[88] In a subsequent report of 12 August 1869 regarding statutes passed by the legislature of Nova Scotia, he noted that Nova Scotia had passed an amendment to the Relief of Insolvent Debtors Act, which Macdonald thought unconstitutional because bankruptcy and insolvency were assigned to the Dominion Parliament. He conceded that the amended act "may be considered more an Act for the relief of indigent debtors, than a law of Insolvency" and recommended that it should be left to its operation with the attention of the Nova Scotia government directed to it. Macdonald then said: "A measure of a similar nature was passed in the session of 1868 by the legislature of New Brunswick and the court there has declared the Act to be unconstitutional. Probably, if the question arises in the courts of Nova Scotia, the same decision will be arrived at."[89]

Thus Macdonald gave fairly explicit approval to Ritchie's initiative in holding a provincial statute unconstitutional on the basis of a failure to conform to the division of powers in the B.N.A. Act. Macdonald probably welcomed the judicial intervention for a number of reasons. The provincial legislatures were enacting a large number of statutes, and insuring that the legislatures remained within their proper sphere became a burdensome task. Another likely reason Macdonald did not object to the sharing of the supervisory task with the judiciary was that he had faith that he had created a centralist constitution and generally speaking only provincial legislation would be held invalid by the courts. As well, relying solely on disallowance would have involved his government in a number of contentious issues. The New Brunswick school question, for instance, was an issue that Macdonald was delighted to leave to the courts. This legislative acquiescence to judicial review was a better explanation of the legitimacy and acceptance of judicial review than reliance on the Colonial Laws Validity Act.

The Canadian courts also followed the lead of Ritchie's vigorous decision. The Quebec Superior Court in *L'Union St. Jacques de Montréal* v. *Dame Julie Belisle* (1872) considered Ritchie's *Chandler* decision favourably and applied it. A widow had challenged the constitutional validity of a provincial act which allowed a financially embarrassed benevolent organization to modify its obligations to its beneficiaries. In a concurring majority opinion, Justice Drummond explored the background of judicial review, quoting extensively from Marshall in *Marbury* and Ritchie in *Chandler*. In holding the legislation *ultra vires* the Quebec legislature, because it infringed on the federal bankruptcy and insolvency power, the judge wrote that the "question under consideration is not the moral character of the Act, but the power, — the authority of the framer. The decision of this court does not tend to impair the supremacy of the Imperial Parliament, but to maintain it, in its full power."[90] In *Re Goodhue* (1872), the first case in which a constitutional challenge was brought to the Ontario Court of Appeal, the court held that while judicial review was inherent in the new federal structure, the impugned legislation was *intra vires* the Ontario legislature.[91] The Privy Council did not have any opportunity to consider the B.N.A. Act until 1873[92] and it was not until 1878 in *A.G. for Quebec* v. *Queen Insurance Co.*[93] that the Privy Council held a provincial statute imposing a tax on certain insurance policies to be *ultra vires* a provincial legislature. The Privy Council assumed the legitimacy of judicial review and consequently did not discuss its propriety. This indicated that judicial review might have been inevitable.

By the time Télesphore Fournier introduced the successful bill in 1875 to establish a Supreme Court of Canada, judicial review of both federal and provincial statutes by all levels of courts was an accepted fact. Sections 54 and 56 of the Supreme and Exchequer

Courts Act[94] clearly recognized that the constitutional validity of an act of Parliament or of a provincial legislature could be impugned in the courts of the provinces, but with the consent of the local legislatures a judge might cause the issue to be removed to the new Supreme Court. Judicial review was much less controversial in 1875 than during confederation debates, and two reasons for this might be surmised. First, the government of Alexander Mackenzie, being more sympathetic to provincial interests than that of Macdonald's, wished to reduce the political flak arising from wide use of a federal power of disallowance. Thus judicial review had greater appeal to them as a mode of keeping provincial legislatures within their proper sphere. Secondly, Ritchie's decision in *Chandler*, and the series of cases that followed on its course, had promoted a new understanding of judicial review.

In 1879 Chief Justice Meredith of the Superior Court of Quebec compared Ritchie's decision in *Chandler* to *Marbury* v. *Madison*, in which Chief Justice John Marshall enunciated that the constitution empowered the Supreme Court of the United States to hold an act of Congress unconstitutional. Marshall had based his decision on the notion that because the Constitution was fundamentally a legal document, and akin to a written contract, the courts were its most appropriate final interpreters. The actions of government institutions must therefore respect its terms or else render the fundamental document a nullity. Chief Justice Meredith made this analogy in *Valin* v. *Langlois* (1879).

> Chief Justice Marshall, than whom a higher authority cannot be cited, in the case of *Marbury* v. *Madison*, speaks of "Legislative acts contrary to the constitution," as not being law, and Chief Justice Ritchie, in *The Queen* v. *Chandler, in re Hazelton*, speaking of legislatures with limited powers, observed, "and if they do legislate beyond their powers, or in defiance of the restrictions placed on them, their enactments are no more binding than rules or regulations promulgated by any other unauthorized body."[95]

Ritchie's decision in *Chandler* for the first time enunciated the power and duty of a Canadian superior court to ensure legislative adherence to the constitutional distribution of power. By the time Steadman's opinion was published in 1873, the issue of judicial review had been effectively determined and Steadman's elaborate reasons for contending that the judiciary lacked the power to determine the constitutionality of a statute could not change the new reality. Had Steadman been a superior court judge instead of a county court judge, judicial review might have been a more contentious issue throughout Canada and not just in New Brunswick.

An early constitutional writer, W.H.P. Clement, said of *Chandler* that:

> The case may well be referred to, as being one of the earliest decisions emphatically enunciating the doctrine that, under the B.N.A. Act, it necessarily devolves upon courts of justice to inquire into the validity of post-Confederation Canadian legislation. The fact that the Governor-General had not disallowed the provincial Act in question, was decisively held by the court to be immaterial, upon an inquiry as to its legal validity.[96]

Yet no modern constitutional law text or casebook, with the sole exception of Strayer's *The Canadian Constitution and the Courts*, even mentions *Chandler*. Why this curious neglect of what was in fact the earliest Canadian case to enunciate the principle that the courts have a duty to engage in judicial review?

One reason may be that it portrayed judicial review in an unfavourable light. Although *Chandler* has never been overruled, even as early as 1892, W.H.P. Clement wrote that it could no longer be "considered a correct exposition of the law." Ritchie had construed "bankruptcy and insolvency" to comprehend all legislation relating to impecunious debtors, whereas a later judicial consensus restricted its ambit to legislation establishing a system for bankruptcy and insolvency. Ritchie himself subsequently held that "there may be many cases where the abolition or regulation of imprisonment for debt is in no way mixed up with or depending on insolvency." A cynic might attribute Ritchie's change of opinion to a desire to avoid precipitating another bitter controversy similar to that which followed in the wake of the *Chandler* decision. The fate of poor Hazleton must surely have caused Ritchie to endeavour to construe the B.N.A. Act so that the benefits of provincial law would be available to debtors unless such law conflicted with federal insolvency legislation. Perhaps more importantly the early judicial attempts to find exclusivity of legislative jurisdiction were giving way to greater recognition of concurrency of legislative powers. This greater acceptance of concurrency might have been partly as a result of the unfortunate outcome of holdings such as that in *Chandler*. Ritchie should not be faulted too much for lack of prescience in this regard: Ritchie relied in large measure on the concluding words of section 91, which stated that any matter falling within the subject enumerated in section 91 "shall not be deemed to come within" the class of matters set out in section 92, to argue for strict exclusivity. As a matter of textual interpretation this is indeed a powerful argument against concurrency. But, the *Chandler* decision was effectively repudiated, and the consensus would be that Ritchie's erroneous decision frustrated the legislature in their efforts to release a poor old man from the Saint John jail. It seemed that the first case to enunciate the principle of judicial review could have provided ammunition for Paul Weiler's thesis that courts often perform this function poorly. Naturally constitutional law scholars, who generally approve of the concept of judicial review, prefer to forget this uncomfortable decision. But there is no doubt that judicial review has both advantages and disadvantages and the *Chandler* case, by revealing its down side, can surely be accommodated rather than suppressed.

The greatest contributing factor for the neglect of the *Chandler* case is that judicial review has been regarded as an inevitable necessity of Canadian federalism. W.R. Lederman has maintained that judicial review flows almost inescapably from the independence of the judiciary and the guaranteed core of substantive jurisdiction which, in his opinion, necessarily flows from sections 96 to 101 of the B.N.A. Act. It remains, according to Lederman, "a matter of governmental necessity that the last word on such distributions and divisions of powers is peculiarly appropriate to superior courts" because "historically ... they determine even the limits of their own powers under the relevant constitutional laws and statutes."[97] B.L. Strayer rejects the idea that jurisdiction to engage in judicial review was "inherent in Anglo-Canadian courts by virtue of the common law" but concludes that:

> While in the abstract it may be argued that judicial review is not inevitable in a federal system as some survive without it, given the Imperial system at the time of Confederation and the prior history of judicial review it was surely implicit that the limitations on legislative power would, where necessary, be enforced by the courts.[98]

If judicial review was either inevitable or as natural as rolling off a log, there was little credit to be earned for engaging in it, even for the first time. However, the *Chandler* case, particularly when read in conjunction with the ensuing debate in the New Brunswick Assembly, and the contemporaneous but even more neglected Steadman opinion, should suggest that acceptance of judicial review was not entirely foreordained. To glorify Ritchie in the way Americans glorify Chief Justice Marshall and his decision in *Marbury* v. *Madison* would do violence to the more modest Canadian psyche. Nevertheless Chief Justice Ritchie and the *Queen* v. *Chandler* deserve a more prominent place in Canadian constitutional law.

Notes to Chapter 10

1. 30 & 31 Vict. c.3 (U.K.). It has been renamed the Constitution Act, 1867, but as the act is discussed in its historical setting, I will refer to it as the British North America Act.

2. For the function and scope of judicial review, see Barry L. Strayer, *The Canadian Constitution and the Courts*, 3rd ed. (Toronto: Butterworths, 1988) and also Jennifer Smith, "The Origins of Judicial Review in Canada," *Canadian Journal of Political Science* 16 (1983).

3. Notes on the Quebec Conference, 10-29 Oct. 1864, as edited by A.G. Doughty *Canadian Historical Review* 1 in (March, 1920), pp. 26-47, reprinted in G.P. Browne, *Documents on the Confederation of British North America*, (Toronto: McClelland and Stewart, 1969), p. 148

4. Ibid., p. 128.

5. Ibid., p. 149.

6. Ibid., p. 86.

7. *Parliamentary Debates on the subject of the Confederation of the British North American Provinces*, 3rd Session, 8th Provincial Parliament of Canada (Quebec: Parliamentary Printers, 1865), p. 433.

8. Ibid., p. 911 (emphasis added).

9. Ibid., p. 404.

10. Ibid., p. 108.

11. Ibid., p. 876.

12. Ibid., p. 502.

13. Ibid., p. 690.

14. William H.P. Clement, *The Law of the Canadian Constitution* (Toronto: Carswell Co., 1892), p. 173.

15. Strayer, *Canadian Constitution*, pp. 17-18.

16. G.V. La Forest, *Disallowance and Reservation of Provincial Legislation* (Ottawa: Department of Justice, 1955), p. 5.

17. *Debates, 1865*, p. 860.

18. Ibid., p. 229.

19. Ibid., p. 51. Benjamin Seymour also described it as a "mongrel Constitution" (p. 205).

20. Ibid., p. 697.

21. Ibid., p. '698.

22. Resolution 29, para. 34 (Quebec Conference Notes, p. 159).

23. Ibid., p. 143.

24. *Debates, 1865*, p. 33.

25. Ibid., p. 42.

26. Strayer, *Canadian Constitution*, p. 16.

27. La Forest, *Disallowance*, p. 6.

28. Quoted in Strayer, *Canadian Constitution*, pp. 18-19.

29. *Debates, 1865*, pp. 500-2.

30. Strayer, *Canadian Constitution*, p .16.

31. Report dated 8 June 1868, found in W.E.Hodgins, *Correspondence, Reports of the Ministers of Justice and Orders in Council upon the subject of Dominion and Provincial Legislation 1867-1985* (Ottawa, Government Printing Bureau, 1896), pp. 61-62.

32. Ibid., pp. 62-64.

33. S.N.B. 1868 c.16, An Act in amendment of Chapter 124, Title xxxiv, of the Revised Statutes, 'Of Insolvent Confined Debtors.': passed 23 Mar. 1868.

34. (1869), 12 N.B.R. 556.

35. In a letter from William Wedderburn, a New Brunswick county court judge to Sir Leonard Tilley dated 28 Dec. 1882 Wedderburn said: "I need not say I am exceedingly glad to hear that Fraser is to succeed Judge Duff. Although it is another instance of how opportunely all those who have conspicuously opposed Confederation (from Chief Justice Ritchie downward) are reaping the benefits of that great Act." NAC, MG 27-I-D15, vol. 21, Sir Samuel L. Tilley 1881-1882.

36. John William Ritchie had been a representative of Nova Scotia at the London conference.

37. (1869), 12 N.B.R 556 at p. 558.

38. Ibid., at p. 557.

39. (1838), 2 N.B.R. 553 at p. 557.

40. Ibid., quoting *Kerr*, p. 557.

41. Ibid., *Chandler* at p. 557. Strayer, *Canadian Constitution* (p. 7, n. 27), indicates that *Chandler* expressly applied the Colonial Laws Validity Act, but this is not correct.

42. Ibid., at pp. 566-67.

43. This decision was made in 1868 although the 25-page paper does not appear to have been printed until 1873, but his strong view would be known to the judiciary in New Brunswick. James Steadman, *Opinion of Judge Steadman of the York County court, Delivered in 1868, upon the power of the Judiciary to determine the Constitutionality of law enacted by the Parliament of Canada or a Provincial Legislature, with his reasons therefor. Also — observations upon two cases involving the same question since determined by the Supreme Court of N.B.* (Fredericton, February, 1873).

44. Ibid., pp. 6-7.

45. Ibid., p. 6.

46. A.V. Dicey, *Introduction to the Study of the Law of the Constitution*, 3rd ed. (London: Macmillan, 1889), p. 155 (emphasis added).

47. Ibid., pp. 155-57.

48. In later editions Dicey toned down his criticism of the preamble by substituting the words "diplomatic inaccuracy" for "official mendacity": see A.V. Dicey, *Introduction to the Study of the Law of the Constitution*, 7th ed. (London: Macmillan, 1908), p. 161.

49. Steadman, *Opinion*, pp. 6, 24.

50. W.R. Lederman, "The Independence of the Judiciary," *Canadian Bar Review* 34 (1956), 769-809, 1139-1179.

51. Steadman, *Opinion*, p. 12.

52. (1869), 12 N.B.R., 556 at p. 566.

53. 28 & 29 Vic., (U.K.) c.63.

54. Steadman, *Opinion*, pp. 3-6,9.

55. Ibid., p. 3.

56. Joseph Doutre, *Constitution of Canada* (Montreal: Lovell & Son, 1880), p. v.

57. In the fifty years before confederation there seem to have been no cases reaching the Privy Council from anywhere in the Empire which challenged local legislation as being *ultra vires*, and only sixteen which challenged other acts of government. See D.B. Swinfen, *Imperial Control of Colonial Legislation 1813-1865* (Oxford: Clarendon Press, 1970), p. 44; L.P. Beth, "The Judicial Committee of the Privy Council and the Development of Judicial Review," *American Journal of Comparative Law* 24 (1976), pp. 34, 42; see also D.O. McGovney, "The British Origin of Judicial Review of Legislation," *University of Pennsylvania Law Review* 93 (1944), p. 1

concerning four cases from the pre-revolutionary Thirteen Colonies which challenged local legislation.

58. See Swinfen, *Imperial Control*, chapter 11, and Beth, "Judicial Review," p. 24.

59. See Swinfen, *Imperial Control*, chapter 8.

60. See, e.g., Macdonald's report of 8 June 1868, in Hodgins, *Correspondence*.

61. William A. Henry, later Ritchie's colleague on the Supreme Court, stated that he and Charles Fisher of New Brunswick wrote the original draft. Justice Strong of the Supreme Court of Canada stated that to his knowledge only a single "verbal" amendment was made in the imperial Parliament. See Canada, Sessional Papers 1885, No.85, p. 144.

62. Swinfen, *Imperial Control*, p. 98.

63. (1869), 12 N.B.R. 556 at pp. 557, 567.

64. Steadman *Opinion*, p. 14, first emphasis added, second in original.

65. (1869), 12 N.B.R. 556 at p. 566.

66. Ibid., at p. 567.

67. Paul C. Weiler "The Supreme Court of Canada and Canadian Federalism" in *Law and Social Change* ed. by Jacob S. Ziegel (Toronto: Osgoode Hall Law School, 1973) at p. 49.

68. *Debates, 1870*, p. 56.

69. Ibid., p. 57.

70. Ibid., p. 58.

71. *Daily Morning News* 12 Mar. 1870.

72. *Debates, 1870*, p. 88.

73. Ibid.

74. Ibid., p. 105.

75. The Legislative Council had amended the maximum period of detention from one year to two years.

76. *Debates, 1870*, p. 121.

77. Ibid., p. 122.

78. Ibid.

79. Ibid., pp. 188-89.

80. Ibid., pp. 121, 123.

81. Ibid., p. 123.

82. Ibid., p. 124.

83. Ibid.

84. The Legislative Council was abolished in New Brunswick by S.N.B. 1891, c.9, but did not come into effect until "after the closing of the first Session of Legislature of 1894, or until the dissolution of the present House."

85. *Debates, 1870*, p. 124.

86. New Brunswick Museum A20, Isaac Allen Jack Journal, 7 April 1870.

87. *Colonial Farmer*, 10 March 1873, "The Legislature and The Supreme Court."

88. Hodgins, *Correspondence*, p. 82.

89. Ibid., p. 256.

90. (1872), 20 L.C.J. 29, pp. 42-45, reversed on appeal (1874), 6 L.R.P.C. 31.

91. (1872), 19 Grant 366.

92. *R. v. Coote*, (1873), L.R. 4 P.C. 599.

93. (1878), 3 App. Cas. 1090.

94. S.C. 1875, c.11.

95. (1879), 5 Q.L.R. 1, pp. 16-17.

96. Clement, *Constitution*, p. 397.

97. Lederman, "Independence of the Judiciary," *supra* footnote 50.

98. Strayer, *Canadian Constitution*, pp. 5, 49.

CHAPTER 11

Women, Denominational Schools and Prohibition

Legislatures in the later half of the nineteenth century began to combat the harshness of the common law and to forge property rights for married women. The common law provided that on marriage all personal property of a woman, including wages, vested in her husband and although she retained ownership of her real property, she forfeited to her husband the right to manage such property and receive the rent. The common law had recognized special exceptions and Blackstone noted that where a husband "had abjured the realm or [was] banished," his wife was restored to the status of a single person. Such a narrow exception proved inadequate in the new world "where the lure of vast expanses of unsettled land caused many men to desert their families and relocate anonymously in relatively unpopulated areas."[1] In 1851 New Brunswick took the lead in enacting protective measures with "an Act to Secure to Married Women Real and Personal Property Held in Their Own Right."[2]

In *Abell* v. *Light* (1867), Chief Justice Ritchie had occasion to interpret this legislation. Mrs. Abell, whose husband was insane and confined in the provincial lunatic asylum, operated a boarding house and sued in her own name to recover an amount due for board and lodging. The defendant, who had contracted with Mrs. Abell, urged that because there was no desertion or abandonment by the husband, the wife had no right to maintain the action. Section 2 permitted a married woman to sue in her own name for debts owed to her but only if she were deserted or abandoned. However, section 3 provided that "When any married woman deserted by her husband, or compelled to support herself, shall acquire any property, it shall vest in her and be at her disposal, and not subject to the debts, interference or control of her husband."

Counsel for the defendant argued that because the furniture in the house belonged to the husband and the husband was also entitled to his wife's services, the husband was entitled to the debt for the lodging — a combination of the husband's property with the wife's services meant the husband was entitled to her wages. Ritchie indicated the absurdity of the contention by posing the following hypothetical: "Suppose the husband was to leave her a dress which she wears, he afterwards goes away, and she goes out to service, wearing this dress, for she could not go naked, would she not be entitled to the wages of her service?"[3] Ritchie certainly disapproved of the defendant's attempt to renege on his contract and indicated his hearty approval of the statute saying that it was remedial, "enlarging the rights of married women compelled to support themselves, extricating them from the too narrow and circumscribed limits of the common law" and therefore merited a liberal construction. To accomplish this Ritchie believed that property in section 3 had to be construed as embracing all property real and personal, including the debt owed by the defendant. Ritchie stated: "it is difficult to understand how a party, by withholding payment from a married woman compelled to support herself, could thereby destroy her right to recover it. To place her in such a helpless position would be entirely to frustrate the humane intention of the Legislature, and to place the result of her labor out of her reach." Ritchie also thought that "[t]here is certainly no more legitimate way by which a married woman, left destitute, and compelled to support herself, could acquire property than by keeping a boarding house."[4]

In spite of the decision, Mr. Light continued to refuse to pay Mrs. Abell the board he owed and Mrs. Abell refused to permit him to remove his furniture. Light sued to obtain his furniture and a judge ruled that a boarding-house keeper, unlike an innkeeper, had no lien on the goods of a guest. Mrs. Abell appealed this decision and while her counsel was absent on the appeal, the defendant again asked for the furniture and threatened to take proceedings against her and to ruin her house if she refused. Mrs. Abell claimed to hold the furniture as of right and refused to do anything in the absence of her counsel. Light had Mrs. Abell arrested for fraudulently detaining his property and converting it to her use and for want of bail she was imprisoned for a day. The charge was dismissed and Mrs. Abell then sued Light for malicious prosecution and false imprisonment. Ritchie acknowledged that she had no legal right to retain the furniture but held that her *bona fide* claim of right could not be converted into a felony. He held that Light "knowingly violated the law, using it wrongfully to accomplish his own purposes, to the injury of the plaintiff's feelings, person and property" and that the jury was "warranted in being liberal in damages" and thus sustained the damage award of £500.[5] The liberality of the damage award can be appreciated by comparing it with the annual salary of the Chief Justice himself which amounted to £800 per year. The damage award in *Abell* v. *Light* must have contributed to a newspaper's subsequent description of Ritchie as "emphatically a terror to evil-doers."[6]

One of the most important cases that Ritchie heard as Chief Justice of New Brunswick was *Ex Parte Renaud* (1873). The constitutionality of the Common Schools Act, 1871, which repealed the Parish School Act 1858, was challenged by a Roman Catholic ratepayer on the basis that it was contrary to 93(1) of the B.N.A. Act. This guaranteed "any Right or Privilege with respect to Denominational Schools which any Class of Persons have by Law in the Province at the Union." The Common Schools Act provided that all schools conducted under the new provisions should be nonsectarian, whereas formerly there existed certain parochial schools established under earlier legislation. All five judges of the New Brunswick Supreme Court held the Common Schools Act to be valid, on the grounds that section 93(1) protected only those legal rights established by virtue of positive legal enactment. It did not protect privileges conferred when a large majority of the ratepayers happened to belong to one particular religion.

Ritchie sympathized with the Roman Catholic ratepayers but contended that they had no legal recourse when a non-sectarian, publicly funded school system existed. He stated:

> It may be a very great hardship, that a large class of persons should be forced to contribute to the support of schools to which they are conscientiously opposed, or be shut out from what they have hitherto, under certain circumstances enjoyed, and be without remedy; but by any such considerations, Courts of Justice ought not to be influenced: hard cases, it has been repeatedly said, are apt to make bad law; and it has also been justly remarked, that if there is a general hardship affecting a general class of cases or persons, it is a consideration for the Legislature, not for a Court of Justice.[7]

Justices Allen and Weldon concurred with Ritchie's judgment but Justices Fisher and Wetmore wrote separate concurring opinions.

The latter two judges wished to dissociate themselves from Ritchie's disapproval of a regulation made under the Common Schools Act. The earlier Parish School Act had declared that the Board of Education was to ensure that the Bible be read to all children whose parents did not object and that Roman Catholic parents could insist on their church's approved Douay version. A similar provision was omitted from the Common Schools Act and the Board of Education declared by regulation 21 that "it shall be the privilege of every teacher to open and close the daily exercises of the school by reading a portion of the scripture (out of the common or Douay version, as he may prefer)." Ritchie's strong religious views, and the importance he attached to the Bible, probably compelled him to speak out against this regulation, even though it was unnecessary to his decision. He stated:

> Why the Board of Education should have departed from the principle and policy of the Parish School Act, and taken from the parents of all the children of the country — Protestant and Roman Catholic alike — the great boon and privilege of insisting on the Bible being read in schools, as they have done, and should have conferred on the teacher, not only the privilege of reading the Bible or not as he likes, but out of the Common or Douay version — not as the children or their parents may choose, but as the teacher may prefer, though he cannot compel the attendance of the pupils, — is not for us to attempt to explain; we simply point out the fact.[8]

The Judicial Committee of the Privy Council dismissed the appeal without even calling upon counsel for the respondents, one of whom was George King, the attorney general for New Brunswick.[9] The fact that it was never officially reported indicated a serious misperception by the Privy Council about the importance of the New Brunswick school question for Canada. Ritchie would later render a decision on the Manitoba separate schools' case while sitting on the Supreme Court of Canada in which *Ex parte Renaud* figured.

Although Ritchie opposed confederation, after it was accomplished he endeavoured to give the distribution of powers contained in the British North America Act a fair and reasonable interpretation. In *Regina* v. *The Justices of the Peace of the County of Kings* (1875), a Mr. McManus applied to the justices for an order to compel the Sessions of King's County to grant him a licence to sell liquor. They had declined his application on the basis that they did not intend to grant any licences that year. An 1873 New Brunswick statute had empowered the General Sessions of the Peace for each county to grant tavern licences to "persons of good character as they in their discretion shall think proper" for a sum not exceeding one hundred dollars, nor less than twenty dollars. Ritchie could have determined the case by simply holding that "empowered" required the session to exercise a sound discretion in granting licences and this they had failed to do by declining to grant any licences that year. Instead, in granting a mandamus to compel the issuing of the licence, Ritchie held that federal Parliament's power under section 91(2), the regulation of trade and commerce,

> must involve full power over the matter to be regulated, and must necessarily exclude the interference of all other bodies that would attempt to intermeddle with the same thing. The power thus given to the Dominion Parliament is general, without limitation or restriction, and therefore must include traffic in articles of merchandize, not only in connection with foreign countries, but also that which is internal between different Provinces of the Dominion, as well as that which is carried on within the limits of an individual Province.[10]

Ritchie thus accorded a broad and reasonable sweep to the federal power over trade and commerce and he also noted that the United States Congress did not enjoy "the same full power of regulating trade and commerce that belongs to the Dominion Parliament."

Ritchie, perhaps for the first time, tentatively advanced the "double aspect" doctrine but did not let it control his decision. This now orthodox constitutional doctrine recognized that a subject which in one aspect falls within federal authority, may in another aspect and for another purpose fall within provincial authority. Ritchie stated that the court wished to indicate that the local legislature had the power to regulate:

> the sale of spirituous liquors in public places, as would tend to the preservation of good order and prevention of disorderly conduct, rioting or breaches of the peace. In such cases, and possibly others of a similar character, the regulation would have nothing to do with trade or commerce, but with good order and Local government, matters of municipal police and not of commerce, and which municipal institutions are particularly competent to manage and regulate.[11]

He noted that if the legislature prohibited the manufacture or sale of any article of trade or commerce, this would be a usurpation of "power which pertains exclusively to the Parliament of Canada." Ritchie then expressed the opinion that an 1871 New Brunswick statute declaring that where a majority in a parish or Municipality voted for prohibition, no licence for the sale of liquor shall be granted was *ultra vires* the local legislature. Ritchie had never looked with favour on prohibition imposed by a majority, for he considered this a sphere for individual choice. In 1855 he had opposed S. Leonard Tilley's bill which, when enacted, led to the defeat of the first Liberal administration in New Brunswick. His strong opposition to prohibition perhaps caused him to render an opinion on the 1871 legislation that was unnecessary to the disposition of the case. Nevertheless, his decision, while according ample scope for the federal trade and commerce power, still recognized some scope for provincial regulation short of prohibition. This balanced interpretation became a hallmark of Ritchie's constitutional adjudication.

Notes to Chapter 11

1. C. Backhouse, "Married Women's Property Law in Nineteenth-Century Canada," *Law and History Review* 6 (1988), p. 217.

2. S.N.B. 1851, c.24.

3. *Abell* v. *Light* (1867), 12 N.B.R. 97 at p. 99.

4. Ibid., pp. 100-1.

5. (1868), 12 N.B.R. 240 at p. 254.

6. *New Dominion* Saint John, 16 Oct. 1875, p. 4.

7. (1873), 14 N.B.R. 273 at p. 293.

8. Ibid., p. 289.

9. The opinion of the Privy Council was never included in the regular law reports and was not in fact fully reported until 1896 by G.J. Wheeler in his *Confederation Law of Canada* from shorthand notes made by the agents of the successful respondent.

10. (1875), 15 N.B.R. 535 at p. 539.

11. Ibid., at pp. 540-41.

CHAPTER 12

From Critic to Founding Member of the Supreme Court of Canada

The Supreme Court of Canada was not created along with the new country when the British North America Act came into force on 1 July 1867. The B.N.A. Act contained an enigmatic provision in section 101 which, in permissive rather than mandatory language, gave the federal government authority to "from Time to Time provide for the Constitution, Maintenance, and Organization of a General Court of Appeal for Canada, and for the Establishment of any additional Courts for the better Administration of the Laws of Canada." At the birth of the Dominion, however, the existing court structures of the provinces were maintained, and the final court of appeal continued to be the Judicial Committee of the Privy Council in London, a recourse that had rarely been used. For nearly a decade following confederation the Dominion carried on with no national appellate court.

The Quebec conference had passed a resolution in favour of such an appellate tribunal. Moreover, the constitution envisaged a highly centralized judicial system. The federal cabinet had power to appoint judges to all superior, district and county courts. The federal Parliament possessed exclusive jurisdiction to enact criminal law and section 94 provided for uniformity of laws relative to property and civil rights in the original three common law provinces, with the concurrence of those provinces. Thus the advent of a supreme court at a national level was more than a spontaneous initiative: "It was surely natural that 'a General Court of Appeal for Canada' would be established to coordinate the pivotal work of the various provincial-level courts. The call for such a central court, however poorly articulated, was no mere afterthought."[1]

The lengthy process of establishing a supreme court really began in the summer of 1868. Sir John A. Macdonald requested Justice Samuel H. Strong of Toronto to draft a bill which would

Sir John A. Macdonald
Prime Minister of Canada
1867-73 and 1878-91
(National Archives of Canada, Neg. no. C10144)

attempt to fulfill the vague directives of section 101. The resulting bill submitted to Parliament on 21 May 1869 envisaged a court composed of six judges and a chief justice which would exercise appellate jurisdiction over all areas of law across Canada. The court was given original jurisdiction in revenue, admiralty and other matters where the federal crown was a potential party. More controversially the court was to have "exclusive original jurisdiction" where any provincial statute was challenged on the basis that the province did not possess the power to enact it under the B.N.A. Act. It was widely felt that this provision placed undue power at a federal level to engage in judicial review of provincial legislation.[2] Notable also was the failure of the bill to ensure representation on the court by those trained in Quebec civil law.

In the face of various objections to the proposed legislation Macdonald withdrew the bill, but he would not drop this initiative. In his view the 1869 draft "was rather more for the purpose of suggestion and consideration than for a final measure" intended to become law.[3] To stimulate further discussion he had copies of the bill distributed to judges and lawyers throughout the Dominion for comment and criticism. Ritchie, at that time Chief Justice of New Brunswick, certainly ranked as one of the most prominent of the many figures to respond to Macdonald's request to review the bill. In his vigorous and perceptive critique of the proposed Supreme Court legislation, Ritchie covered a wide range of issues and expressed concerns similar to those of other critics (See Appendix 2, p. 339). Among the most important of these was the extensive original jurisdiction proposed for the court. He had noted that although only one court was to be established, the bill would create three distinct and separate jurisdictions: an appellate court from the highest provincial courts, a constitutional court of original jurisdiction, and a court of original common law, equity and admiralty jurisdictions. Although Ritchie strongly supported the need for some sort of federal appellate tribunal of last resort "whose precedents would be a rule of decision for the Courts of all the Provinces," he equally strongly disapproved of giving the Supreme Court exclusive or concurrent original jurisdiction.[4]

He did so for two basic reasons. Parliament under section 101 of the B.N.A. Act, was empowered to create a general court of appeal, but any court of original jurisdiction had to be confined to administering only the federal law. Ritchie maintained that "a grave objection then to this Bill would seem to be that in many

149

particulars it exceeds those limits." Even if Parliament had such power, he would oppose the bill as injurious to the interests of New Brunswick because its effect would "weaken and enfeeble the Supreme Court [N.B.], by depriving it of many of its present powers, and rendering it substantially an inferior Court of comparatively limited jurisdiction; thereby crippling its usefulness, destroying its prestige, and necessarily lowering it in the estimation of the public."

In determining the composition of the court, Ritchie believed that, before experimenting or looking to the United States, consideration should be given to the judicial system of Britain as a model for a supreme court. He advocated adhering more closely to the model of the Judicial Committee of the Privy Council. This suggested that the final appellate judges be drawn exclusively from existing provincial courts. He also objected to a bill that allowed appeals irrespective of the amount or principle involved. He severely criticized retaining an unlimited appeal to the Judicial Committee of the Privy Council because it unnecessarily multiplied appeals, especially those of the most expensive character, and he expressed concern that ordinary litigants would not be able to afford the expensive chain of appeals. Taking one's case to the Supreme Court of Canada in Ottawa, then to the Privy Council in London, would mean that "the unfortunate suitor will stand a chance of being a gray headed man with empty pockets, before he gets through." He believed that resort to the Privy Council should only be permitted in very exceptional cases, "in which questions of a national character are involved." His emerging sense of Canadian nationalism, and his firm belief in local self-government, clearly lay behind his effective use of rhetorical questions, a characteristic of his judicial prose. "Does it not sound very like a reproach to our Dominion to say that there is not sufficient legal talent within its boundaries to decide finally the legal rights of the parties in all ordinary suits? Does it not ignore the principle so largely conceded, that we are fit for Local self Government?"

Ritchie recognized that such a position could be attacked as an interference with the royal prerogative. He anticipated this by saying that if it was in the interest of the Dominion that appeals be abolished or limited, this should be readily conceded. With a new appellate tribunal in Ottawa "the necessity for its continuance not only ceases, but its retention would subject our system to the imputation of encouraging a multiplicity of appeals, which is directly opposed to the policy of the law."

Ritchie opposed the wide appeal which the 1869 bill would have given in criminal cases. By present-day standards, this seems reactionary. However, from the perspective of his time, it was that of a cautious reformer, not some commercial lawyer's lack of concern for the integrity of the criminal law process. In New Brunswick the only procedure in the nature of an appeal in a criminal case was that a trial judge could reserve any question of law which might arise during a trial for determination by a higher court. (England would not allow appeals in criminal cases until 1907.) Ritchie thought the current mode of proceeding in criminal cases was plain and simple, producing no inconvenience or injustice. Anyone improperly convicted, Ritchie noted, could always petition the prerogatives of the crown which, in a proper case, "never will be invoked in vain." He recognized that it was difficult to justify Canada's unlimited appeals in civil cases with a very limited scope for appeal in criminal cases: "It cannot be denied that it is an anomaly, that in a civil suit involving no great principle, and of comparatively trifling amount, a new trial can be obtained, when the same is denied in cases involving liberty, reputation, life and death. Theory is clearly with the appeal."

However, Ritchie's pragmatism led him to conclude that one should accept what in theory was imperfect when it worked well in practice, particularly where, in his opinion, the alternative was injury to the administration of justice. In regard to criminal appeals, time has shown Ritchie to have been too cautious; but in his desire to limit appeals to the Privy Council, he was a far-sighted reformer.

It has been said that Ritchie's objections to the Supreme Court Bill of 1869 "went far to prevent the idea from being carried out at that time."[5] This probably overstated the impact of his criticism, but Macdonald did postpone introducing his second Supreme Court bill, acknowledging in the Commons that the New Brunswick submissions were "worthy of full consideration" and that "he wished carefully to read them before he brought down the bill."[6]

Macdonald introduced a second bill to establish a Supreme Court on 18 March 1870 which responded to the criticisms of the original bill. In this revised attempt certain proposed areas of original jurisdiction were removed. Most importantly, he dropped the provision which would have vested the court with original and exclusive jurisdiction to determine the constitutionality of provincial legislation. In the House of Commons the prime minister conceded that by the terms of section 101 of the B.N.A. Act, the federal government did not have the authority to confer such a power.[7] Thus, cases for judicial review would have to arise out of actual cases in the provincial courts and proceed in the usual course to a national appellate court. This process was exemplified by Ritchie's earlier *Chandler* decision although at that time there was no national appellate court. Thus Ritchie concluding that decision had stated:

> If any doubt exists as to the correctness of the conclusions at which we have arrived, we should, though entirely clear in our own minds, earnestly desire that an appeal should be taken, so that this important constitutional question may be forever set at rest by a final determination of Her Majesty, under the advice of the judicial committee of the Privy Council of Great Britain.[8]

Unfortunately Hazleton lacked the resources to pursue an appeal to the Privy Council and even had the Supreme Court been in existence, resort to it would probably have been beyond his means.

Shortly after the tabling of this new bill, John H. Cameron, member for Peel (Ontario), raised a concern which foreshadowed a long-standing tension surrounding the proposed court. Cameron asked the prime minister whether the government intended to make the supreme court the final court of appeal for Canada, and thus displace the Judicial Committee of the Privy Council. Was Canada to ask the British Parliament to repeal the statute which gave that imperial body its jurisdiction? Macdonald, ever loyal to the empire, replied that the Dominion government did not have the power to deprive British subjects of their right to seek redress at the foot of the throne. Capacity aside, Macdonald adamantly opposed the severing of this imperial connection. And in practical terms the former Kingston lawyer reminded the House of the great benefits gained from "resort to the body of great and good men who compose the Courts of England."[9]

The question of abolition of the appeal to the Privy Council did not die, as Macdonald's bill did. The reasons for the government's withdrawal of the proposal were not entirely clear. Macdonald, speaking in 1880, commented that the main impediment to the legislation was obtaining sufficient support from Quebec. He stated that:

Télesphore Fournier, Minister of Justice 1874-75
Justice of the Supreme Court 1875-95
(National Archives of Canada, Neg. no. C39959)

> The difficulties connected with the establishing of a court satis-
> factory to the Province of Quebec was one of the great reasons
> that made me hesitate so long in presenting a measure for the
> establishment of a Supreme Court which I twice submitted to
> the Parliament of Canada, and that hesitation induced me to
> postpone pressing the measure while I held the office of Minister
> of Justice.[10]

That lack of support might have partially arisen from the failure
of the 1870 bill to protect Quebec's unique civil law system in the
national appeal court of a primarily common law country. There
was no provision for a minimum Quebec representation on the
court. Even with a minimum of two Quebec judges on the court,
it was pointed out that a litigant could succeed in three levels of
Quebec courts before losing three judges to two at Ottawa. Theo-
retically, on a civil law matter, three judges from the common law
tradition could effectively overrule eleven Quebec judges in a
dispute;[11] the Supreme Court bill needed further refining. The
Macdonald government had planned a third attempt in 1873 but
instead found itself out of office on the heels of the Pacific Scan-
dal.[12]

Support for establishment of a supreme court was found
among members of both national parties. Thus defeat of
Macdonald's government did not involve shelving the initiative
until the Conservatives were returned. Indeed, Liberal leader
Alexander Mackenzie, who became prime minister in 1873,
believed that a national court of appeal was an important part of
a strong national structure. Such an institution "was a necessary
complement to our system of self-government in this country,"
said Mackenzie, and "it [was] desirable that there should be a
Canadian tribunal of the highest character, to which our people
would appeal."[13]

Télesphore Fournier, Mackenzie's minister of justice, had the
responsibility to make another attempt to establish the court. He
was a highly regarded lawyer and former Legislative Assembly
member from Quebec. His supreme court bill, based largely on
the earlier Macdonald versions, was introduced to Parliament in
February 1875 and succeeded where Macdonald's had failed. A
provision making the 1875 bill more palatable was the severance
from the Supreme Court of any exclusive, original jurisdiction by
the concurrent creation of an Exchequer Court, which would deal
with suits by or against the federal government and be staffed by
Supreme Court judges. By and large the new Supreme Court

would have only appellate jurisdiction.[14] At the same time its role as constitutional arbitrator was refined so that, with coordinating provincial legislation, questions about the division of powers arising in the course of regular litigation could be immediately referred to the Court for a determination. This provision was more acceptable because it contemplated the determination of the validity of both provincial *and* federal laws, and lower courts could be bypassed only with provincial authorization.[15] However, the 1875 bill also allowed the Governor in Council to refer any matter, including the validity of provincial statutes, to the court for its opinion.[16]

Fournier's legislation reflected more sensitivity to Quebec's legal concerns. It prohibited any appeal to Ottawa in Quebec cases involving less than $2,000.[17] More significantly, it required at least two of the court's six judges to be members of the Quebec bar.[18] French Canadians thus had more assurance that their civil law system would receive a competent hearing in the Supreme Court, and this helped Fournier enlist the support of his Quebec colleagues. The minister of justice was well connected with prominent Quebec Liberals such as T.A.R. Laflamme and Wilfrid Laurier, through common affiliation with Rouge politics and their aspirations for a strong and progressive Quebec. These ties, and a shared conviction that the new court should soon replace the Judicial Committee of the Privy Council as the truly final appellate tribunal, helped the bill obtain necessary Quebec support where Macdonald had failed.

Fournier's bill, however, did not mention the issue of appeals to the Privy Council. The absence of such a reference no doubt contributed to its early momentum, but the matter remained a sensitive one. Continued access to London was an emotional and symbolic issue for many on both sides. Appeals to the Privy Council represented, or were perceived to represent, a strong and enduring link to the empire. But the controversy involved more than symbolism; powerful and wealthy litigants, particularly English Canadian interests in Quebec, saw resort to a tribunal across the Atlantic as an important negotiating tool when opposed to less wealthy adversaries susceptible to threats of a costly appeal to London. Such practical considerations also informed the views of those opposed to the retention of the appeal. Some lawyers concerned with the integrity of the Quebec civil law system were apt to find more hope in a Canadian court, with at least some

Aemilius Irving, M.P. 1874-78
Treasurer of The Law Society of Upper Canada 1893-1913
(Portrait painted by Edmund Wyly Grier)

assurance of judges trained in Quebec law, than a panel staffed by British justices.[19]

The minister of justice himself was in favour of abolishing the appeal to London, but maintained that the bill's silence on the matter was crucial to its passage. While Fournier "did not desire to put any unnecessary obstacle in the way of exercising the right of petition, he wished to see the practice put an end to altogether."[20] For the time being his goal was establishing a national court, not abolishing the Privy Council appeal. But passage of the bill could not proceed independently of the Privy Council issue. On third reading on 30 March a private member from Hamilton, Aemilius Irving, proposed an amendment, seconded by T.A.R. Laflamme and accepted by Fournier. Clause 47 appeared to make the decisions of the Supreme Court final by abolishing appeals as of right to the Privy Council. The amendment declared:

> The judgment of the Supreme Court shall in all cases be final and conclusive, and no appeal shall be brought from any judgment or order of the Supreme Court to any Court of Appeal established by the Parliament of Great Britain and Ireland, by which appeals or petitions to Her Majesty in Council may be ordered to be heard, saving any right which Her Majesty may be graciously pleased to exercise by virtue of Her Royal Prerogative.[21]

The amendment allowed Macdonald to mobilize the loyalist sentiment and earn some political points by denouncing this measure to sever ties with England. The Tory leader, in rhetorical flight in the Commons, referred to the link with the empire as "a golden chain, and he, for one, was glad to wear the fetters."[22] He warned that "this was the first step towards the severance of the Dominion from the Mother Country." Somewhat prophetically he noted that clause 47 probably "insured the disallowance of the Bill in England. The Minister of Justice by assenting to this amendment defeated his measure. He would find that within six months it would be thrown aside in disgrace."[23] The Liberals' strong majority in the House of Commons meant the bill, with clause 47, passed easily. The Senate, however, was evenly divided on whether to allow the amended legislation to proceed. A motion to strike the amendment resulted in a tie vote of twenty-nine on each side. By virtue of section 36 of the B.N.A. Act, 1867 this meant the motion was lost, and the amendment survived.[24]

Edward Blake
Minister of Justice 1875-77
(National Archives of Canada, Neg. no. C30426)

On 8 April 1875 Lord Dufferin gave royal assent to the Supreme and Exchequer Court Act. Shortly after this, despite his success in piloting the bill through the Commons, Fournier was replaced as minister of justice by Edward Blake.[25] Blake, a fierce Canadian nationalist and a divisive force within the Liberal caucus, had been impatient with Mackenzie over the prime minister's approach to the Colonial Office and other provinces. Blake believed Mackenzie to be too subservient. The strained relationship between the two men caused other Liberals to attempt a reconciliation and Mackenzie responded by offering Blake the chief justiceship of the new court. Blake, however, was more interested in political life and accepted the offer of minister of justice in May 1875.[26]

Around the same time as Blake took up his new post, the Colonial Office warned the Mackenzie government that clause 47 of the Supreme and Exchequer Court Act was not being well received by the law officers of the British government, and that the entire act might be disallowed. Later, Colonial Secretary Lord Carnarvon confirmed this possibility during Mackenzie's summer trip to England:

> This possibility, which so strikingly confirmed Macdonald's predictions, came as a shock to the Prime Minister. It was made doubly unwelcome by the fact that the Conservative leader, in campaigning during that summer was continuing his criticism of the appeal clause and confidently prophesying the Act's disallowance. To Mackenzie, therefore, it became essential for the Government's prestige that the Act be not disallowed.[27]

Mackenzie obtained an informal understanding from the imperial authority that the bill could be enacted as it was, but that Canada might have to amend clause 47 should it be found offensive by the imperial law officers. On Mackenzie's return to Canada he and Blake decided that quick action on this agreement might make British disallowance more difficult. If they moved swiftly to establish and staff the new court, the imperial government might be more hesitant to intervene. Apart from the political and symbolic repercussions of disallowance, once the judges were appointed delays or disallowance would create real difficulties for all levels of judicial administration in the Dominion. That is, appointments and promotions would have been made to fill the vacancies left by the new Supreme Court judges. As Snell and Vaughan note in their history of the court, "once the process of

William Johnstone Ritchie 1873
Justice of the Supreme Court of New Brunswick 1855-65 and
Chief Justice of the Supreme Court of New Brunswick 1865-75
(Notman Photographic Archives, McCord Museum of Canadian History)

Grace Vernon Ritchie
born Nicholson, married W.J. Ritchie 6 May 1856
(Notman Photographic Archives, McCord Museum of Canadian History)

appointment began, any delay could throw into chaos the judicial calendars of the various provinces, but that situation was of the government's deliberate making."[28]

Blake was not long in selecting a list of proposed judges. The cooperation of the vice-regal representative was necessary to appoint them, as the act provided for implementation of the court in two phases. First, proclamation by the governor-in-council was required to allow for the appointment of judges, clerks and a registrar and to proceed with the drafting of court rules. A second proclamation was required before the court could actually begin to perform its judicial functions. With Lord Dufferin out of the country it fell to General O'Grady Haly, commander of the forces at Halifax, to issue the necessary first proclamation. He did this with some reluctance, due to the Colonial Office's continued concern about clause 47. On 17 September 1875 he assented to the appointment of the judges, but hesitated to come to Ottawa to swear in the new chief justice. Eventually, after Blake threatened to resign, Haly came to Ottawa and swore in the first chief justice of the Supreme Court of Canada, William Buell Richards, formerly the chief justice of the Ontario Court of Queen's Bench, on 8 October 1875.

By this time, Justice Ritchie had already received an offer of appointment as a Supreme Court judge from the Department of Justice. It had dispatched the following message to him on 11 September 1875.

> My Dear Sir
> I have pleasure in asking whether I may be allowed to submit your name to His Excellency in Council for appointment to one of the Puisne Judgeships of the Supreme Court of Canada. I shall take it as a favor if you will let me have an early answer as circumstances make it desirable that the Court should be organized as soon as practicable.[29]

It was addressed to Ritchie in Saint John but as he was on circuit it was readdressed to Madawaska County and finally caught up with him in Victoria County. However, Edward Blake, the minister of justice, must also have telegraphed Ritchie with the offer, for on 13 September 1875 Ritchie sent a collect telegram from Saint John which read: "Much obliged for your telegram my services are at the disposal of the government am this moment leaving for upriver circuits and have not opportunity of writing."[30] Ritchie revealed his decision for the first time in an address to the grand jury for the County of Carleton which coincided with the twentieth anniversary of the first court which Ritchie had held in Carleton. The grand jury presented a lengthy address to Ritchie which read in part:

> Your elevation does an honor to the Province in which you have during so many years labored in the several capacities at the Bar, in the Legislature, and on the Bench, while it is a deserved acknowledgment of your abilities and worth....
>
> Permit us to express the hope that the future of your Honor may be one of many years of still ripening wisdom of increasing usefulness and happiness in all the associations of life.[31]

Ritchie replied stating that he could never forget the hearty greeting from the grand jury received twenty years before nor the courtesy and assistance he had subsequently received when carrying out his duties in the county. He assured them that "while he was about to make Ottawa his judicial residence, his heart and home would still be in New Brunswick." Although Ritchie would enthusiastically enter into the life of Canada's capital, he never forgot his roots in New Brunswick.

Many factors, doubtless, contributed to Ritchie's continuing attachment to New Brunswick, but perhaps the most important were his fondness for his estate, Kawatcoose, at Quispamsis and for his grandchildren who lived in Rothesay. His daughter by his first marriage, Martha Margaret Strang Ritchie, married David Dobie Robertson, a Saint John merchant, in August 1876. David Robertson was the son of John Robertson, a Saint John banker and merchant who had served as mayor of Saint John, as a member of the New Brunswick Legislative Council and as a Liberal senator in Ottawa. John Robertson was intimately involved in organizing the European and North American Railway and this may have brought the two families together. When John Robertson retired to England, David acquired his father's very substantial home in Rothesay called "the Cottage." David Robertson and Martha had five daughters, Mary, Muriel, Grace, Sophia and Madge. Four of these five Ritchie grandchildren would spend the rest of their lives in this house. Only Grace married and she wed George Nicholls but had no children. The eldest grand-daughter acquired the name "Fire Engine Mary" because she smoked "like a chimney" and perhaps as a result was instrumental in obtaining a fire truck for the village of Rothesay. Madge, the youngest, had artistic abilities and once exhibited her water colours in Saint John. The Robertsons were often referred to as the "aristocracy" of Rothesay and in 1934 donated the land known as the "Common" to the village.[32] These five grand-daughters, growing up in Rothesay a few miles from Quispamsis while Ritchie was serving on the Supreme Court of Canada, exerted a strong force which attracted Ritchie back to New Brunswick each summer.

Ritchie was one of two Maritimers to be appointed to the Supreme Court; the other was William Alexander Henry of Nova Scotia. Under the Supreme Court Act two judges were required to be from Quebec. Appropriately, Télesphore Fournier received one of the seats on the new court which he helped to establish. The other Quebec position was filled by Jean-Thomas Taschereau. The remaining place on the new bench was filled by Justice Samuel Henry Strong from Ontario. He had been partly responsible for the initial draft of Macdonald's proposed Supreme Court bill in 1869. Thus three of the six judges of the first Court had played notable roles in the creation of the institution. Ritchie had critiqued the early bill which Strong had drafted, and Fournier finally obtained enactment of a more finely tuned version. Of the original members, these three were to make the most significant and enduring contributions to the new court.[33]

Edward Blake had selected a politically balanced court. Richards, Ritchie and Fournier had political roots in the reform or Liberal party, and S.H. Strong and J.-T. Taschereau in the Conservative party and Henry had originally been a reformer but had switched sides. The selection, however, did not satisfy L.H. Holton, Liberal member for Chateauguay who on 10 November 1875 wrote to Alexander Mackenzie:

> Very frankly I think Blake made a great mess of the judicial appointments. He pleased the Tories it is true and adverse criticism from our side was suppressed on Party grounds. The Supreme Court is thoroughly Tory. The only provincial Liberal in it is Fournier who for obvious reasons can not occupy a leading position in it for several years.[34]

Holton also complained that the appointment of Thomas Moss, a Liberal member of the House of Commons, to the Ontario Court of Appeal had occasioned some political flak and asked "why was he [Moss] not put on the Supreme Bench and the Tory Strong left where he was?"

Edward Blake had some reservations about appointing William Buell Richards as chief justice. In a confidential letter to Alexander Mackenzie on 12 November 1875 he wrote:

> Richards and Morrison [Joseph Curran of the Ontario Queen's Bench] have been at open feud in Court for a long time. They are both coarse grained men who don't know how to use the rapier and fight with the bludgeon and they have bruised each other's heads several times in the presence of the Courthouse crowds .... I am very sorry that Richards should have said what he did. I do not think it was worthy of him.[35]

Richards's reform credentials were excellent, for in 1848 he had defeated in Leeds the Reformers' arch-villain, Ogle Robert Gowan, a leader of the Orange Lodge. In 1851 Richards became attorney general in the reform administration of Francis Hincks and Augustin-Norbert Morin. On 22 June 1853 Richards was appointed a puisne judge of the Ontario Court of Common Pleas and chief justice of that court on 22 July 1863. On 16 November 1868 he became chief justice of Ontario's Court of Queen's Bench.[36] Richards, a popular judge and widely acclaimed as "a man of large common sense," would probably have made a good chief justice for the new Supreme Court of Canada but for his ill health. He suffered from diabetes and asthma. As early as 1 May 1877 Richards wrote to Alexander Mackenzie in "strictest confidence" about a proposal to retire saying: "For some time past I have become apprehensive that the state of my health will compel me 'ere long to ask to be allowed to retire from the position of Chief Justice of the Supreme Court."[37] Nevertheless, in 1875 he launched into his duties as chief justice with vigour.

Chief Justice William Buell Richards had responsibility for the administration and organization of the new court and he quickly began the task. On 13 October 1875, five days after being sworn in, Richards sent a letter to Ritchie and the other puisne justices, asking them to come to Ottawa in early November for their own swearing in, and advising them that it would be necessary to meet in order to formulate the rules of both the Supreme and the Exchequer Courts, on which they would also sit. Richards wrote that:

> On consulting with Mr. Justice Fournier, who is now here, we thought it better that we should meet to swear in the Judges and organize with a view of framing Rules under the statute in the beginning of November. We thought we might, by meeting then be able to prepare Rules, so that the Government could issue the

Sir William Buell Richards
Chief Justice 1875-79
Portrait painted by Frances Richards 1884
(National Archives of Canada, Neg. No. C80528)

166

Sir William Johnstone Ritchie
Justice of the Supreme Court 1875-79
Chief Justice 1879-92
(Notman Photographic Archives, MᶜCord Museum of
Canadian History, No. 51, 127-BII)

Chief Justice Ritchie

Sir Samuel Henry Strong
Justice of the Supreme Court 1875-92
Chief Justice 1892-1902
(National Archives of Canada, Neg. No. PA25835)

168

Jean-Thomas Taschereau
Justice of the Supreme Court 1875-78

William Alexander Henry
Justice of the Supreme Court 1875-1888
(National Archives of Canada, Neg. No. C11349)

necessary proclamation for bringing into effect the whole act by the commencement of the New Year, if they desired to do so.[38]

The chief justice asked the appointees to bring copies of the Rules of the Courts in their own provinces to assist in drafting. The judges would also have to deal with the important subject of a tariff of fees for the new Supreme Court.

On 8 November 1875 Chief Justice Richards administered the oath of office to Ritchie and the four other puisne justices in the Senate chamber in the presence of members of the cabinet and of the bar. At the conclusion of the brief ceremony, the chief justice, the newly sworn justices together with the cabinet ministers and several other gentlemen "proceeded to the residence of the Premier, where they were entertained at lunch."[39]

Together with Richards and newly appointed registrar Robert Cassels Jr., the court moved expeditously to draft rules and procedures necessary to allow it to begin its judicial functions. It occupied temporary space in the Senate wing of Parliament. The judicial section of the Supreme Court Act was proclaimed on 10 January 1876. Thus eight and a half years after confederation, Canada finally had a national appellate court.

While the practical details were being resolved, Edward Blake had turned his attention to drafting a formal argument in support of clause 47 for the Colonial Office's consideration. The justice minister's feisty and determined opposition to the Privy Council appeals left no doubt among his adversaries that he not only believed Canada was competent to abolish such appeals, but also that Canada should abolish them. As David Farr noted in his detailed discussion of the issue:

> Blake's arguments, inflexibly logical and direct, were illumined at all times by the ardour of his faith in the progressive extension of Canadian autonomy. The problem of appeals to the Privy Council was more than the subject of a lawyer's brief; it was an opportunity to vindicate Canadian self-government.[40]

In October 1875, Blake wrote a memorandum on the appeal question which the Mackenzie government transmitted to the Colonial Office. The essence of Blake's argument was that making the judgment of the Supreme Court of Canada final in all cases was a logical extension of powers already held by Canada over its judicial administration. Appeals to London had long been regulated, usually by the imposition of monetary limits by the provinces and the minister of justice contended, therefore, that "if it was competent to Provincial authority, and is competent to Canada, to make the judgment of Local Courts final in the vast majority of cases, it must surely be, by the same process of reasoning, within its competence to make that judgment final in all cases."[41]

While sentiment in the Colonial Office was not altogether unsympathetic toward the Canadian view, any hope of swift settlement of the issue was dashed by Lord Cairns, the lord chancellor. In November, Lord Cairns made clear to the Colonial Office his distaste for the Canadian position. He wrote to Lord Carnarvon:

> I venture to hope you will not decide on the Canadian Appeal [question] without further consideration. What is desired appears to me to be equivalent to a complete severance of the strongest tie betw. our Colonies and the Mother Country. The Minister of Justice's Memo. is a mass of inaccuracy and bad reasoning. It may be summed up in one proposition:
> Canada had a power given her to *regulate* appeals: Ergo she may enact that there shall be no appeals whatever...![42]

The appeals question had a dual nature; there were important legal and political questions. For the statesmen the legal issues had an unfortunate tendency to subvert attempts to come to an amicable, political resolution. Lord Cairns may have been a strong judicial figure but he was no diplomat, and his legal analysis of clause 47 was harsh and unshakeable. Similarly Edward Blake had a strong commitment to the abolition of appeals. Rejection of the Supreme Court Act by Whitehall would not only damage the government's credibility, but would also be a personal affront to his legal competency. Thus, what was for Lord Carnarvon and Lord Dufferin a sensitive but resolvable diplomatic question was for Lord Cairns a matter of imperial legal hegemony and for Blake an issue of Canadian autonomy. The resulting intransigence of Lord Cairns caused Carnarvon to confide in Dufferin that "I have had a great deal of trouble in inducing the Chancellor to take a political instead of a merely legal view of the question.... I have no respect for lawyers or the language with which they delight to darken common sense."[43]

The language may have seemed to darken common sense because the appeals issue was shrouded in complexity. Moreover, the wording of clause 47, the Irving amendment to the Supreme Court bill, although clear to some, was the source of a year-long controversy. Appeals to the Judicial Committee of the Privy Council were historically rooted in the notion of the king as the fountainhead of justice.[44] The king-in-council, or Privy Council, served as the basis of courts of royal prerogative. Thus a British subject could always appeal by leave of the king to his council, a right which could only be deprived by express imperial statute. An act of Parliament in 1641 abolished this right to appeal to the king-in-council in England, but left the right intact in the colonies. Supplementing this appeal by prerogative was the development through imperial legislation of appeals as of right in certain circumstances from the colonies to the Privy Council. The colonies in British North America were permitted to regulate such appeals. In 1833 the Judicial Committee of the Privy Council was created by imperial statute to hear the appeals to the king-in-council. Fundamentally, however, the essence of the appeal remained unchanged. The new body "advised" the king; it was not a court of law. In 1844 the appeal by leave based on the prerogative was affirmed. Thus in 1875 there were two bases of appeal to the Judicial Committee: one was based on the prerogative, and one based on imperial legislation. The later appeals, those of right created by imperial legislation could be regulated by the provinces and presumably by the dominion.

Against this background, the British government proposed major revisions to its appellate courts between 1873 and 1876. The reorganization would create a new, final court of appeal to replace the House of Lords and other existing appeal courts. The proposed legislation also included a provision for the transfer of the Privy Council's jurisdiction over empire appeals to this new statutory court. It was to this restructured court — "to any Court of Appeal established by the Parliament of Great Britain and Ireland,"[45] to which a part of section 47 of the Supreme Court Act purported to abolish appeals.

However, in February 1876 the British government dramatically rethought these measures. While a new court of appeal was established in England, the proposal to end the jurisdiction of the House of Lords and the Privy Council was withdrawn. Hence the court which was contemplated by clause 47 did not materialize. This development ultimately created the potential for defusing the political repercussions of a disallowance of the Supreme Court Act over clause 47. The first part of the controversial provision was nullified by the last-minute reaffirmation of the Judicial Committee. It remained an advisory body to the queen, not a court established by Parliament, and was unaffected by the reference in clause 47. The remaining part of the section expressly saved a right to appeal granted "by virtue of Her [Majesty's] Royal Prerogative."[46] Thus, the historical appeal with leave to the throne was preserved.

The lord chancellor seized upon these circumstances in a memorandum of 9 March 1876, issued by the Colonial Office. He had arrived at the conclusion that clause 47 was inoperative, and asserted that every appeal to the queen-in-council constituted an exercise of the prerogative. The Colonial Office had also included a memorandum reiterating the virtues of the Judicial Committee, including the thought that a truly "impartial and independent tribunal" ensured respect for all in a country with "strong divisions of race, religion, and party."[47]

Blake replied indignantly that nothing could more deeply "wound the feelings of Canadians than an insinuation that impartial decisions are not to be expected from their Judges." Despite Blake's continued nationalistic resolve, by the time he sailed for London on 3 June he had conceded in his own mind the correctness of Lord Cairns's view respecting the application of clause 47 to an unrestructured Privy Council. In a 3 May letter to David Mills, a friend and prominent Liberal, Blake wrote that in the Lord Chancellor's "arguments there seems to me much force. If they prevail it is obvious that the clause is, with reference to appeals to the Privy Council, inoperative."[48]

On his arrival in London the minister of justice found imperial authorities occupied with many matters other than the abolition of Privy Council appeals. Blake himself had other government business to address, and only after several weeks did he have an audience with colonial secretary, Lord Carnarvon. His most significant interview, however, was with the lord chancellor on 5 July. At this meeting Lord Cairns reaffirmed the view that clause 47 was inoperative, and that there was no need for either modification or disallowance. Blake tenaciously argued the case for abolition of London appeals, referring "to the unfamiliarity of judges and counsel here [in London] with our laws and constitutional system, to the loss of power and prestige in the Supreme Court if not made final." Lord Cairns remained unmoved by the Canadian's arguments, which prompted Blake to write to Prime Minister Mackenzie on the next day that "they will not commit themselves to abolition and probably would kick against it."[49]

Blake waited another week and a half before receiving Lord Cairns's proposed resolution of the dispute. A 17 July memorandum from the lord chancellor proposed a dispatch pronouncing that clause 47 did not affect the prerogative and that the Supreme Court Act could be left to its operation. Furthermore, the draft dispatch recommended Canadian regulation of these appeals to prevent abuse. Blake, who realized he had to concede the point on clause 47, moved to control the political ramifications of the imperial decision. He negotiated with the Colonial Office to create two dispatches. One public announcement would state only that the act would be left to its operation. The second would be private, to the Canadian government, explaining the imperial position on the appeal with the recommendation of further regulation. Confidentiality of the second dispatch was necessary as publicity over the suggestion of regulation would emphasize Blake's failure to secure abolition of the appeal. Agreement was reached on these terms, and by the end of August 1876 the atmosphere of uncertainty over the Supreme Court was dispelled. The unfortunate, lingering result was continued deference to the judicial authority of the Privy Council.

Aemilius Irving's section 47 had accomplished practically nothing. It meant only that a person appealing a judgment of the Supreme Court of Canada first had to seek leave of the Privy Council before launching the appeal. Another amendment proposed by Irving would have prevented any appeals from provincial courts directly to the Privy Council. It read:

> No error or appeal shall be brought from any judgment or order of any Court of any of the Provinces, subsequent to the commencement of the said Act, to HER MAJESTY in Council, but every decree and order of all Courts of final resort within the several Provinces, in respect of any subject matter or proceeding wherein appeal now lies from any such Courts to HER MAJESTY in Council, shall and may be appealed to the Supreme Court.[50]

There was no doubt that this amendment would have been within the legislative competence of the federal Parliament under section 101, the constitution of a general court of appeal for Canada. It would have prevented litigants bypassing the Supreme Court of Canada and thus enabled the court to pass judgment on all issues even though the Privy Council would still have had the last word. This amendment, however, had been defeated in the House of Commons on 30 March 1875.

While the appeal issue was being resolved, the new court had begun to hear cases in June 1876. Reaction to the selection of judges had been mixed, but Ritchie's appointment was greeted with widespread approval. In Saint John it was announced that the wisdom of the "eminent jurist" was to be "extended to a wider and more important sphere."[51] Meanwhile the Toronto-based *Canada Law Journal*, unenthusiastic about the other appointments of non-Ontario judges to the new court, praised Ritchie as being of "strong will and decided views, of large judicial experience .... This appointment is an excellent one." Commenting on his background in New Brunswick, the paper noted that while he was at "one time strongly opposed to confederation, his court has probably gone further than any of the provincial courts in limiting the jurisdiction of the local legislatures."[52]

The Supreme Court of Canada's first chief justice, William Buell Richards, was in poor health when appointed. By contrast, Ritchie, only a few days short of his sixty-second birthday and its eldest member, enjoyed robust health. He was "endowed with a splendid physique, tall, well built and athletic in frame, his energetic manner and bearing indicated the great reserve of nervous power which has assisted a fine mind to do its work to the best advantage."[53]

While the bar might have been slow to appreciate the status of Supreme Court justices, the same was not true of Ottawa society. Lord Dufferin had introduced the members of the court in a grand manner.[54] On 18 November 1875, ten days after the swearing in of the court, Lord Dufferin gave a banquet in their honour at Rideau Hall. The illustrious guest list included the lieutenant-governors of all seven provinces, the prime minister and most of the cabinet, the Speakers and other prominent members of the Senate and the House, the premiers of all the provinces, senior members of the judiciary, church leaders, senior bureaucrats and military men.

Lord Dufferin had emphasized the political significance of the court: "The establishment of that court marks another epoch in the progressive history of the Dominion; it exhibits another proof and pledge of the stability of our confederation." In proposing a toast to the members of the new court, he continued effusively:

A great court thus becomes the author of its own supremacy — nay, it can extend its ascendancy beyond the limits of its natural jurisdiction, and impress foreign codes of jurisprudence with its own interpretations of equity and justice .... Such a court is the parent of peace, order and good government; it is the guardian of civil, political and religious liberty. It is like the sun at noon-day; it shines with its own light; and happily human passion and prejudice, executive tyranny, and popular phrensy, are as impotent to intercept the beneficial influence of the one as to shear the beams from the other.[55]

The justices, perhaps anxious to live up to such a billing, attended the first major social event of the season, a "Drawing Room" held by the governor general and Lady Dufferin in the Senate chamber, attired in their official robes. Whether this instilled respect for the dignity of the court remained unknown, but a social column noted that "the official robes of the judges attracted more attention than the dresses of the ladies."[56] In their robes or otherwise, the Supreme Court justices soon found their place in Ottawa social circles; in official protocol they went after the governor general and members of the cabinet, but before members of the Senate and the House of Commons.[57] Even before Ritchie became chief justice, he assumed some formal functions of the office because Richards was unwell. In the autumn of 1878 Ritchie administered the oath of office to the new governor general, the Marquis of Lorne, when he disembarked from the *Sarmation* in Halifax. Although Lorne had sat in the British House of Commons as a Liberal, Disraeli, the Conservative prime minister of Britain, selected him largely because he had married Princess Louise, the fourth daughter of Queen Victoria. For Disraeli, sending the couple to Canada represented an "experiment in statecraft by which the Crown was employed as an instrument to proclaim the greatness and unity of the Empire."[58]

Ritchie might have been overly impressed with the dignity of his position, at least immediately after his appointment as chief justice, judging from the following report of his behaviour at the first state ball held by the new governor general on 19 February 1879:

> It is also said that Chief Justice Ritchie under the influence no doubt of champagne, made himself somewhat conspicuous in the Dressing Room, standing on his dignity as Chief Justice of Canada, and saying that he had been standing 10 minutes and no one had brought him his clothes. At last, in some despair, he thrust his ticket (which up to then he had kept in his pocket) through the hole — like any common mortal — and got his clothes.[59]

Grace Ritchie
attired for a fancy dress ball.
(National Archives of Canada, Neg. No. PA138390)

William Ritchie
(National Archives of Canada, Neg. No. PA27038)

Ritchie's family also became part of the social scene. His wife and daughters were among those invited to the reserved area of the floor of the Senate for the opening of Parliament. They attended the state balls, and the grand vice regal fête — which the headlines reported as "the Crowning Triumph of Social Life in Canada."

Richards remained chief justice for just over three years before retiring. Ritchie succeeded him as chief justice and after this promotion only a knighthood could enhance Ritchie's social credentials. Queen Victoria granted this on the occasion of her sixty-second birthday, 24 May 1881. The governor general conferred this honour at Quebec City. Hector Langevin received a knighthood at the same time and become a companion of the Order of St. Michael and St. George. This overshadowed Ritchie's knighthood in the press.

The queen's conferral of a knighthood did not overawe Ritchie. Lord Kimberley, the colonial secretary, had written to the Marquis of Lorne requesting that he inform Ritchie that "the Queen has on my recommendation been pleased to give directions for the dignity of Knight Bachelor being conferred on him" but added that the "Patent will be proceeded with on his remitting to the Chief Clerk of the Home Department the sum of ninety-seven pounds fifteen shilling and six pence, the amount of the usual charge on such Patents."[60] Ritchie had no qualms about accepting the knighthood but had no intention of paying for the honour and so informed the governor general. The Colonial Office, perhaps unaccustomed to such independence of spirit, backed down. On 28 November 1881 Lord Kimberley dispatched Ritchie's letters patent of knighthood and requested that Ritchie be informed that "in the circumstances of the case the Lord Commissioners of the Treasury have consented to the remission of the Fees."[61]

The promotion to chief justice itself brought increased status off the bench, through its accompanying vice-regal functions. Ritchie acted as deputy for three governors general — the Marquis of Lorne (1878-83), the Marquis of Lansdowne (1883-88) and Baron Stanley of Preston (1888-93). He opened sessions of Parliament and gave assent to parliamentary bills. His first opening of Parliament occurred early in his chief justiceship under a commission dated 13 February 1879. During the absences of the governor general from 6 July 1881 to January 1882, and again between September and December 1882, Ritchie acted as deputy governor of

Canada. Each time an elaborate commission was prepared authorizing Ritchie to act and this was usually preceded by an informal hand-written letter from the governor general requesting him to do so.

Judging from the letters Ritchie received from the three successive governors general, he enjoyed a friendly easy going relationship with them. The Marquis of Lansdowne for instance wrote:

> Cascapedia R.
> New Richmond
> June 16, [18]85

My Dear Chief Justice

> I came here last Saturday for a few days fishing, being informed that my presence was not required at Ottawa. I have just heard by telegram that the Royal assent is necessary for the Bill under which Sir L. Tilley is to be authorized to raise his loan. Will you allow me once more to trespass upon your good nature and to ask you to act as my deputy for this purpose?
> I have telegraphed to you this afternoon in order to prepare you for this request.
> I have been punished for my desertion by a heavy flood which has for the present put fishing entirely out of the question.
> With my apologies for the trouble I am giving you.
> I am
> dear Sir William Ritchie

> Yours truly,

> Lansdowne[62]

Ritchie, who also enjoyed salmon fishing, undoubtedly sympathized with Lansdowne over the interruption of his fishing.

Undoubtedly the growing stature of Ritchie and the other judges in official Ottawa brought increased expenses. While the salaries of the time could not be described as meagre — the salary of the chief justice was $8,000 and puisne judges received $7,000 — there was some suggestion that they might not have been fully adequate to meet the social demands placed upon them and their families. The judges of the Supreme Court did not receive any salary increase throughout the seventeen years that Ritchie was in Ottawa. Inflation, however, did not eat into the real purchasing power of their salaries. Although prices did fluctuate the general trend over the period was downward. In real terms, their salaries increased significantly. Nevertheless, Charles Hibbert Tupper reported in a private letter to Sir John Thompson in 1883 the rumour that "every Sup. Ct. Judge but Ritchie C.J. has drawn his salary nine months ahead at the Bank."[63]

Ritchie's apparent immunity from financial problems might have been the result of his prosperous legal career in Saint John or the result of a life lived by Calvinist ethics taught him at Pictou. But in addition his father, Thomas Ritchie, was a wealthy man. The inventory of his estate, taken after his death on 13 November 1852, revealed that he had total assets of £11,241 4s 6d.[64] Thomas provided for his daughters in land and money, while his six sons benefitted only when the life estate of his widow, Anne, came to an end on 4 February 1869.[65] This inheritance undoubtedly assisted Ritchie. The 1891 census revealed that they did not want for expenses. There were ten family members in the Ritchie household, including three adult children. The Ritchies also employed four servants, two cooks and two maids.

In addition to the residence at 285 Metcalfe Street in Ottawa, Ritchie maintained his home at Quispamsis, in New Brunswick. Each year the family escaped the heat and humidity of an Ottawa summer by returning to Kawatcoose. Here Ritchie enjoyed his hobby of gardening and just relaxing from the work of the court.

Ritchie had brought twenty years of judicial experience to Ottawa, and provided stability and strength to the new court for its first seventeen years. He rarely missed a sitting, except for the period from 25 January 1889 to 30 April 1889 when ill. During the year prior to the resignation of Chief Justice Richards, Ritchie bore the major burden of providing reasons for judgment in the court. The chief justice's absence for part of the sittings began in January 1878 and lasted for all of the June sittings. Of thirteen reported decisions rendered in Richards's absence, Ritchie alone wrote one judgment for the whole court and what must be regarded as the most significant majority decisions in the remaining cases. In only one case was he in dissent. The quantity of Ritchie's judicial prose was evidence of his energy and devotion to his work. In the thirteen judgments, the total number of pages of reasons from each of the five judges were Ritchie sixty-four, Strong nineteen, Fournier fifteen, Taschereau twelve and Henry fifty-four. In only one of the thirteen cases was Ritchie content with a simple concurrence, whereas Fournier entered a simple concurrence in eleven cases, Taschereau in nine, Strong in four, and Henry in one. On the eve of Chief Justice Richards's resignation, no one could doubt who was in charge.

Notes to Chapter 12

1. James G. Snell and Frederick Vaughan, *The Supreme Court of Canada: History of the Institution* (Toronto: Osgoode Society, 1985), p. 4.

2. Ibid., pp. 6.

3. Commons, *Debates*, 18 Mar. 1870, p. 502.

4. W.J. Ritchie, "Observations of the Chief Justice of New Brunswick on A Bill Entitled 'An Act to Establish a Supreme Court for the Dominion of Canada'" (Fredericton: G.E. Fenety, 1870) (Presented to Parliament on 21 May 1869 by the Hon. Sir John A. Macdonald).

5. Lawrence, *Judges of New Brunswick*, p. 495.

6. Commons, *Debates*, 24 Feb. 1870, p. 175.

7. Ibid., p. 503.

8. (1869), 12 N.B.R. 556 at p. 567.

9. Commons, *Debates*, 18 Mar. 1870, p. 507.

10. Ibid., 26 Feb. 1880, p. 240.

11. Peter H. Russell, *The Supreme Court of Canada as a Bilingual and Bicultural Institution* (Ottawa: Queen's Printer, 1969) pp. 7-10.

12. Frank MacKinnon, "The Establishment of the Supreme Court of Canada," *Canadian Historical Review* 26 (1946), p. 260.

13. Snell and Vaughan, *Supreme Court*, p. 5.

14. Ibid., p. 8; Supreme and Exchequer Court Act, S.C. 1875, c.11, s.17 (Here after Supreme Court Act).

15. Supreme Court Act, s.54.

16. Ibid., s.52.

17. Ibid., s.17.

18. Ibid., s.4.

19. See Russell, *Supreme Court*, pp. 14-15 for a discussion of Quebec views on the abolition of Privy Council appeals.

20. Frank H. Underhill, "Edward Blake, the Supreme Court Act and the Appeal to the Privy Council, 1875-6" *Canadian Historical Review* 19 (1938), p. 247.

21. Commons, *Debates*, 30 Mar. 1875, p. 976. The amendment became s.47 of Supreme Court Act.

22. Commons, *Debates*, 30 Mar. 1875, p. 981.

23. Ibid., p. 976.

24. A number of writers, including Underhill (p. 248), have been mistaken regarding the Senate vote on clause 47. He states that the Senate tie vote was broken by the Speaker's casting vote. In fact the Speaker in the Senate does not have a casting vote. The B.N.A. Act provides in section 36, that: "Questions arising in the Senate shall be decided by a Majority of Voices, and the Speaker shall in all cases have a vote, and when the voices are equal the Decision shall be deemed to be in the Negative."

25. M. Brassard and J. Hamelin suggest Fournier was dropped as justice minister in part because of his involvement in a tavern brawl. See *Dictionary of Canadian Biography*, vol. 12, p. 325.

26. Underhill, "Blake," p. 249.

27. Quoted in David M.L. Farr, *The Colonial Office and Canada, 1867-1887* (Toronto: University of Toronto Press, 1955), p. 139.

28. Snell and Vaughan, *Supreme Court*, p. 17.

29. NAC, MG 29, E 121, W.J. Ritchie Papers.

30. NAC, Reel No. M-243, Edward Blake Papers, 13 Sept. 1875.

31. *Saint John Daily News*, 4 Oct. 1875, p. 3.

32. Robert Hook, Ann Condon and Charles Grant, *Rothesay — An Illustrated History 1784-1920* (Rothesay: Rothesay Area Heritage Trust, 1984), pp. 13-14.

33. J.-T. Taschereau resigned in 1878 and Richards left the court in 1879. Henry's career in Ottawa has received a mixed reception at best. By contrast, Fournier sat on the court until 1895, while Ritchie and Strong both served as chief justice.

34. Queen's University Archives, Alexander Mackenzie, Papers Collection #2112, pp. 1039-42.

35. Ibid., pp. 1043-45.

36. Ian MacPherson, "Sir William Buell Richards," *Dictionary of Canadian Biography*, vol. XI, pp. 730-31.

37. Mackenzie Papers, Collection #2112, pp. 1580-81.

38. NAC, MG 29, E 121 W.B. Richards to Ritchie, 13 Oct. 1875.

39. *Ottawa Citizen*, 8 Nov. 1875, p. 1.

40. Farr, *Colonial Office*, p. 141.

41. Ibid.

42. Quoted in Ibid., p. 144.

43. Ibid., p. 146.

44. The following account is based on M.J. Herman, "The Founding of the Supreme Court of Canada and the Abolition of Appeals to the Privy Council," *Ottawa Law Review* 8 (1976), pp. 14-17.

45. Supreme Court Act, s.47.

46. Ibid.

47. Herman, *Founding of Supreme Court*, p. 22.

48. Quoted in Underhill, "Blake," p. 256.

49. Blake to Mackenzie, 5 July 1876, reproduced in *Canadian Historical Review* 19 (1938), pp. 292-94.

50. Commons, *Debates*, 30 Mar. 1875, p. 974.

51. *New Dominion*, 16 Oct. 1875 , p. 4.

52. *Canada Law Journal* 11 (1875), pp. 265-66.

53. Robert Cassels, "The Supreme Court of Canada," *The Green Bag* 2 (1890), p. 245. Cassels was the court's first Registrar.

54. *Ottawa Citizen*, 19 Nov. 1875, p. 4.

55. George Stewart, Jr., *Canada under the Administration of the Earl of Dufferin* (Toronto: Rose-Belford, 1879), 2nd ed., pp. 429-30.

56. *Ottawa Citizen*, 11 Feb. 1876, p. 4.

57. See N.O. Côté, *Political Appointments, Parliaments and the Judicial Bench in the Dominion of Canada 1867-1895* (Ottawa: Thorburn & Co., 1986), p. 434 for a full table of precedence for Canada. See also the order of presentation to the Marquis of Lorne at the inaugural social event of his tenure, reported in *Ottawa Citizen*, 6 Dec. 1878. Also see guest lists for various social events, e.g., the Governor General's Drawing Room, in ibid., 6, 7, 8, Feb. 1878, Governor General's "At Home" and Opening of Parliament, ibid., 14, 15 Feb. 1879.

58. W. Stewart MacNutt, *Days of Lorne* (Fredericton: Brunswick Press, 1955), p. 8.

59. Sandra Gwyn, *The Private Capital: Ambition and Love in the Age of Macdonald and Laurier* (Toronto: McClelland and Stewart, 1984) p. 190. Gwyn quoted Edmund Meredith, a senior civil servant and diarist.

60. NAC, MG 29, E 121 Kimberley to Lorne, 20 June 1881.

61. Ibid., Kimberley to Lorne, 28 Nov. 1881.

62. Ibid., Lansdowne to Ritchie, 16 June 1885.

63. NAC, Sir John Thompson Papers, No. 3007, C.H. Tupper to Thompson (1883); Snell and Vaughan *Supreme Court*, p. 45.

64. Provincial Archives of Nova Scotia, Thomas Ritchie Estate Papers.

65. Mary Ritchie, "The Beginnings of a Canadian Family," Nova Scotia Historical Society *Collections* 24 (1938), p. 151.

Alexander Mackenzie
Prime Minister of Canada 1873-78
(National Archives of Canada, Neg. No. C96)

CHAPTER 13

Priests, Politics and Quebec's Free Franchise

In one of the Supreme Court's earliest reported cases, the judges handed down a unanimous decision in the controverted election of January 1876 in the County of Charlevoix, Quebec. Ritchie put to use some of the liberal principles which he had expounded since his days as a New Brunswick reformer. Undoubtedly his was an easier task than that of the writer of the other reported judgment, Jean-Thomas Taschereau, for the case symbolized the struggle between secular liberal and Catholic ultramontane views in Quebec.

In *Brassard* v. *Langevin* (1877), the petitioner contested the election of Hector Langevin, a Father of Confederation who, following Cartier's death, was to become one of Macdonald's chief lieutenants in French-speaking Canada. The principal issue was whether certain sermons and threats made by parish priests during the election constituted undue influence within section 95 of the Dominion Controverted Elections Act of 1874; and if so, whether the priests were to be considered agents of Langevin. The message which the sermons conveyed was that to vote for P.A. Tremblay, the Liberal candidate, was to commit a grievous sin for which one could be deprived of the sacraments of the church. Free exercise of the franchise was the basic issue, but this involved the more fundamental question of whether Quebec was to be a theocracy or a liberal democracy. The Liberals regarded the case as of vital importance. The prime minister, Alexander Mackenzie, during the hearing of the case wrote to George Brown: "I am certain that if Langevin retains his seat we cannot win ten seats in Quebec at the coming federal election. That power must now be firmly met and conquered or it will conquer us."[1] Counsel for the petitioner stated in argument, "The question is, after all, which policy is to be supreme, the Church or Parliament?" Counsel for Hector Langevin contended that "[p]reaching ... is within the exclusive jurisdiction of the Church, and the State is not a competent judge...."[2] The Supreme Court reversed the decision of Justice A.-B. Routhier and held that Langevin was not duly elected and declared the seat vacant.

Ritchie rejected both the contention that priests did no more than what they had a right to do and also that what they did was in the exercise of their spiritual functions and outside the jurisdiction of the civil courts. He asserted that the electoral franchise was a statutory civil right, that its exercise was regulated and protected by statute and that any infringement had to be determined by the civil tribunals. He considered the case to involve "grave questions of constitutional law, in which all in this Dominion are deeply interested."

> It has long ago been said by a standard legal authority as a common law doctrine that "It is essential to the very existence of Parliament that elections should be free, wherefore all undue influences on electors are illegal." The rights of individual electors are the rights of the public. All, without distinction of class or creed, are alike interested in the good government of the country, and in the enactment of wise and salutary laws, and therefore the public policy of all free constitutional governments in which the electoral principle is a leading element, (at any rate of the British Constitution) is to secure freedom of election; and it has been truly said a violation of this principle is equally at variance with good government and subversive of popular rights and liberties, and therefore the Legislature has, with the greatest care, made stringent provisions to prevent any unconstitutional interference with the freedom of elections, by prohibiting anything calculated to interfere with the free and independent exercise of the franchise.[3]

Ritchie noted that the free exercise of the Roman Catholic religion was guaranteed to the inhabitants of Quebec, but "like every member of every other Church, is subordinate to the law. There is no man in this Dominion so great as to be above the law, and none so humble as to be beneath its notice." He elaborated that clergymen of all churches had all the freedom and liberty belonging to laymen and that "while there may be free and full discussion, solicitation, advice, persuasion, the law says ... there shall be no undue influence or intimidation to force an elector to vote or to restrain him from voting in a particular manner." Ritchie continued:

> So a clergyman has no right, in the pulpit or out, by threatening any damage, temporal or spiritual, to restrain the liberty of a

voter so as to compel or frighten him into voting or abstaining from voting otherwise than as he freely wills. If he does, in the eye of the law this is undue influence. But, as I intimated before, legitimate influence can be denied neither to the clergy nor to the laity.[4]

Ritchie found that Langevin, before deciding to be a candidate, stipulated that he should have the support of the clergy and, receiving the assurance of this support, became a candidate. Langevin then called upon the clergy — five curés were named — received confirmation of their support, and at a public meeting proclaimed that the clergy favoured his candidature and that the public should obey the voice of the clergy. Ritchie held that the clergy had exerted undue influence and that they were Langevin's agents within the provisions of the act.

Although it was a unanimous decision, except on the matter of costs, Justice Jean-Thomas Taschereau, the brother of the archbishop of Quebec, also rendered a decision. He also held that the five priests exerted undue influence and because they were the agents of Langevin, the election must be annulled. His decision differed from Ritchie's only in that he indicated his "great misgivings" and "deep feeling of regret" in having to determine such a conflict. He indicated that three eminent Quebec judges had in a very similar case held an election void, but the basis for their holding had "been commented on, and severely blamed as opposed to the faith by an eminent member of the Canadian Episcopate." He said he mentioned "this circumstance in order to show the difficulty of the position in which I, together with one of my colleagues upon this Bench, am placed as a Catholic."[5]

The court, although declaring the seat vacant, did not disqualify Langevin from running in a subsequent election. Ritchie concluded his judgment by saying:

> In view of the *quasi* penal nature of the enactment, I think, that before inflicting consequences so serious, the evidence should be most clear and conclusive; and though we have found it somewhat difficult to arrive at the conclusion that the Respondent was not aware of what his agents, the curés, were saying and doing on his behalf, still we are not prepared to say there is not such a reasonable doubt on the point as to justify us in adopting the milder view, and reporting that the undue influence was not with the Respondent's actual knowledge and consent.[6]

The voters, called back to the ballot box on 23 March 1877, once again elected Langevin. The Conservatives and the church regarded Langevin's return as a significant triumph. Edmond Langevin, Hector Langevin's brother wrote to Canon Godfrey Lamarche in Rome:

> I am in a position today to give you news that will show the worth of the accusations of undue influence brought against the clergy of Charlevoix. ...The voters were so free, and the clergy had so little violated the desires of the faithful in their civil behaviour, that when called to elect a new member (and despite the corruption, the money and the drink that the Liberals used to try to influence the people), they re-elected the one who for them personified good principles.[7]

But because Langevin's majority fell from 211 to 56 votes, the Liberals claimed that such a close vote was a victory for them as well. The Charlevoix election case focused attention upon the serious problem created by the Quebec clergy meddling too strongly in the realm of politics. Ritchie probably enjoyed the opportunity to affirm the need for free and open elections, but Fournier's concurrence and Taschereau's opinion show that he was not insensitive to Quebec culture.

When allegations first arose that priests had exerted undue influence in elections, Archbishop Taschereau took the same hardline adopted by bishops Bourget and Laflèche, the ultramontane leaders in Quebec. Taschereau wrote the pastoral letter issued by the Quebec bishops on 22 September 1875 condemning in the strongest terms Catholic liberalism. He also signed a declaration issued after the *Charlevoix* case strongly affirming the freedom of the church and requesting changes in the election act. However, Archbishop Taschereau came to appreciate the risk of precipitating a confrontation with the Protestant majority of Canada and unilaterally published a pastoral letter that put the Liberal and Conservative parties on the same footing. He exhorted Catholics to pray and work to ensure honest elections. The other bishops felt betrayed and openly revolted. To end this dissension the apostolic delegate Bishop George Conroy came to Canada in 1877-78 and "issued a declaration publicly exonerating the Liberal party and had a circular letter sent to the clergy ordering them to take the course of 'discreet reserve' and 'great prudence'."[8]

The Supreme Court of Canada in the *Charlevoix* case, by defining the boundaries between legitimate and undue influence,

helped to promote liberal democratic values and to stem the ultramontane tendency of the Roman Catholic church in Quebec, but
by not disqualifying Langevin they prevented a backlash against
perceived meddling by the central authorities. The court also
assisted Archbishop Taschereau to pursue a moderate line.

The beneficial results achieved by the Supreme Court in the
Charlevoix case should be compared with the impact of the Privy
Council's decision in the earlier *Guibord* case. Joseph Guibord, a
founding member of the Institut Canadien, died on 18 November
1869 and the Catholic authorities of Côte des Neiges cemetery in
Montreal refused to bury him in consecrated grounds. The widow,
born Henriette Brown, sought a mandamus to compel them to do
so and thus began the most significant nineteenth-century Quebec
case involving church-state conflict. The contest proceeded
through four levels of courts over a six-year period, a period
corresponding roughly with the gestation and birth of the
Supreme Court of Canada. The nominal parties in this unseemly
dispute were the widow of Joseph Guibord and the curé and lay
church officers of the cemetery, but the Institut Canadien and
Bishop Bourget of Montreal were the real antagonists.

The Institut Canadien, founded in Montreal in 1844 by young
radical liberals, sponsored debates, held public lectures and accu-
mulated a substantial library. As there was no French-Canadian
university in Montreal at this time, the Institut fulfilled an important need. However, Bishop Bourget became its implacable foe
because the Institut espoused such liberal values as the separation
of church and state and its library contained books prohibited by
the church. The clash symbolized the larger struggle between liberal and ultramontane tendencies in the Catholic church. L.A.
Dessaulles, one of the leading members of the Institut, depicted
Pope Pius IX as a despot and enemy of liberty and progress.[9] This
preceded the pope's publication on 8 December 1864 of the encyc-
lical *Quanta cura* with its attached Syllabus of Errors denouncing
"'the principal errors of our times' including the view that the
pope 'can or should reconcile himself to, or agree with, progress,
liberalism and modern civilization.'"[10] Bishop Bourget enthusiastically endorsed these authoritarian views and successive confron-
tations occurred between him and the Institut in the 1850s and
1860s. The feud culminated in the summer of 1869 when Bishop
Bourget, with papal approval, declared that "two things are specifically and strictly forbidden; firstly to take part in the activities

of the Institut Canadien, as long as it teaches pernicious doctrines, and secondly, to publish, keep, save or read the Yearbook of the said Institut for 1868." Anyone who maintained his membership in the Institut or read or kept its yearbook of 1868 deprived "himself of the sacraments, even the sacrament of the dead, for to be worthy of approaching it one must detest sin that kills the soul."[11]

Before his death Joseph Guibord had explicitly refused to renounce his membership in the Institut. Therefore Father Victor Rousselot, the curé of the parish of Montreal and clerk of the cemetery, refused burial in the consecrated section but offered interment in the part reserved for those dying out of the faith and for executed criminals who had not made a confession. The widow's suit focused on "the proper standards for the distribution of honour and dishonour"[12] and on whether the civil courts had the power to question the church's determination. The trial judge, Justice Charles Mondelet, found that Guibord had been unjustly deprived of ecclesiastical burial and granted the mandamus. The officers of the cemetery appealed to the Court of Review which reversed the trial decision. The widow then unsuccessfully appealed to the Court of Queen's Bench. In the two intermediate appellate tribunals all eight judges decided in favour of the cemetery authorities for a variety of reasons.

The widow died on 2 April 1873 and was interred in the plot owned by her late husband in the consecrated portion of the cemetery. She made the Institut her heir and it decided to proceed with the appeal. Joseph Doutre obtained leave to appeal to the Judicial Committee of the Privy Council in June 1873. The Privy Council found that "although the Roman Catholic Church in Canada may have ceased to be an Established Church in the full sense of the term, it nevertheless continued to be a Church recognized by the State; retaining its endowments, and continuing to have certain rights....enforceable at law."[13] The Privy Council rejected the fundamental contention by the cemetery authorities that the denial of burial in consecrated ground constituted an ecclesiastical decision which could not be questioned in a civil court. The Privy Council harboured no doubt that the civil courts were and must be supreme. It stated:

> The payment of *dîmes* to the clergy of the Roman Catholic Church by its lay members; and the rateability of the latter to the maintenance of parochial cemeteries, are secured by law and statutes. These rights of the Church must beget corresponding obliga-

tions, and it is obvious that this state of things may give rise to questions between the laity and clergy which can only be determined by the Municipal Courts.[14]

As the widow had not asked for burial with religious rights but only burial in consecrated ground, the Privy Council found it unnecessary to consider whether it had the power to order interment with the usual religious rights.

Whether the Privy Council applied civil or ecclesiastical law remained ambiguous. It said that "it has been their Lordships' duty to determine the question in accordance with what has appeared to them to be the law of the Roman Catholic Church in Lower Canada." If the court applied ecclesiastical law, the assumption and superiority of the civil courts appeared somewhat problematic. The order of civil burial in consecrated ground seemed to involve some internal contradiction. The Privy Council, anticipating some problems, said:

> If, as was suggested, difficulties should arise by reason of an interment without religious ceremonies in the part of the ground to which the mandamus applies, it will be in the power of the ecclesiastical authorities to obviate them by permitting the performances of such ceremonies as are sufficient for that purpose, and their Lordships hope that the question of burial, with such ceremonies, will be reconsidered by them, and further litigation avoided.[15]

The first attempt to comply with the order on 2 September 1875 proved unsuccessful. An angry mob closed the cemetery gates and a barrage of stones caused those in charge of the hearse to retreat, taking Guibord's coffin back to the Protestant cemetery of Mount Royal where it had been for six years. On 16 November 1875, with the aid of most of the Montreal police force and over a thousand local militia, Joseph Guibord was interred beside his wife. The Institut appeared to have scored an important victory over its implacable opponent, Bishop Bourget. It was a short-lived triumph, for the bishop declared the ground in which Guibord was buried to be a profane place and forever separate from the consecrated portions of the cemetery. Also the Quebec legislature, in response to the Privy Council's decision, passed an act in 1875 respecting interment in Roman Catholic cemeteries. In its preamble it recited the expediency of preventing conflict between ecclesiastical and civil authority respecting Roman Catholic cemeteries. The statute provided that:

It belongs solely to the roman catholic ecclesiastical authority to designate the place in the cemetery, in which each individual of such faith shall be buried after death; and if the deceased, according to the canon rules and laws, in the judgment of the ordinary, cannot be interred in ground consecrated by the liturgical prayers of such religion, he shall receive civil burial, in ground reserved for that purpose and adjacent to the cemetery.[16]

The wisdom of the Privy Council in granting leave to appeal in the Guibord case could certainly be questioned. The Privy Council presumably wished to strike a blow for liberal democratic values and against the theocratic views of the ultramontanes. The issue, however, came too close to the border between ecclesiastical and civil power and constituted poor tactical ground for a battle. The decision antagonized and promoted more militancy within the ultramontane wing of the Roman Catholic church. The Privy Council came under fire from much of the French-Canadian press. *La Minerve* of Montreal said:

Brute force, backed up by the judges' decision — judges who were either perverse or ignorant of the organization of our Church, attempted on Tuesday to put into practice the abominable claim that one may demand privileges for an individual who did nothing during his lifetime for procuring, after his death, of the prayers and honours reserved by the Church for those who depart this life in her bosom. If someone should make up his mind to demand the same privileges for a pagan, we would not be surprised.[17]

The Privy Council in the *Guibord* case did not cope with the church-state conflict in Quebec as competently as did the fledgling Supreme Court of Canada in the *Charlevoix* case three years later. The torrent of criticism in Quebec following the Privy Council's 1874 decision did, however, facilitate the passage of the Supreme Court Act in 1875.

Notes to Chapter 13

1. Alexander Mackenzie to George Brown 25 Jan. 1877, quoted by Andrée Désilets in *Hector-Louis Langevin* (Quebec: Laval University Press, 1969), p. 301.

2. (1877), 1 S.C.R. 145 at pp. 173-74, 181.

3. Ibid., pp. 215-16.

4. Ibid., pp. 220-23.

5. Ibid., pp. 188-89.

6. Ibid., p. 230.

7. Désilets, *Langevin*, p. 300 (translation).

8. Nive Voisine, "Elzéar-Alexandre Taschereau," *Dictionary of Canadian Biography*, Vol. 12, p. 1022.

9. Rainer Knopff "Quebec's 'Holy War' as 'Regime' Politics: Reflections on the Guibord Case," *Canadian Journal of Political Science* 12 (1979), p. 316.

10. J.N.D. Kelly, *The Oxford Dictionary of Popes* (Oxford: Oxford University Press, 1986), p. 310.

11. Lovell C. Clark, *The Guibord Affair* (Toronto: Holt, Rinehart & Winston, 1971), pp. 27-28.

12. Knopff, "Quebec's 'Holy War,'" p. 316.

13. *Brown v. Curé et Marguilliers de l'Oeuvre et Fabrique de Notre Dame de Montreal* (1874), 6 L.R.P.C. 157 at p. 206.

14. Ibid., p. 207.

15. Ibid., p. 219.

16. An Act respecting interment in roman catholic cemeteries S.Q. 1875, c.19, s.1.

17. Clark, *Guibord*, p. 116.

CHAPTER 14

The Second Chief Justice and the Court's Integrity

Ritchie's industry and leadership as a puisne judge were rewarded on 11 January 1879 when two days after Richards's resignation he was named the second chief justice of the Supreme Court of Canada. On the preceding day Sir John A. Macdonald wrote to Ritchie as follows:

Dear Sir,

Chief Justice Sir W.B. Richards has resigned his office, and I am authorized to inform you, that I shall be glad to submit your name to His Excellency the Governor General as the successor of the late Chief Justice.

I am assured that the appointment of a gentleman of your distinguished ability and recognized professional eminence will command the confidence of the Country and the approval of the profession.

Will you allow me to add my personal satisfaction and believe me to be always

Yours faithfully

J.A. Macdonald

Later in January Macdonald acknowledged in a letter to A.L. Palmer that the move was based on merit, and not politics: "Ritchie was an anti-Confederate and a strong one, but he is a good lawyer and makes a good judge .... I am strongly of the opinion that the Supreme Court should be comprised of judges who have had judicial training in Courts of the first instance."[1] The legal community also appeared pleased by the newly appointed chief justice. "Mr. Ritchie is admitted to be an excellent lawyer and will, we trust, in his new position develope [sic] many of the qualities which rendered the appointment of his predecessor so acceptable to the country.... We congratulate him on his promotion."[2] For his part, Ritchie assured Macdonald that "I shall honestly try to

Sir Henri Elzéar Taschereau
Justice of the Supreme Court 1878-1902
Chief Justice 1902-1906.
(National Archives of Canada, Neg. No. PA42230)

John Wellington Gwynne
Justice of the Supreme Court 1879-1902
(National Archives of Canada, Neg. No. P27242)

discharge the [position] in such a way as not to bring discredit on your recommendation."[3] The positive reaction to Ritchie's appointment reflected the reputation he had earned for solid judicial work both in New Brunswick and his early years in Ottawa.

One of Ritchie's first acts as chief justice was the swearing in of two new puisne judges, Henri Elzéar Taschereau and John Wellington Gwynne. Jean-Thomas Taschereau had resigned from the Supreme Court on 6 October 1878 ostensibly on the grounds of ill health. However, earlier in the year the *Canada Law Journal* had drawn attention to the requirement that a judge of the Supreme Court must reside in Ottawa or within five miles of the city.

> There is a rule, however, that law-makers should not be law breakers; and in the same way a judge ought not wilfully to bring himself into judgment. It so happens that Mr Justice Taschereau resides not "in Ottawa or within five miles thereof," but in the city of Quebec. During the two-and-a-half years' existence of the Court he has failed to comply with the law; and, so far as the public know, no notice has been taken of this fact by the Government. We understand that the learned judge only comes to Ottawa to attend the sessions, and leaves immediately after. We know of no reason why he should not comply with the law, as do the other judges. It may be inconvenient for him, but he knew the law when he accepted office.[4]

Taschereau perhaps preferred Quebec City to Ottawa described by Goldwin Smith, a Toronto history professor, as a "sub-Arctic lumber-village converted by royal mandate into a political cock-pit." Following his resignation he lived on in Quebec City until his death in 1893. His resignation occurred after the Mackenzie government had been defeated at the polls in September 1878 and before Macdonald had reassumed the reins of power. After the defeat of his party Mackenzie appointed Henri Elzéar Taschereau to the Supreme Court to replace his cousin, Jean-Thomas Taschereau. Jean-Thomas's son, Henri Thomas, was appointed to the Superior Court for the district of Kamouraska which had formerly been held by Henri Elzéar Taschereau. This Taschereau shuffle did not entirely represent Liberal party patronage, as J.-T. Taschereau had in December 1857 sought to run for the Conservatives for the Legislative Assembly, but bowed out in order to assure the election of Dunbar Ross, the incumbent Conservative.[5] J.-T. Taschereau's replacement in the Supreme Court of Canada, H.E. Taschereau, had been the Conservative member for

Beauce from 1861 to 1867 and then on 12 January 1871 was appointed a judge of the Superior Court of Quebec. Henri Thomas Taschereau, the only Liberal thus involved in the shuffle, had been the Liberal member for Montmagny from 1872 to 1878.[6]

These appointments, carried out after the Mackenzie administration had been defeated at the polls, and justified on the basis that the efficiency of the judiciary required them, came under scrutiny when the new justice of the Supreme Court of Canada could not be sworn until 1879 because of the absence of Chief Justice Richards. Alexander Mackenzie replied rather inadequately that he "found it absolutely necessary to take immediate action" and Sir John A. Macdonald retorted, "It is a family affair."[7]

Ritchie administered the second oath of office to John Wellington Gwynne. He had been born in Ireland in 1814 and educated at Trinity College, Dublin, before coming to Canada in 1832. He was noted for his remarkable knowledge of both law and equity at a time when there were few who practised at both bars. He became a puisne judge of the Ontario Court of Common Pleas in 1868 and his appointment to the Supreme Court in 1879 received wide acclaim from the Ontario bar. Gwynne, of all the early judges, had the most centralist vision of the constitution.

With the B.N.A. Act just over a decade old, constitutional questions were of fundamental importance for the new Court. Ritchie's judgments indicated his attempt to strike a balanced interpretation of the 1867 document and an appropriate division of powers between the federal and provincial governments. In *Severn* v. *The Queen* (1877) the issue was whether the Ontario legislature had the power to raise revenue from brewers by requiring them to obtain a licence to carry on their business and sell their beer in Ontario. The majority held that the Ontario statute was *ultra vires* because it was in conflict with the federal power under section 91(2), the regulation of trade and commerce, and did not fall within the power of the provincial legislature under section 92(9), shop saloon, tavern, auctioneer, and other licences covering the raising of a revenue for provincial, local or municipal purposes. Justices Ritchie and Strong dissented. Ritchie specifically disapproved of the expansive approach adopted by Chief Justice Richards in construing the B.N.A. Act, which took into account the knowledge of the framers and their desire to avoid the difficulties caused by the state's rights thrust of the United States constitution. Ritchie, as a proud Maritimer, also took exception to reading the act "by the light of an Ontario candle alone, that is, by the state of the law at the time of Confederation in that Province." He construed the words "and other licences" to give the local legislature the power to raise substantial revenue for provincial as well as for municipal purposes. Ritchie said, "He [a brewer] could not sell by wholesale in New Brunswick at the time of Confederation without a license, and I do not think he can do so now in Ontario."[8] He conceded that licensing necessarily interfered with trade and commerce but he regarded it as legitimate, provided its object was to raise revenue for a provincial purpose. The majority decision of the Supreme Court of Canada was subsequently repudiated by the Privy Council and thus Ritchie's dissent prevailed.

In *City of Fredericton* v. *The Queen* (1880), a party sought a mandamus to compel the city to issue a licence to permit him to sell liquor in his hotel. However, the Canada Temperance Act, 1878, had been brought into force in Fredericton and thus the city council contended that it could not grant the licence. Ritchie held that section 91(2), the regulation of trade and commerce, included the power to prohibit the trade in intoxicating liquor and only the Parliament of Canada had such power to exercise either absolutely or conditionally.

> I think it equally clear, that the Local Legislature have not the power to prohibit, the Dominion Parliament having, not only the general powers of legislation, but also the sole power of regulating as well internal as external trade and commerce ... to allow the Local Legislatures, under pretence of police regulation, on general grounds of public policy and utility, by prohibitory laws to annihilate such trade and traffic, and practically deprive the Dominion Parliament of a branch of trade and commerce from which so large a part of the public revenue was at the time of confederation raised in all the Provinces ... which never could have been contemplated by the framers of the B.N.A. Act.[9]

Only Justice Henry dissented from this decision; but the Privy Council in later cases repudiated the proposition that trade and commerce included intraprovincial trade and commerce and that regulation included the power to prohibit a trade altogether.[10]

In another 1880 decision Ritchie upheld provincial legislation but did so cautiously, possibly to avoid undue impact on federal powers. In *Citizens' Insurance Co.* v. *Parsons* (1880), the constitutional validity of the Fire Insurance Policy Act of Ontario, prescribing standard conditions, was questioned. The Supreme Court in a four to two split upheld the Ontario legislation regulating fire insurance contracts. This decision survived appeal to the Privy Council but in such a way that section 91(2), the trade and commerce power, was greatly circumscribed so that it no longer comprehended intraprovincial trade or the right to regulate a particular business or trade. This was not the thrust of the decision rendered by Ritchie. He held the Ontario legislation valid but without sapping the vitality of section 91(2). Ritchie tried to give a balanced interpretation to the B.N.A. Act which would have recognized a substantial area of concurrent jurisdiction.

> I do not think the local legislatures are to be deprived of all power to deal with property and civil rights, because parliament, in the plenary exercise of its power to regulate trade and commerce, may possibly pass laws inconsistent with the exercise by the local legislatures of their powers — the exercise of the powers of the local legislatures being in such a case subject to such regulations as the Dominion may lawfully prescribe.[11]

Ritchie did, however, say that in his opinion the act was not a regulation of trade and commerce; it dealt with the contract of fire insurance, as between the insurer and the insured, but then he went on to say:

> If an insurance company is a trader, and the business it carries on is commercial, why should the local legislature, having legislative power over property and civil rights, and matters of a private and local character, not be enabled to say to such a company: "If you do business in the province of Ontario, and insure property situate here, we have legislative control over property and over the civil rights in the province, and will, under such power, for the protection of that property and the rights of the insured, define the conditions on which you shall deal with such property," it being possibly wholly unconnected with trade and commerce, as a private dwelling or farming establishment, and the person insured having possibly no connection with trade or commerce?[12]

Thus, while upholding the legislative competence of the province, Ritchie did not emasculate the federal power over trade and commerce as did the Privy Council.

In *Mercer* v. *A.G. for Ontario* (1881) the question was whether land belonging to a person who died intestate and without heirs escheated to the crown in the right of Canada or of the province. The majority of the Supreme Court held in favour of the Dominion but Ritchie and Strong dissented. Ritchie displayed intimate knowledge about public revenue procedures that he had gained in New Brunswick. He regarded as illogical the idea that lands never owned by the Dominion could revert to it by failure of heirs, rather than "reverting to the original grantor to be held for the benefit of the province to whom the rights of the Crown, the original grantor, had been surrendered, in other words, to be placed in the same position and held for the Crown for the benefit of the province as if they never had been granted."[13] Ritchie refused to give a wide reading to section 102 so as to include escheats within duties and revenues that were to become part of the Consolidated Revenue Fund belonging to Canada. Ritchie conceded that lieutenant-governors did not represent the crown in the same manner that they had prior to confederation, but he insisted that they still represented the crown, "though doubtless in a modified manner." Ritchie again desired to achieve an appropriate balance in the interpretation of the B.N.A. Act:

> The executive and legislative powers of the Dominion are large, and so of necessity should be, and while it behoves all courts in the Dominion to recognize and give full force and effect to all executive and legislative acts within the scope of such powers, it is at the same time equally the duty of all courts, especially this appellate tribunal, to recognize and preserve to the executive governments and local legislatures of the provinces their just rights, whether political or proprietary, and not to permit the provinces to be deprived of their local and territorial rights on the plea that Lieutenant-Governors in no sense represent the crown, and therefore all seignorial or prerogative rights, or rights enforceable as seignorial or prerogative rights, of necessity belong to the Dominion.[14]

The Privy Council reversed the majority of the Supreme Court of Canada and thus agreed with Ritchie, that the lands escheated to Ontario. The Privy Council reached this conclusion by holding that royalties in section 109 included the feudal incident of escheat.[15] Jeremiah Travis, in an early treatise on constitutional law, compared Ritchie's decision to the opinion of the Privy Council and concluded that Ritchie's decision remained the better one.[16]

Despite the competence of Ritchie and the rest of the Court in early constitutional cases, the Supreme Court's early years remained a struggle for identity and authority. It suffered, in Bora Laskin's words, an "uneasy infancy," and experienced difficulties in establishing itself in several parts of the legal community.[17] In Parliament there were attempts between 1879 and 1882 to abolish the tribunal completely.[18] These debates mainly resurrected early grievances and the court was never seriously threatened because the leaders of both parties supported it. However, Mackenzie and Macdonald differed in the debates themselves. The Liberal leader considered talk of abolition of the Supreme Court tantamount to repeal of the B.N.A. Act. Macdonald believed the institution could withstand the scrutiny:

> I must admit that I do not think there is any advantage to be gained in shutting our eyes to the fact that the Court, by some accident or misfortune, has not obtained that confidence which such a tribunal ought to have succeeded in obtaining .... But it is a new Court, a court established early in our history as a Dominion .... I have no doubt that, as the Court grows older, the people of the country will become more accustomed to consider it as one of the tribunals of which they should be proud, and of which they would not willingly be deprived.[19]

That pride, however, had been slow to develop. Contemporaries in the legal community were, in a very Canadian way, reluctant to accept the homegrown institution. In 1882 the Supreme Court was characterized as having "so far been a failure, partly owing to the inherent difficulties of our confederation ... and partly owing to the difficulties and infirmities of a personal nature which we do not care to enlarge upon."[20]

There was discontent about delays in the rendering and printing of decisions. "May I ask the reason why the Supreme Court is so excessively slow?" wrote one Montrealer, adding "they have comparatively little to do."[21] Interestingly, Justice Strong accused Ritchie of delays in a letter to the prime minister: "The Chief seems to think of anything rather than his judicial work and is never ready with his judgments."[22] Yet it was apparently Strong who, among the early members of the Court, was most likely to cause problems in the reporting process; in one case the reporter recorded that although Strong had delivered a written judgment he could not obtain it.[23] In *Provincial Insurance Co. v. Connolly* (1879)[24] and in *McLeod v. The New Brunswick Railway Co.* (1880)[25] the reporter simply stated that Strong "read a written judgment stating his reasons for that conclusion" in the first case reversing and in the second case affirming the judgment of the court below. But apparently he did not give his judgment to the reporter for no reasons were printed. In another case a footnote recorded that the "learned judge, having mislaid his judgment, directed the reporter to report the case without it."[26] *Sewell v. British Columbia Towing and Transportation Co.* (1883)[27] revealed a lack of communication between Ritchie and Strong. In this case Ritchie simply concurred with Strong both as to the facts and the law. This simple concurrence must have surprised Strong for a footnote to his judgment stated that "This judgement is not prefaced with any statement of the facts for the reason that it was intended to follow a judgment of the Chief Justice, in which the facts were stated."[28]

Ritchie's term as chief justice from 11 January 1879 until his death on 25 September 1892, a period of nearly fourteen years, is the longest tenure of any chief justice of the Supreme Court of Canada. Also notable is the fact that the longest period of stability in the personnel of the Court occurred during his tenure. From the appointment of Mr. Justice Gwynne on 14 January 1879 until the death of Mr. Justice Henry on 3 May 1888, a period of over nine years, there was no change in the Court's membership.

Such stability of personnel might be thought to encourage a united and harmonious court. This was not the case, primarily because the individual justices did not appear to prize cooperation. Snell and Vaughan, in their book on the Supreme Court of Canada, held Ritchie to blame for the friction under his tenure, and concluded that the "Chief Justice had clearly failed to mould the individual justices into an effective, harmonious unit .... [T]his was the central weakness of the Supreme Court in the 1880's".[29] What did colleagues expect of Ritchie, and what should we now expect? How could he compel the five other justices to subordinate differences in background, language and outlook, to achieve this harmonious unit? Furthermore, William Alexander Henry, Henri Elzéar Taschereau and John Wellington Gwynne could not be described as easy colleagues. Their jurisprudential views differed greatly. For instance, on the matter of interpreting the B.N.A. Act, Gwynne was the most centralist of judges, while Strong staunchly upheld provincial powers.[30]

The most troublesome personality on the Ritchie court was clearly Justice Strong. The best evidence of his disruptive influence was in his letter to Macdonald, which included a scathing attack on the judicial capabilities of Justice Henry.[31] Strong was described by an Ontario lawyer as "one of the best appeal judges we have but he is blessed with a shocking bad temper."[32] He did not suffer fools gladly and was prepared to question the abilities of other members. In *Attorney General of Canada* v. *City of Montreal* (1885), Strong said, "If I was not a single dissentient judge in this court I should have thought this argument is so obviously fallacious as scarcely to call for observation, but as I differ from the other members of the Court I am bound to assume that it is not so untenable as it appears to me and is entitled to respectful consideration."[33]

It has been said that Chief Justice Ritchie was himself "guilty of inappropriate courtroom behaviour."[34] However, the only evidence adduced for this was in a book review written by Jeremiah Travis, assessing his own book on the Canadian constitution. Travis wrote that "it would have been much more pleasant for me to have been generally able to agree with the very able Judge, and one of the kindest and most courteous of gentlemen" [Gwynne] "than with one whose proverbial rudeness amounts at times to almost boorishness [Ritchie]."[35] But Travis's assessment of Ritchie's behaviour should not be uncritically accepted. P.B. Waite described Travis as "agreeable and pleasant on the surface but underneath vindictive, unreasonable, inexhaustible, and treacherous as a snake."[36] Ritchie, as chief justice of New Brunswick, had sat in *Ex Parte Travis* (1866) in which Travis sought an order to compel the New Brunswick Barristers' Society to examine him after three years rather than four because he had obtained an LL.B. from Harvard. Ritchie held that a student could only claim to have his time of study reduced to three years if during the whole period of articles he had been a university graduate, and as Travis had interrupted his articles to obtain a degree, he had to serve for four years. This may have antagonized Travis towards Ritchie.

Nevertheless, reading between the lines of other commentators still leaves the impression that Ritchie might not always have shown limitless patience and understanding. Recalling his New Brunswick years, George Fenety wrote:

> Those who understood Ritchie found in him a companionable, confiding man. Those who did not understand him thought him still and unapproachable, and with all his liberal professions a great Tory at heart. Nevertheless we can only judge politicians by their actions, and by this standard I always found this gentleman a true man."[37]

The *Canada Law Journal* remarked that the chief justice had a "temper quick and ardent," but added that he kept it "well under control, and his relations with all who came in contact with him were most happy." This journal also remarked that Ritchie "was extremely jealous of what he considered the dignity" of the Court and noted "where counsel failed to appear promptly when a case was called for argument he was especially severe; sometimes ... not fully appreciating the fact that a court is intended for the purpose of trying cases and not merely disposing of them."[38] In June 1888 the chief justice remarked that the absence of counsel when the Court delivered judgments was "not indicative on their part of the respect which was due to the tribunal" and also indicated that their presence without robes represented a failure "of their obligations to the court they appeared before."[39]

Ritchie might also have attached too much importance to the mode of addressing judges. In Upper Canada, until John Beverley Robinson became chief justice in 1829, barristers traditionally addressed a superior court judge as "Your Honour."[40] On the basis of rooting out creeping Americanisms, Robinson insisted on "Your Lordship."[41] In Quebec advocates addressed the bench as "Your Honour" or "Votre Honneur" until 1901, when judges of the superior courts indicated their preference for the higher sounding title of "Your Lordship" or "Votre Seigneurie." However, Pierre Beullac, registering his disapproval, stated "Quant à 'Votre Seigneurie,' le mot est trop d'un autre âge et il jure trop avec nos ideés democratiques pour que l'on puisse s'étonner de le voir mal accueilli."[42]

In 1969, Justice Laskin questioned the mode of addressed superior court judges:

> So far as I have been able to determine, the present-day salutation of "Your Lordship" has no formal basis; it rests on exaggerated courtesy, and perhaps on an assumed enhancement of prestige to mark the superior courts off from the inferior county and district courts whose presiding officers are "Their Honours." I cannot forbear to note that a judge of the High Court of Australia is "His Honour" despite the fact that he may be knighted. A judge of the Supreme Court of the United States is also "His Honour" without the redeeming possibility of a title. It may strike others, as it strikes me, to be pretentious for Canadian society, which rejects titles of honour in the formal gift of the British monarch, that any class of judges should be addressed as "My Lord."[43]

In New Brunswick the tradition was that superior court judges were addressed as "Your Honour" and this continued until 1930.[44] However in 1889, a proposal was made to use the term "My Lord." A Saint John newspaper denounced this as a "piece of unhealthy flunkeyism" and said:

In the old colonial days, when there were lords in this country who had no business to be here, when there was no responsible government, and the people had very little to say, the practice of the courts was as near as possible like that of the courts in England. In some of the provinces the title of a supreme court judge was "my lord," and it so continues to this day. In New Brunswick it never was so, and to make it so at this period of the nineteenth century is to take a step backward and downward.[45]

One reason suggested for the change was that New Brunswick lawyers appearing in Ottawa might, through habit, be "guilty of addressing their lordships of the Supreme Court of Canada as 'your honor'." The *Progress* noted that "Chief Justice Ritchie takes special umbrage when this happens." Ritchie, although defending the dignity of the Court, might have been overly pompous. He was, however, fortunate because his wife, a naturally warm, unpretentious woman, would have combatted this tendency at home. Lord Frederick Hamilton, brother-in-law of Lord Lansdowne, the governor general, recorded that he called at the home of a high official and was

> told at the door that Lady R [Ritchie] was not at home. Recognising my voice, a cry came up from the kitchen-stairs, "Oh, yes! I am at home to you. Come right down into the kitchen," where I found my friend, with her sleeves rolled up, making with her own hands the sweets for the dinner-party she was giving that night, as she mistrusted her cook's capabilities.[46]

The integrity that she brought to her family was matched by the similarly unified mission that Ritchie struggled to bring to his fledgling Court.

Notes to Chapter 14

1. NAC, Sir John A. Macdonald Papers No. 21-232, John A. Macdonald to A.L. Palmer, 30 Jan. 1879.

2. *Canada Law Journal* 15 (1879), p. 41.

3. NAC, Sir John A. Macdonald Papers No. 163361-64, W.J. Ritchie to Sir John A. Macdonald, 11 Jan. 1879.

4. *Canada Law Journal* 14 (1878), p. 5.

5. Christine Veilleux, "Jean-Thomas Taschereau," *Dictionary of Canadian Biography*, vol. 12, pp. 1024-25.

6. Pierre-Georges Roy, *Les Juges de la Province de Québec* (Quebec: R. Paradis, 1933), p. 533.

7. Commons, *Debates*, 17 Mar. 1879, p. 506.

8. (1878), 2 S.C.R. 70 at pp. 99, 102.

9. (1880), 3 S.C.R. 505 at p. 542.

10. See, for example, *Citizens' Insurance Co.* v. *Parsons* (1881), 7 App. Cas. 96; *Bank of Toronto* v. *Lambe* (1887), 12 App. Cas. 575; and *A.G. Ontario* v. *A.G. Canada* (Local Prohibition), [1896] A.C. 348.

11. (1880), 4 S.C.R. 215 at p. 243.

12. Ibid., p. 251.

13. (1881), 5 S.C.R. 538 at p. 646.

14. Ibid., pp. 643-44.

15. (1883), 8 App. Cas. 767.

16. J. Travis, *A Law Treatise on the Constitutional Powers of Parliament and of the Local Legislatures under the British North America Act, 1867* (Saint John: Sun Publishing, 1884), p. 33.

17. Bora Laskin, "The Supreme Court of Canada: A Final Court of and for Canadians," *Canadian Bar Review* 29 (1951), p. 1039.

18. Snell and Vaughan, *Supreme Court*, pp. 29-32.

19. Frank MacKinnon, "The Establishment of the Supreme Court of Canada," *Canadian Historical Review* 27 (1946), p. 270.

20. *Canada Law Journal* 18 (1882), p. 88.

21. *The Legal News* 1 (1878), p. 140.

22. NAC, Sir John A. Macdonald Papers No. 148624-640, S.H. Strong to John A. Macdonald, 9 Feb. 1880.

23. *Clark* v. *Scottish Imperial Insurance Co..* (1879), 4 S.C.R. 192 at p. 212. The reporter finally obtained a copy of Justice Strong's judgment and included it as an appendix at p. 706.

24. (1879), 5 S.C.R. 258 at p. 267.

25. (1880), 5 S.C.R. 281 at p. 299.

26. *Milloy* v. *Kerr* (1884), 8 S.C.R. 474 at p. 486. Justice Strong was responsible for the lion's share of cases unaccounted for by 1887. See Snell and Vaughan, *Supreme Court.* p. 37.

27. (1884), 9 S.C.R. 527.

28. Ibid., p. 543.

29. Snell and Vaughan, *Supreme Court*, p. 40.

30. F. Murray Greenwood, "Lord Watson, Institutional Self-Interest, and the Decentralization of Canadian Federalism in the 1890's," *University of British Columbia Law Review* 9 (1974-75), p. 271.

31. NAC, Sir John A. Macdonald Papers, Strong to Macdonald, 9 Feb. 1880.

32. Queen's University Archives, A. Mackenzie Papers, Collection 2112 No. 795-8, T. Hodgins to A. Mackenzie, 29 Apr, 1875.

33. (1885), 13 S.C.R. 352 at p. 363.

34. Snell and Vaughan, *Supreme Court*, p. 40.

35. J. Travis, "Travis on Constitutional Law," *Manitoba Law Journal* 2 (1885), p. 43.

36. P.B. Waite, *The Man from Halifax: Sir John Thompson, Prime Minister* (Toronto, University of Toronto Press, 1985), p. 195. Travis appeared before the Supreme Court in *Vernon* v. *Oliver* and although he succeeded in the appeal his factum was struck off the files of the court because it was "framed in such a scandalous manner, in fact, in such a virulent and malignant spirit of invective of the judgments of the learned judges whose decision is appealed from, as to disgrace not only the counsel by whom it was prepared, but this court also, if it should be permitted to remain upon its files or among its records." (1885), 11 S.C.R. 156, p. 163. The decision of the court was written by Justice Gwynne. Chief Justice Ritchie did not sit on *Vernon* v. *Oliver* because he was related to one of the litigants. Travis's short and very unsuccessful career as a stipendiary magistrate is set out by W.F. Bowker in "Stipendiary Magistrates and Supreme Court of the North-West Territories, 1876-1907" *Alberta Law*

Review 26 (1988), pp. 270-72, and by Max Foran in "The 'Travis Affair,'" *Alberta Historical Review* 19 (1971).

37. Lawrence, *Judges of New Brunswick*, p. 486.

38. *Canada Law Journal* 28 (1892), p. 484.

39. *Ottawa Citizen*, 24 June 1884, p. 2.

40. W.R. Riddell, *The Bar and the Courts of the Province of Upper Canada or Ontario* (Toronto: Macmillan, 1928), pp. 152 and 159, n. 23.

41. Patrick Brode, *Sir John Beverley Robinson: Bone and Sinew of the Compact* (Toronto: Osgoode Society, 1984), p. 167.

42. *La Revue Legale* 7 (1901), p. 393.

43. Bora Laskin, *The British Tradition in Canadian Law* (London: Stevens & Sons, 1969), p. 32.

44. Franklin O. Leger, *One Hundred Years in the Practice of Law: 1888-1988* (Saint John: Lingley Printing Co., 1988), p. 40.

45. *Saint John Progress*, 16 Feb. 1889, p. 1.

46. Frederic Hamilton, *The Days Before Yesterday* (London: Hodder & Stoughton, 1920), pp. 257-58. Lord Hamilton does not specifically identify Lady R as Lady Ritchie, but Sandra Gwyn in *The Private Capital* indicates at p. 236 that the reference probably was Lady Ritchie.

CHAPTER 15

Judicial Ethics and the Double Sitting

Ritchie's career as a judge spanned some thirty-seven years, offering a substantial perspective for his and his contemporaries' conception of judicial ethics. The modern judiciary must be, and be perceived to be, impartial, disinterested and fair in dealing with litigants. Thus a judge should not try a case which might cast doubt on his ability to decide the case fairly. A lawyer who has advised, commenced an action, or participated in defending an action on behalf of a client, and subsequently becomes a judge, has no business judging such a case, even though he might still be capable of judging such a case impartially. The principle that a judge must determine a case solely on the basis of evidence adduced in court has supported the judge who declines to sit on a case in which he has previously advised either party. He might be aware of facts and circumstances which might or might not come out at trial.

It was clear that a judge would not sit on a case in which he previously participated as counsel. For example, on 20 November 1856, Justice Robert Parker of New Brunswick wrote to Chief Justice Brenton Halliburton of Nova Scotia thanking him for sending a copy of a published poem and in a postscript noted: "Our business centres much at St. John. Our new Judge, Ritchie, has a docket before him of 15 remands and 105 new cases for trial, leaving a residue of 14 for me to take up in which he was concerned as counsel — but in other parts our business is not heavy."[1] This also indicated that on Ritchie's appointment to the Supreme Court of New Brunswick in 1855, he had acted as counsel in more than ten per cent of the litigation occurring in Saint John, at a time when the bulk of New Brunswick litigation occurred in that city. Eight years after his appointment there was the notation in *Myers* v. *St. Andrews and Quebec Railroad Co.* (1863) that "Ritchie J., having been counsel in the case, took no part."[2]

Ritchie's uncle, Justice James W. Johnston, an equity judge of Nova Scotia, in *Wallace* v. *Young* (1868) said that there was a principle of natural justice "by which no Judge shall sit in his own cause or in a cause in which his relation to the parties, or to the facts of the case, or the result of the adjudication has a necessary tendency to create a strong bias on his mind."[3] He emphasized that this principle not only protected the interest of litigants but looked beyond them to the public interest that "the administration of justice should not only be pure, but unsuspected."

A judge must also disqualify himself where he has a pecuniary interest in the case to be tried. This was based on the ancient concept that a person cannot be judge in his own cause. Ritchie fastidiously adhered to this notion. In *Ex Parte Nowlin* (1864) certain property owners in Saint John challenged an assessment and Justice N. Parker in his judgment stated:

> The case having been heard in the absence of His Honor the Chief Justice and Mr. Justice Parker, and Mr. Justice Ritchie having, on consideration felt himself precluded, as being an owner of property assessed, from taking part in the judgment, we do not think it desirable to go at large into the various questions raised.[4]

Similarly in *Coram* v. *The Mayor of Saint John* (1869)[5] Ritchie and Weldon took no part in the case because they were ratepayers of Saint John and the issue was whether its royal charter mandated the keeping of wharves and sea-walls in repair. Ritchie believed it was his duty to insure that others also respected this principle of justice. In *Ex Parte Calhoun* (1863), Chief Justice Carter delivered a judgment for all members of the court but Ritchie held that the commissioners of sewers of the Germantown Lake district could undertake improvements and then assess and tax the owners of land even though they themselves were owners of land in the district. In his dissent Ritchie maintained that the duties of the commissioners were of a judicial character and therefore he could not be a judge in his own cause. Six years later precisely the same issue came before the court in *The Queen* v. *The Commissioners of the Germantown Lake District*. Ritchie, now chief justice of New Brunswick, had to choose between adhering to precedent or to the principle that a man must not be a judge in his own cause. He wrote the majority decision and acknowledged that "great stress was laid on the fact that there had been already an adjudication on the very point in controversy, and that until reversed by an Appellate Court that decision was binding." Nevertheless, Ritchie continued saying:

It is no doubt generally most convenient and desirable to adhere strictly to the decisions of the Court once pronounced, leaving further discussion and reversal, if found wrong, to a higher tribunal, and this observation would be entitled to more weight if such Appellate Court was practically accessible to the great body of suitors in this Province. But we can discover no arbitrary and inflexible rule requiring this in all cases ... if the decision ignores, or is in our opinion inconsistent with, the right applica- tion of a clear and well-established and important principle, we think the case should give way to principle .... And therefore, though we think a decision once deliberately declared should not be lightly disregarded or disturbed unless by Court of Appeal, except for cogent reason and upon a clear manifestation of error, there are occasions when we should be wrong to shut our ears or refuse our judgment, and this, we think, is one of those exceptioned cases.[6]

Thus the owner of land in a district became disqualified from acting as a commissioner of sewers for that same district.

By adopting a flexible approach to precedent and making it subservient to principle, Ritchie transformed his dissenting judg- ment of only six years earlier into the majority decision. The fact that Chief Justice Carter had retired, Robert Parker had died, Lemuel A. Wilmot had become lieutenant-governor and Neville Parker did not sit helped Ritchie to achieve this alchemy. Never- theless, only Justice Weldon joined Ritchie in his decision for the majority of the court and Justice Allen felt himself "bound by the former decision, holding that it [owning land in the district] is not such an interest as will prevent them from acting."[7] Ritchie did believe in *stare decisis*, adhering to decided cases. For instance in *Spears* v. *Walker* (1884), he tersely stated that "unless we are pre- pared to overrule that case (which most certainly I am not pre- pared to do), the non-suit must stand."[8] But occasionally in Ritchie's judicial world precedent had to give way to principle, particularly if Ritchie himself fervently adhered to that principle. One of these principles was that a man could not be judge in his own cause and in applying it Ritchie was prepared to give wide scope to what constituted a judicial proceeding and what amounted to an interest which would result in disqualification.

In order to avoid any appearance of partiality, judges would not sit if related by blood or marriage to any of the litigants. Since most of Ritchie's relatives resided in Nova Scotia, Ritchie had little occasion to disqualify himself on this basis, until his own family became older and he sat in the Supreme Court of Canada. The first such case in which Ritchie declined to sit was *Lenoir* v. *Ritchie* (1879); the defendant was his half-brother, Joseph Norman Ritchie. In 1874 Nova Scotia passed two statutes, one authorizing the lieutenant-governor to appoint queen's counsel for the province and another authorizing him to determine the order of precedence of members of the bar in the courts of Nova Scotia. By letters patent dated 26 May 1876, seventeen members of the bar were appointed queen's counsel for Nova Scotia. It also purported to establish a new order of precedence such that several persons obtained seniority over Joseph Norman Ritchie Q.C., who previously did not have this precedence. J.N. Ritchie, who received his federal Q.C. in December 1872, challenged the new order of precedence of 1876. The Supreme Court of Nova Scotia interpreted the statute as applying only prospectively and therefore the letters patent could not validly affect J.N. Ritchie's precedence. Peter H. Le Noir, among others, appealed the order confirming J.N. Ritchie's precedence.

It was unfortunate that J.N. Ritchie was a litigant because it deprived Ritchie of an opportunity to speak to an important constitutional question. Three of the five judges of the Supreme Court held that Her Majesty did not form a constituent part of provincial legislatures, that no provincial statute could impair the prerogative right to appoint queen's counsel in Canada directly or through the governor general. Therefore, the Nova Scotia statutes conferring authority on the lieutenant-governor to appoint Q.C.s and to determine their precedence were *ultra vires*. The proposition that the queen was not a part of the provincial government was not accepted by the Judicial Committee of the Privy Council in London and was clearly repudiated in *Liquidators of the Maritime Bank of Canada* v. *Receiver General of New Brunswick* (1892). Lord Watson stated that there was neither principle nor authority for the contention that the effect of the B.N.A. Act was "to sever all connection between the Crown and the provinces; to make the government of the Dominion the only government of Her Majesty in North America; and to reduce the provinces to the rank of independent municipal institutions."[9] Yet clearly *Lenoir* v. *Ritchie* was such an authority, even though not binding on the Privy Council. Perhaps if Chief Justice Ritchie had been able to sit, and if he had joined the majority in *Lenoir* v. *Ritchie*, it might have been slightly more difficult for Lord Watson to ignore the clear holding in that case. The Privy Council, intent on supporting a co-ordinate federal system for Canada, probably felt compelled to find that the Crown was an inherent part of the provincial government.

There were at least four other known cases in which Ritchie did not sit because he was related to a litigant. *Almon v. Lewis* (1881) involved the construction of the will of John Robertson, his daughter Martha's father-in-law. In *Lewin v. Wilson* (1884) the plaintiffs were the surviving trustees of Martha's marriage settlement, and presumably for that reason he did not sit. In *Vernon v. Oliver* (1885) a notation at the bottom of the report stated "[t]he Chief Justice being related to some of the parties in the cause, took no part in the hearing of the appeal." Ritchie was related by marriage to the Vernon family through his second wife Grace. In *Diocesan Synod of Nova Scotia v. Ritchie* (1890), the Reverend James Johnston Ritchie, rector of St. Luke's Church, Annapolis, and brother to William Ritchie, claimed to be entitled to participate in a fund established to supplement the salary of certain Anglican clergymen.

If a judge was related to one of the counsel in the case, in Ritchie's time there evidently was no need for disqualification. The chief justice sat on the case of the *Controverted Elections for the Electoral Districts of Shelburne N.S.* (1891) even though his son, John Almon Ritchie, was one of the two counsel appearing for the appellant. Ritchie's contemporaries on the Supreme Court of Canada also felt no obligation to disqualify themselves because they were related to counsel. Chief Justice Richards sat in *Gray v. Richford* (1878) even though his brother, Stephen Richards, Q.C., was a counsel in the case. Also in *Windsor and Annapolis Railway Co. v. The Queen* (1885) and in *McDonald v. McPherson* (1886), Justice Henry sat when his son, Hugh McDonald Henry, Q.C., appeared as counsel.

The fact that judges did not disqualify themselves when related to counsel may have been a holdover from earlier colonial times. When lawyers and judges were drawn from a few families, there would have been considerable inconvenience to the administration of justice if a judge thought it necessary to disqualify himself in such circumstances. For its first fifty-three years, the Supreme Court of Canada consisted of only six judges but the quorum to hear a case was five as it is today. Because of illness the court occasionally had difficulty obtaining a quorum and this perhaps militated against the recognition of additional grounds for disqualification. Also since champerty was illegal, a lawyer

217

had no pecuniary interest in the outcome of litigation and was in a very different position than the litigant. This ignored the reality that a lawyer could charge a client a fatter fee when he had been successful; however, with contingent fees not permitted, the quantification of the benefit which accrued to the successful counsel was more difficult and the benefit more remote. The ban on contingent fees in Ritchie's time probably helped judges to conclude that there was nothing improper in sitting on a case in which they were related to counsel. However, when a judge related to counsel heard a case, there was the appearance of partiality about which the court should have been concerned. In *Rollings* v. *Gallant* (1983), Justice MacDonald set out the modern view when he stated that "the practice that has existed in this court has been that the sons, daughters, son-in-law or daughter-in-law of a judge do not appear before that judge."[10] A modern author wrote that "it is a ground for disqualification if counsel in any case is a near relative of the trial judge (third degree of relationship)."[11]

Perhaps one of the most remarkable features of late nineteenth-century judicial ethics, viewed from a current perspective, was that judges considered it permissible to sit on an appeal from their own trial judgment. However most of these judgments were rendered in jury trials. For all of Ritchie's career on the New Brunswick bench, and for most of his tenure in the Supreme Court of Canada, judges had no apparent qualms about such double sittings in the same case. By present-day standards, this would be a clear denial of natural justice, so their tolerance, let alone active practice, is difficult to understand.

Sitting on an appeal from one's own trial judgment might have been in part due to inertia. It had always been done in England and in the Maritime provinces. The positivist tradition in the law even reinforced this practice. If judges simply applied rules in an impersonal way to a factual situation, what objection could there be to sitting on an appeal from your own decision? Not only did this ignore the considerable scope which a judge had in selecting the particular rule, and in moulding and modifying that rule to make it applicable to the particular fact situation, it also failed to recognize the considerable intellectual commitment which a judge made when rendering a judgment and the difficulty that might be encountered in persuading a judge to alter an opinion once formally expressed in a judgment.

Exchequer Court Decisions Appealed to the Supreme Court of Canada 1875-1887

(when Judges of the Supreme Court were also Exchequer Court Judges)

Case	Name of Exchequer Court judge	Number of judges hearing appeal	Did Exchequer Court judge sit on appeal?	If no, why did Exchequer Court judge not sit on appeal?	Affirmed or reversed in the Supreme Court
1. *Chevrier v. The Queen* (1880), 4 S.C.R.1	Taschereau J.-T.	5	No	Resigned before appeal	A
2. *O'Brien v. The Queen* (1880), 4 S.C.R.529	Fournier	5	Yes		A
3. *The Queen v. Robertson* (1882), 6 S.C.R. 52	Gwynne	5	No	Questions its propriety	A but rev'd in part
4. *The Queen v. Doutre* (1882), 6 S.C.R. 342	Fournier	6	Yes		A
5. *The Queen v. Belleau* (1881), 7 S.C.R. 53	Fournier	5	Yes		A but varied
6. *The Queen v. McFarlane* (1882), 7 S.C.R. 216	Henry	5	Yes		R
7. *The Queen v. McLeod* (1883), 8 S.C.R. 1	Henry	5	Yes		R

Case	Name of Exchequer Court judge	Number of judges hearing appeal	Did Exchequer Court judge sit on appeal?	If no, why did Exchequer Court judge not sit on appeal?	Affirmed or reversed in the Supreme Court
8. *The Queen v. MacLean* (1882), 8 S.C.R. 210	Henry	5	No	?	A in part
9. *The Queen v. Smith* (1882), 10 S.C.R. 1	Henry	6	Yes		R
10. *Windsor & Annapolis Railway Co. v. The Queen* (1885), 10 S.C.R. 335	Gwynne	6	Yes		R
11. *The Queen v. Dunn* (1885), 11 S.C.R. 385	Fournier	5	Yes		R
12. *Berlinquet v. The Queen* (1886), 13 S.C.R. 26	Taschereau J.-T.	5	No	Resigned before appeal	A but varied
13. *The Queen v. Farwell* (1887), 14 S.C.R. 392	Henry	5	Yes		R
14. *The Queen v. Hubert* (1887), 14 S.C.R.737	Taschereau H.E.	?	?		R
15. *McQueen v. The Queen* (1887), 16 S.C.R. 1	Gwynne	6	Yes		A 3 x 3 split

Case	Judge	No.	Participation	Note	Result
16. *Grinnell v. The Queen* (1888), 16 S.C.R. 119	Gwynne	5	Yes (present but took no part in judgment)		R
17. *Charland v. The Queen* (1889), 16 S.C.R. 721 (1887), 1 Ex.C.R. 291*	Taschereau H.E.	5	Yes (no indication of his participation in judgment)		A
18. *The Queen v. Starrs* (1889), 17 S.C.R. 118	Henry	5	No	Henry had died before appeal	R (but without costs throughout)
19. *Merchants Bank of Canada v. the Queen* (1881), 1 Ex.C.R. 1	Gwynne	5	No	?	R
20. *Paradis v. The Queen* (1887), 1 Ex.C.R. 191	Taschereau H.E.	5	No	?	R
21. *The Queen v. McGreevy* (1890), 18 S.C.R. 371	Fournier	5	No	Appeal heard after Judges statutorily barred from sitting on an appeal from own judgment	

* (Ex.C.R. indicates Taschereau present on appeal but S.C.R. indicates only Strong, Fournier, Gwynne and Patterson present)

From 1875 to 1887, when the judges of the Supreme Court of Canada were also the judges of the Exchequer Court, there were twenty-one reported decisions in which the judgment of the Exchequer Court was appealed to the Supreme Court of Canada. As the table indicates, in twelve of these cases the Exchequer Court judge sat in the Supreme Court of Canada to hear the appeal from his own decision. In at least ten of these cases the Exchequer Court judge rendered a decision in the Supreme Court which in every case confirmed his trial decision, even though the majority of the court reversed six of them. In one case, Justice Gwynne was present at the appeal but took no part in the judgment, and in another Justice H.E. Taschereau was present but there was no indication of whether he participated in the judgment. In five of the ten cases the full court of six judges sat on the appeal and yet the trial judge still participated. This indicated that it was considered to be perfectly correct for the Exchequer Court judge to sit and that he was not sitting merely to satisfy the quorum requirement of five judges. In eight of the twenty-one decisions, the Exchequer Court judge definitely did not sit on an appeal from his own judgment. Two of these cases were appeals from Exchequer Court decisions of Justice J.-T. Taschereau and were brought after he retired from the court in 1878. One was an appeal from the Exchequer Court judgment of Justice Henry, and by the time the appeal was heard Henry was dead. In another case the appeal was not heard until March 1890, after the amendment to the Supreme and Exchequer Courts Act had provided that no judge whose judgment was under appeal should sit or take part in hearings in the Supreme Court. Of the four other cases in which the Exchequer Court judge did not sit on an appeal from his own judgment, two were rendered by Justice Gwynne, one by Justice H.E. Taschereau and one by Justice Henry. Since all three judges in other cases sat on appeals from their own decisions, and Gwynne and Henry sat even when the full court heard the appeal, their absence in the four cases cannot be attributed to any conviction that it was improper to sit on an appeal from one's own decision, but more likely because of illness or some other extraneous factor. However, Justice Gwynne once questioned the propriety of sitting on appeal from his own decision and refused to do so, though he subsequently did resume the practice.

Judges of the Supreme Court of Canada, from its inception in 1875 until the appointment of Christopher Salmon Patterson on

Christopher Salmon Patterson
Justice of the Supreme Court 1888-1893
(National Archives of Canada, Neg. No. PA27280)

First Supreme Court Building, used by the Court from 1881 to 1946. It was erected in 1874-75 as the Board of Works Workshop, designed by Thomas Seaton Scott and demolished in the 1950s.

Interior of first Supreme Court Building
(National Archives of Canada, Neg. No. PA27195)

2 October 1888, generally did not question the propriety of sitting on an appeal from their own decisions. Patterson, prior to his appointment, sat for four years as a judge on the Ontario Court of Appeal. In 1889 Sir John Thompson, Macdonald's minister of justice, introduced a bill to amend the Supreme and Exchequer Court Act, one section of which provided that no judge whose judgment was being appealed should sit or take part in hearing such an appeal and where, as a consequence of this provision, a judge was unable to sit, the quorum would be reduced to four. On second reading, Thompson explained why this provision was introduced: "the learned judge [C.S. Patterson] who has recently come to that court, having heard a large number of cases in the Appeal Court in Toronto, held that he should not sit on hearing appeals, and he was obliged to sit for lack of any provision of the law to relieve him." Thompson, however, indicated that he "had the benefit of communicating with the learned judge, and I understand this is not his view, and that he thinks legislation of this kind is not necessary."[12] Consequently, Thompson withdrew the section. However, it was reinstated by the Senate.

J.J.C. Abbott, government leader in the Senate, indicated that it had been struck by the Commons because there was fear that "this provision might be taken as offensive in some degree to some of the gentlemen on the bench of that court." Abbott then indicated that the cabinet had reconsidered and said, "On further reflection, and on conference with advocates practising in the court and the judges themselves, it has been determined by my colleagues that in their opinion it would be an advantage to have the clause replaced." Abbott moved that the clause be reinserted and commented that

> in Lower Canada it has always been our law that no judge could sit in judgment in appeal on a case on which he had given a decision. It is thought that the natural disposition of a man to adhere to an opinion that he has given is so strong that it is an influence to which suitors ought not to be subject in appealing to a higher court; but I believe it has not been the rule in Ontario. Now, it seems that the universal consensus of opinion of the Bench and members of the Bar, who have been seen in reference to the matter, is that it is expedient to create this disqualification against a judge who originally delivered the judgment.[13]

The Commons accepted the amendment and the act received royal assent.

The insertion, withdrawal and reinsertion of the provision that a judge of the Supreme Court of Canada should not sit on an appeal from his own decision indicated the minister of justice, cabinet and legislature did not perceive that there was a necessary denial of natural justice. Surprisingly, Justices Fournier and H.E. Taschereau, in spite of a Quebec civil law tradition to the contrary, thought it permissible to sit on appeals from their own Exchequer Court decisions and did so; the early Quebec judges, when appointed to the Supreme Court of Canada, readily accepted the common law tradition. The early Ontario judges Richards, Strong and Gwynne might also have been expected to object to such a procedure. A statute of Upper Canada passed in 1794 provided that a judge whose judgment was under appeal might give his reasons but "he shall not be at liberty to give his vote in the decision before the Court."[14] But more significantly, in 1874 Ontario had enacted that "No Judge of that Court against whose judgment, decree or decision any error is assigned or appeal brought, shall sit or take part in the hearing of or adjudication upon the proceedings in Error and Appeal, in case such judge took part in the hearing in the court below."[15] Instead of recognizing that the Ontario statute embodied the principle that courts should scrupulously avoid any reasonable apprehension of bias, the statute apparently was considered only a special rule imposed on Ontario courts. It was possible that Patterson saw the Ontario legislation in a broader context.

How did Ritchie perceive the issue of sitting on an appeal from his own decision? There was no New Brunswick legislation comparable to that of Ontario which might have sensitized his judicial conscience. In addition, New Brunswick had no separate Court of Appeal, so appeals from trial court judgments were simply taken to the full court. It was customary for the trial judge to sit on the appeal from his own decision, and this Ritchie did while on the New Brunswick bench.

For example, Ritchie tried the case of *Humphreys* v. *Helmes*, (1861),[16] an action for trespass and for cutting down and carrying away trees. The defendant was the heir of the original grantee of the wilderness land, but it had been conveyed without authority by the father of the original grantee and had subsequently been purchased by the plaintiff, who was in possession. The issue was what significance should be attached to registered deeds. Ritchie instructed the jury that what would constitute continuous possession was different for a party who relied on a claim of possession under a registered deed than for a person without title or claim of title. The jury found for the plaintiff. On an appeal to the full court, Ritchie's direction to the jury was upheld by a bare majority of three to two, with Ritchie himself constituting the majority. Ritchie, in his judgment, stated that he adhered to the opinion that he expressed at trial. However, if Ritchie had not participated the court would have split evenly and Ritchie's trial decision would have been upheld anyway.

The practice of hearing an appeal from one's trial decision continued in New Brunswick until the legislature amended the Judicature Act in 1913 by inserting a new section which provided that "no Judge shall sit as a Judge on a hearing of an appeal from any judgment or order made by himself, and no Judge shall sit on the hearing of any motion for a new trial in any cause or matter tried before himself, with or without a jury."[17] The judiciary of New Brunswick may already have concluded that the practice was inappropriate and recommended the change to the legislature.

Although the chief justice together with the puisne justices of the Supreme Court of Canada did sit singly as judges of the Exchequer Court until 1887, there was no reported case in which an Exchequer Court decision rendered by Ritchie was appealed. Thus Ritchie never had to face the issue of the propriety of sitting on an appeal from his own judgment while on the Supreme Court of Canada. The quality of Ritchie's judgments may have discouraged the losing litigant from appealing, or the lack of an appeal may have been fortuitous given the small number of reported cases in which there was an appeal, or Ritchie may have tried fewer Exchequer Court cases than did the puisne justices.

One notable case tried by the chief justice in the Exchequer Court was *The Queen* v. *J.C. Ayer Co.* (1887). The J.C. Ayer Co., a manufacturer of proprietary medicines in the United States, established a branch in Quebec and openly imported liquid compounds, paying duty at the fair market value at the time of importation. Subsequently the ingredients were mixed, bottled and sold in Canada and had they been imported in the final form, higher duty would have been levied. The customs authorities in Montreal seized large quantities of the company's patent medicines and alleged that the company had evaded the payment of duty. Ritchie branded this contention as "monstrous" and held that the form in which material was first imported determined the duty. The case caused considerable controversy because Ritchie was very critical of the customs officials. He insisted that in discharging their public duty they should do justice both to the crown and to importers. They "should not act, as their conduct would seem to indicate in this case, as partizans having a deep pecuniary interest in the result, and with an apparent determination to effect, at all hazards, a condemnation."[18] This was the exemplary case used by one commentator who maintained that Ritchie was not only an able and impartial judge but that "he was a fearless Judge, and little disposed to be influenced by the question of expediency. *Fiat justitia, ruat coelum*, was his motto — 'let justice be done though the heavens should fall.'"[19] Although customs officials were very unhappy with the result in the *Ayer* case, no appeal occurred.

A judge hearing an appeal from his own judgment virtually became a judge in his own cause. He had to assess the intellectual merit of his own judgment. There must be reasonable apprehension of bias in such a circumstance, for it was unlikely that he would deviate from his trial decision, as the table shows. In *The Queen* v. *McLeod*, Justice Henry, wishing to convey the idea that he retained an open mind, said:

> I have considered this case very fully, to some extent before I gave my judgment in the Exchequer Court, and since very fully, with a view to changing my opinion, if I could do so conscientiously, and coming to the same conclusion as my learned brothers. I have not been able to do so, but, on the contrary, consider that the verdict I gave in the first place is the right one.[20]

Some judges can retain on appeal an open mind about issues that they have decided at trial. A striking example occurred in *McLean* v. *McKay* (1873). The Judge in equity, James W. Johnston, the uncle of W. J. Ritchie, held at trial that McLean was entitled in equity to an order requiring the removal of a structure from adjacent land, where the vendor had agreed that such land "should never be sold, but left for the common benefit of both parties and their successors." There was an appeal to the Nova Scotia Supreme Court and Justice Johnston sat with four other judges to hear an appeal from his own judgment. Two judges including J. W. Ritchie, the brother of W. J. Ritchie, thought the clause invalid, being in their opinion a perpetual restriction on the sale of land. The decision thus lay with the trial judge himself and he rendered a judgment reversing himself. However, on an appeal to the Privy Council, the appellate decision was reversed and the trial decision restored. Sir Montague E. Smith speaking for the Privy Council said: "Their Lordships regret that the learned Judge should have found occasion to change the opinion to which he had originally come, for after full discussion of the case, their Lordships are of the opinion that his first judgment was right in its reasoning and sound in its conclusion."[21]

Some judges were open minded and did possess sufficient humility to be influenced by contrary opinions of other judges expressed in the course of an appeal, although no judge ever questioned his Exchequer Court decision in the Supreme Court of Canada. In any event, what was important was not only impartiality but also maintaining the appearance of impartiality. As Chief Justice Laskin, dissenting in *Law Society of Upper Canada* v. *French* (1974), said: "The key issue is surely impartiality, to be evidenced not by *post-facto* review of proceedings to determine whether there was bias in fact but by a scrupulous *a priori* regard for any reasonable apprehension of bias or of interest."[22]

The early judges of the Supreme Court of Canada deserved criticism for not being sufficiently sensitive to the possibility of bias and certainly to the appearance of bias. Criticism of the Supreme Court should, however, be tempered by an appreciation that judicial ethics evolve through time and cannot be judged only by present-day standards. After all, as late as 1951 in England in *R.* v. *Lovegrove*, a person convicted by Justice Lynskey at the Bedford assizes found that the same judge was one of the three judges sitting on his appeal. The chief justice, Lord Goddard, did not seem to believe that this was a serious problem and said:

> There are cases in which, no doubt, it would be desirable that the trial judge should not sit, but where the ground of appeal is nothing but an argument by the appellant that the verdict was wrong there is no reason whatever why the trial judge should not sit. In fact, it might be very useful sometimes that he should.[23]

Notes to Chapter 15

1. New Brunswick Museum, Webster Collection, 157-4.

2. (1863), 10 N.B.R. 577 at p. 588.

3. (1868), 7 N.S.R. 173 at p. 177.

4. (1864), 11 N.B.R. 141 at p. 143.

5. (1869), 12 N.B.R. 443 at p. 452.

6. (1869), 12 N.B.R. 341 at pp. 354-5.

7. Ibid., p. 368.

8. (1884), 11 S.C.R. 113 at p. 116.

9. (1892) A.C. 437 at p. 441.

10. (1983), 43 Nfld. & P.E.I.R. 320 at p. 324.

11. J.O. Wilson, *A Book for Judges* (Ottawa: Supply and Services Canada, 1980), p. 26.

12. Commons, *Debates* 22 March 1889, p. 787.

13. Senate, *Debates* 3 Apr. 1889, p. 403.

14. An Act to establish a Superior Court of Civil and Criminal Jurisdiction, and to Regulate the Court of Appeal, S.O. 1794, c.2, s.34.

15. An Act to make further provision for the due Administration of Justice, S.O. 1874, c.7, s.9.

16. (1861), 10 N.B.R. 59.

17. S.N.B. 1913, c.23, s.4.

18. (1887), 1 Ex.C.R. 232 at p. 287. An appeal was filed in this case, file numbers 802 and 803, however, it was discontinued on 20 December 1888. See Louis William Coutlée, *A Collection of Notes of Unreported Cases in the Supreme Court of Canada* (Toronto: Carswell, 1907), p. 88.

19. Lawrence, *Judges of New Brunswick*, p. 497.

20. (1883), 8 S.C.R. 1 at p. 64.

21. (1873), L.R. 5 P.C. 327 at p. 330.

22. (1975) 2 S.C.R. 767 at pp. 771-72.

23. (1951) 1 All E.R. 804 at p. 805.

CHAPTER 16

Collision with the Courts of British Columbia

The case of *Re Sproule* (1886) illustrated how the lack of a consistent legal philosophy not only caused friction on the Court but could have much wider implications. In 1886 there was an extraordinary clash of judicial authority between Justice Henry of the Supreme Court of Canada and the full bench of the British Columbia Supreme Court, with the sheriff of Vancouver Island caught in the crossfire.[1]

In June 1885 Robert Evan Sproule was charged with a murder committed near Kootenay Lake, British Columbia. He was tried at Victoria, found guilty, and sentenced to death. A writ of error was heard by the full bench of the B.C. Supreme Court, including Justice Gray, the trial judge. All five judges unanimously rejected all of the alleged errors. As section 49 of the Supreme and Exchequer Courts Act provided that no appeal should lie "where the court affirming the conviction is unanimous," it seemed that Sproule's judicial remedies had been exhausted. However, his counsel, Theodore Davie, relied on section 51 of the same act which said:

> Any Judge of the Supreme Court shall have concurrent jurisdiction with the Courts or Judges of the several Provinces, to issue the writ of Habeas Corpus *ad subjiciendum*, for the purpose of an enquiry into the cause of commitment, in any criminal case under any Act of the Parliament of Canada.

Sproule's counsel made a *habeas corpus* application before Justice Henry. It was an excellent tactical choice because Henry had, in the *Trepanier* case,[2] indicated his belief that judges of the Supreme Court not only had the power but the duty to go behind a conviction to insure that the party had been legally convicted.

Henry ordered the sheriff for Vancouver Island to show cause why *habeas corpus* should not issue. Consistent with the majority decision in the *Trepanier* case, Henry held that if the prisoner had been tried and convicted by a court possessing the necessary jurisdiction he could not interfere. However, he was intent on minutely examining every link in the chain constituting jurisdiction. He found the order for a change of venue from the Kootenays to Victoria to be a weak link. The legislature had provided that such orders should only be made conditional upon payment of any additional expense thereby caused. The initial order issued by Chief Justice Begbie had omitted this condition, but Begbie's bench book showed that he provided for the additional expense. The subsequent order, Henry said, was "intended to supply what was considered to be a fatal defect in the previous one."[3] Henry held that the trial of the prisoner was improperly and illegally removed to Victoria because the first order was defective and the subsequent order was not made until after the trial. Henry also found that the lieutenant-governor had no authority to issue a commission to hold court in a matter of criminal procedure. Accordingly, he ordered the sheriff to deliver Sproule to him at his chambers in Ottawa to be discharged.

This placed the sheriff in an exceedingly difficult situation. Required to hold the prisoner under a death sentence of a competent court, confirmed by the full bench of the British Columbia Supreme Court, he was now ordered by a single judge sitting in chambers to deliver the prisoner to Ottawa for a discharge. The attorney general of B.C. drafted a return in the name of the sheriff, declining to produce the prisoner and stating that the affirmed conviction was paramount to the writ of *habeas corpus* and that the costs for the conveyance of the prisoner to Ottawa had not been received or tendered. Counsel for the prisoner then applied to Henry for an order that the sheriff's return was insufficient and that the prisoner be discharged. Henry concluded that the return was not in the handwriting of the sheriff and stated: "Whoever wrote that endorsement seems to be of opinion that a sheriff — a Queen's officer — can refuse to execute the Queen's writ, and usurp judicial authority to decide as to the validity of the writ."[4]

On 6 August 1886 Henry ordered the sheriff to discharge the prisoner rather than deliver him to Ottawa. The attorney general of B.C. then applied to the Supreme Court of Canada to have the writ of *habeas corpus* quashed on the ground that it had been issued improvidently. Chief Justice Ritchie was on his annual holiday with his family in New Brunswick. The deputy minister of justice,

George Burbidge, contacted him and a special session of the court was arranged for 1 September 1886 to cope with the escalating controversy.

Five judges sat for the first four days of September 1886 to sort out this clash of judicial power between Justice Henry and the British Columbia Supreme Court. There was considerable attention paid to the two change of venue orders issued by Chief Justice Begbie. During argument, Justice Strong with his usual penchant for stirring up trouble, was reported by the press to have said: "It is a dreadful thing to do, after a man has been tried and sentenced, that an order should be altered, and if I had done it I think I had laid myself open to impeachment." The Supreme Court moved very expeditiously and nine days later handed down its judgment on 13 September 1886. By a three to two majority it quashed the *habeas corpus* order, with Henry and Fournier dissenting.

Ritchie held that the writ had been issued out of the Court and therefore the Court had an inherent right to judge the regularity or abuse of its process. He also noted that section 51 of the Supreme and Exchequer Courts Act empowered Supreme Court judges to issue the writ of *habeas corpus,* but only "for the purpose of an enquiry into the cause of commitment in any criminal case under any Act of the Parliament of Canada." As this was prior to the enactment of the federal Criminal Code, murder was a common law offence and not an offence under any act of the Parliament of Canada. Ritchie questioned why such a limitation was imposed by Parliament. Indeed, it was anomalous because it deprived those people charged with the most serious crimes, and therefore perhaps in the greatest need of protection, from obtaining a writ of *habeas corpus,* at least from a Supreme Court of Canada judge. However, Ritchie held that "the legislature having limited the jurisdiction we are bound to give effect to that limitation."[5] Therefore Henry had no authority to issue the writ. But should that conclusion be incorrect, Ritchie then considered whether Henry was justified in issuing the writ. He found it unnecessary to decide whether it was the lieutenant-governor or the governor general who should issue a commission for holding of an assize, because the holding of such a court was clearly authorized by provincial legislation. This decision avoided the chaos which would have resulted had the sittings of these British Columbia courts been ruled invalid.

With respect to the change of venue to Victoria, Ritchie said that the judge had the power to change the place of trial: "The order said to have been signed in the first instance was a good and sufficient order for that purpose, as was the order which appears on the record." Ritchie held that Henry had no authority to go behind the record of a superior court which must be "treated as absolute verity so long as it stood unreversed." He was clearly disturbed that the administration of the criminal law might be paralysed by a single judge of a superior court using the writ of *habeas corpus* to review and nullify a judgment of superior courts. This he thought would be "subversive of all law and order." He said that he had "an abiding confidence that the laws of this Dominion have not entrusted to any single judge, however high his legal status, a jurisdiction fraught with such dreadful consequences."[6]

Although during argument Strong had firmly implied that substituting the second order for a change of venue for the first was so reprehensible that it might justify impeachment of Chief Justice Begbie, he, like Ritchie held that the writ of *habeas corpus* should be quashed. Begbie had been greatly incensed by any suggestion that he had acted improperly. In Begbie's view, there was simply a formal defect in the first order, a failure to record the condition about the crown undertaking to bear any additional cost that the trial judge might think just. This condition he had in fact made and noted in his bench book at the time of the first order. Strong wrote: "We are bound to consider the record as importing absolute verity, and the order must, therefore, be assumed to have been actually made on the day it bears date."[7] It is unlikely that Strong's decision would undo the aspersion upon his judicial integrity felt by Chief Justice Begbie. Strong had implied that Begbie's conduct could not be challenged simply because there was a rule that one could not go behind the record of a superior court. Taschereau said that he was "perfectly satisfied" that the "prisoner in this case has had a fair and legal trial."[8]

Both Ritchie and Taschereau tried to calm the judicial waters that had been stirred up by Henry's compelling but undisciplined desire to right every wrong. Strong's ill-considered interjection had only added waves to the storm. The majority recognized that there had to be limitations upon the writ of *habeas corpus* and that it could not be used to circumvent the ordinary appeal procedure in criminal cases without creating chaos. The *Sproule* case remained a leading case on the availability and limitations of the writ of *habeas corpus*, even though since 1970 the concurrent jurisdiction of the Supreme Court of Canada to hear *habeas corpus* applications has been abolished. It illustrated how divergent legal views of some members of the court could embroil it in controversy. It also illustrated the capacity of the court to recover expeditiously from such controversy, and considerable credit for that was due to Ritchie's sound judgment.

Notes to Chapter 16

1. For an exhaustive and fascinating account of this case, see Wilbur F. Bowker, "The Sproule Case: Bloodshed at Kootenay Lake, 1885," in Louis A. Knafla, ed., *Law and Justice in a New Land: Essays in Western Canadian Legal History* (Toronto: Carswell, 1986), pp. 233-66.

2. *Re Melina Trepanier* (1885), 12 S.C.R. 111.

3. (1886), 12 S.C.R. 140 at p. 154.

4. Ibid., pp. 171, 173.

5. Ibid., p. 185.

6. Ibid., pp. 192, 194, 201-2.

7. Ibid., pp. 206-7.

8. Ibid., p. 250; the scholarly authority on this subject remains Robert J. Sharpe, *The Law of Habeas Corpus* (Oxford: Clarendon Press, 1976; 2nd ed., 1990).

CHAPTER 17

The Ritchie Court, its Critics and Character

Legal journals recorded regular complaints about a perceived lack of consultation among the justices. This concern largely resulted from the tendency to issue multiple judgments in most cases. Judges of the House of Lords, the Supreme Court of the United States and Canadian appellate courts were free to write either concurring or dissenting opinions. Nevertheless, in the United States, beginning during John Marshall's term, that court usually rendered one majority judgment, together with any dissents. In New Brunswick when the Supreme Court sat *en banc*, it too customarily rendered one judgment, often written by the chief justice. Controversial cases could result in multiple majority decisions and dissents, but these were exceptional. Why judges of the Supreme Court of Canada almost invariably wrote multiple majority decisions until relatively recently cannot be answered. The Court might have consciously modelled itself on the House of Lords, where multiple judgments prevailed, and not on the Privy Council, which always issued a uniform "advice" to the queen in each case. The lack of cooperation and consultation among the judges, and the initially small case load, might have been factors. However, it appeared that Canadian lawyers had been spoiled by the single opinions written by the Privy Council. Bemoaning the multiplicity of decisions from Ottawa, and the resulting difficulty of establishing the ratios of the cases, the *Canada Law Journal* observed: "How notably different is their course from that which obtains in the other court of ultimate appeal for the colony (the Privy Council) where one judge alone clearly and fully gives the decision of the Court."[1]

It was thought that the single opinion created certainty, even though the one unanimous opinion may only have been achieved by glossing over difficulties and suppressing differences. The issue of whether the Supreme Court should render only one judgment arose in the House of Commons on an amendment to the Supreme Court Act in 1891 requiring judges to give reasons for their decisions in reference cases. Wilfrid Laurier said:

> Is it the settled opinion of the Minister of Justice that a judge should express his dissent when he does dissent? Would he not prefer the system that prevails in other courts, of having the report of the court, and not the opinion of Mr. Justice so-and-so, and so-and-so, who may dissent. In the Privy Council and in the *Cour de Cassation* in France, the question is deliberated upon by the judges — and I presume that they have to settle amongst themselves that the majority must rule — the report is given as the opinion of the court.[2]

However, another member thought that compelling the court to render only one decision would be disadvantageous to the losing litigant.

> Mr. *CAMERON* (Huron). I think that would be a mistake. If this were a court of final resort, and if there was no appeal from it, then the suggestion of the hon. member for Quebec East (Mr. Laurier) would be quite correct; but this is not a court of final resort, and therefore the opinion of the dissenting judge or judges, and their reasons for dissenting, and the authorities upon which they dissent, should be given as a guide to litigants as to whether it would be judicious to appeal or not. In every other court that I know of, from which there is an appeal, the judge who dissents gives his reasons, and as a general rule gives his reasons, perhaps, more fully than the judges in the majority. I do not see any reason why the same rule should not apply to the judgment of this court, when it is not final.[3]

Law Journal (London) wrote critically about the Privy Council's adherence to a single opinion, referring to a Canadian appeal dealing with the issue of the right of a barrister to sue for fees.

> In reading the formal judgment of the Committee, which in style and manner is half-way between the recitals of a French judgment or the note to a Scotch interlocutor and the judgment of an ordinary English Court of law, whether at home or abroad, one is struck with the loss sustained by the prohibition of *seriatim* opinions. On a subject of so much interest the judgments in the Court of Appeal and the House of Lords would have been doubly interesting.[4]

Legal News of Montreal thought that this case should have been finally determined in Canada, but if it had to go to the Privy Council, it regretted the one-opinion rule. It preferred the procedure of the House of Lords and English Court of Appeal, saying,

"We should then have the opinions, seriatim, of judges responsible for their utterances, instead of a rambling note, over which no one but the registrar has an individual influence."[5] The *Canada Law Journal* remained committed to the single judgment and in 1892 said:

> It is most desirable that such a court should (as has before been pointed out) give its judgment *as a court*, without referring to dissenting opinions, if any such there be —in the same way as is done by the Judicial Committee of the Privy Council. If this should necessitate a consultation among the members of the court before the delivery of each judgment (which, as is generally supposed, is not the case at present), no harm would result.[6]

During Ritchie's tenure as chief justice there were fourteen reported cases in which the court split three to three. This averaged out at only one per year during his thirteen-and-a-half year tenure as chief justice. The quorum for the court was five and in many cases the full court of six judges did not sit owing to the illness or absence of one of the judges. Thus, when the full court sat, the three/three splits were not that rare an occurrence. These even splits represent some evidence that conferences to thrash out difficult issues presented to the court either did not occur or were frequently unsuccessful. The three/three splits must have been disturbing to the prevailing positivist tradition of the common law. In the light of these splits, it became more difficult to contend that judges simply applied rules in a scientific way to the facts of a case, and thus produced an impersonal result. The three/three splits led to uncertainty in the law. The litigant who had succeeded in the court below would win, but reasons for judgment which justified that result were now highly doubtful because they had failed to win acceptance by a majority in the Supreme Court and no new rationale had been substituted.

Column two of the accompanying table indicates that the even split did not occur with regard to a particular kind of case but arose across the full spectrum of cases which the Supreme Court of Canada heard: contracts, torts and public law. The even splits also reasonably represented the volume of cases flowing to it from the various courts with six from Ontario, six from Quebec, one from New Brunswick and one from the Exchequer Court.

Poitras v. *LeBeau*(1888)[7] warrants attention because of the unusual nature of the dispute. It resulted from the failure of Hermas Poitras to kneel on both knees whilst high mass was being

Three/Three Splits in the Supreme Court of Canada During Ritchie's Term as Chief Justice (1879-1892)

Citation	Type of Case	Source of Appeal	Judges Upholding Judgment	Judges Wishing to Reverse
McLeod v New Brunswick Railway Co. (1880), 5 S.C.R. 281	Interpretation of a lease	N.B.S.C.	S, T, G	R, F, H
Coté v Morgan (1881), 7 S.C.R. 1	Public Law availability of writ of prohibition	Q. B. Que. (Appeal Side)	H, T, G	R, S, F
McCallum v Odette (1882), 7 S.C.R. 36	Maritime tort	Maritime Ct. of Ont.	R, F, T	S, H, G
Megantic Election Case (1883), 8 S.C.R. 169	Election case	Superior Ct. Que.	F, H, G	R, S, T
Milloy v Kerr (1880), 8 S.C.R. 474	Warehouse receipt and insolvency	Ont. C. A.	S, T, G	R, F, H
Shields v Peak (1883), 8 S.C.R. 579	Purchase of goods and insolvency	Ont. C. A.	R, F, G	S, H, T
Poulin v Corporation of Quebec (1884), 9 S.C.R. 185	Liquor licence offence	Q. B. Que. (Appeal Side)	R, S, F	H, T, G

Case	Subject	Court		
Giraldi v LaBanque Jacques-Cartier (1883), 9 S.C.R. 597	Creditor-debtor	Q. B. Que. (Appeal Side)	S, T, G	R, F, H
Trust and Loan Co. v Lavrason (1882), 10 S.C.R. 679	Mortgage and distraint	Ont. C. A.	S, F, H	R, T, G
Mackinnon v Keroack (1887), 15 S.C.R. 111	Fraudulent preference	Q. B. Que. (Appeal Side)	R, F, T	S, H, G
Poitras v LeBeau (1888), 14 S.C.R. 742	Malicious prosecution	Q. B. Que. (Appeal Side)	R, S, T	F, H, G
Lynch v Seymour (1888), 15 S.C.R. 341	Interpretation of lease or licence	Ont. C. A.	S, F, G	R, H, T
McQueen v The Queen (1887), 16 S.C.R. 1	Interpretation of deed	Ex. Ct.	R, S, G	F, H, T
Grand Trunk Railway v Beckett (1887), 16 S.C.R. 713	Negligence and contributory negligence	Ont. C. A.	R, F, H	S, T, G

R = W.J. Ritchie   S = S.H. Strong   F = T. Fournier   H = W.A. Henry   T = H.E. Taschereau   G = J.W. Gwynne celebrated at the Church of St. Anne, Bout de L'Isle, on 9 August 1885. He maintained that he had been sick all night and when he attempted to kneel on both knees it caused him pain so he knelt on one knee only. Dolphis LeBeau, a former church warden, requested him to kneel on both knees to which Poitras replied that he was sick and LeBeau retorted that he would take him to a doctor after mass. At the conclusion of the service Poitras disclosed his name and LeBeau said he was a blackguard and he would fix him. Later that same afternoon Poitras was arrested by a bailiff who had a warrant for his arrest for having committed an irreverent act in kneeling on one knee only. He decided to accompany the bailiff but his wife and friends persuaded him to put an end to the matter by paying the amount the bailiff requested. Poitras paid the penalty of $8.20 under protest but then sued LeBeau for illegally and maliciously instigating the charge of irreverence against him, and sought damages of $2,000 for injury to his good reputation.

A trial by jury found that the plaintiff, Poitras, had not suffered any damage but some findings made by the jury appeared contradictory. The plaintiff appealed and the Court of Review ordered a new trial. The defendant appealed and the Court of Queen's Bench allowed the appeal and quashed the order for a new trial. The plaintiff appealed to the Supreme Court for a new trial. Justice Henry held that "anyone who went into a Catholic chapel would find a picture of St. Andrew with his hand on a staff and resting on one knee and if it were not an act of irreverence for St. Andrew to be represented in that position he did not see that the appellant acted irreverently in kneeling as he did."[8] Henry thought that the judgment of the court below should be reversed and a new trial granted, as did Fournier and Gwynne. However, Ritchie, unreceptive to the plaintiff's action for malicious prosecution, held that "Had the plaintiff wished to contest this matter and to show that he was guilty of no offence for which he was answerable to the law, he should have done so before the justice, the proper judge, having jurisdiction to try the merits of the case: if the merits were not tried it was by reason of the plaintiff's own voluntary conduct, and from which, if he has suffered any inconvenience, he has only himself to blame."[9] Strong and Taschereau also refused to order a new trial. As the court split three to three, the judgment of the lower court refusing to grant the plaintiff a new trial prevailed.

Like *Johnston* v. *The Minister and Trustees of St. Andrew's Church*(1877), a case the Court decided early in its history, which involved the right of a person to occupy a church pew, *Poitras* v. *LeBeau* might be regarded as an example of the insignificant issues the Court considered in its early years. However, religion occupied a very prominent place in nineteenth-century Canadian life and arbitrary and insensitive conduct on the part of church officials was keenly felt. Poitras thought he had been badly treated by LeBeau and thus it was important for him to have a forum to air his deeply felt grievance. Perhaps the three Quebec courts should have been sufficient. However, Ritchie's lack of sympathy for Poitras might not have stemmed from a belief that this dispute was too unimportant for the Supreme Court but because he thought Poitras was partly the author of the unfortunate incident. Had Ritchie been in the position of Poitras, his dogged nature would probably have caused him to refuse to pay the fine and to challenge the whole matter initially rather than permitting it to fester. This may have influenced Ritchie's decision.

Since these fourteen cases caused the judges particular difficulty, a look at their voting pattern is suggested. It is admittedly a small number of cases but it does include all the cases in which there was an even split. If there were no forces at work which would influence their voting pattern, one would expect, in fourteen cases in which the court divided evenly, that each judge would concur with each of his fellow judges 5.6 times and dissent 8.4 times (ratio of 2 to 3 adding to 14). The table, however, reveals that Ritchie and Gwynne concurred with one another in only three cases and thus dissented in eleven.

	Pattern of Concurrences, 1880-1887					
	Ritchie	*Strong*	*Fournier*	*Henry*	*Taschereau*	*Gwynne*
Ritchie		5	9	5	6	3
Strong	5		4	4	7	8
Fournier	9	4		8	3	4
Henry	5	4	8		5	6
Taschereau	6	7	3	5		7
Gwynne	3	8	4	6	7	

This marked departure from a random distribution appears significant. Ritchie and Gwynne took diametrically opposite sides in a controversy that erupted in St. George's Church about the authority of the rector and the table suggests that their approach to law must have been equally divergent. An equally marked and interesting divergence occurred in the voting pattern of Fournier and Taschereau. They concurred with one another in only three cases and thus dissented in eleven. This indicates that the different approach between the common law and the civil law of Quebec was not one of the major factors in contributing to the even splits in the Supreme Court, for the two civilian jurists tended to vote differently from one another. The different political views held by Fournier and Taschereau may have coloured their perception of legal rights. Fournier had been a leader of the *parti rouge* or Liberal party in Lower Canada. He possessed a scrappy disposition. At a time when he combined newspaper work and law, he had fought a duel and later as a member of Alexander Mackenzie's cabinet he engaged in a barroom brawl which tarnished his reputation with his dour leader. He was, however, an able lawyer and had become a leader of the Quebec bar. Henri Elzéar Taschereau had represented the county of Beauce in the old united Parliament of Canada from 1861 to 1867 and was a *bleu* or Conservative who generally supported Macdonald, except with regard to confederation, which he believed failed to offer sufficient guarantees for French Canadians. He was a refined scholar who had written several legal treatises. Fournier and Taschereau were very different in temperament and it was not surprising that this coloured their perceptions of the law. Even with regard to the six appeals from Quebec among the even splits, they concurred with each other only once.

The table also indicates that Fournier concurred only four times with Strong and also only four times with Gwynne. Strong was the exception among the early judges of the Supreme Court in not having held a political office or been a political candidate. However, he had a reputation for being a Tory and a confidant of Macdonald and other conservative politicians. John Wellington Gwynne was not a member of the original Supreme Court but was appointed to fill the Ontario vacancy caused by Chief Justice Richards's resignation in 1879. This vacancy gave Sir John A. Macdonald his first opportunity to make an appointment to the Supreme Court. Gwynne, his appointee, had spent a number of years as solicitor for the Great Western Railway in Hamilton and then had carried on a commercial practice in Toronto before being appointed to the Court of Common Pleas by Macdonald in 1867. In 1847 Gwynne, as a relatively young man, had run unsuccessfully in Huron County for a seat in the Legislative Assembly as a reformer. The fact that he was twice sought out for judicial preferment by Macdonald indicates that his political views may have become more conservative with age. Fournier, a federal Liberal cabinet minister, probably had little in common with either Strong or Gwynne and therefore it is not surprising that he differed from each of them in eleven of the fourteen cases. The only other significant divergence which the table reveals is that William Alexander Henry and Samuel Strong concurred with one another only four times. Strong disliked Henry and held his legal ability in such low regard that he wrote to Macdonald in an effort to get rid of Henry. Whether this personal antagonism influenced their voting pattern or whether it resulted from a different philosophy about law cannot be determined. The other differences in voting pattern would all appear to be within a range that would be expected, given the small number of cases considered.

The Supreme Court of Canada continued to have a number of critics during the Ritchie era. Some thought it an unnecessary expense. Ontario critics generally thought that their own Court of Appeal was competent and doubted that a court remote from the stimulation of a large and active bar would prove as good as the courts centred in Toronto. French Canadians feared that a court with only two civilian lawyers out of six would be less capable than Quebec's own Cour d'Appel. The prevalence of the criticism has led some commentators to conclude that the quality of early decisions must have been a source of this discontent. For example, Snell and Vaughan argued that the early constitutional judgments of the Supreme Court of Canada were reasonably good but that the Court's quality was not apparent in other areas of the law.[10]

This was not altogether persuasive and their evidence was weak. The authors appeared to be in a dilemma of their own making: they wished to accord general approval to the constitutional law decisions of the Supreme Court, because they preferred the more centralist interpretation of the constitution to the provincial bias of the Privy Council, but they were unwilling to reject the traditional view of a weak Court. Peter Russell might be closer to the mark when he attributed the early discontent "more on the Court's anticipated performance than on its actual performance."[11] The court displayed more than reasonable competence overall, taking into account the state of legal education and the dearth of scholarly criticism.

Snell and Vaughan selected *R. v. McLeod* (1883) as the case to reveal that the "intellectual quality" of the Supreme Court was not high. In this case a passenger who sustained injury in a derailment sued the crown for negligent operation of the Prince Edward Island Railway, which was owned by Canada and was under the management of the minister of railways and canals. Had the railway been operated by a private company, it would have been liable because the roadbed was "in a most unsafe state from the rottenness of the ties" and "the safety of life had been recklessly jeopardized by running trains over it."[12] In the Exchequer Court, Juctice Henry held the crown liable because the claim was not founded solely on negligence but also upon breach of contract for safe carriage. Henry said

> a contract to carry safely was by legal implication entered into in this case, and unless it can be found that Her Majesty in all cases of contract is above the law, I cannot arrive at the conclusion that because the injuries complained of were caused by the bad management, unskilfulness or negligence of those entrusted with the working of the railway, the suppliant must be denied redress.[13]

In essence the only issue that confronted the Court was whether crown immunity was an available defence. The Supreme Court split four to two, reversed Henry's decision, and held that the crown was not liable.

Ritchie refused to find a contract for safe carriage and said that the only evidence of any contract was that McLeod paid his fare and received a ticket which read "Ticket, P.E.I. Railway, first class, Charlottetown to Souris and return. August 25th, 1880." He considered that it indicated "neither more nor less than that the holder had paid his toll and was entitled to passage between the points indicated." Ritchie considered that government railways, like the Post Office, were "created by statute for purposes of public convenience, and not entered upon or to be treated as private mercantile speculations". An old railway advocate, he considered the Intercolonial Railway and the P.E.I. Railway to be "a great public undertaking essential to the consolidation of the union of British North America"[14] and stated that:

> being thus established for public purposes, it is subordinate to those principles of public policy which prevents the Crown

being responsible for the misfeasances, wrongs, negligences, or omissions of duty of the subordinate officers or agents employed in the public service on these public works, and therefore the maxim *respondeat superior* does not apply in the case of the Crown itself, and the Sovereign is not liable for personal negligence, and, therefore, the principle *qui facit per alium facit per se*, which is applied to render the master liable for the negligence of his servant, because this has arisen from his own negligence or imprudence in selecting or retaining a careless servant, is not applicable to the Sovereign, to whom negligence or misconduct cannot be imputed, and for which, if it occurs in fact, the law affords no remedy;[15]

Ritchie indicated that the crown, in relation to the railway, was like a private individual who made an express stipulation that he was not liable for the negligence of his servants. Ritchie then emphasized that the negligent servant was still personally liable to the injured person, and therefore there was nothing unreasonable in freeing the crown from the liability of its servants. Ritchie believed that crown immunity was an important prerogative and said:

To say that these great public works are to be treated as the property of private individuals or corporations, and the Queen, as the head of the government of the country, as a trader or common carrier, and as such chargeable with negligence, and liable therefor, and for all acts of negligence or improper conduct in the employees of the Crown, from the stoker to the Minister of Railways, is simply to ignore all constitutional principles. These prerogatives of the Crown must not be treated as personal to the sovereign; they are great constitutional rights, conferred on the sovereign, upon principles of public policy, for the benefit of the people, and not, as it is said, "for the private gratification of the sovereign" — they form part of and are generally speaking "as ancient as the law itself."[16]

Ritchie also indicated that in the United States the government could not be sued in an action sounding in tort and was not liable for the tortious acts of its officers.

Ritchie also drew attention to the fact that section 19 of the Petition of Right Act, 1876, gave power to the court to hear petitions of right after a fiat had been granted, subject to the proviso that nothing was to prejudice or limit the prerogative of Her Majesty except as otherwise provided. He added that no remedy was given except as allowed in England prior to the imperial Petitions of Right Act, 1860. In *R. v. McFarlane* (1882) Ritchie had held that in England "a petition will not lie for a claim founded upon a tort on the ground that the Crown can do no wrong."[17]

Ritchie has been severely criticized for this decision in *McLeod*. Snell and Vaughan have said that he made "repeated appeals to 'constitutional principles,' none of which he identified," that he "took a strict constructionist stance" and used "narrow and superficial reasoning."[18] These criticisms do not seem fair. Today we would regard as preferable the dissenting judgment permitting the injured person to recover against the crown. However, in line with the prevailing view of the times, Ritchie clearly identified encouraging the state to undertake public works for the good of all as being of paramount concern. We might not agree with this assessment of the best balance of interests, but it is unfair to characterize it as superficial.

As well, while some might prefer to see a more activist court, eager to remould and reform the law so as to better meet social needs, this was not the nature of nineteenth-century courts (or for that matter courts during the first half of the twentieth century). Ritchie was of the view that the Court "must not attempt to make laws; it must administer the law, constitutional, local, public or private, as it is" and leave the reform of the law to Parliament and the legislatures.[19] The "law application" and "law reform" dichotomy has always been a slippery one, which is not easily drawn; nevertheless, crown immunity was a constitutional principle that could not simply be ignored, and we should not assess Ritchie too harshly for drawing the line where he did.

Perhaps Ritchie should have questioned the legitimacy of subsidizing a public enterprise through the denial of recovery to persons injured by it. Even if a public enterprise was conducted for the benefit of the public and not for commercial gain, an unfair subsidy extracted from negligently injured persons should not be condoned.

Ritchie in *R. v. McLeod* slavishly followed English and American precedent and failed to appreciate that the much larger public sector could justify curtailing crown immunity. Ritchie's judgment in *McLeod* was also certainly less impressive than that of Justice Fournier. On the sale of a railroad ticket, Fournier insisted that "the law engrafts an obligation to convey the passenger with sufficient care, skill and foresight to ensure his safety." He believed that immunity should be confined "to agents in the public service for acts committed in their official capacity, as forming part of the political government of the country." When a government operated a railroad, Fournier maintained it "ceases to exercise its political authority and undertakes an ordinary civil transaction, and in such transaction is not above, but under and subject to the ordinary rules of the common law."[20] Fournier anticipated A.V. Dicey's *Law of the Constitution*, first published in 1885, which emphasized that equality was an important element of the rule of law and government should be under the same law applicable to others because special exemptions lead to unfairness and tyranny. Perhaps rather than chastizing Ritchie for rendering a conventional decision, the emphasis should be on giving credit to Fournier for espousing a greater and better vision for the common law, an even more significant accomplishment for Fournier because he came from Canada's other legal tradition.

We might bear in mind that until 2 August 1946, the United States was not (generally speaking) liable for the torts of its agents. The Federal Torts Claims Act 1946 made that federal government liable for the negligent or wrongful acts or omissions of federal employees, when acting within the scope of their employment "in the same manner and to the same extent as a private individual under like circumstances." The Crown Proceedings Act, 1947 achieved a comparable result for the United Kingdom.

Canada's own Parliament did not sweep away the last vestige of *R. v. McFarlane* and *R. v. McLeod* until 1952, with the passage of its Crown Liability Act. Section 3(1) of the act provided that "The Crown is liable in tort for the damages for which, if it were a private person of full age and capacity, it would be liable a) in respect of a tort committed by a servant of the Crown." To have expected the Supreme Court of Canada to sweep away crown immunity in 1884 was simply too much.

Two years later, the chief justice modified his view on the question of crown immunity, finding that it must not be applied in a purely contractual setting. In *The Windsor and Annapolis Railway Co. v. The Queen and the Western Counties Railway Co.* (1885), certain branch lines and running powers over the Intercolonial Railway were leased to the suppliants by the Government of Canada in September 1871. Some six years later, the superintendent of government railways ejected the suppliants and leased the same line and running powers to the defendant, the Western Counties Railway Company. Justice Gwynne in the Exchequer Court held that the ejectment of the suppliant was a tortious act for which a petition of right did not lie. On appeal Ritchie, with Strong and Gwynne dissenting, concluded that although the crown thought it had the right to terminate the lease, it did not. The case was one to which the petition of right was applicable. Ritchie stated:

> It must be admitted that the maxim that the Queen can do no wrong does not apply to breaches of contract entered into by the Crown. To turn, then, the deliberate and advised action of the Crown on its construction of this agreement into a simple tort by an officer of the Crown would be to make the maxim applicable to breaches of contract as well as torts, and in my humble opinion to enable a salutory prerogative to be used for the perpetration of the greatest injustice.[21]

While the crack made in the notion of crown immunity in this case may have been progressive, it made Ritchie vulnerable to attack because he was a former railway lawyer. When an ordinary citizen had been injured, the crown was not liable, but when a railway was the plaintiff the crown became liable. Ritchie, however, might better be faulted for maintaining the tort/contract dichotomy and not simply for giving preferential treatment to a railway, as he rendered progressive decisions in torts cases, even when the defendant was a railway.

One case still cited today with approval is the *St. Lawrence and Ottawa Railway Co. v. Lett* (1885). Mrs. Lett died when a train moving in reverse struck her carriage. The railway had negligently failed to ring a bell or blow a whistle, did not have a man on the rear of the car and had proceeded at a speed greater than six miles per hour. At trial the jury found the railway company negligent and awarded damages of $5,800, of which $1,500 was apportioned to the husband and the balance divided among the children.

The Queen's Bench Division set aside the verdict but the Ontario Court of Appeal restored the trial judgment. The railway company then appealed to the Supreme Court of Canada. There was no dispute about negligence, so the sole issue was the meaning to be attached to the word "injury" in the statute. It provided that "the Judge or jury may give such damages as they think proportioned to the injury resulting from such death, to the parties respectively for whom and for whose benefit such action has been brought."[22] The railway contended, and Chief Justice Haggarty and Justice Burton accepted in the Ontario Courts,[23] that the loss of the wife and mother, no matter how careful and conscientious she was in managing the household affairs and looking after the children, was still a sentimental loss and not of a sufficient pecuniary character to support an action. Chief Justice Ritchie, in forcefully rejecting this argument advanced by the railway company, said:

> I must confess myself at a loss to understand how it can be said that the care and management of a household by an industrious, careful, frugal and intelligent woman, or the care and bringing up by a worthy loving mother of a family of children, is not a substantial benefit to the husband and children; or how it can be said that the loss of such a wife and mother is not a substantial injury but merely sentimental, is, to my mind, incomprehensible. And if the injury is substantial, the only mode the law could provide for reimbursing the husband and children is by a pecuniary compensation, and so, in my opinion, in the eye of the law, the injury is a pecuniary injury.[24]

Fournier and Henry concurred in the decision of the chief justice but Justices Gwynne and Taschereau refused to attach monetary significance to the services rendered by the average mother and wife. The more reasonable and expansive meaning which Ritchie attached to "injury" in this case may have reflected the fact that he was happily married to an especially capable, intelligent and industrious woman, or that Ritchie himself had become the single parent of two young children when his first wife died. His decision in favour of the children's claims may also have been influenced by the fact that his own mother died when he was five years of age. For one or all of these reasons, he simply could not accept that the death of a wife would not be a great injury to the surviving family members.

Another case in which Ritchie ruled against railway interests was *Grand Trunk Railway Co. v. Vogel* (1886), in which the court had to construe an amendment to the General Railway Act providing that "the company shall not be relieved by any notice, condition or declaration, if the damage arises from any negligence or omission of the company or its servants." It was argued that the statute prohibited only the limitation of liability where there was a public or general notice but did not prevent the railway from limiting its liability by contract. The majority, led by Ritchie, refused to accept this argument and held the legislation prevented the railway from freeing itself from liability by way of contract or otherwise. Ritchie said: "To limit the clause as contended for would, in my opinion, entirely frustrate the intention of the legislature, or enable the companies to do so with impunity."[25] Strong and Taschereau dissented. Taschereau stated: "Why should parties desirous of making such contracts be deprived of their common law right to do so?"[26] and held that it would require express words to prohibit exculpatory clauses which he did not find in the statute. Ritchie, on the other hand, found this prohibition and by giving it a large liberal construction he manifested his receptivity to the regulatory state. As a proponent of responsible government, the secret ballot and the extension of the franchise, one would expect Ritchie to be respectful of legislative initiatives.

A decision which might have stood the test of time, had it not been overruled by the Privy Council, was *Beatty* v. *North-West Transportation Co.* (1886). Ritchie believed that company directors should behave with absolute integrity towards their shareholders. The case turned on whether a director of the company, who was also a major shareholder, could use his votes at a shareholders' meeting to ratify a breach of his fiduciary duty. The director had sold the company a ship which he personally owned. In a direct and pragmatic judgment Ritchie refused to allow this, saying:

> Is it not somewhat of a mockery to say that this by-law and sale were invalid and bad, and not enforceable against the company as being contrary to the policy of the law by reason of a director entering into the contract for his personal benefit where his personal interests conflicted with the interests of those he was bound to protect, but that it can be set right by a meeting of the shareholders, by a resolution carried by the vote of the director himself against a large majority of the other shareholders? If this can be done how has the conflict between self-interest and integrity ceased?[27]

Ritchie would have refused to allow the ratification unless the interested director had refrained from voting on the issue at the shareholders' meeting.

The Privy Council rejected this view, holding that the shareholders' meeting could ratify such an abuse, and that as a shareholder the defendant had a perfect right to vote on this or any other issue as he pleased. This separation of the roles of shareholder and director, neat in theory, had the unfortunate effect of allowing a majority of directors, who also controlled a majority of the stock, to milk the corporation at the expense of the minority shareholders. Implicitly recognizing this, the Privy Council added the proviso that the dealing could not be "oppressive towards those shareholders who oppose it."[28] This pragmatic addendum destroyed the theoretical neatness. It also meant that while the Privy Council appeared to be upholding the principle of judicial non-interference in corporate affairs, it was in fact inviting examination of the motives and effects of the director's actions to determine whether the dealing was oppressive.[29]

Ritchie's judgment would require judicial examination of the internal affairs of the company, but only to the extent of determining if the director had any interest in the matter. This was a much simpler question than whether the dealing was in the best interests of the company. The latter was a matter of business judgment, arguably best left to the disinterested shareholders. A director who wished to ratify a transaction in which he had an interest would have to convince a majority of the disinterested shareholders that it was in the best interests of the company.[30]

The opinion of the Privy Council possessed an illusory tidiness which contributed to the legal confusion. At least one contemporary was of the opinion that the Privy Council had rendered an "extraordinary decision, wholly unsupported by authority," which was a glaring example of a judgment which "give[s] us inverted equity so adulterated with common law notions that it would require a chemical test to indicate the presence of any legitimate equity doctrine."[31] Statutory intervention has since been required to remedy in part the situation. Ritchie's judgment attacked the real problem directly and would better insure that decisions of the board remained in the best interests of the corporation.[32]

Notes to Chapter 17

1. *Canada Law Journal* 16 (1880), p. 74.

2. Commons, *Debates*, 7 Aug. 1891, pp. 3588-89.

3. Ibid.

4. Quoted in *Legal News* 7 (1884), p. 241.

5. Ibid., p. 265.

6. *Canada Law Journal* 28 (1892), p. 481.

7. (1888), 14 S.C.R. 742. Only a very brief summary of the decision was reported. More details can be found in the NAC, RG 125, vol. 63, file 712.

8. As reported in the *Ottawa Free Press*, 15 Mar. 1888, p. 1.

9. NAC, RG 127, vol. 63, file 712.

10. Snell and Vaughan, *Supreme Court*, pp. 42-43.

11. Russell, *The Supreme Court of Canada*, p. 24.

12. (1883), 8 S.C.R. 1 at p. 6.

13. Ibid., p. 15.

14. Ibid., pp. 22-23.

15. Ibid., pp. 24-25.

16. Ibid., p. 26.

17. (1882), 7 S.C.R. 216, p. 240.

18. Snell and Vaughan, *Supreme Court*, p. 43.

19. (1883), 8 S.C.R. 1 at p. 27.

20. Ibid., 1 at pp. 48, 43, 54.

21. (1885), 10 S.C.R. 335 at pp. 364-65.

22. An Act respecting Compensation to the Families of Persons killed by Accident, and in Duels, R.S.O. 1877, c.128, s.3.

23. (1884), 11 Ont. App. R.1.

24. (1885), 11 S.C.R. 422 at p. 435.

25. (1886), 11 S.C.R. 612 at p. 622.

26. Ibid., p. 638.

27. (1886), 12 S.C.R. 598 at pp. 603-4 rev'd *sub nom. North-West Transportation Co. Ltd.* v. *Beatty* (1887), 12 App. Cas. 589.

28. (1887), 12 App. Cas. 589 at p. 594.

29. See criticism on this point by S.M. Beck, "Corporate Opportunity Revisited" in Jacob S. Ziegel, ed., *Studies in Canadian Company Law* (Toronto: Butterworths, 1973), II particularly p. 236.

30. See ibid. for support for this view. The Privy Council decision has been criticized in Bruce Welling, *Corporate Law in Canada* (Toronto: Butterworths, 1984).

31. A.H. Marsh, *Canada Law Times* 14 (1894), p. 93.

32. Opinions were also written by Henry and Gwynne, who apparently would not have allowed the contract to be ratified under any circumstances. They considered Beatty to be acting as buyer and seller in the same transaction, which was therefore illegal.

CHAPTER 18

The Court's Illusion of Supremacy

Despite the fact that the Ritchie Court made good law in a variety of areas, in judgments that have continued to shape twentieth-century jurisprudence, many Canadians at the time saw no need for the Supreme Court. British nationalists and monarchists placed trust in Queen Victoria's Judicial Committee of the Privy Council. Provincial lawyers and judges preferred to contain and control decisions of law locally, to their own courts of appeal. Criminal law would remain entirely underdeveloped and uncodified until the end of the Ritchie era, so the Court could offer few visible signs of leadership on "law and order" disputes. Canadians were still adjusting to their very recent status as a Dominion. As the struggle to achieve confederation had shown, people remained primarily identified with their own province and only secondarily with the new national structure.

Not surprisingly, the legal communities, particularly in Ontario and Quebec, looked more favourably on the courts in Toronto, Montreal and Quebec City than to the Supreme Court in Ottawa. These regional prejudices began with complaints about the location of the new Court. An 1880 article in the *Canada Law Journal* expressed dismay over the distances between Ottawa and major cities. Advocating removal of the Court to Toronto, the journal noted the advantage to suitors and judges alike of the vast wealth of legal experience and talent around Osgoode Hall. It was also feared that its location would make the country's best legal minds unwilling to accept an appointment to the Court:

> It is unnecessary to dilate upon the results which would flow from an inferiority in point of talent of those composing the Court of last resort. We are not, of course, speaking of those at present on the Bench, but of those who may be appointed after the glamour of the thing has disappeared.[1]

Chief Justice Ritchie and his colleagues faced more significant concerns relating to the "inherent difficulties of our confederation."[2]

Specifically there was uncertainty about the competence of the Court to deliberate on decisions of Quebec courts in civil law matters. Conversely, was a six-person court which included two Quebec judges capable of overturning an Ontario common law decision? Interestingly, some of the strongest questioning came from within the Supreme Court itself. H.E. Taschereau, who had been appointed to replace his cousin, J.-T. Taschereau in 1878, wrote to Prime Minister Macdonald in 1882 stating: "It is obvious that Ontario will not submit any longer to having the decisions of its own Courts reversed by Quebec judges, and that Quebec cannot be expected to consent any longer to having its civil law administered by English law judges." He added:

> Perhaps it would be better to abolish the Court altogether ... the Government would be unfettered by the existing organization, and could establish a Court on a new and more satisfactory basis. As the Court stands, it may never give satisfaction.[3]

The Supreme Court of Canada had a unique, early chance to foster cross-fertilization between our two great legal cultures but unfortunately failed to grasp this opportunity.[4] In this regard Chief Justice Ritchie appeared as much at fault as any of the other common law judges. To his credit, at age seventy he entered into a systematic study of French "in order to fit himself more thoroughly for his duty."[5] Ritchie may have earlier acquired some facility with the French language, for when he was sixty-eight he wrote in *Dupuy* v. *Ducondu* (1881) that it was unnecessary to go behind a deed because "My brother Fournier has made this so manifest in the judgment he is about to deliver, which he has kindly permitted me to peruse, and in which I entirely agree, that it would be a waste of time for me to discuss the question at greater length."[6] As Fournier almost invariably wrote in French, and did so in this case, it would appear that Ritchie had already acquired a basic ability to read French.

There is, however, no indication that he was ever receptive to or even knowledgeable about the Quebec civil code. He gave no encouragement to cross-fertilization and often seemed to insist on applying common law solutions to disputes arising in Quebec. For instance, in *Sweeny* v. *Bank of Montreal* (1885), Dame Emily Sweeny brought an action against the Bank of Montreal to recover the value of stock which had been wrongfully pledged to it. Funds had been originally sent out from England to James Rose at Montreal to be invested for the plaintiff. James Rose subscribed for stock as "J. Rose in trust" and paid the dividend he received to the plaintiff. Subsequently, Rose became indebted to the Bank of Montreal and transferred the shares as security for his loan, with the transfer showing that he held the shares "in trust." Rose became insolvent and the plaintiff, who was no longer receiving the dividend, sued the bank for an account. Although the trust was a product of the English court of chancery and foreign to the civil law, Ritchie simply applied the English law of trust with no reference to the civil law. He stated:

> There can be no doubt the transfer of this stock by Rose for securing his private indebtedness was a flagrant breach of trust, and the simple question is which of two innocent parties must bear the loss caused by the gross fraud of Rose.

Ritchie concluded that the bank had to bear the loss, because the bank had notice that the shares were held "in trust." Therefore, it was "bound to account for it to the plaintiff as the *cestui que trust* entitled to the beneficiary interest therein."[7]

The civil law system placed much greater emphasis on the principle of absolute ownership than Ritchie acknowledged, and did not recognize any dichotomy of legal and equitable title. Justices Fournier and Taschereau also decided that the bank was liable, but for civilian reasons. Taschereau held that:

> The original mandate was to invest her moneys. Having done so, his powers as to the capital had lapsed. He was *functus officio*, art. 1755 C.C., and he had no right thereafter to dispose of or deal in any way with this investment without a new authorization or mandate.[8]

Reasons mattered more than results, particularly for common law precedent. The two civilian judges applied the Quebec code's concept of mandate or agency, whereas Ritchie and Henry applied the English concept of equitable trust. Strong held that "the decision in this case must depend entirely upon the law of the Province of Quebec, as embodied in the Civil Code, and that the English law of trust, and analogies derived from that law, are entirely inapplicable, and cannot be resorted to for the purpose of determining the rights of the parties."[9] Such right reasoning, however, did not produce a right result. Strong's respect for the civil code caused him to find that the bank was not liable, whereas four colleagues, including the two civil jurists, concluded that it was. Nevertheless, Strong "was the only common law judge with whom Taschereau could have carried on a reasonable dialogue about the civil law."[10]

261

Monahan v. *Horne* (1882) presented the Court with an opportunity to explore the ideas and principles of the civil law in an appeal from an admiralty decision by the Maritime Court of Ontario. A mother claimed $2,000 in damages arising from the death of her son in a steamboat collision in the Detroit River caused by the negligence of the officers of the *Garland*. Counsel for the mother argued that an admiralty court applied the rules of the civil law except as specifically required to apply the common law, and a mother could recover for the death of her thirteen-year-old son and consequent loss of service without relying on the Fatal Accidents Act which conferred a statutory cause of action in favour of the deceased's dependants. Ritchie and the majority of the court would not accept that the Canadian legal system could be anything but a statutory modification of the common law. Ritchie began his short judgment by stating that "no civil action can be maintained at common law for an injury which results in death,"[11] and then decided there could be no such cause of action in admiralty because none had been given by statute.

Taschereau and Fournier thought that the Maritime Court had jurisdiction in personal injury claims even when death resulted, and moved easily to general principles to find that a claim for damages should lie. Taschereau regarded the common law doctrine that the death of a human being did not give rise to a cause of action to be "utterly indefensible" and thought that an admiralty court could and should circumvent such an absurd rule. He subjected the common law rule to scathing criticism:

> A widow, for instance, has a minor son who is her only support. A physician, whom she has called to attend him for a slight indisposition, gives him a violent and deadly poison instead of a soothing draught. He dies on the spot, and she is deprived, by the gross negligence of this physician, of the only support for existence she had in this world. That she suffers damages by the loss of her son's services till at least he would have been of age, is undeniable. That this physician is the author of these damages is also clear. That these are her damages, not her deceased son's damages, is as clear. Yet, says the defendant, "this mother would have no action against the physician." And why? because he killed her son instead of disabling him only, or only rendering him ill, say, for a month. "But, just because he killed my son" (would think this mother) "I am entitled to heavier damages." "No," says the defendant, "the law exonerates this physician just because he killed your son. Had he disabled him for a short space of time only, you would be entitled to damages, but as he killed

him, though he must admit that you suffered damages, and that he caused you these damages, yet the law says that he is not answerable for these damages."[12]

Taschereau asked, "Upon what principle can this doctrine be upheld?" and observed that under Roman law, French law and Scots law an action would lie. He and Fournier wanted to determine "this question by the best established principles of justice."[13] But the intransigence of the common law majority prevented the grasping of an opportunity to apply broader perspectives to the development of the law.

Without a common law recognition of the civil code there was no possibility of cross-fertilization. Quebec had long since learned to use and work with common law, especially in criminal matters. The early Supreme Court of Canada could have started the process of breaking down the legal separation between Canada's two great legal traditions. But Chief Justice Ritchie did not possess the necessary knowledge or sensitivity for the civil code. This failing still persists among Canadian common lawyers; as Jules Deschênes recently maintained, another century has failed to take sufficient "interest in Quebec doctrine and jurisprudence."[14]

Dissatisfaction with the new Court was by no means universal. While the legal communities in Toronto and Montreal had major reservations, Maritime jurists embraced the institution with enthusiasm. Provincial supreme courts in the Maritimes did not have formal appellate divisions during this time, and they maintained low monetary requirements for cases to qualify for appeal to Ottawa. Maritime judgments also had a greater likelihood of reversal in the Supreme Court, than did appeals from other regions.[15]

If this Maritime support was heartening for Ritchie, the new Supreme Court still failed to command broad national respect. Regardless of the other problems which troubled the Ritchie Court, one overriding factor lay beyond its control. Despite its impressive title, the Supreme Court of Canada simply was not the true Court of last resort for the new Dominion. Its decisions could be appealed to the Judicial Committee of the Privy Council in England by leave. Also cases at the option of the litigant could be appealed directly (*per saltum*) from the highest provincial court to the Privy Council. The bypassed Supreme Court of Canada had no way of influencing the outcome of such cases. It was "supreme" in name only.

A later chief justice, Bora Laskin, would write that such factors stifled the tribunal's development, as it was, "in fact, an intermediate appellate court which could neither compel resort to its facilities nor control further appeal from its decisions."[16] Thus the hands of Chief Justice Ritchie and his colleagues remained tied. A further consequence of the continued Privy Council appeal was that the Supreme Court of Canada had to adhere to the principles and decisions made in London. "The real effect of this complete subjection of the Supreme Court's jurisprudence to the authority of English decisions was to sap the Court's initiative for developing its own distinctive solutions to Canadian legal problems."[17]

There was no better example of the early Court's potential, and of the damaging impact of continued appeals to London, than *Barrett* v. *City of Winnipeg* (1891). In the year prior to his death, Ritchie had the opportunity to consider the matter of denominational school rights once again. Ritchie held that the Public Schools Act 1890 of Manitoba was invalid because it was in conflict with section 22(1) of the Manitoba Act 1870, a provision comparable to section 93(1) of the B.N.A. Act, which had been in issue in *Ex parte Renaud* (1873). Ritchie carefully distinguished his earlier decision, noting that the denominational school rights and privileges granted by the Manitoba Act were not simply those "which any class of person have by law," as in the B.N.A. Act, but also those enjoyed by "practice" in the territory at the time of union. He said that in *Renaud* he had held only that in New Brunswick there were no legal rights in regard to denominational schools in 1867 and therefore no rights protected by the constitution. Chief Justice Ritchie wrote that Parliament was well aware that no class of persons had by law any rights and privileges in Manitoba in 1870 concerning denominational schools; but in fact such schools did exist and were supported by particular religions. Therefore, in regard to Manitoba one had to look at the practice relating to denominational schools in 1870, at their time of union. He stated that by rejecting "the words 'or practice' as meaningless or inoperative we shall be practically expunging the whole of the restrictive clause from the statute."[18]

The Manitoba Public Schools Act 1890 would totally abolish the denominational character of the school system, and the chief justice concluded that it was *ultra vires*:

> Does it not prejudicially, that is to say injuriously, disadvantageously, which is the meaning of the word "prejudicially", affect

them when they are taxed to support schools of the benefit of which, by their religious belief and the rules and principles of their church, they cannot conscientiously avail themselves, and at the same time by compelling them to find means to support schools to which they can conscientiously send their children, or in the event of their not being able to find sufficient means to do both to be compelled to allow their children to go without either religious or secular instruction?[19]

This unanimous decision of the Supreme Court of Canada reflected great credit and character. Frank Scott wrote that "if ever the Protestant majority on the bench of the Canadian Supreme Court might be expected to show its religious and racial prejudices, this was the moment par excellence." Then, after noting that the strong Protestant feeling prevailing in the country had been completely set aside, he said: "By this decision the highest Canadian Court vindicated its right to be considered a truly impartial court of justice."[20] The Court had spoken as a strong nationalist court, proud of its bicultural and bilingual nature.

Unfortunately, the Privy Council brushed aside the unanimous Court. Lord Macnaghten, speaking for the Privy Council, said that the purpose of the Manitoba Act 1870 was "to preserve every legal right or privilege and every benefit or advantage in the nature of a right or privilege, with respect to denominational schools, which any class of persons practically enjoyed at the time of the Union." As there were no legal rights or privileges, he considered what rights or privileges would have existed had the practice in 1870 been established by law. Persons would have had the right to establish denominational schools at their own expense, and he added that "this right, if it had been defined or recognized by positive enactment, might have had attached to it as a necessary or appropriate incident the right of exemption from any contribution under any circumstances to schools of a different denomination." But, the Privy Council thought that tax immunity from "a national system of education upon an unsectarian basis" was going much too far.[21] Because one could not envisage a legislature taxing Roman Catholics to establish an Anglican school, the interpretation conferred no effective tax immunity. It was only immunity from a tax levied to establish a public school system that could make denominational schools feasible in the practical and meaningful way that existed in 1870. The Privy Council thus rendered almost totally nugatory the denominational school guarantee of the Manitoba Act, by holding that only if Roman Catholic children were compelled by law to attend the public school system would their customary rights and privileges be prejudicially affected.

The Privy Council's decision was popular in Manitoba but it caused French Canadians to believe that only under the protection of Quebec would their cultural rights be protected. Thus the Privy Council's decision in *Barrett* helped to nurture the growth of political separation. The Conservative League of Montreal, angered by the decision, called for the abolition of appeals to the Privy Council. On 3 November 1892 the league said:

> The present crisis would have been avoided if the Privy Council in England had rendered a decision according to equity, and based on the true state of the case. Unfortunately in the present instance, as in every other where the interests of the Catholics of this country and of the French Canadians have been involved, that high tribunal has rendered an arbitrary judgment. Since unhappily this appears to be true, it is most opportune to consider whether indeed the Privy Council has jurisdiction in such matters and to have it taken away if it exists: for the time has gone by and is past when a country or a people can be made to suffer injustice indefinitely.[22]

The Privy Council's provincialism only reinforced Canadian critics of the Court, at a time when Canada itself remained incomplete, judicially and politically. Sir John George Bourinot, an authority on the constitution and Canadian history, wrote in 1890:

> ...the Court can be considered only a general Court of Appeal for the Dominion itself in a limited sense, since there is in every province the right to appeal from its Appellate Court directly to the Privy Council. But the general sense of the people is tending more and more to make the Supreme Court, as far as practicable, the ultimate Court of Appeal in all cases involving constitutional issues. It is felt that men, versed in the constitutional law of Canada and of the United States, and acquainted with the history and the methods of government, as well as with the political conditions of the country at large, are more likely to meet satisfactorily the difficulties of the cases as they arise, than European judges who are trained to move in the narrower paths of ordinary statutes.[23]

Bourinot and men such as J.S. Ewart may have been premature in detecting a sense that the people wished to make this Court the ultimate court of appeal for Canada. After all, these same people, Canadians all, remained reluctant to cut completely away from the colonial past that still captivated and inspired their laws and public institutions. The Ritchie Court's apparent disunity was a microcosm of Canada's fragmented constitutional scene in 1892.

Notes to Chapter 18

1. *Canada Law Journal* 16 (1880), p. 99.

2. Ibid., 18 (1882), p. 88.

3. NAC, Sir John A. Macdonald Papers, No. 148652-661, H.E. Taschereau to John A. Macdonald, 1882.

4. It has recently been contended that the growth of a parochial spirit concerned with the preservation of the integrity of the civil law, which replaced the late nineteenth century tradition of "principled eclecticism," was caused by the failure of English-speaking judges to take an open and expansive view of the law. Common law judges failed to respect the Quebec civil law and as a result failed to take advantage of the opportunity for the cross-fertilization. This absence of reciprocity, it is argued, produced the inward-looking spirit of P.-B. Mignault and caused the universalist approach of H.E. Taschereau to wither. David Howes, "From Polyjurality to Monojurality: The Transformation of Quebec Law, 1875-1929," *McGill Law Journal* 32 (1987), p. 523.

5. Lawrence, *Judges of New Brunswick*, p. 497.

6. (1881), 6 S.C.R. 425 at pp. 440-41.

7. (1885), 12 S.C.R. 661 at pp. 667, 670.

8. Ibid., p. 704.

9. Ibid., pp. 670-71.

10. Howes, "Polyjurality," p. 544.

11. (1882), 7 S.C.R. 409 at p. 420.

12. Ibid., p. 444.

13. Ibid., pp. 445, 451.

14. Jules Deschênes, *The Sword and the Scales* (Toronto: Butterworths, 1979), p. 41.

15. James G. Snell, "Relations between the Maritimes and the Supreme Court of Canada: The Patterns of the Early Years," *Dalhousie Law Journal* 8 (1984), pp. 146, 148.

16. Bora Laskin, "The Supreme Court of Canada: A Final Court of and for Canadians", *Canadian Bar Review* 29 (1951), p. 1039.

17. Russell, *The Supreme Court of Canada*, p. 26.

18. (1891), 19 S.C.R. 374 at p. 384.

19. Ibid., p. 388.

20. F.R. Scott, "The Privy Council and Minority Rights," *Queen's Quarterly* 37 (1930), p. 671. See also Russell, *The Supreme Court of Canada*, pp. 23-24.

21. *City of Winnipeg* v *Barrett*, [1892] A.C. 445 at pp. 453-54.

22. The statement of the Conservative League of Montreal is reproduced in *In Re Certain Statutes of the Province of Manitoba Relating to Education* (1894), 22 S.C.R. 577 at p. 620.

23. "The Federal Constitution of Canada: Part 2," *Judicial Review* 2 (1890), p. 216.

CHAPTER 19

High Art and Low Church

Chief Justice Ritchie became a significant figure in Ottawa's fledgling cultural circles soon after his arrival in 1875. In response to Lord Lorne's initiative in promoting a Royal Canadian Academy and a National Gallery, a small group of men which included Chief Justice Ritchie, Sandford Fleming and Colonel Allan Gilmour assembled at the Rideau Club on 29 May 1879 to discuss establishing an art association as a precursor to the gallery.[1] They felt that Ottawa needed such an organization for its large proportion of persons of culture and refinement. Three weeks later Ritchie chaired a committee and promoted the idea of an art association:

> His Lordship the Chief Justice, at this point, entered the room, and after explaining that he had been unavoidably detained in court, he proceeded in an admirable address to enforce the necessity of proceeding actively in the formation of an association which commended itself so strongly to every mind. He dwelt, particularly on the want, very severely felt, of a school where our young people might be taught drawing, painting and sculpture, under good professional teachers, and he fully expected that under the association this great *desideratum* would be speedily supplied.[2]

The Ottawa Art Association came into existence at about the same time as the Royal Canadian Academy and the National Gallery. While the Association's art school had only eighteen students in its first year, this number increased to sixty-five in 1882-83, the year Ritchie was president.[3]

Ritchie was doubtlessly among the crush of six hundred guests who attended the opening of the first exhibition of the Royal Canadian Academy on 6 March 1880 in Ottawa. A military band played in the corridors and added a touch of pomp. However, "the academicians themselves were overlooked completely, but were probably an unobtrusive group since a decade later some reporter described them as a 'scrubby lot' except for debonair Dickson Patterson, the Academy Beau Brummel."[4] The

Department of Justice in 1890 commissioned Andrew Dickson Patterson to paint the portrait of Ritchie which now hangs in the Supreme Court of Canada. It is a three-quarter length life-size portrait. Patterson, in a letter to the deputy minister of justice concerning the payment of the balance of $100 of the agreed price of $500, stated that Sir John Thompson, the minister of justice, had viewed the almost completed portrait and "approved very highly."[5] A.D. Patterson was the son of Christopher Salmon Patterson who was appointed to Ritchie's court in 1888 by the government of Sir John A. Macdonald. In addition to the portrait of Ritchie, A.D. Patterson painted Macdonald, Oliver Mowat, Casimir Gzowski and Charles Fitzpatrick, who subsequently became chief justice of the Supreme Court in 1906. Patterson was not the only portrait painter with whom Ritchie became acquainted, for the New Brunswick Barristers' Society commissioned Robert Harris to paint his portrait which now hangs in the Justice Building in Fredericton. The Fathers of Confederation probably constituted Harris's most famous commission but he also painted Louis Henry Davies, who succeeded Fitzpatrick as chief justice of the Supreme Court in 1918, and also Ritchie's four immediate successors as chief justice of New Brunswick.

When Ritchie promoted the National Gallery, he probably did not expect that the Supreme Court would have to share its premises with the gallery. However, the first permanent home of the gallery, a room thirty-six feet by twenty feet in the Supreme Court building, opened to the public on 27 May 1882. The *Ottawa Citizen* in 1886 commented that "the halls of the Supreme Court, however well they may echo the sonorous voices of the ermine-clad sages (who by the way have been worked up to a fine frenzy by the ruthless invasion of their domain), are not adapted to the showing of pictures."[6] Ritchie wanted this space for the library of the Supreme Court and in 1888 the gallery was relocated to the room above the Government Fisheries exhibit on O'Connor Street.

Ritchie's interest in the creative arts was genuine, evidenced in part by his affinity for gardening and also for architecture. His interest in building was noted by one writer, who commented on plans Ritchie had for property he had owned when still residing in Saint John:

> The judge, whose taste for architecture is well known, often planned the style of building he would like to put up. In the evenings, after reading awhile, it was no uncommon thing for

him to draw near to a table, and with pencil and paper plan buildings of infinite variety. It was good employment for the mind, and less expensive than actual building, and the paper houses could be altered and improved and altered again at very little cost.[7]

The chief justice displayed his architectural bent again during discussions about Supreme Court facilities in 1889. After reviewing plans for improvements to the existing, unsatisfactory situation, he wrote to the minister of justice, Sir John Thompson: "It appears to me that the contemplated expenditure with a moderate amount added would be quite sufficient to defray the cost of a building suitable and proper for holding the sittings of the highest Court in the dominion. I do not think any amount expended on the present building will make it satisfactory."[8] Unfortunately for Ritchie and his colleagues, a new structure was not built at this time. Perhaps the repercussions of the Charlevoix election decision were still being felt. Sir Hector Langevin said in 1889 "that a new Courthouse will never be built in his day."[9]

For the first session of the Court in Ottawa in 1876, Ritchie boarded at 88 Sally Street, now Lyon Street. After this temporary lodging, Ritchie moved into "Gleniffer," a house in Rideau Terrace near Rideau Hall with his large and growing family of five boys and four girls. While living there from 1877 to 1883, he attended St. Bartholomew's Church. An 1880 vestry meeting requested Chief Justice Ritchie together with the bishop and wardens, "to frame an address thanking Princess Louise for her munificent gift of three bells to the Church" and to express sorrow about her sleighing accident.[10]

It was not certain what caused the Ritchie family to move in 1883. Ritchie might simply have wished to live closer to the Supreme Court building, or his increasing family might have necessitated the move. While living at "Gleniffer," Grace Ritchie gave birth to three more children — Eliza Wildman on 9 March 1878, William Johnston on 20 May 1880 and Douglas Vernon on 16 December 1881. Ritchie's fathering of three children while a member of the Supreme Court of Canada, two of them while chief justice, attested to his vigour and love of family. When Douglas Vernon Ritchie, the last of the Ritchie children was born in 1881, Ritchie was sixty-eight. Such fecundity has not been surpassed by any judge of the Supreme Court of Canada.

274 Daly Street, Ottawa

285 Metcalfe Street, Ottawa
(demolished about 1910)
(National Archives of Canada, Neg. No. PA27093)

In 1883 Ritchie rented 274 Daly Street for three years from Richard Scott, a former mayor of Bytown and a senator. Located on the south side of Daly between Friel and Chapel, the house built originally for Alfred Patrick was sold to Dr. Charles Tupper in 1867 who sold it to Scott in 1874. This large yellow brick house has been described as recently as 1970 as having an air of Victorian elegance. The following description of the interior of the home with its ten bedrooms indicated that it was adequate even for Ritchie's large family.

> The very large drawingroom on the west side, with a marble fireplace, has four deeply-set windows, high ceilings, ample skirting boards and a very attractive french door leading onto the verandah with a stained glass panel at the top.
> On the other side of the wide centre hall, is a former reception room with a large arch (now closed in) connecting it to the dining room. There was also a morning room and large pantry downstairs. The staircase, also now enclosed, was almost a spiral, winding upwards to the two upper floors.
> There are five fireplaces, three on the ground floor and two in bedrooms on the second. There are three other bedrooms here plus five more on the third floor, where the charming dormer windows from outside lend an air of vivacity and quaintness.[11]

During this time Ritchie attended St. John the Evangelist Anglican Church where, on 30 October 1883, his daughter Eleanor married Captain William Egerton Hodgins, a widower with a family. The church was "crowded to its utmost capacity;" Sir John and Lady Macdonald, Sir Alexander Campbell, the minister of justice, and all five judges of the Supreme Court of Canada were among the guests. John Campbell Allen, who had succeeded Ritchie as chief justice of New Brunswick, Judge J.W. Weldon and Judge Clarke, as well as many relatives and friends from the Maritimes, attended the wedding. Following the service, the bridal party and invited guests proceeded to the Ritchie residence on Daly Street, "where a *recherche* and bountiful *dejeuner* was partaken of and the health of the newly united pair cordially drunk."[12]

On 14 July 1885, Ritchie purchased lots 5 and 6 on the east side of Metcalfe Street and lots 1 and 2 on the west side of Beaconsfield Place from James MacLaren, a lumber merchant, for $2,500. On this large block of land, he built a handsome three-storey house, with a large verandah extended along the south side, and adjacent to this a grass tennis court. As the chief justice was seventy-three when he took up residence on Metcalfe Street, his prowess on his tennis court might not have been great. He also had a large stable constructed for his horses, carriage, cutter and one jersey cow. Ritchie would live at 285 Metcalfe Street for the rest of his life, but his summers were consistently spent at Quispamsis in New Brunswick.

He bought a pew in St. George's Anglican Church on the corner of Metcalfe and Gloucester streets. St. George's was established in 1885 by dissenters from nearby Christ Church, who objected to the introduction of high church ritualism in the Anglican services. John Lewis, the bishop of Ontario, although a supporter of ritualist tendencies, acceded to the founding of this new parish in order to stem the discord that already had lead to a schism in the church with the establishment of the Reformed Episcopal Church in Ottawa a decade before.[13]

Whether because of this low church orientation, as Ritchie was later to insist,[14] or because it was conveniently located in prosperous and growing downtown Ottawa, by 1889 St. George's had become the largest Anglican congregation in the city. But religious concerns were as important as those of convenience in his choice of church, as was demonstrated by his prominent part in an intriguing controversy that arose in St. George's late in 1889. Besides the firmness and nature of his religious convictions, this dispute showed Ritchie to be uncompromising in matters of principle, almost to the point of tactlessness, but also open and forthright in debate.

The focus of the controversy was the practice, introduced in early October of 1889 by the rector, the Reverend Owen-Jones, of chanting rather than speaking the Kyrie, or responses to the reading of the commandments during the communion service. The practice continued even after protestation by the church wardens on behalf of the congregation. On 3 November 1889, when the chanting of the Kyrie began, "the local founders of the church headed by Chief Justice Ritchie got up and walked out."[15]

The discord at St. George's was a microcosm of the underlying church-wide dispute. In his service after the walkout the rector explained that he had merely exercised his discretion as arbitrator of the assembly. His avowed reasons for exercising his discretion in this particular fashion were that it would brighten the service, and many of the congregation desired that. This was a feeble reason to introduce knowingly such discord, and there was no evidence that any of the congregation asked for chanting to be introduced, although many objected to it.

Owen-Jones was entirely cognizant of the low church origins of St. George's and his expressed bewilderment that such a "trifling cause should have such a serious effect"[16] was entirely disingenuous. The ritualist tendencies of the Anglican clergy of the time, and in particular those of Bishop Lewis, who gave unstinting support to Owen-Jones, made it more plausible that Owen-Jones wished to make the changes for doctrinal reasons.

Many parishioners objected to this because of a combination of simple conservatism and a strong distrust of authority. Change which tended towards authoritarian Romanism was therefore doubly suspect. Ritchie exemplified both these attitudes. He announced quite firmly that he "objected on principle to any alterations or innovations in their service,"[17] and was also reported as saying that "he did not believe in people singing on their knees. It was the Protestant Church of England that he belonged to and by the grace of God he would keep it Protestant, so far as his efforts could do it, till he died." He went so far as to stop attending communion, complaining that "when he [the rector] turned his back to the people during the prayer of consecration it gave out the key note of that party which they did not want."[18]

It was one thing to dislike such changes, and another to express one's disapproval so forcefully. The righteousness which had Ritchie after the walkout "quivering with excitement" and ready to "subscribe to carry the question through every court in the land,"[19] was that of a strong willed man unwilling to submit to arbitrary authority. That same trait had made him a strong supporter of responsible government.

Ritchie and the other dissenters were aware of the power of the congregation and not ready to let it be abused. In newspaper interviews they concentrated, not on theology, but on the right of the congregation to have services as they wished and on their power to enforce this right. The people's warden stated that "what we want is a low church service, and it is certainly a mistake when the church is paying better than any other in the diocese for the rector to try and make changes which cause dissensions among the congregation." Another dissenter was even more blunt, opining that the rector "should know the feelings of his congregation and they have it in their power to vote him $1 a year at the next vestry meeting as salary."[20] Later another parishioner remarked that he "did not know the rubrics, but he did know that their rector was an employee of their church."[21] Sheep was an unlikely metaphor for this particular flock.

The ensuing congregational meetings strengthened the impression that the dispute centred as much on attitudes to authority as on the questioned religious practices. The meetings also indicated a conflict between Ritchie and Justice Gwynne, his colleague at the Supreme Court of Canada and also a member of the congregation. At the meeting of 18 November 1889, called to discuss the rector's changes, Gwynne moved that "this vestry has no jurisdiction to determine upon the legality or illegality of the course pursued by the Rector."[22] Ritchie retorted to the effect that "he did not think there was the slightest doubt as to the legality of holding the meeting."[23] He then complained of the rector's absence by asking rhetorically if they had been brought together "to be made fools of,"[24] and made an amendment that the meeting proceed to business. He refused to address the merits of Gwynne's position. Ritchie's amendment was carried, and the exchange portrayed differences of opinion on the value of respecting authority versus one's own opinion. We are left to wonder whether the discussions in chambers partook of the same direct spirit.

Support for the rector centred on the "scant courtesy" accorded the rector, and emphasized that it was "a matter of taste" in which "a principle of give and take" would be wise. The opposition felt more strongly about the substantive issue and were disinclined to accept the rector's authority. They railed against the "rod of iron" with which they were ruled, contending that it "leads to Rome,"[25] and complained of the rector's refusal to call a meeting. The end result was a measure of support for the rector, a motion expressing not a desire for the responses to be chanted but "confidence in [Owen-Jones] as their pastor" and that "the changes ... be done at such times as in his discretion may seem expedient and in the best interests of the congregation."[26] This motion carried, fifty-two to forty-six.

Having won his point, the rector announced the following week that the responses would no longer be sung. The reconciliation was only cosmetic, however. Both the rector's warden and the people's warden had announced their resignations, and on 2 December a meeting to elect their replacements took place. Acrimony over trivial points showed that divisions persisted and tempers still rode high. First it was moved that reporters be excluded from the meeting. Ritchie showed little patience for secrecy, and at the same time ruled out face-saving measures which a closed meeting might have permitted. An even more pointless dispute followed when Owen-Jones declined to nominate his warden first, as was the custom. Ritchie suggested, with what must have been considerable irony, that "out of respect to the rector" the people should refuse to nominate their warden before the rector had named his candidate, and that the meeting would be reconvened at a later date if need be. Justice Gwynne came to Owen-Jones's defence, countering Ritchie's position with the procedural point that since the motion had already been made and seconded, the election of the people's warden had to proceed. This was sidestepped with an amendment, and the rector somewhat ungraciously agreed that he was in fact quite prepared to submit the name of his candidate. A simple uncontested election had turned into a test of wills, with Ritchie winning on both counts.

In this atmosphere Owen-Jones's next move seemed designed to bring matters to a final head. During a sermon soon after, he suggested that members of the congregation rise at the entrance and exit of the clergy, as well as for the presentation of the offertory. This was a departure from low church tradition, which could hardly be justified as brightening up the service. Dissenters did not have to leave the church to register their disapproval. They simply remained sitting. The rector also began to turn his back during communion which caused profound offence to those attaching importance to the visibility of the manual acts of consecration. To express his displeasure Ritchie also stopped taking communion. These symbolic protests were supplemented by a sharp drop in donations, which the rector and the Church could not ignore.[27]

This uneasy state continued until the Easter vestry, when the church's formal financial report showed a marked decline in revenues. This was directly attributed by some to the division occasioned by the rector's conduct, and on this basis a motion was made that "the services should be conducted in every particular as they were previous to the first of October last."[28] Passionate speeches followed, the one side accusing the rector of being divisive by refusing to abide by the wishes of his flock, the other accusing the dissenters of being divisive by refusing to follow the wishes of the rector. "In characteristically mild language," Gwynne advocated compromise by suggesting "that they appeal to the people themselves to rise and thus find an easy solution to the trouble," adding that "the rector was not at fault." Ritchie immediately countered Gwynne's suggestion. He showed no interest in easy solutions if they involved prevarications and "in warm tones claimed that it was the fault of the rector for he had coerced them into standing." Ritchie also pointed out, with considerable merit, that if the issue was divisiveness then as "the rector had said the innovations were immaterial ... why should he not abandon them to secure peace. He [Ritchie] believed they were most material."[29] Ritchie would have no truck with allowing individuals to save face when issues of principle were involved.

This meeting ended with a surprising show of harmony, when the motion requesting a return to the simpler service was amended by the addition of the words "and the vestry extend to the rector and the curate the kindliest feelings of confidence."[30] The motion in this form was carried overwhelmingly, illustrating again that the main issue for the rector's supporters was proper respect.

This was not enough for Owen-Jones, however, and within a day he resigned. The bitterness was such that many of his congregation left with him. Justice Gwynne, prominent among them, chaired the meeting at which the rector's supporters decided to build a new church, eventually to be known as Grace Church. It may have been Gwynne, perhaps seeking revenge, who suggested as one of the possible locations for the new church a vacant lot directly across the street from Ritchie's Metcalfe Street home. St. George's itself did not suffer financially from this split, and in March of 1891 Ritchie chaired a meeting which led to the extension and reseating of the church. The Reverend Owen-Jones did not take a position in Grace Church, but, no doubt with the assistance of his staunch supporter, Bishop Lewis, secured a good position in a prominent Halifax parish.

The dispute showed Ritchie and Gwynne in strongly opposed positions, with each in turn consistently opposing any initiative of the other. Ritchie appeared strong in his convictions, and confident in his judgment. Sometimes he seemed tactless and almost rude, but this indicated a preoccupation with the issues at stake rather than with the personalities of those involved, surely an asset in a judge. Ritchie, separating issue from personality, shook hands with the rector, and even expressed surprise at the rector's resignation.[31] If this was not simply *pro forma*, it shows a peculiar, but not unappealing, insensitivity to questions of prestige and face. The healthy mistrust of authority, which Ritchie consistently exhibited, might shade easily into excessive respect for one's own opinion, but Ritchie's repeated willingness to have the reporters present indicated that he was willing to trust his opinion to an open process. That his self-confidence did not lead to blind arrogance was also illustrated in a different context by a remark to a counsel at the end of a case, that when the case had opened he had been quite certain as to where the result lay, but after hearing the argument he had completely reversed his opinion.[32] A combination of faith in his own opinion and in the value of open debate meant Ritchie had the spirit of a reformer, not that of a tyrant.

Notes to Chapter 19

1. Sandra Gwyn, *The Private Capital*, p. 210.

2. *Ottawa Daily Citizen*, "Art Association of Canada," 18 June 1879 p. 2.

3. Ibid., 10 Apr. 1883.

4. J. Russell Harper, *Painting in Canada: A History* (Toronto: University of Toronto Press, 1966), p. 176.

5. NAC, RG 13, A2/vol.77/#579 letter from A.D. Patterson to R.G. Sedgewick [n.d.][1891].

6. Jean Sutherland Boggs, *The National Gallery of Canada* (Toronto: Oxford University Press, 1971), p. 2.

7. George Stewart, *The Story of the Great Fire in St. John N.B.: June 20, 1877* (Toronto: Belford Bros., 1877), p. 133.

8. NAC Sir John Thompson Papers No. 10302, W.J. Ritchie to Thompson, 3 Aug. 1889.

9. Ibid., No. 10324, R. Sedgewick to Thompson, 9 Aug. 1889.

10. Zita Barbara May, *St. Bart's of the Village 1867-1967* (Ottawa, 1967), p. 16.

11. *Ottawa Journal*, 1 Apr. 1970.

12. *Ottawa Citizen*, 31 Oct. 1883, p. 4.

13. See Bruce S. Elliott, "Ritualism and the Beginnings of the Reformed Episcopal Movement in Ottawa," *Journal of the Canadian Church Historical Society* 27 (1985), p. 31, and Clive Clapson, "John Travers Lewis: An Irish High Churchman in Canada West," ibid., 22 (1980).

14. See the minutes of the Vestry of St. George's Church for 16 Mar. 1891, p. 90.

15. *Ottawa Free Press*, "Trouble in St. George's," 4 Nov. 1889, p. 1.

16. *Ottawa Journal*, "St. George's Services," 18 Nov. 1889, p. 1.

17. *Ottawa Free Press*, "The Easter Vestries," 8 Apr. 1890, p. 2.

18. *Ottawa Journal*, "The Rector Sustained," 19 Nov. 1889, p. 4; ibid., "Tempest and Calm," 8 Apr. 1890, p. 4.

19. Ibid., "Walked Out of Church," 4 Nov. 1889, p. 1.

20. *Ottawa Free Press*, "Trouble in St. George's", 4 Nov. 1889, p. 1.

21. *Ottawa Journal*, "The Rector Sustained," 19 Nov. 1889, p. 4.

22. Minutes of St. George's Church congregation meeting, 18 Nov. 1889, p. 67.

23. *Ottawa Citizen*, "The Pastor Endorsed," 19 Nov. 1889, p. 4.

24. *Ottawa Journal*, "The Rector Sustained," 19 Nov. 1889, p. 4.

25. Ibid.

26. Minutes of St. George's Church congregation meeting, 18 Nov. 1889, p. 67.

27. See minutes of the Vestry of St. George's of 7 Apr. 1890, and also *Ottawa Journal*, "Tempest and Calm," 8 Apr. 1890, p. 4, *Ottawa Free Press*, "The Easter Vestries," 8 Apr. 1890, p. 2, and *Ottawa Citizen*, "Meeting of the Vestries," 8 Apr. 1890, p. 4.

28. Minutes of the Vestry of St. George's of 7 Apr. 1890.

29. *Ottawa Journal*, "Tempest and Calm," 8 Apr. 1890, p. 4.

30. Minutes of the Vestry of St. George's of 7 Apr. 1890.

31. *Ottawa Free Press*, "St. George's Church," 9 Apr. 1890, p. 1.

32. *Ottawa Citizen*, "Editorial Notes," 1 May 1882, p. 2.

CHAPTER 20

Death and Survivors

Although William Ritchie had been the oldest member of the court when appointed in 1875, he enjoyed better health than most of his colleagues. Indeed, only once before 1892 did the chief justice have to apply for extended leave as a result of illness. But in May 1892, Ritchie was stricken with bronchitis. It seemed initially that he only needed recuperation away from Ottawa. However, on returning to the capital on 6 September, Ritchie suffered a relapse from which he never recovered. He died at home on 25 September 1892 at the age of seventy-nine.

The funeral service was held at St. George's Church, followed by burial in Ottawa's Beechwood Cemetery. The remaining Supreme Court justices — Strong, Gwynne, Fournier, Taschereau and Patterson — and Sir John Thompson, the minister of justice, acted as pallbearers.[1] On 4 October 1892, all the justices of the Supreme Court of Canada forwarded the following letter of condolence to Lady Ritchie:

> The judges of the Supreme Court of Canada, at their first sitting since the decease of the great man who so long presided over the court, while they have deemed it proper not to deviate from the rule which he himself laid down, and which was observed on the occasion of the death of Sir William B. Richards and of Mr. Justice Henry, by publicly addressing any observations to the members of the bar and others attending the court, desire to express to you their sense of the loss sustained by the court which for the long period of seventeen years enjoyed the benefit of the extensive learning, the untiring industry and the large judicial experience of Sir William Johnstone Ritchie, and their personal deep regret at the event which deprived them of an esteemed friend and a courteous, dignified and efficient chief, and to convey to you and to the family of the late Chief Justice of Canada their warm sympathy in your bereavement.[2]

Ritchie went to the Supreme Court of New Brunswick on 17 August 1855 and thus at the time of his death had completed

St. George's Church, Metcalfe Street, Ottawa.

Ritchie's grave, Beechwood Cemetery, Ottawa.

more than thirty-seven years of judicial service. This term of service exceeded that of any of his contemporaries either in Canada, Britain or the empire. He had been chief justice of the Supreme Court of Canada for over thirteen years, a term which has not yet been surpassed.

When Ritchie died there was no obvious successor to him and the chief justiceship remained vacant for more than two and a half months until the minister of justice named Samuel Henry Strong. On 29 September 1892, Senator J.R. Gowan, a former Ontario county court judge, wrote to Thompson:

> The poor Chief has gone I see — I suppose Strong will be looking for the place. He at one time professed anxiety to retire. It might be expedient to enable him to leave with a better retiring allowance....
> I do not myself see that the public interest could suffer if the appointment of a new Chief was postponed for a season. Gwynne and Patterson are great workers anyway.[3]

Senator Gowan returned to the topic of the vacant chief justiceship in a subsequent letter in which he said:

> The Supreme Court needs badly no doubt a general accession of working men — but unless Strong has turned over a new leaf his appointment as C.J. would not help much I think. I have no faith in the man in any way. Why not leave things as they are for a time — courts have been left without a head before now![4]

Lack of enthusiasm for Strong did not constitute the only reason for delay. Sir John Thompson would have been happy to give up politics and return to the bench. The *Canada Law Times* reported that "There seems to be a general consensus of opinion that Sir John Thompson would be a great acquisition to the court."[5] An Ottawa newspaper stated:

> There is no doubt that, in accordance with usage, the position will be offered by the premier [J.J.C. Abbott] to Sir John Thompson, the latter being now attorney general of Canada. Sir John's family and personal friends will no doubt urge him to accept the office, but strong party pressure will be used to keep him in political life. The Montreal Herald of today says: A leading Montreal Conservative, who was once a candidate for parliamentary honors, assured our reporter that Sir John Thompson would take the supreme court, as he was well aware that he could never secure the premiership.[6]

Thompson did not take the chief justiceship, but on the retirement of Sir John Abbott he became prime minister. He filled the puisne judgeship for the Maritime provinces made vacant by Ritchie's death by appointing his own deputy minister, Robert Sedgewick, who was also a lawyer from Nova Scotia.

Thirteen of Ritchie's fourteen children survived him, one by his first marriage and all twelve by his second marriage. Three of his seven sons, by his second marriage, followed their father into the legal profession. Robert Rankin Ritchie, the first born son, enrolled in the Harvard Law School in 1881. After attending Bishop's College, Lennoxville, Quebec, and the University of Toronto, he commenced in 1879 or 1880 his articles with Charles W. Weldon in Saint John. The chief justice in a letter dated 20 September 1880 wrote Weldon seeking his opinion as to whether Robert "can pass the necessary examination to enter Harvard University with a view to obtaining a degree or whether you think it would be more desirable that he should remain with you for another year."[7] The reply does not survive, but Ritchie's concern proved well founded as his son did not gain admission as a regular student. He remained a special student for the academic years 1881-82 and 1882-83 and returned to Saint John without a degree. On his return he became an attorney in 1883 and received his call to the New Brunswick bar one year later. He continued to practise his profession until 1901 when he received the appointment of high sheriff of the City and County of Saint John. He died on 30 July 1911.

John Almon Ritchie, born in Saint John on 31 March 1863, attended Bishop's College School, Lennoxville, Quebec, Trinity College School, Port Hope, Ontario, and graduated with a B.A. degree from the University of Toronto in 1885. He obtained his legal training in Ontario under the apprenticeship system in the same way that his father received his training in Nova Scotia, but perhaps with somewhat greater supervision by the Law Society. He received his call to the bar in September 1890 and seven years later entered into the partnership of Belcourt and Ritchie. For many years he was the crown attorney for the County of Carleton. Witty and charming, Dick, as he was known to his many friends, wrote poetry and drama. At least three of his plays were produced on the American stage, *Dinner at Eight*, *The After-Glow* and *The Worldlings*.[8] His early poetry received good reviews, but it did not live up to its early promise. However, he did achieve immortality through his authorship of the verse inscribed over the entrance to Parliament's centre block:

The wholesome sea is at her gates,
Her gates both east and west.   [See Appendix 4]

Another son, Owen Ritchie, born in New Brunswick on 6 May 1865, also pursued a legal career and received his call to the bar of Ontario in September 1889. He died 14 August 1913 in Vancouver.

Of the four other male children of Ritchie's second marriage, Frank William became an Anglican cleric, Hazen attended the Royal Military College and became an electrical engineer, young William Johnston went off to the Boer War then settled in the West and Douglas Vernon, who was about eleven years of age when his father died, enlisted in the First World War and was killed on 3 July 1916.

None of the five Ritchie girls by his second marriage went to boarding schools or university or received any training to earn a livelihood. They appear to have received their education at home with a governess.[9] Ritchie, in legal decisions involving women, adopted a progressive view and, therefore, one is surprised that he did not encourage his daughters to obtain more formal education or training. However, he could afford to keep them at home and this accorded with the accepted norm of the time. W.H. Tuck, one of Ritchie's successors as chief justice of New Brunswick, held in 1905 that Mabel P. French was not entitled to be admitted as an attorney because she was not a "person" within the meaning of the statute. Not content to deny French access to the legal profession, Tuck expressed his lack of "sympathy with the opinion that women should in all branches of life come in contact with men. Better let them attend to their own legitimate business."[10] Ritchie would probably have held a more progressive view but Tuck's opinion illustrated that women's employment opportunities were severely limited by both law and social conventions at the time Ritchie's daughters were growing up. Of his second family Ritchie would live to see only one of his five daughters, Eleanor, marry. The next daughter to marry was Amy Maud, whose wedding to James Smellie of Brockville took place on 12 October 1904. Amy was then thirty years old and her father had been dead for twelve years. Eight months later, Beatrice wed Francis Macnaghten, son of Lord Macnaghten of Antrim, Ireland when she was thirty-seven. The last daughter to marry was Eliza Wildman, who at thirty-three married William H. Rowley of Ottawa on 25 October 1911. Grace Nicholson Ritchie remained unmarried.

None of the daughters rushed into an early marriage. Perhaps they were too particular about their choice of partners or perhaps they enjoyed their social life too much. At that time, Ottawa society largely revolved around Rideau Hall, the residence of the governor general. The Ritchies' social position assured their entrée to this privileged set. Lady Ritchie's charitable endeavours, urged upon her by Lady Aberdeen while her husband was governor general from 1893 to 1898, would have further solidified their standing. Later, when the Earl of Minto occupied Rideau Hall from 1898 to 1904, skating parties became the rage and the Ritchie girls were all very accomplished skaters, like their father. They knew Agnes Scott, the niece of Sir Richard W. Scott, the flamboyant, enigmatic journalist who wrote under the pseudonym of Amaryllis for the *Ottawa Free Press*. Sandra Gwyn, writing of the Minto period, indicated that the atmosphere for the in set "had never been more salubrious" and that

> these intimates were a youngish, sporting, unmarried set. Amaryllis was in, not because she was a working journalist but in spite of it because back in the eighties, as a debutante, she had belonged to "The Wanderers", an exclusive snowshoeing coterie of which the Mintos had been founders. In also were the four vivacious Ritchie sisters, Beatrice, Elsie, Grace and Amy, all daughters of a former Chief Justice....[11]

Even after Earl Grey took up residence at Rideau Hall in 1904 the skating parties continued. He developed a particular fondness for the Ritchie sisters, especially Elsie, a petite young lady. Grey arranged a skating tournament, the result of which had been predetermined, because at its conclusion, he presented a small sterling silver cup engraved with the words, "This cup given by His Excellency Lord Grey to Miss Elsie Ritchie who obtained the highest marks in Grace, Pace and Space, Skating Competition, March 1906."[12] The Rowley family contend that this is the original Grey Cup as the larger and more famous cup was not presented until 1909.

The Ritchie daughters thus enjoyed their social life and may not have yearned for marriage. But when their marriages did take place, they were very fashionable. Guests at Amy's wedding to James Smellie included the Earl of Minto, W.S. Fielding, the minister of finance, A.G. Blair, minister of railways and canals, R.W. Scott, secretary of state, Sir Sandford Fleming, the famous civil engineer, and three judges of the Supreme Court of Canada and their wives. A daughter of this marriage is Sylvia, who married Charles Ritchie, the diplomat-diarist and brother of Roland Almon Ritchie who sat on the Supreme Court of Canada from 1959 to 1984.

Lady Ritchie had accompanied her husband's rise to prominence in Ottawa, and continued for more than eighteen years after his death to play an active role in the capital city's society. She was a founder and first president of the Ottawa chapter of the National Council of Women. Lady Aberdeen, who started the association, recalled Mrs. Ritchie "as a dear sweet-faced elderly woman." Lady Ritchie remained exceedingly active on behalf of the National Council of Women until her death on 7 May 1911.

Other philanthropic causes occupied Lady Ritchie's time. In 1895 she sat on a committee which organized the Associated Charities for Ottawa. And she was also very involved in another of Lady Aberdeen's projects — the establishment of the Victorian Order of Nurses. Lady Ritchie was a member of the provisional committee of the V.O.N., which included such prominent individuals as Sir Sandford Fleming and served as an original board member and a governor.

There were no pensions for widows of Supreme Court justices. An order-in-council passed on 29 September 1892 authorized the payment of $1,333.32 to the widow, representing two months' salary of the chief justice, to be charged to unforeseen expenses.[13] Lady Ritchie continued to move in the highest social circles of Ottawa and it was said that life, while not uncomfortable, was lived on limited means by this active woman.[14]

In his will Ritchie left his wife all furniture and personal effects in the Metcalfe Street house in Ottawa and at Kawatcoose in New Brunswick. All other property he gave to his wife Grace and his eldest son, Robert Rankin Ritchie, to hold in trust. They were to pay $1,000 to Martha Margaret Robertson, the daughter of his first marriage and a like sum to Eleanor Jaffray Hodgins, the eldest daughter of his second marriage. His will directed that his two trustees pay $500 "to each of any other children who being a son may be of the age of twenty-one years or being a daughter may be of that age or married."[15] Lady Grace, so long as she did not remarry, received all rents and profits from the balance of the estate and the right to occupy the Metcalfe Street house and, Kawatcoose or to receive the rent from them as "may seem best and most for her benefit." If she remarried, her life estate ceased but she became entitled to $5,000. Upon her death or remarriage, the estate was to be divided equally among all his children. The will conferred full discretionary power to manage the estate, but with the proviso that "any building or buildings shall be kept fully insured; as I have suffered so much loss by fire I wish this particularly attended to." Doubtless, the two fires that had previously consumed the Ritchie building in Saint John prompted him to impose this condition.

Lady Ritchie continued to live at 285 Metcalfe Street. However, on 5 December 1906 the trustees of the estate sold the back portion of the lot on which the stable and part of the tennis court had been located for the sum of $7,000. Then on 9 May 1910, the remainder of the lot was sold for $15,000 and shortly after the Ritchie home was demolished to make way for a nondescript building, the Gainsborough Apartments, which still occupies the site. Lady Grace, her son John, her daughters Grace and Elsie and her sister Ellen Nicholson, moved to 417 Laurier Avenue East in 1910. On 7 May 1911, Lady Ritchie died of pneumonia and typhoid fever. All her children survived her except Frank who had died in 1907. Robert Rankin Ritchie died on 30 July 1911 and as he was then the sole trustee of Sir William Ritchie's will, the Royal Trust Co. became the trustee of the estate. On 21 March 1919, the Royal Trust Co. sold Ritchie's summer retreat Kawatcoose near Quispamsis to W. Malcolm Mackay Limited and the final distribution of Ritchie's estate occurred.

Notes to Chapter 20

1. *Ottawa Citizen*, 28 Sept. 1892, p. 5.

2. *Ottawa Free Press*, 5 Oct. 1892, p. 7.

3. NAC, John S.D. Thompson Papers, 29 Sept. 1892.

4. Ibid., Gowan to Thompson 13 Oct. 1892.

5. *Canada Law Times* 28 (1892), p. 481.

6. *Ottawa Free Press*, 26 Sept. 1892, p. 7.

7. New Brunswick Museum, Weldon and McLean Papers, s.52, box 5, p. 25-11.

8. Henry J. Morgan, *The Canadian Men and Women of the Time* 2nd ed. (Toronto: W. Briggs, 1912), at p. 944.

9. Letter of C.S.A. Ritchie dated 5 Sept. 1989 to the author.

10. In *re Mabel P. French* (1905), 37 N.B.R. 359 at pp. 361-62.

11. Gwyn *The Private Capital*, p. 302.

12. Major General Roger Rowley, a son of Elsie Ritchie still has the cup in his possession.

13. NAC, RG 2-1, vol. 607, PC 2582, 29 Sept. 1892.

14. Interview with Sylvia Ritchie, a granddaughter of the chief justice.

15. Will of William Johnston Ritchie.

CHAPTER 21

Conclusion

Sir William Johnstone Ritchie has been a neglected figure in Canadian history. Thirty-seven years on the bench, including ten as chief justice of the Supreme Court of New Brunswick and more than thirteen as chief justice of the Supreme Court of Canada, did not prove sufficient to overcome the usual neglect accorded our earlier judges. Had Ritchie wished to ensure his place in history he might have done better to have kept to his political career, which, even though cut short by his appointment to the bench, brought him some recognition. James Hannay, for instance, said of Ritchie:

> He possessed, what few members at that time had, a clear knowledge of the true principles of Responsible Government. Mr. Ritchie had an eminently practical mind; he was a forcible and impressive speaker, and he was bold in the enunciation of those Liberal principles to which he held.[1]

In New Brunswick, Ritchie was a clearer and more consistent advocate of the principle that the government be responsive to the will of the people, speaking through their elected representatives, than others, particularly Lemuel A. Wilmot, who received disproportionate credit for the advent of responsible government. From the beginning of his career Ritchie advocated not only the principle, but also the specifics, such as the need for the executive to have control over decisions about taxation and expenditure.

Both in politics and on the bench, Ritchie was a pragmatic incrementalist. While he could be a forceful advocate of change, his goal was not to change society, but rather to spread the opportunity for individual hard work and dedication which could lead to the same comfortable prosperity he enjoyed. He saw the need for change in the practical workings of society, not in grand schemes or utopian visions.

This does not mean that Ritchie was a conservative masquerading as a reformer. For instance, Ritchie spoke at great length in the New Brunswick House of Assembly in support of the secret ballot. He supported the extension of the franchise, but stopped short of advocating universal male suffrage. He believed it was unfair to tie the vote to ownership of land because he recognized that, as New Brunswick became more urbanized, many prosperous and respectable men did not own land, but had personal property or a salary instead. He did believe that some such guarantee of success was needed to ensure a responsible electorate.

In his opposition to prohibition in 1855 he clearly enunciated all the dangers that flow from such a significant social experiment if it does not have overwhelming popular support. Ritchie enjoyed a drink and his opposition to prohibition had strong personal motivation; but he also presciently foresaw the rejection of the first Liberal administration of New Brunswick over this issue.

Ritchie was not adverse to government help in promoting economic development, as is shown by his sponsorship of railways, particularly the European and North American Railway. His active participation in the Saint John Mechanics' Institute revealed the importance he attached to education and training. Recognizing that economic development was critically dependent on savings, he helped launch the Saint John Savings Bank, and even after his elevation to the bench he continued his active participation in its supervision.

Ritchie's belief in hard work and study as a route to success was reflected in his extremely successful law practice. Sir John C. Allen, the chief justice of New Brunswick at the opening of the courts following Ritchie's death, said "To many members of the Bar, Sir William Ritchie was well known for his great legal ability, and while practising at the Bar, was, with perhaps one exception, the most able and successful advocate in the Province." At the time of his death a newspaper noted that his first marriage strengthened his professional position, but it acknowledged that he had previously established a prosperous commercial practice because of his "practical acquaintance with general principles of commercial business" and "his deep knowledge of the law."[2] Ritchie's occasional forays in the criminal courts, particularly to defend an unpopular person such as Dennis McGovern, indicated his dedication to the rule of law. His refusal to fight a duel in 1845 also indicated a progressive stand and a repudiation of outdated social values about honour.

As a puisne judge on the Supreme Court of New Brunswick, he wrote many notable judgments and did not hesitate to dissent when necessary. When the power of the city of Fredericton to tax the lieutenant-governor's salary was challenged, Ritchie, in dissent, refused to allow the rich to escape their share of the burden, and espoused the modern principle that taxing statutes, like any other statute, must be construed to achieve their object and purpose. Ritchie's healthy attitude towards the higher authorities extended to more personal matters; in 1881 when he received a knighthood he refused to pay the British government for the patent, forcing the Colonial Office to back down.

During his tenure as chief justice of New Brunswick, Ritchie became the first superior court judge in Canada to hold a duly enacted provincial statute invalid, thereby determining that the courts should enforce the division of powers set out in the B.N.A. Act through judicial review of legislation. Ritchie's decision in *Chandler* challenges the current orthodoxy that the introduction of judicial review of legislation was inevitable and came quietly and naturally. This was not so in New Brunswick, where it promoted intense controversy and a period of almost open warfare between the legislature and the judiciary in the early 1870s. Nor were the courts united on the question. Judge Steadman, a county court judge, developed an argument based on parliamentary supremacy and the inclusion of the power of disallowance in the B.N.A. Act which denied the legitimacy of judicial review of legislation. While little attempt has been made to assess the relative merits of the two sides of this debate, the arguments of Judge Steadman's are sufficiently cogent to show that debate was warranted. It may be that judicial review became entrenched not because of convincing arguments in its favour, but precisely because there was no argument at all; Ritchie and judges like him simply assumed that the power of judicial review was theirs to exercise. Had Steadman been the superior court judge who heard the *Chandler* case rather than Ritchie, his arguments might have lead to a rejection of judicial review.

In the field of constitutional law, Ritchie maintained a relatively even hand between the powers of the federal Parliament and the local legislatures. An early biographer of Macdonald acknowledged this when he wrote:

> Owing to obscure definition of certain provincial powers upon the one hand, and of federal jurisdiction upon the other, in the

British North America Act, there is in this quiet way some conflict of opinion among the judges as to "provincial rights," much
as there is among the politicians; but the trying task of holding
the balance evenly between the aggregate of the provinces, and
each province singly, at once calls for the highest talent and the
keenest discrimination. And in this important respect, as in all
others belonging to his sphere, Sir W.J. Ritchie gives a lustre and
a prestige to our highest Canadian seat of justice.[3]

The table which summarizes the Court's interpretation of the
B.N.A. Act from 1875 to 1892, shows that Gwynne gave the most
centralist interpretation, with twenty-two holdings in favour of
federal power and five for the provincial power for a centralist
score of 81 percent. Strong is located at the other end of the spectrum with only ten holdings in favour of the federal power and
sixteen for the provincial power for a centralist score of 38 percent.
We find Ritchie located in the middle of the spectrum with fifteen
centralist holdings and fifteen provincialist holdings, representing
a centralist score of 50 percent. The whole Court in a total of
thirty-one holdings held eighteen times for the federal power and
thirteen times for the provinces, resulting in a 58 percent centralist
score. Ritchie's holdings were slightly more oriented towards the
provinces than that of the whole Court.

J.M. Clark in 1909 claimed that the Privy Council had saved
the nation because "what is too well known to require argument,
namely, that the earlier decisions of our Supreme Court would
have rendered our Constitution quite unworkable."[4] This thesis is
difficult to sustain in light of the summary of early constitutional
law cases indicating that the Supreme Court together with Chief
Justice Ritchie gave a balanced and reasonable interpretation to
the B.N.A. Act. The Court did not share the Privy Council's strong
bias in favour of the provinces, but it nevertheless recognized the
need to provide the provinces with substantial legislative competence. It seems unlikely that the Canadian Supreme Court's interpretation would have caused the country to disintegrate. For
instance, in *Barrett* v. *The City of Winnipeg* (1891) the court showed
considerable sensitivity to minority rights by holding Manitoba's
school legislation *ultra vires* for taxing Roman Catholic separate
school supporters, many of whom were French Canadians, to
finance a non-sectarian common school system to which they
could not in conscience send their children. The approach of the
early Supreme Court to minority rights was consistent with that
of the modern Court, which in the 1980s, freed from the dictates

Interpretations of the B.N.A. Act by the Supreme Court of Canada during the Ritchie Years, 1875–1892

Case	Holding	C/P	A/R	G	T	F	H	R	S	Other
In re: *The Brothers of the Christian Schools in Canada* (1876) 1875–1906 Coutlée 1.	The incorporation of a society of teachers is *ultra vires* the Dominion.	P	-	-	-	P	-	P*	P	-
Severn v. *The Queen* (1878) 2 S.C.R. 70.	Held *ultra vires* an Ontario statute requiring a licence of liquor wholesalers.	C	REP.	-	-	C	C	P	P	Richards C J.-T.Taschereau C
Valin v. *Langlois* (1879) 3 S.C.R. 1.	Upheld the Dominion Controverted Elections Act.	C	A	C	C	C	C	C	-	-
Lenoir v. *Ritchie* (1879) 3 S.C.R. 575.	Held *ultra vires* a Nova Scotia statute granting precedence in the provincial courts to provincially appointed Queen's Counsel.	C	REP.	C	C	P*	C	-	P*	-
McCuaig v. *Keith* (1879) 4 S.C.R. 648.	Held that the establishment of a court of maritime jurisdiction is *intra vires* the Dominion. (Ritchie said the point was not even arguable).	C	-	C	-	C	C	C	C	-

Case	Holding	C/P	A/R	G	T	F	H	R	S	Other
The City of Fredericton v. The Queen (1880) 3 S.C.R. 505.	Upheld the Canada Temperance Act under s. 91(2).	C	REP.	C	C	C	P	C	-	-
The Citizen's Insurance Co. v. Parsons (1880) 4 S.C.R. 215.	Upheld an Ontario statute regulating fire insurance contracts (under s. 92(13)).	P	A	C	C	P	P	P	-	-
Holman v. Green (1881) 6 S.C.R. 707.	The foreshore of a harbour belongs to the Dominion under s.108.	C	-	C	-	C	C	C	C	-
Mercer v. A.G. Ontario (1881) 5 S.C.R. 538.	Held that the lieutenant-governor does not represent the crown for the purposes of escheat.	C	R	C	C	C	C	P	P	-
The Queen v. Robertson (1882) 6 S.C.R. 52.	1. S. 91(12) of the B.N.A. Act does not confer proprietary rights on the Dominion.	P	-	-	P	P	P	P	P	-
In re: Quebec Timber Co. (1882) 1875-1906 Coutlée 43.	Parliament can incorporate a manufacturing and trading company to transact business throughout Canada.	C	-	C	C	C	C	C	-	-
In re: Canada Provident Association (1882) 1875-1906 Coutlée 48.	Parliament may incorporate a mutual benefit society.	C	-	C	C	C	C	C	C	-

Shields v. *Peak* (1882) 8 S.C.R. 579. Per Ritchie and Fournier; section 136 of the Insolvent Act 1875 is *intra vires* the Dominion. The other judges did not find it necessary to address the question.	C	*	*	*	*	C	*	-
Queddy River Driving Boom Co. v. *Davidson* (1883) 10 S.C.R. 222. The province does not have the power to authorize a company to obstruct a navigable river. Taschereau concurring, but doubtful.	C	-	C	P	C	C	C	-
Reed v. *A.G. Quebec* (1883) 8 S.C.R. 408. Held *ultra vires* a Quebec tax on exhibits filed in court.	C	A	C	P	C	C	P	-
A.G. Can. v *Flint* (1884) 16 S.C.R. 707. Dominion can confer jurisdiction to hear inland revenue cases on Court of Vice-Admiralty; *Valin* v. *Langlois* followed (reversing S.C.N.S.).	C	-	C	-	C	C	C	-
Poulin v. *The Corporation of Quebec* (1884) 9 S.C.R. 185. Three judges upheld provincial jurisdiction to regulate opening and closing hours of taverns; three judges refused to deal with the constitutional issue.	-	-	C*	C*	P	C*	P	-
Sulte v. *City of Three Rivers* (1885) 11 S.C.R. 25. Upholding Quebec License Act (foll. *Hodge* v. *The Queen*).	P	-	P	-	P	P	P	-

Case	Holding	C/P	A/R	G	T	F	H	R	S	Other
McCarthy Act Reference (1885), Canada, Sessional Papers, 1885, no. 85a.	1: held *ultra vires* the Dominion Liquor License Act in so far as it dealt with retail licensing.	P	A	P	-	P	P	P	P	-
	2: upheld the provisions of the act dealing with wholesale licensing.	C	R	C	-	C	P	C	C	-
St. Catherines Milling and Lumber Company v. The Queen (1887) 13 S.C.R. 577.	Held that the beneficial interest in certain Indian lands was vested in Ontario, not the Dominion.	P	A	C	P	P	P	P	C	-
Central Vermont Ry. Co. v. Town of St. Johns (1887) 14 S.C.R. 288.	Held that a town can extend its limits to the centre of a navigable river (not the main question).	P	-	P	P	P	P	P	P	-
A.G. British Columbia v. A.G. Canada (1887) 14 S.C.R. 345.	Held that British Columbia's grant to the Dominion of land to further the construction of the C.P.R. included mineral rights.	C	R	C	C	P	P	C	-	-
The Queen v. Farwell (1887) 14 S.C.R. 392.	Held that British Columbia ceased to have any interest in the land covered by the C.P.R. grant (decided day after A.-G. B.C. v. A.-G. Can; Fournier decides this case differently).	C	-	C	-	C	P	C	C	-

Molson v. Lambe (1888) 15 S.C.R. 253.	Upheld a Quebec liquor licensing statute.	P	-	C*	C*	P	P	P	-
Forsyth v. Bury (1888) 15 S.C.R. 543.	Per Ritchie: Dominion act professing to confer right to sell Anticosti Island is *ultra vires*. Per Gwynne, obiter: act is not *ultra vires*. No other opinions expressed on the question.	-	-	C	*	*	P	*	-
Longueuil Navigation Co. v. City of Montreal (1888) 15 S.C.R. 566.	Municipal taxation of local ferries *intra vires* the province.	P	-	*	*	P	P	P	-
Liquidators of the Maritime Bank v. Receiver General of N.B. (1889) 20 S.C.R. 695.	Held that the prerogative of prior payment in an insolvency was vested in the crown in right of New Brunswick.	P	A	C	P	P	-	P	Patterson P
Danaher v. Peters (1889) 17 S.C.R. 44.	Upholding provincial licensing act.	P	-	P	P	P	-	P	Patterson P
Pigeon v. The Recorder's Court (1890) 17 S.C.R. 495.	Provincial business licensing act upheld.	P	-	P	P	-	P	P	Patterson P
Lynch v. The Canada North-West Land Company (1891) 19 S.C.R. 204.	Upheld a Manitoba statute imposing a 10% penalty for late payment of municipal taxes.	P	-	C	P	P	P	P	Patterson P

Case	Holding	C/P	A/R	G	T	F	H	R	S	Other
Barrett v. The City of Winnipeg (1891) 19 S.C.R. 374.	Held *ultra vires* a Manitoba statute taxing Roman Catholic separate school supporters for the purpose of financing a common school system.	C	R	-	C	C	-	C	C	Patterson C
Quirt v. The Queen (1891) 19 S.C.R. 510.	Insolvency with regard to a bank *intra vires* the Dominion.	C	-	C	C	C	-	C	C	Patterson C
Total C/P		18/13	-	22/5	12/9	16/15	12/11	15/15	10/16	
Percentage of centralist holdings		58	-	81	57	52	52	50	38	

* indicates that the decision was not based on constitutional considerations. In cases where the constitutional argument was strong, the refusal to deal with the constitutional question could be taken as indicating a provincialist or centralist bias, which is indicated. In other cases it is not plausible to infer such a bias from the decision, and none is indicated.

Column headings
C/P: centralist (C) or provincialist (P) holding
A/R: affirmed (A), reversed (R) or later repudiated (REP.) by the Privy Council
G: Gwynne
T: H.E. Taschereau
F: Fournier
H: Henry
R: Ritchie
S: Strong

of the Privy Council, finally accorded recognition to French-language rights in Manitoba. Had the early court not been overruled by the Privy Council, its decision would more likely have bound the country together rather than torn it apart.[5]

Alan Cairns has mounted a powerful defence of the Privy Council. His major thesis is that interpretation of the constitution should be applauded for injecting a "decentralizing impulse into a constitutional structure too centralist for the diversity it had to contain"[6] and in so doing placated Quebec. There are two major problems with this thesis. First, even if one believes in province-building, there is no hard evidence that the Privy Council had the knowledge and understanding of Canadian life to engage intelligently in this enterprise. Secondly, by what right did the Privy Council assume the power to remake, under the guise of interpretation, a constitution which had been largely determined at the Quebec conference in 1864? Cairns concedes the first problem but nevertheless insists that "the provincial bias of the Privy Council was generally harmonious with Canadian developments." Cairns states that "the clear divergence between the act as written and the act as interpreted makes it impossible to believe that in practice the Privy Council viewed its role in the narrow, technical perspective of ordinary statutory construction."[7] This is certainly true, but it would be difficult to argue that the Privy Council usually engaged in a broad liberal interpretation appropriate to a constitution.[8] For some reason, the Privy Council simply brought a strong provincial bias to the B.N.A. Act[9] and this may have inhibited the growth of a strong national loyalty.

Further, even if the constitution was too centralist for the strong regional forces that existed, this mandated a constitutional amendment agreed upon in Canada, or required the mobilizing of political forces to compel Parliament not to exercise some of its broad powers. It does not justify unprincipled interpretation by a court or an advisory body in the nature of a court. Chief Justice Ritchie would never have condoned the interpretation of the trade and commerce power to exclude internal trade. Interpretation may comprehend much, but some inferences must be beyond the pale. As late as 1885 Ritchie categorically stated that "the Local Legislature has nothing to do with trade and commerce, external or internal, in this country."[10] He also recognized a wide ambit for concurrent power, and had his view prevailed Canada might have been a more united country without sacrificing the benefits of diversity possible in a federal system.

In interpreting the B.N.A. Act Ritchie disapproved of the admission of some kinds of legislative history. He did not accept the approach adopted by Chief Justice Richards in *Severn* v. *R.* (1878). In that case Richards considered a wide range of matters, including the desire of the framers of the B.N.A. Act to avoid the United States example, which accorded much more power to the states. Ritchie's condemnation of this approach made it much easier for the Privy Council to superimpose its own classical theory of a decentralized federalism upon the B.N.A. Act. The framers' intention of a highly centralized federation had been seriously undermined by Ritchie. However, Ritchie did regard other forms of legal history as relevant in determining the division of power. In the *McCarthy Act Reference* in which the court was asked to determine whether the federal Liquor License Act, 1883 was within the authority of Parliament, Ritchie said:

> The question narrows itself down to this — are the regulations which the Dominion Government have undertaken to enact regulations of trade and commerce, or subordinate regulations, which are understood as police regulations, which are the subject, not of general legislation, but the subject of municipal control?[11]

In answering this question Ritchie insisted that it was necessary to consider how life had been lived prior to confederation to determine what was a matter of a local or private nature. If the colony had previously delegated powers to municipalities or if there were no municipality to the quarter sessions, this was good evidence that the matter fell within section 92(16), "matters of a merely local or private nature." Ritchie recognized that one key to constitutional interpretation involved the weighing of the need for national uniformity and the desirability of local diversity:

> Speaking of the uniformity of this Act with reference to hotel keepers and tavern keepers, and the propriety of uniformity throughout the Dominion, the history of Nova Scotia and New Brunswick shows that it is not desirable that there should be that uniformity; because in the olden time the Quarter Sessions had the authority to grant free licenses in sparsely settled parts of the country with a view to inducing people to take out licenses to afford accommodation to travellers; and in some cases not only a free license, but money was given. Take at that time one of the leading roads of the Province — the road which connects the

city of St. John with the then town of Fredericton, the seat of Government of the country. A new short road was opened there, but it was not settled, and a man named Gillen was given thirty pounds a year by the Legislature and a free license, to hold a tavern on that road so that the judges, lawyers and the legislators travelling up there might have accommodation as they went along this road. Otherwise they would have had to travel sixty or seventy miles and carry their refreshments with them. It shows that you cannot have uniformity. What was more perfectly and purely a matter of police regulation than that? Fortunately, now we have a railroad between those two cities.[12]

Ritchie and the majority of the court held that the federal Liquor License Act was *ultra vires* except for sections dealing with wholesale and vessel licences.

Ritchie, in common with most judges of the time, was a confirmed positivist. He regarded it as his duty to apply the rules of the common law, and where any rule required reform it was the function of the legislature, not the courts, to effect the change. While this approach robbed the courts of much creativity, Ritchie usually applied rules in an enlightened fashion. Despite occasional woodenness, his common sense and pragmatism usually enabled him to reach a reasonable result. In *R. v. Doutre* (1881) a member of the Quebec bar, retained by the minister of marine and fisheries in Ottawa to render services in Halifax, Nova Scotia, became dissatisfied with his remuneration and sued the crown.[13] The Exchequer Court awarded Doutre $8,000 in addition to the amount he had already received. The Supreme Court dismissed the appeal by the crown, with Ritchie dissenting, on the grounds that the contract made in Ottawa was to be performed in Nova Scotia. He concluded that the English rule that a barrister cannot maintain an action for his fees applied in both Ontario and Nova Scotia. Recognizing that the great majority of the Canadian profession practised both as barristers and solicitors, Strong concluded that the English rule was not part of the common law of England introduced into the colonies. Ritchie, however, mechanically applied the English rule in spite of differing circumstances. The explanation for this probably lies in the fact that in *Kerr v. Burns* (1860) he had concurred with the judgment of the New Brunswick court rendered by Chief Justice Carter upholding this same rule. Ritchie always strove for consistency with his former decisions, a quality he prized on some occasions more than adherence to precedent.

Ritchie contributed much to the early Supreme Court of Canada and although it might not have been a great court, it compared not unfavourably to other courts of the time in both Britain and the United States. Without Ritchie, the Court would not have withstood its early critics nearly as well. He left behind a Supreme Court which was functioning much more smoothly than when he had succeeded to the top post more than thirteen years earlier. Parliamentary calls for the abolition of the Supreme Court had ceased. The Court still did not enjoy the whole-hearted support of the bar, but few courts do.

One newspaper obituary said that "Sir William Ritchie has been to the Dominion of Canada what Chief Justice Marshall was to the United States." This assessment appeared based on Ritchie's "most masterly grasp of ... constitutional questions."[14] This probably overstated Ritchie's significance, but there was force in the analogy to Marshall. A comparison of Ritchie's judgment in *R. v. Chandler* with *Marbury v. Madison*, shows that his vigorous and clear exposition of the necessity for judicial review of legislation compared favourably with that of Marshall. Ritchie deserves recognition as a father of judicial review in Canada. He also merits recognition as one of the few to keep alive the movement towards reform and responsible government in New Brunswick, where, in the critical years from 1846 to 1855, he stood firm in the face of apathy, opportunism and outright hostility to that cause.

While Ritchie's judgments were perhaps not strikingly original, he generally showed a solid and practical progressiveness, combined with an even-handed respect for the rule of law. Such steady worthiness may not be glamorous, but it was arguably appropriate to the new and growing country in which William Johnstone Ritchie played so active a part.

Notes to Chapter 21

1. James Hannay, *The Life and Times of Sir Leonard Tilley* (Saint John, 1897), p. 189.

2. Saint John *Globe*, 26 Sept. 1892.

3. J.E. Collins, *Life and Times of the Right Honourable Sir John A. Macdonald* (Toronto: Rose, 1883), p. 426.

4. J.M. Clark, "The Judicial Committee of the Privy Council," *Canadian Law Times* 29 (1909), p. 348.

5. Gordon Bale, "Law, Politics and the Manitoba School Question: Supreme Court and Privy Council" *Canadian Bar Review* 63 (1985), p. 461.

6. Alan C. Cairns, "The Judicial Committee and Its Critics" *Canadian Journal of Political Science* 4 (1971), p. 323. See also Frederick Vaughan "Critics of the Judicial Committee of the Privy Council: The New Orthodoxy and an Alternative Explanation," (1986), ibid., 19(1986), p. 495, and "Comments" by Alan C. Cairns and by Peter H. Russell, ibid., pp. 521 and 531.

7. Ibid., pp. 322, 327.

8. There were the exceptional cases such as *Edwards* v. *Attorney General for Canada*, [1930] A.C. 124 and *In re Regulation and Control of Aeronautics in Canada*, [1932] A.C. 304.

9. There are many explanations for this. One of the best is F. Murray Greenwood, "Lord Watson, Institutional Self-Interest, and the Decentralization of Canadian Federalism in the 1890's," *University of British Columbia Law Review* 9 (1974), p. 244. The table in this chapter is an expanded version of a table presented in Greenwood's article.

10. Canada, Sessional Papers, 1885, no. 85, p. 120.

11. Ibid., p. 156.

12. Ibid., p. 119.

13. (1881), 6 S.C.R. 342.

14. *St. John Daily Sun*, 26 September 1892, p. 4.

Appendices

OPINION OF

JUDGE STEADMAN

OF THE YORK COUNTY COURT

Delivered in 1868, upon the

POWER OF THE JUDICIARY

TO

DETERMINE THE CONSTITUTIONALITY

of a Law enacted by the Parliament of Canada or
a Provincial Legislature, with his reasons therefor.

Also — observations upon two cases involving the same
question since determined by the Supreme Court of New Brunswick

PRINTED BY ORDER OF THE LEGISLATURE

Opinion of

JUDGE STEADMAN

Of the York County Court,

Delivered in 1868, upon the power of the Judiciary to determine the Constitutionality of a Law enacted by the Parliament of Canada or a Provincial Legislature, with his reasons therefor.

Also — observations upon two cases involving the same question since determined by the Supreme Court of N.B.

---

p. 1 A question touching the constitutionality — and binding force of laws enacted by the Parliament of Canada and the Provincial Legislatures having been raised before the legal tribunals in some of the Provinces, and an application involving the legality of a law passed by the Legislature of this Province in the Session of 1868 in amendment of the Insolvent Confined Debtors law, having been made before me, and I having declined to take jurisdiction to determine a question of that nature, I now propose to state the reasons, in as brief a manner as the great importance of the subject will admit, which influenced my judgment upon that occasion, with a few general observations upon two cases involving the same question, which have since been determined by the Supreme Court of this Province.

In stating my views I desire it to be understood, that I do so with the greatest possible respect for the admitted legal ability of the Court, and also with a proper deference to the opinions of a number of eminent legal gentlemen at the Bar who differ from me. But speaking respectfully, as I have not yet heard any reason advanced sufficient to convince me that the conclusion at which I first arrived was erroneous, I am induced to state the principles and reasons which it still seems to me ought to obtain in the determination of this (to the people of the Dominion) most important question.

It is necessary in order to a correct understanding of the nature of the question involved, first, to inquire in what character we are to view the British North American Act. Is it in the nature of a written constitution, adopted by the people of the Dominion as the foundation and basis of a new Government, by which several distinct bodies of Executive and Legislative authority are created, with limited and exclusive powers granted to each, and each executing its authority independent of the other, providing also for a judiciary, with extraordinary powers, reserving to themselves all other powers and authority not expressly granted?

Is it in the nature of an Act of Parliament by which the long estab-   *p. 2*
lished political rights and legislative authority of the people are swept away, and new and limited powers granted, and investing the judiciary with extraordinary powers, establishing a system of government different in its character from the British Parliamentary system?

Or shall we view it as an Act of Parliament not granting any new political rights or legislative powers not previously possessed by the people, but rather as establishing an additional body of Executive and Legislative authority, having relation to that already existing through the negative legislative power of the Governor General, and distributing the legislative authority between the Dominion and Provincial Legislatures for the greater convenience of each in the work of legislating for the peace, good order and government of the Dominion and Provinces, leaving the judicial power as it was before the passing of the Act, viz: an authority subordinate to the legislative, created for the purpose of interpreting and administering the laws?

It will scarcely be contended that the British North America Act should be regarded in the character stated in either of the first two propositions, but rather in that stated in the last proposition; that is to say, as an Act of Parliament passed for the purpose of reorganizing the several Provincial constitutions and governments then in existence, each possessed of complete and ample powers of legislation within the respective Provinces.

Viewing it then in this light, it is necessary to examine what were the powers of the several Provincial Legislatures, prior to the Act coming into force, and whether the legislative was in any way subordinate to the judicial authority.

The Parliament of Great Britain, consisting of the Queen, Lords and Commons, is the Supreme power of the nation, and whatever Parliament does no other power can undo. The Colonial Legislature, before Confederation, consisted of the Governor, Legislative Council and House of Assembly as the affirmative legislative authority within the colony, with the negative legislative power in the Sovereign. These four branches constituted the supreme legislative authority of the colony, possessed of the same power within the colony that the Parliament of Great Britain possessed within the United Kingdom, and whatever the legislative authority enacted, no other power within the colony could refuse to give effect to; the negative legislative supremacy of the Sovereign being always presumed in the affirmative, until signified to the contrary. The judiciary

313

of the colony could no more assume negative jurisdiction over the laws enacted by the Legislature than the judiciary of England, Ireland and Scotland could assume a negative jurisdiction over the laws enacted by Parliament.

The Royal Commission to the Governor, prior to Confederation, and the Royal Instructions accompanying it, (an authority not to be questioned), establish this proposition too plainly to be controverted. The

p. 3 Royal Commission authorized the Lieutenant Governor, by and with the advice and consent of the Legislative Council and Assembly, to constitute and ordain laws, statutes and ordinances, for the public peace, welfare and good government of the colony, and the people and inhabitants thereof, &c., which said *laws, statutes,* and *ordinances* were not to be repugnant, but as near as local circumstances, would admit agreeable to the *laws* and *statutes* of the kingdom.

The Royal Instructions expressly declare what the Imperial authorities intended by this statement of legislative powers contained in the Royal Commission, and the authority by which alone the Legislature was to be restrained in the exercise of such powers, and is expressed in the following words:— "Whereas great mischief may arise, from passing Bills of an unusual and extraordinary nature and importance in our Plantations, which Bills *remain in force there from the time of enacting until our pleasure be signified to the contrary,* we do will and require you, not to give your assent to any Bill or Bills of an unusual or extraordinary nature and importance wherein our Prerogative, or the property of our subjects may be prejudiced, or the *trade* and *shipping of our Kingdom* in any way affected, until you shall have transmitted unto us through one of our principal Secretaries of State the draft of such Bill or Bills, and shall have received *Our Royal pleasure thereupon,* unless you take care that there be a clause inserted therein *suspending and deferring the execution thereof* until our pleasure shall be known concerning the same." Trade and Shipping were always regulated by laws enacted by the Imperial Parliament applying to and having force in all the colonies. Yet by this authority either of them might have been affected by laws enacted by the Colonial Legislatures. And so it is laid down in Dwaris and Amyotts on Statutes "that all laws of the Colonial Legislature remain in force within the colony until disallowed by the Sovereign." The clause in the Royal Commission "which laws, statute, etc., are not to be repugnant but as near as local circumstances will admit agreeable to the laws and statutes of the Kingdom," is only directory, and the Colonial Legislature is to judge in the first place of the necessity according to the local circumstances of the Colony, subject to the approval or disapproval of the Sovereign.

There is no instance on record in any of the Provinces, that I am aware of, where the Courts before Confederation assumed jurisdiction to declare the *Sovereign will* and to disallow a law enacted by the Legislature. On the contrary the Courts in New Brunswick have recognized and acted under a law passed by the Legislature in 1850, which, after reciting a section of an Act of Parliament, having force in this Province, in express words declared it to be repealed and of no force or effect *within the Province*. It did not occur to any one at that time, not even the law officers of the crown, by whom all colonial laws are carefully examined, that the legislature had no power to legislate in that way, that is, by expressly repealing an Act of Parliament so far as it related to the Province. In the case of the Queen *vs.* Kerr,— determined by the Supreme Court of this Province, the late Chief Justice Chipman in delivering the judgement of the Courts, speaking of laws passed by the Provincial Legislature said: *p. 4* "It is a thing unheard of under British institutions, for a judicial tribunal to question the validity, or binding force of any such law; when duly enacted, a law so passed goes into force, subject to be disallowed by the Sovereign." This fourth branch of the legislative authority of the colony was incorporated into the colonial constitution for the express purpose of preventing mischief or injury to the general interests of the Kingdom, and unnecessary conflict with the laws of Parliament. But the Colonial Legislative authority has often and repeatedly been exerted to alter and repeal laws enacted by Parliament, so far as they related to the colony, whenever it was deemed necessary in the interests of the colony. If the Colonial Legislature could not do this then there would be no such thing as Colonial self-government.

By the comity of nations, the laws of the country where a contract is made, and upon which an action is brought in a foreign country, govern the Judicial Tribunals of that country. This rule has long been extended to the Colonies by the Courts in England, and if an action be brought in England upon a contract made in any of the colonies, the law of that colony where the contract was made obtains, unless it be repugnant to some law of Parliament made in regard to such colony, then the comity is denied and the law of the colony rejected because by the Act 7 & 8, Wm. III, it is made void in England. But the law within the colony is of binding force and is there enforced by the legal tribunals.

It is well established that no statute of the Imperial Parliament extends to the colonies unless it is expressly so declared. The Act 7 and 8 Wm. III, enacts that all laws, usages and customs *which shall be in practice* in any of the Plantations repugnant to any law made or to be made in this kingdom, *relative to the said plantation* shall be utterly void and of no effect. But it does not say it shall be utterly void and of no effect *within the* Plantation, and therefore it never was considered that that Act interfered with the Supreme constitutional power of the Sovereign to enact laws with the advice of the Legislature to be in force within such colony.

Nor was it ever supposed that it could be inferred from the provisions of that Act that Parliament had invested the colonial legal tribunals, from the highest to the lowest, with jurisdiction over the Acts of the Supreme legislative authority of the colony, which possessed the power to constitute such courts and to add to and take from their jurisdiction as might be considered necessary or expedient.

It is laid down as the rule by the Commission of Legal Enquiry for the Colonies, that *"no colonial law can be disallowed except by order of the Queen in Council,* and when disallowed, and so signified by the mode pointed out in the Royal Instructions, it is void within the colony, as well as in England. This is the legal and constitutional principle upon which the Royal instructions are based, wherein it is stated that *laws passed in the Colony remain in force there until the pleasure of the Crown is signified to the contrary;* the Governor being directed not to give his assent to any Bills of an unusual or extraordinary nature or affecting trade and shipping.

p. 5   By the Act of Parliament 28 and 29 Vic. the word "repugnant" as used in the 7 and 8, Wm. III. is explained, and it is therein declared that laws of a colony *repugnant* to an Imperial Statute relating to the colony shall be void only to the extent of such repugnancy, and shall be read subject to the Imperial Statute.

The Legislature of Upper Canada, in the year 1839, passed an Act providing for the sale and disposal of the Clergy Reserves, making provision for the application of the money arising from the sale thereof. Numerous petitions from the clergy and others interested were presented to the House of Lords in the Session of Parliament, 1840, praying that House to pass an Address to Her Majesty that the Act of the Legislature be disallowed. Four questions were submitted by the House of Lords to the Judges of England, one of which was, whether the Act so passed was repugnant to the provisions of the 7 & 8, Geo. IV, and consequently void. The Judges answered that it was, but did not say, neither were they asked to say, whether if the Queen did not declare her dissent to the law passed by the Legislature of Upper Canada, but left it to *its operation,* it would be of binding force or void in that Province.— Her Majesty disallowed the law and so declared it void *within the Province of Upper Canada.*

In an action brought in the Court of Queen's Bench, England, against the late Governor of Jamaica, on account of excesses alleged to have been committed by him in quelling the rebellion that took place in that colony during his administration, under the Act of Parliament 11 & 12, Wm. III., which rendered him liable to an action in England for oppressive acts committed upon her Majesty's subjects in the Colony while governor thereof. The Legislature of Jamaica, after the rebellion, had passed an Act of Indemnity, relieving the Governor and all others from all actions brought against them for or on account of any act committed in putting down the rebellion. But it was contended on the part of the Plaintiff that the Act of Indemnity was repugnant to the Imperial Statute 11 and 12, Wm. III, giving the Plaintiff a right of action, in England, and must therefore be read by the Court subject to that Act, according to the provisions of 28 & 29 Vic., and not according to the rule of comity. It was never contended that the Act of Indemnity was void in Jamaica because repugnant to the 11 and 12 Wm. III, or that it must be read by the Courts in Jamaica subject to the Imperial Act, had an action been brought there against any party engaged in quelling the rebellion. It was admitted that the Act would be an answer to any action brought in the Colony. The Court decided, as did the Court of Exchequer Chamber on appeal from the Queen's Bench "that the Crown as well as Parliament had power to establish a Colonial Legislature with supreme Legislative powers within the Colony over all acts done or to be done within its territorial jurisdiction. That the comity extended to the law of foreign nations must be extended to the law of the colony. But if a law passed by the Colonial Legislature was repugnant to an Imperial Statute relating to that Colony, it must be read by the Courts in England by the 28 and 29 Vic., subject to such Imperial Statute, and that the right of action in the case before   *p. 6* the Court must be determined by the law of Jamaica, which took away the right to bring the action and not by the law in England under the Statute 11 and 12 Wm. III, which gave the right to bring an action in England. If an action brought in any colonial court be taken by appeal to the Judicial Committee of the Privy Council, the controversy will be determined according to the comity, and the law of the colony where the cause of action accrued will be applied and not the law as in England.

This being the rule before Confederation is there anything in the British North America Act, either expressed or implied, conferring upon the judiciary, in conjunction with the Sovereign, a *negative jurisdiction* to determine what laws passed by either of the legislative bodies of the Dominion shall or shall not be of binding force?

It is true that the Royal Commission to the Governor of a colony, under which the two Houses of the Legislature were summoned, conferred general legislative powers. The subjects in regard to which it was not considerable [sic] desirable the legislature should pass any Bills were pointed out in the Royal Instructions accompanying the Commission, while the British North America Act names the particular subjects exclusively assigned to each of the legislative bodies. Although the rule which governs the construction of ordinary statute law is, that "what is exclusively given to one person to do is necessarily prohibited to all others," still without express jurisdiction is conferred upon the judiciary, it is not within their province to determine a question involving the constitutional exercise of that authority. By the Act the *negative legislative power* of the sovereign was preserved over laws passed by the Parliament of Canada, transferring the same power to the Governor General over laws passed by the Provincial Legislatures. It is a clear principle, that jurisdiction cannot be taken by one Court where it is expressly conferred upon another and a higher tribunal, which the sovereign authority is, possessing power to create a judiciary. It is not consistent to submit the judgment of a supreme sovereign tribunal to the investigation of any subordinate tribunal, however competent it may be to determine the question.

The British North America Act is not the supreme law in the sense that the constitution of the United States is the supreme law in that Republic. It *is* supreme in as much as it is the authority by which the different departments of our Confederate government are organized, and the central power created, and to which each must look for the authority which it is to exercise, and by which each department must, under the restraining control of the prerogative, be governed in the exercise of its particular functions. But it is not the supreme law in the sense that it controls through any inherent authority in the judiciary, all Statute Law of the Dominion Parliament and Provincial Legislatures. It could not be such without taking from the Constitution the principle which affirms the supremacy of the legislative authority. The object and aim of the Act *p. 7* is not to restrict the legislative prerogative of the Sovereign but to extend that power. The legislative authority of the Dominion therefore can alter the British North America Act, as it can any other Act of Parliament, so far as it affects the internal government of the Dominion or any Province thereof, if not, self-government, the most vital principle of the British colonial system of government, is taken away. If Parliament had intended the British North America Act to work such a change in our Constitution, and to make it the standard by which the legal tribunals were to judge and determine all statute law, it would have been considered a matter of sufficient importance to have been made a subject of special enactment as involving a principle so entirely adverse to the theory of all British institutions. If the provisions contained in that Act had been enacted by each of the Provincial Legislatures instead of by Parliament, and had received the assent of the Sovereign, and the government of the Dominion had been organized under such laws, the judiciary would not have possessed any inherent power to place any limit to the legislative authority. Nor can it be argued that the Provincial Legislatures did not possess the right and authority with the assent of the Sovereign to organize of themselves the confederacy as now established, or in other words that the Crown had not power to establish the Parliament and Government of Canada. That the Crown possesses co-ordinate power with Parliament to establish a Legislature in any Province of the Empire is fully stated in the case of Philips *vs.* Eyre. Surely then since it is established they have not

318

lost the right, subject to the same assent, to alter or amend its constitution. There is no restriction in the Act. It was not from want of power in the Provinces that application was made to Parliament to pass the British North America Act, it was because of the great difficulty of bringing so many minds to agree upon the details of so important a subject.

By the Act of the Imperial Parliament for the Union of Upper and Lower Canada it was declared that each Province should have an equal number of representatives in the House of Assembly, with a proviso that the legislature of Canada, might alter the number if the Bill proposing such alteration should be adopted by a two-thirds vote of the members of the Legislative Council and House of Assembly. But for fear this restriction might not be sufficient, it was further enacted that it should not be lawful for the Governor to *assent in Her Majesty's name* to any Bill *altering* the *number of* representatives unless it was passed on the second and third reading with the concurrence of the two-thirds majority, and upon addresses of the Legislative Council and House of Assembly declaring that the Bill had been so passed. It was also provided in the Act of Union, that Her Majesty's assent should not be given to any Bill relating to Ecclesiastical rights and matters, waste lands of the Crown, etc., until such Bills were laid before Parliament. What was the object of these restrictions upon the Governor General? They must have been intended to serve some useful purpose. Is it not a recognition by the Imperial Parliament of the supreme legislative power of the Sovereign to enact any law, with the advice and consent of the Legislative Council and Assembly, to be in force within the Province of Canada? Were it not for these restrictions, had the Legislative Council and House of Assembly, though not by a two-thirds vote, passed a Bill altering the number of representatives, or affecting Ecclesiastical rights, the Governor assenting and the Sovereign not afterwards signified her dissent, it would have become law in Canada, but it is not at all likely that either the Governor or Her Majesty would have assented to a Bill of that nature so passed. The hostile elements in these Provinces on the question of representation could not afford to leave anything in doubt in a matter of such vital importance.

p. 8

An Act was passed by the Imperial Parliament 17 and 18 Vic., authorizing the Legislature of Canada to alter the constitution of the Legislative Council, not because the Legislature was without power, with the assent of the sovereign, to effect such change. But for the reason that the assent of the Queen could not be had to a Bill so repugnant to the Act of Union, and so opposed to the theory upon which all British Parliamentary institutions are based, without the authority of Parliament first obtained. Such measures are always the result of a party triumph, and usually adopted after a long party struggle.

If the Courts can declare a law of the legislative authority void, it ought to follow that they can exercise a control over the Chief Magistrate, who, by the advice of the Council and Assembly enacts the law, and it has been suggested by eminent counsel that the Lieutenant Governor might be compelled by a writ of Mandamus to do an official act within his official authority. If so it must follow that by a writ of prohibition he might be enjoined under pains and penalties not to do an act beyond the scope of such authority. It is true that the judiciary power of the United States, though possessing jurisdiction to declare a statute law void, have never exercised jurisdiction over the official acts of the Chief Magistrate of the State. But the jurisdiction there is expressly conferred by the Constitution, and does not include jurisdiction over the official acts of the Chief Magistrate. But the jurisdiction here is claimed as inherent in the original and constitutional powers of the judiciary. If so, as a natural result, the Supreme Judicial Tribunals must include both, and the rule applicable to municipal governments must apply in regard to both the legislative and executive authorities. There can be no doubt that the judiciary has jurisdiction to declare a law made by any municipal authority void, if repugnant to the law of the land, and that the Supreme Judicial Tribunals have jurisdiction over the official Acts of the chief municipal officers, and may compel them to do any official act within their authority and to prevent them from doing any act not within their authority. Now there is no very good reason to be assigned why if the Courts can take part of this jurisdiction as applicable to the legislative, they should not take it as applicable to the executive authority and all officers of the executive government. The clear result of the principles involved in these propositions are rather startling, and I think ought to convince all that the jurisdiction must fail in both cases and for like reasons.

Mr. Justice Story in his work on the Constitution of the United States, says, "The propriety of the delegation of jurisdiction in cases arising under the constitution, rests on the obvious consideration that there ought always to be some constitutional method of giving effect to constitutional provisions. What, for instance, would avail restrictions on the authority of the State Legislatures without some constitutional mode of enforcing the observance of them. The States are by the Constitution prohibited from doing a variety of things.****No man of sense will believe that such prohibitions would be scrupulously regarded without some effectual power in the government to restrain or correct the infractions of them. *The power must be either a direct negative on the State laws, or an authority in the national courts to overrule such as shall manifestly be in contravention to the Constitution.* The latter course was thought by the convention to be preferable to the former: and it is without question by far the most acceptable to the States. The same reasoning (he says) applies with equal force to cases arising under the law of the United States. " The soundness

p. 9

of the reason here given for some power in the Constitution capable of restraining the several legislative bodies within the constitutional limits cannot be questioned. But the reason which influenced the members of the United States convention when framing the Constitution for vesting that power in the judiciary, instead of the highest executive authority of the nation, is not applicable to the British Parliamentary constitution, or to the British Colonial constitution. The prerogative power vested in the Sovereign, has always been found sufficient to restrain the colonial legislatures within proper limits, and to prevent unnecessary conflict with the laws of Parliament. In these days of constitutional government the prerogative is only exercised in the best interests of the people. If under the British North America Act the Judiciary can assume this negative jurisdiction, then we have two separate restraining authorities instead of one as heretofore.

It will be observed that the reason assigned by Mr. Justice Story for vesting in the judiciary of the United States, the jurisdiction to declare laws enacted by either of the legislative bodies void, when in contravention of the constitution, was the absence of any negative power in the constitution. If there had been any such power, and no express jurisdiction conferred upon the judiciary, it is quite clear from his reasoning that the courts would not have assumed it. This is a power greater than the legislative power and cannot be exercised by judicial supremacy. The question involved cannot be considered in the light of a conflict of laws, nor as a conflict between municipal authorities. A conflict of laws arises only where there is found to exist in different countries, or in different localities of the same country, rules of law conflicting with each other upon the same subject, or where two statutes are found in conflict in prescribing a rule of law in respect to the same matter. Now the British North America Act establishes no rule of law upon any of the subjects of legislation named in the Act. It only declares what authority may enact a rule of law in regard to such subjects. And until two different laws are enacted concerning some one subject, there can be no conflict. The conflict raised is purely on the question of legislative authority between the Parliament of Canada and the Provincial Legislature, and not a conflict with an Imperial Statute, which has prescribed no rule of law and must *p. 10* be determined by the negative legislative power; in cases of doubt before the law is finally enacted.

There are abundant reasons for retaining the prerogative power in the confederate constitution of the Dominion; the absolute necessity for fixing with certainty the binding force of all statute law, which could never be if a final jurisdiction is to be exercised by the legal tribunals. For instance, a law may be enacted which in the judgment of the negative tribunal is entirely within the authority as declared by the British North

321

America Act: the public accept it as law, individuals invest money under its authority, and important interests become involved; after a time a question is raised by some individual anxious to avoid a responsibility; the validity of the law is brought into question before the Courts and pronounced void, because in the opinion of the judges it is in contravention of the authority of the Act. It is needless to say that in such a case great injustice and great loss of property to individuals with great public injury is the result. Nor is it a sufficient answer to say that the best or only remedy for such a calamity is to be found in the legislature keeping strictly within the delegated authority, as that is next to an impossibility. Legislators like judges and all other men are fallible, and the question must be determined by mere opinion *not by facts*, and different minds may arrive at very different conclusions. However anxious then the legislators and the Sovereign power may be to keep within the constitutional provisions, they can only exercise their best judgement. It is impossible to know what the opinion of the Court will be if called on to pronounce upon the validity of their Act.

A case that arose in the Town of St. Stephen in this Province completely illustrates what I have just stated. The Legislature passed a law authorizing the inhabitants of that town to issue bonds to raise money and apply the proceeds to the Houlton Branch Railway; and authorized assessments upon the inhabitants from time to time for the payment of the interest and the ultimate redemption of the debt. The bonds having been issued an assessment was ordered. A case was brought before the Supreme Court, on an application for a writ of certiorari, with a view to quash the assessment on the ground that the law was *ultra vires* and therefore void. The Court determined that it was void and ordered the writ to issue. An application was made to the Dominion Parliament for a remedial Statute to enable the Town to keep faith with the bond holders, Parliament refused to pass any law for various reasons, one of which was that the subject involved in the Act in question was entirely within the powers of the Provincial Legislature; the ablest legal minds in Parliament entertaining an opinion different from that expressed by our Supreme Court. Now if the position assumed by the Court in regard to the jurisdiction, and the law as declared in this case, be correct, then a wrong has been done for which the Constitution and laws afford no remedy, and such cases must frequently occur if the *validity* of the law is to be made a subject of judicial investigation. The powers given to the Dominion
p. 11 Parliament to levy taxes is confined to raising money for the general purposes of the Dominion. The power of levying taxes for a local purpose is exclusively assigned to the Provincial Legislatures. By the rule of construction adopted by the Court in the case referred to, any law enacted by Parliament in regard to local taxation must also be declared void.

Another reason why the courts should not assume this jurisdiction is to be found in the fact that it must often bring them in direct collision with the legislative authority, certainly a state of things not very desirable. In the case of the Queen *vs.* Chandler, which arose under a law passed by the Legislature of this Province, in amendment of the Insolvent Confined Debtors Law, in which the Supreme Court granted a prohibition to Judge Chandler, forbidding him to discharge a confined debt or under the authority of the amended Act, for the reason that it was *ultra vires*, and therefore void. The Legislature being determined to defeat the action of the Court, passed another law requiring all sheriffs and gaolers to discharge from their custody all prisoners for debt who had been confined for a period of two years and upwards. An Act was also passed whereby all officers were indemnified from all actions or suits on account of such discharge, or of any other act done in pursuance of the authority and direction of the first Act. An injunction was granted forbidding the Sheriff of the City and County of St. John to discharge a debtor in his custody under the authority of that law. The Sheriff, however, did discharge the debtor in defiance of the injunction, and I think it was discovered that the Court was unable to enforce obedience or to effectually impose any penalties for the disobedience to its writ. It is hardly to be supposed that the legislature in such a case would be disposed to invest the Court with the necessary power of enforcement. Such a conflict of authority between the judiciary and the legislature ought never to occur. If it does occur it must cease whenever the latter chooses to assert its supremacy. If the legislature in the case of the Town of St. Stephen, should pass a law declaring the judgment of the Court void, and without force, (for which a precedent can be found in Imperial Legislation), and as in the case under the Insolvent Confined Debtors Law, pass an act of indemnity, and restrain the Court in the exercise of jurisdiction by injunction, or otherwise, and such law should receive the assent of the Governor General (of which there could be no doubt, His Excellency having already sustained the authority of the legislature by the assent to the first law) the Court would be powerless to interpose and prevent the collection of the assessment, or the application of the money. This is a proceeding that ought never to be resorted to unless the emergency of the case justifies it. In this case the bondholders have no right of appeal to the Judicial Committee of the Privy Council, the local authorities may not desire it, and the only Court of Appeal open by right to the creditors of the Town, is the Provincial Legislature. In this view then of the case any attempt on the part of the judiciary to restrain the legislative authority must fail for any useful or practical purpose.

Questions of great public importance must often arise in the legislation of the Parliament of Canada, as well as in the Provincial Legislatures, in which the most important interests of the Dominion or Province may *p. 12* be involved, and if the validity of a statute is to remain in a state of uncertainty until determined by the legal tribunals it must necessarily lead to great public inconvenience, and it may be in the end to great confusion, preventing the successful carrying out of the most important laws.

It will be readily admitted that the legislative and judiciary power in every well constituted government should act in harmony with each other; the legislative always aiding the legal tribunals in the execution of judicial authority, the Courts interpreting and administering the laws enacted by the legislature. But under any government where the judiciary power exercises a control over the legislative, and a collision of authority occurs, the former (though it may be right) will be compelled to yield, as in the case I have stated, and as it was in the United States between Congress and the Supreme Court in regard to the duties to be performed by the Judges in the Circuit Courts. Is it wise then under our constitution for the judiciary to assume jurisdiction over the legislative power of the Dominion, especially as the British North America Act has provided an authority entirely independent of the legislative body capable of restraining each within the constitutional provisions, or, to adopt the language of Chief Justice Chipman, it retains in the Sovereign a legislative power distinct and separate from that of the legislative bodies, *and which affords a remedy for any improper legislation.* Jurisdiction in the judiciary to declare a law void can only be sustained upon the theory that the British North America Act has reduced the respective legislatures of the Dominion to the character and capacity of ordinary municipal governments. If the Superior Courts can take this jurisdiction, it follows as a matter of course that all inferior courts must take it also, and the constitutionality and binding force of every legislative act may be brought in question before a Justice of the Peace exercising civil or criminal jurisdiction, and the Justice like the Judges of the Superior Courts will be bound to determine according to his judgement whether a law enacted is within the exclusive legislative authority, or whether it is beyond that authority and so *absolutely void.* It would appear very unseemly in a Justice of the Peace to declare a law, enacted by the legislative authority, void; but if the law be void and the courts have this jurisdiction, *it must not be enforced.* In point of fact then it is no more unseemly in a Justice of the Peace doing what his oath of office requires of him, viz: decide what the law is according to his best judgement, than in the Judges of the Supreme Court declaring a law void. Now it may be that the Imperial Parliament intended so to degrade the supremacy and power of the Parliament of Canada and of the Provincial Legislatures, as to render the exercise of their powers subordinate to the jurisdiction of the least or the highest in authority of the legal tribunals of the Dominion, but I have not yet heard a reason advanced, nor have I been able to discover any reason, upon which such an assumption can be founded.

I do not wish to advance anything that might have the appearance of ridicule in discussing a great question like this; but I cannot forbear saying that it does not tend to elevate the character of the Provincial *p. 13* Legislature to hear Counsel learned in the law arguing before a legal tribunal upon the constitutionality of a permissive liquor license law passed by the Provincial Legislature, urging upon the court the profound argument, "that to prohibit the granting of a license to a country tavern, to sell liquor within the municipal authority, interferes with the regulations of *trade and commerce*, the right to export and to import, to buy and sell, in the foreign market; that it affected the general revenues of the Dominion and robbed the government of Canada of its just dues. That to impose a pecuniary penalty for selling liquor without a license, and imprisonment for its non-payment when imposed, was making the offence of so selling *in a legal sense* a criminal act under the term *Criminal Law* in the British North America Act, and therefore void." Truly weighty arguments to advance upon such a question, apparently forgetting that all trade and barter within the Province must necessarily be governed by the laws relating to property and civil rights, and that the only principle involved in such a law is the civil right of the subject to sell within the municipal jurisdiction; a civil right *the most important of all rights*, and forgetting also the sound principle that the greater right must never be merged in the minor right. If the two rights are inseparable, the minor must merge in the greater, which the Provincial Legislature has. Such occasions lead one to imagine that the Provincial Legislature is reduced to a mere Parochial Government, instituted for the sole purpose of regulating the sale of intoxicating liquors and like subjects within the limits of its Parochial Authority, and with very doubtful powers for even that.

The Dominion Parliament is supposed to pass no law except necessary in the general interests of the Dominion and of like effect in all the Provinces, except in a few instances in the case of Quebec. There ought, therefore, to be no arbitrary rule laid down by which any desired alteration in the laws of any Province could not be effected by its legislature, though such alteration in the opinion of some legal minds encroached upon the powers delegated to the Parliament of Canada, if, in the opinion of the tribunal invested by the British North America Act with *the negative* jurisdiction, such alteration did not infringe upon the powers so delegated. If experience should subsequently prove that the nature of any such alteration had been misapprehended, it would be in the power of either legislative body to correct the error, as was done in the case of a law passed by the legislature of this Province in regard to the Central

Bank, which being found to conflict with the authority assigned to Parliament was repealed at the next session of the legislature.

Where a Bill is passed by the Legislative Council and House of Assembly, it is the duty of the Lieutenant Governor to declare that he assents thereto, or that he withholds his assent, according to his discretion, subject to the provisions of the British North America Act, that is as stated in Sections 91 and 92. He is required first to determine, which he does with the aid of the Attorney General, whether the Bill so presented for his assent is in contravention of the authority as declared in the two

p. 14 sections named. If so his duty is plain, either to declare his dissent or reserve it for the consideration of the Governor General. When a bill so reserved or assented to is presented to the Governor General, he also is required to consider the question of *ultra vires*, which he does with the aid of the Minister of Justice and Privy Council, and determines in like manner according to his discretion and either assents thereto or declares his dissent. In the language of Chief Justice Chipman, when a Bill is so assented to and duly enacted it goes immediately into force, and so remains, and the legal tribunals are bound to give effect to it. If disallowed (by the words of the Act as it was before Confederation), it must be signified by message to the legislature, if in session, or by proclamation, and the Act is declared to be null *after the day of such signification*, negatively declaring that *until such signification* the Act is valid, not only recognizing but incorporating into the Act the rule laid down in the Royal Instructions. The same rule is adopted with the bills passed by the Senate and House of Commons, the Governor General acting with the aid of the Minister of Justice, instead of the Lieutenant Governor, and the Sovereign with the aid of the law officers of the Crown, and the Queen's Privy Council, instead of the Governor General.

It is urged that the consent of the Queen in the one case and of the Governor General in the other, cannot extend the powers of legislation or render valid a law not within the authority conferred by the British North America Act. It is not to be supposed that the exercise of the negative authority, in its assent or dissent, has the effect of extending or limiting the legislative jurisdiction. The office and purpose of the negative power is to determine what is within the powers conferred. And the Act having placed this jurisdiction in the Sovereign and Governor General, the question involved in the proposition does not arise. By the assent the law is declared and affirmed to be within the authority, and no other tribunal is created by the Act or invested with jurisdiction to question the correctness of that decision. It is wholly a question of legislative authority, and having been once determined by the jurisdiction specially named for that purpose, and always aided by high legal authority, *why raise it again?* Surely it will not be urged that Parliament intended to establish a constitution for the Dominion, out of which such a conflict (not of law) between the judiciary and legislative powers of the country should arise, and from which no possible good, but much uncertainty, confusion and injury would result.

The Queen and the Governor General are not invested by Parliament with a negative legislative power for the mere purpose of exercising an arbitrary will over laws passed by the respective legislative bodies. It would be inconsistent to suppose that after conferring certain exclusive authority upon each legislative body, Parliament would confer any other power by which it might be intended that any act clearly within such authority could be arbitrarily defeated. It is much more rational to suppose that the Queen in the one case, and the Governor General in the other, were invested with this power for the purpose of determining what laws were or were not within the authority as declared by the Act, and so determine by either assenting thereto or declaring their dissent, and *p. 15* thereby settle all doubt and finally determine that question. It is not the personal will of the Sovereign or of the Governor General that they are authorized by the Act to signify. It is the sovereign will of the people declared by express authority of Parliament, and when so declared it must remain until Imperial enactment, or the legislative authority within the Dominion, chooses to alter it.

It is said that the sections of the British North America Act relating to the allowance and disallowance of Bills only apply to such as the legislative body is empowered to pass. But this does not affect the argument. It is still a question of legislative jurisdiction which the *negative legislative power*, as before stated, is authorized to determine. If the Act had not preserved this power the judiciary could not assume jurisdiction to say what was or was not within the legislative authority, and to declare void a law which in the opinion of the Judges was *ultra vires*. The British North America Act is not declared to be the supreme law within the Dominion, not to be changed or altered except by the authority which enacted it. It is as before stated like all other statutes relating to the colonies subject to alteration in so far as it relates to the Dominion and the government thereof by the legislative authority of the Dominion, restrained only by the prerogative power. It is a question of a political nature, growing out of a conflict between legislative authorities, and therefore not within the sphere of ordinary judicial inquiry or judicial control.

Assuming for the sake of argument that if Parliament intended by the use of the word "exclusive" in the ninety first and ninety second sections of the Act, that all laws passed by either legislative body which in any way encroached upon the subjects of legislation so exclusively assigned to the other should be void, the legal tribunals would be called upon to ascertain and declare what law was void and what valid. Let us see whether we can be justified in implying such an intention in the absence of any express declaration to that effect. If that was the intention of Parliament the general rule of law which governs the courts in such cases is that "when exclusive authority is given to one person to do an act it cannot be executed by another," and when the same law confers exclusive authority upon one person to do a particular act and upon another person authority to do some other act, each is confined to the execution of his own authority, and cannot, as incident thereto, execute any part of the authority so exclusively given to the other. There is another rule that where a law directs a thing to be done in a particular manner, the direction must be implicitly followed. To this rule, however, there are some exceptions. For instance, if the law relates to an authority already held and exercised, and is only declaratory of another mode of executing some of such powers, any act done though not in strict conformity with the direction of the law, would not be void unless so expressly declared, or some strong negative words are used that necessarily render it void. The word "exclusive" in a law only declaratory of the authority is not sufficient. But there is another reason why the word "exclusive" does not render a law void because *ultra vires*. Parliament has expressly stated for

p. 16 what purpose the word is used. In the ninety-first section it is stated, "and for greater certainty, but not so as to restrict ＊ ＊ ＊ it is hereby declared that the exclusive authority of the Parliament of Canada extends etc., etc." The word is not therefore used for the purpose of rendering a law void not enacted strictly within the letter of the authority, nor in the vain hope of securing absolute certainty, but to enable each legislative body to ascertain with a *greater degree of certainty*, what may or may not be fairly and reasonably within its authority — Surely it is not used for the purpose of rendering the binding force of *all law uncertain*. The unavoidable uncertainty in the interpretation of the law is enough, we should not unnecessarily add thereto. The last named rule then is the one to be applied in the construction of the British North America Act. It is evident that Parliament did not intend that all laws should be void not enacted strictly within the authority conferred, for the reason, that in the subjects assigned to the Parliament of Canada, such only were selected in regard to which a uniformity of law was deemed requisite. But if the ninety-first and ninety second sections of the Act are construed according to the two first named rules, it must follow that in regard to many of the subjects assigned to Parliament no uniform law can be enacted. In order to do so the authority must be exercised in conjunction with some of the powers expressly assigned to the Provincial Legislatures. In regard to "Bankruptcy and Insolvency" the Dominion Parliament could not exercise authority over "Property and civil rights" as incident to the enactment of a uniform law upon the former subject, the latter being exclusively assigned to the Provincial Legislatures. It would be compelled to confine legislation upon that subject to declaring what persons should be subject to the Bankrupt and Insolvent laws, what acts by such persons should be deemed acts of Bankruptcy, and what acts by bankrupt or insolvent debtors should be deemed criminal, leaving the respective Provincial Legislatures to deal with the liberty of the person and subsequently acquired property of a Bankrupt whose estate had been subjected to compulsory liquidation by the law of Parliament. The power to make laws relating to Bankruptcy and Insolvency cannot be construed into an authority to take away the right of a creditor who is neither Bankrupt or Insolvent, to pursue his remedy to recover his debt against either the person of his Bankrupt debtor or his future assets. What may be taken as incident to any subject under the last clause of the ninety-first section of the Act is a question that would necessarily lead to great diversity of opinion and endless legal conflict, if it be left subject to judicial inquiry.

Laws relating to "property and civil rights" are the most important and most sacred of all temporal laws by which a people are governed, and include more than all the other subjects named. The laws relating to bankruptcy and insolvency are so vastly inferior in importance, it cannot be contended for a moment that authority to deal with the latter subject can take with it, as incident thereto, the right to make laws upon the former subject; the minor right cannot merge the greater. The application then, of the two first mentioned rules of construction, would entirely defeat the clear intention of Parliament.

There is one case stated in the British North America Act, which *p. 17* renders a law enacted by either Legislative body null and void, viz: where a law passed by the Parliament of Canada is disallowed by the Sovereign, and where a law passed by any Provincial Legislature is disallowed by the Governor General; then such disallowance being signified to the legislature or by proclamation within the time stated in the Act, the law in each case is declared to be null from and after the day of such signification. In regard to the power given to the Parliament of Canada to provide for a uniform law in the three Provinces upon the subject of property and civil rights, it is expressly declared by the ninety-fourth section, that no law providing for such uniformity shall have any effect in any Province until the legislature thereof shall have enacted such law. Now it is not unreasonable to suppose that in an Act of the peculiar nature of the British North America Act, if Parliament had intended that laws enacted by either legislative body should in any other case be absolutely void and of no effect, it would have been stated. If the negative power is left to determine the question of legislative authority, that tribunal would not necessarily be bound by the construction which the judiciary might feel compelled to adopt, and would treat the sections named as declaratory only, and not in restraint of the general powers of legislation. Under this construction, it would be competent for the Parliament of Canada to deal with property and civil rights in the enactment of a uniform law on any of the subjects assigned to that body. But whichever construction may be considered most in accordance with the general rule for construing statutes, if there be any reasonable doubt of the intention of Parliament in regard to what laws should be void, or of the authority to determine what laws enacted are, or are not within the scope of the legislative authority, then I say public interest and public convenience require that such doubt should be given in favor of the legislative jurisdiction. By the legislative jurisdiction, I mean the negative power of the Sovereign and the Governor General, which Chief Justice Chipman in the case before cited said, was in the nature of a legislative power, retained for the express purpose of restraining and controlling the colonial legislatures.

There is another reason why we should not give to the word "exclusive" the full legal force claimed for it. We must not mistake the real nature of the authority conferred by the British North America Act upon the Parliament of Canada and the Provincial Legislature. It is not an authority to enact laws. It is only an "exclusive" right and authority to the Senate and House of Commons for the Dominion, and the respective Legislative Councils and Assemblies of the Provinces to tender advice and consent to the Sovereign to enact laws, in regard to the subjects named in the Act. The Sovereign ever did by the legislative prerogative power enact all law for the United Kingdom by the advice and consent of the Lords and Commons, and for the Provinces by the advice and consent of the Legislative Council and Assembly. The latter always had the right to give such advice and consent. No grant was therefore required for that purpose. The Lieutenant Governor now, as formerly, assents to *p. 18* Bills passed by the Legislative Council and Assembly in the name of the Queen in the same manner as the Governor General by authority of the fifty-fifth and ninetieth sections of the Act.

In Cooley, on Constitutional Limitations, it is stated "where by the theory of any government, complete sovereignty is vested in the same individual or body to enact law, any law enacted could not be void, but if it conflicted with any existing constitutional principle must have the effect to modify or abrogate such principle instead of being nullified by it. This must be so in Great Britain, with every law not in harmony with pre-existing constitutional principles." This is an admirable illustration of the law making power under the British Constitution. Let us see how far it is applicable to the Dominion under the British North America Act. The same sovereign authority enacts all law for the United Kingdom, the Dominion, and the Provinces. In exercising the legislative prerogative power of enacting laws for the United Kingdom, the Sovereign is governed by the advise [sic] and consent of the Lords and Commons; for the Dominion, the Senate and House of Commons; for any Province by the Legislative Council and Assembly. Though the advice and consent is tendered by "exclusive" right and authority by respective legislative bodies of the Empire, the sole enacting power is centred in one and the same sovereignty. Hence whatever law is enacted by that sovereign authority either modifies or abrogates any pre-existing constitutional principle or law relating thereto. The *Legislative prerogative power* of the Sovereign can no more be subject to judicial supremacy when enacting laws for the Dominion or any Province, than when in enacting laws for the United Kingdom.

If we give to the word "exclusive" the full force claimed for it, it would carry us farther than any would be willing to go. The Lords and Commons by the British North America Act advised and consented that the Queen should confer upon the Senate and House of Commons for Canada the "exclusive" right and authority to advise and consent to the enactment of laws to be in force within the Dominion, and *in a legal sense* these two Houses of Parliament are as much excluded from the right to tender that advice and consent as the Legislative Councils and Assemblies in the respective Provinces, and cannot of *strict legal right* resume it. Therefore if a law enacted by the advice and consent of the Legislative Council and Assembly or Senate and House of Commons is subject to judicial supremacy, because repugnant to any "exclusive" authority conferred, the law enacted by the advice and consent of the Lords and Commons, alike repugnant, must also be subject to judicial supremacy. This is the fair *legal* result of the claim on behalf of the judiciary, not only to declare what the law is, but to restrain the sovereign authority which alone can declare what shall be the law. There are certain acts performed by virtue of the prerogative subject to judicial inquiry, but that of enacting laws is not one of them. There is nothing in the British North America Act that can be construed to render it so subject. On the contrary, the sovereign prerogative to enact the law in the fullest sense, to dissent from and declare null a law passed by either of the legislative authorities within the Dominion, is expressly preserved and confirmed by Parliament. If Parliament had said it *shall not* be lawful for the Queen to enact laws with the advice and consent of the Legislative Council and Assembly of any *p. 19* Province, except upon the subjects assigned to each, and had not preserved the negative power for the purpose of determining what was within the subjects so exclusively assigned, there might be some force in the claim put forth on behalf of the judiciary to assume that jurisdiction.

None will deny that it is most desirable for each legislative body to confine its legislation to the subjects assigned to it by the British North

America Act, so far as it is possible to do so, consistent with the general interest of the Dominion, or of any Province. But it would be very unwise in the commencement of our confederate system of government to surround the constitution with a *legal band* rendering it unable to yield to any public necessity or public pressure, save only that capable of rending it asunder and reducing it to its original fragments. It is not a sufficient answer to say that a remedy can be found to meet such a difficulty in an application to the Imperial Parliament. The people of the Dominion, through the Legislative authority, always did, and do now, possess the power within themselves necessary to effect any change they may deem desirable in the constitution or laws, and no other power within the constitution other than the negative power can prevent them.

The Constitution of the United States is a grant of executive and legislative and judicial powers and authority to these three departments of the Government organized under its authority, with certain specified subjects upon which no law is to be enacted, and reserving all other powers not expressly granted. It provides the mode of appointing and electing all officers of the state, and among a great variety of provisions an article is inserted declaring that the Constitution is the *supreme law of the land*. It makes special provisions in regard to the mode or proposing and effecting amendments to the constitution by the people through delegates elected for that purpose, and so *depriving the legislative authority* of any such power it expressly requires that the judiciary shall determine all questions according to the authority as declared by the constitution. The oath of office taken by the Judges before entering upon their judicial duties, compels them to decide every question by the standard of the constitution as the *supreme law*. The legislature under that constitution does not represent the people in the same sense in which Parliament represents the people under the British constitution, nor in the sense in which a colonial legislature represents the people under the colonial constitution. A rule of construction therefore applied to the former in regard to its restraining powers must not be applied to the British North America Act. That Act does not contain a grant of powers from the people to the legislatures, nor from the Imperial Parliament acting on their behalf to the legislatures, for the reason that Parliament does not act in its dealings with the colonies in a representative capacity, but as a sovereign power. The people of the colonies are not represented in Parliament. But the action of Parliament in regard to the colonies is governed by the same principles, as if it acted in a representative capacity, and therefore subject to be altered or repealed by the legislative authority of the colony to which

p. 20 it relates, in so far as it affects the internal interests of that colony. The theory of the British Constitution is that Parliament represents the people in the fullest possible sense, and can do whatever the people themselves could do were they personally present. Parliament can add to or take from the constitution whatever it deems proper. The law enacted by the sovereign with the advice and consent of the two Houses of Parliament is the *supreme law*. The colonial legislature in like manner represents the people and may add to or take from the Colonial Constitution. All laws enacted by the Queen, (represented by the Governor) with the advice and consent of the Legislative Council and Assembly is the *supreme law within the Colony*.

The seventeenth section of the British North America Act says, "there shall be one Parliament for Canada," meaning for the people of Canada. Neither the term "Parliament" in the ninety-first section, nor the term "legislature" in the ninety-second section is used to designate a body distinct from, but as a body representing the people, and must be read in the same sense as if the words "the people in Parliament" and the words "the people in the legislature" had been used. Inasmuch, therefore, as all the powers of legislation mentioned in the Act were possessed before and at the time of its enactment, these sections are not to be taken as granting powers already possessed, nor in an arbitrary sense as restraining the exercise of such powers. Whatever language is used to express it, it must be taken as declaratory only in pointing out for the purpose of *greater convenience*, the particular subjects upon which the people, through each legislative body, are to exercise the legislative authority, to be controlled only by the negative legislative power of the Sovereign. In reading the Act then we must not treat Parliament or the legislature as distinct from the people, but like all statutes involving the rights of the subject or the public good, it must receive the most full and liberal construction the language and intention of the legislature will admit of, and best to attain that end. No man will be found to say that the public interests or the rights of the subject will be best promoted by the judiciary exercising jurisdiction to declare an act of the legislative authority void, thereby rendering uncertain the binding force of all statute law. All must agree that both objects will be best attained if that question be determined as heretofore, by the negative authority, and the binding force of the law, when enacted, rendered certain. Certainty in the binding character of the laws is a matter of the greatest importance in every well governed country. The judiciary ought not, therefore, to attempt to restrict the powers of Parliament or of the legislature in a mistaken belief that such restriction is necessary in the interests of the people, or the liberty of the subject.

Whenever, under any Constitution, the people cannot rely upon their representatives in Parliament to protect their personal liberties, their "property and civil rights" from unjust or oppressive laws, but are compelled to flee to the judicial authority for protection, depend upon it despotism reigns somewhere. We may rest assured, however, it has no abiding place in our Constitution.

p. 21   The supreme authority of the Imperial Parliament will be as well guarded from intrusion, and the interests of the nation as well protected in the keeping of the Sovereign and Queen's Privy Council, as in the keeping of the Judiciary of any Province. If that high authority find no reason for the exercise of the royal veto upon the act of the Parliament of Canada, the constitutional calls for no exercise of a judicial veto. The authority of the Parliament of Canada and the interests of the Dominion will be as carefully watched over and preserved from all undue interference by His Excellency the Governor General, and the Queen's Privy Council for Canada, as by the legal tribunals of any Province, and if that high authority in the Dominion find no reason for the exercise of the Royal veto by the Governor General upon the Act of the Provincial Legislature, the British North America Act requires no *legal* veto to be exercised by the Courts.

No Provincial Court can arrogate to itself authority to declare void any law enacted by the Queen, with the consent of the two Houses of Parliament or the two Houses of a Provincial Legislature, without assuming a jurisdiction and responsibility neither called for nor justified by the constitution. It is a weak argument to urge in justification of this jurisdiction that unless the courts take it, the Dominion Parliament may by its legislation override the authority of the Provincial Legislatures. The negative legislative power of the Sovereign over the Parliament of Canada (which has ever been exerted to protect the weak and maintain the right) will not permit any encroachment injurious to the Provincial authority, or to the interests of the people of any Province. Further the Provinces may safely rely upon each other to protect their respective as well as their mutual interests, the latter not created but united by the confederate compact. Their representatives constitute the Parliament of Canada, and it must be that the safety and permanency of the central power depends, constituted as it is, upon the protection afforded to the rights and powers secured to each of the several Provincial governments. It is asking too great a sacrifice of the legislative powers of the people to permit the exercise of any such negative jurisdiction in the judicial tribunals, in addition to the negative legislative power of the Sovereign.

Under a constitution which provides a constitutional system of government, combined with a direct executive responsibility, the judiciary is never called upon to say what Parliament is or is not authorized to do, but simply to interpret and determine upon what Parliament has done. The language of Chief Justice Chipman is, as applied to our confederate constitution, as it was to that of the Province at the time he gave utterance to it. If it be asked how this principle can apply under a constitution where the legislative authority is divided between two several bodies, each possessing certain designated powers, when a law enacted by the one is found to be in conflict with a law enacted by the other, the answer is plain. The question of legislative jurisdiction having been *once* settled by the authority before pointed out, there can be no good reason assigned why the rule applied to different statutes enacted by the same legislative body, should not be applied here, and preference given to that law which *p. 22* is found to be last in order of time. If it should happen that any public inconvenience is occasioned by the passage of laws subsequently found to be in conflict, the legislative authority is, and always will be, the best adapted to remedy the difficulty, as was done in regard to the law relating to the Central Bank before referred to. If it be asked what rule is to be applied if an action should be brought in the Courts of this Province upon a contract made in Nova Scotia, if the law of Nova Scotia, by which it was claimed the matter in dispute should be determined, was found to be in conflict with the law of the Dominion, then, I think, as there is nothing in the British North America Act to restrain the Courts, the *Comity* should be extended to the law of Nova Scotia, and the cause determined according to the law in that Province; that in turn we may have justice administered to us by the Courts in Nova Scotia upon contracts made here according to the law as in New Brunswick.

The necessity for the adoption of this rule by the legal tribunals is obvious, that the conflict of law, which must inevitably occur, may be rendered as little *burdensome* and as little *uncertain* to the people of the Dominion in the prosecution of their individual rights as the constitution will admit.

There is nothing in the view which I have taken in regard to the supremacy of the colonial legislature within the colony, that derogates in the slightest degree from the supreme legislative power of the Imperial Parliament over the colonies or over the Dominion of Canada. That Parliament may, if it choose, deprive the sovereign of the power to assent to a Bill passed by a colonial legislature repugnant to an Imperial Statute, as it did in the case of the Act 3rd and 4th Vic. for the Union of the two Provinces of Canada. It may enact any law upon any subject and declare that it shall be in force and binding upon the inhabitants of the Dominion. It may, if it will, repeal the Act of Confederation and all other laws in force in the Dominion. In short destroy all law and order and reduce society to a state of chaos. The sovereign is possessed of the same constitutional right to refuse to enact into a law any Bill passed by the two Houses of the Imperial Parliament, as any bill passed by the two Houses of the Parliament of Canada or the two Houses of any Provincial Legislature, and if the Lords and Commons of Great Britain should pass a Bill to overrule any law enacted or in force in the Dominion, Her Majesty may withhold Her assent, and protect from the power of the Imperial Parliament the rights of the people and legislature of the Dominion. The propriety of doing so might be questioned; not the constitutional right. And when a Bill is passed by the Senate and House of Commons of Canada or by the Legislative Council and House of Assembly in any Province, repugnant to an Imperial Senate [sic], relating to the Dominion, the Queen may either enact into a law or withhold Her assent, and as before the propriety of the act in either case may be questioned, not the constitutional right.

But we need not be alarmed at this sovereign power. The wisdom of Parliament will bend its future policy towards the Dominion in quite a different direction. The Imperial Parliament will not be likely to take the trouble of legislating for the Dominion unless desired by the legislative authority thereof to do so. It has constituted the Provinces of British North America a *Dominion* with full dominion powers within its territorial limits, and will leave it to the legislative authority to shape and direct its internal policy and prescribe such laws for the government of the inhabitants thereof, as may from time to time be deemed necessary, unrestrained by any imaginary power in any subordinate department of the government.

p. 23

It is a political axiom that the judiciary power of any well constituted government must be co-extensive with the legislative power, and must be capable of deciding every judicial question which grows out of the constitution and laws. While we admit the truth and force of this axiom we must not forget the vast difference there is between interpreting and administering the law and determining what rule of law the sovereign authority shall or shall not prescribe. The latter is exclusively within the province of the Houses of Parliament and the two Houses of the respective Provincial Legislatures.

The legislative power is always the supreme and the creative power in any well constituted government. The judicial is a power created by and subordinate to the legislative. It does not appertain to the created power to make or to unmake the law; its duty is confined to interpreting and administering the law. If the judiciary can declare a law enacted by the legislature null and void, it must necessarily possess the greater power, and it ought to follow capable of being enforced in opposition to the legislative authority. This could not be because the judiciary must depend upon the legislature for the ability to enforce its decrees. This jurisdiction in the judiciary of the United States being expressly conferred by the constitution and deemed necessary under their peculiar system of government the courts were bound to accept it, and it is capable of being enforced over the State Legislatures, because the Supreme Court of the nation is aided by the power of the national government. Notwithstanding this power is given by the constitution, the court is utterly helpless when asserting its authority in opposition to that of the government. Whenever Congress asserts its authority the court must yield, whatever the opinion of the Judges may be of the constitutional right. It must submit to the power without the aid of which it cannot enforce its judicial authority. In short, it must execute the will of the national Legislature or do nothing. This jurisdiction in the judiciary is admittedly a weak point in the constitution, because it cannot always be enforced, and it renders the binding character of the laws uncertain. It can only be remedied by incorporating into the constitution two elements of the British Colonial system of government, viz: a negative legislative power in the Executive Head of the nation over all laws enacted by the state legislatures, (one of the modes suggested by Chief Justice Story), and the principle of direct Executive responsibility in the national government.

The British North America Act does not confer this jurisdiction upon the judiciary, nor could it be enforced if it did. The legislative authority of the Province always had, and still has the power to constitute courts for the administration of Justice. It always had the power, and has now, *p. 24* to abolish entirely any court, and to constitute any other court in its stead with such jurisdiction as it may choose to confer.

It seems to me a strange proposition that the County Courts, created by the Legislature of this Province for the purpose of aiding in the administration of Justice, with such jurisdiction as it was deemed necessary in the wisdom of the legislature to confer upon them, should, because a branch of the judiciary power under the constitution, assume jurisdiction to declare void any act of the authority by which they were so created and by a single breath of which they may be swept out of existence. Yet this is the theory upon which all the legal tribunals are to take such a jurisdiction. The judiciary does by its original and constitutional powers possess jurisdiction to restrain the *individual* will and action of the people, but not the *sovereign will*. The sovereign power of the people or the major part of them, as declared through the sovereign head of the nation or its representative, may make lawful whatever it will, and every department of the government is bound to give effect to it.

If the Parliament of Canada should establish a Supreme Court of Appeal for the Dominion, and by the Act organizing the court should require the court to be governed in its judgments and decisions by the law enacted by Parliament, or by any Provincial Legislature, preferring that law last in order of time, and declaring that it should be deemed a good ground for the reversal of the judgment of any Provincial court if found to be in conflict with any such law, could there be any doubt that the court would implicitly obey the authority and execute the powers conferred upon it by the law which created it. If not, could the courts in any Province resist the authority of the Court of Appeal upon the ground that the Parliament of Canada had no constitutional right or power to take away or destroy any of the jurisdiction inherent in the original and constitutional powers of the judiciary of the Provinces. It seems to me not. If the attempt were made, it would fail for two reasons, firstly, the right could not be maintained upon any sound constitutional principle, and secondly, the court possesses no power within itself to enforce its authority. The Provincial Legislature could not be relied upon for aid because the Court in the position assumed sets aside the latter authority also. If the British North America Act had expressly conferred this jurisdiction, though the power to enforce it in opposition to the will of the legislature would be wanting, yet it would be reasonable to suppose that as the constitution had invested the judiciary with this power, the legislature, in deference to the constitution, would yield a willing compliance to the opinion of the Judges, and provide the necessary authority to enable the judgments of the Courts to be put into execution. But if the judiciary in the entire absence of such an authority should refuse to administer the law as declared by the legislative authority, we need not be surprised if the legislature, acting in the best interests of the country, should feel constrained to assert its supremacy, and insist upon its administration without any question of the authority from which it emanated, leaving *p. 25* that to be determined by the only authority known to the Colonial constitution and the one provided by the Act for that purpose. This is a jurisdiction peculiar to the judiciary of the United States under their *constitution,* in which the prerogative power as known to our constitution forms no part. The written constitution is the prerogative authority through which the people have declared their will, which is paramount to that of their representatives expressed in any law. This high authority is not claimed by the Judges by virtue of judicial supremacy, but as administrators of the public will. This judicial jurisdiction is a theory altogether foreign to the spirit of the British constitution, by virtue of which the sovereign declares the will of the people in every law enacted in regard to the subjects embraced therein. Hence when the Judges in any Province claim to exercise this high authority by virtue of judicial supremacy, they act not as administrators of the public will but as restrainers of that will, declared by the only authority through which the people speak.

In conclusion, to use the language of Blackstone, "what Parliament does no power on earth can undo," and so what the Parliament of Canada does or the Legislature of any Province does, no power within the Dominion, save the legislative, can undo or successfully resist.

JAMES STEADMAN
J. C. C.
Fredericton, February, 1873.

OBSERVATIONS

of

THE CHIEF JUSTICE OF NEW BRUNSWICK

on

A BILL ENTITLED "AN ACT TO ESTABLISH A SUPREME COURT FOR

THE DOMINION OF CANADA."

———————

*Presented to Parliament on 21st May 1869, by the Hon.
Sir John A. Macdonald, K.C.B. Minister of Justice, &c. &c. &c.*

———————

FREDERICTON:

G.E. FENETY, PRINTER TO THE QUEEN'S MOST EXCELLENT MAJESTY.

1870

OBSERVATIONS

of

THE CHIEF JUSTICE OF NEW BRUNSWICK

on

A BILL ENTITLED "AN ACT TO ESTABLISH A SUPREME COURT FOR

THE DOMINION OF CANADA."

———————

Presented to Parliament on 21st May 1869, by the Hon. Sir John A. Macdonald, K.C.B. Minister of Justice, &c. &c. &c.

———————

Under this Bill, though only one Court is proposed to be established, three entirely distinct and separate jurisdictions are raised; and though presided over by the same Judges, the Bill really creates three Courts, entirely different, one from the other, viz:—

1. An Appellate Court.

2. A Court for settling certain Constitutional questions, in the nature of a Court of Original Jurisdiction.

3. A Court of original Common Law, Equity and Admiralty Jurisdiction.

In dealing with the Bill, this must be kept clearly in view, and the Court of Appeal discussed independently of the Courts of Original Jurisdiction, or confusion is unavoidable.

"The British North America Act, 1867," is the Supreme Law of the Dominion, and must be universally and implicitly obeyed. All Acts of the Parliament of Canada, or of the Legislatures of the respective Provinces, repugnant to the Imperial Statute, are necessarily void; and of like necessity when cases come before the legal tribunals, it pertains to the judicial power to determine and declare what is the law of the land. It is said to be "a political axiom, that the judicial power of every well constituted government must be co-extensive with the legislative power, and must be capable of deciding every judicial question which grows out of the Constitution and Laws."

The Parliament of Canada is no doubt supreme in all cases in which it is empowered to act. If therefore the Constitution of the Dominion is "The British North America Act, 1867," we must look there for authority for constituting and organizing Courts.

The portions of the Statute which bear on this subject are—   *p. 2*

Division VI.—*Distribution of Legislative Powers.—Powers of the Parliament.*

By section 91, it is enacted that "It shall be lawful for the Queen, by and with the advice and consent of the Senate and House of Commons, to make laws for the peace, order and good government of Canada, in relation to all matters not coming within the classes of subjects by this Act assigned exclusively to the Legislatures of the Provinces; and for greater certainty, but not so as to restrict the generality of the foregoing terms of this section, it is hereby declared that (notwithstanding any thing in this Act) the exclusive Legislative authority of the Parliament of Canada extends to all matters coming within the classes of subjects next hereinafter enumerated."

Then follows the enumeration of twenty nine classes, one only of which refers to the matter in question, vis. the 27th—"The Criminal Law, except the constitution of Courts of Criminal Jurisdiction, but including the procedure in criminal matters."

Under head—*"Exclusive powers of Provincial Legislatures,"*—Section 92 enacts that "In each Province the Legislature may exclusively make laws in relation to matters coming within the classes of subjects next hereinafter enumerated." They are sixteen in number, of which is—

No.1. "The amendment from time to time, notwithstanding any thing in this Act, of the Constitution of the Province, except as regards the office of Lieutenant Governor."

No.13. "Property and Civil rights in the Province."

No.14. "The administration of justice in the Province, including the constitution, maintenance and organization of Provincial Courts, both of Civil and Criminal jurisdiction, and including procedure in Civil matters in those Courts."

No.15. "The imposition of punishment by fine, penalty or imprisonment, for enforcing any law of the Province made in relation to any matter coming within any of the classes of subjects enumerated in this section."

Under Division VII—*"Judicature,"*—after providing that the Governor General shall appoint the Judges of the Superior, District and County Courts in each Province; specifying the Bars from which they shall be selected; the tenure of office of the Judges of the Superior Courts; and that their salaries, &c. shall be fixed and provided by the Parliament of Canada; section 101 provides that "The Parliament of Canada may, notwithstanding any thing in this Act, from time to time provide for the constitution, maintenance and organization of a General Court of Appeal for Canada, and for the establishment of any additional Courts *for the better administration of the Laws of Canada.*"

Under Division IX—*"Miscellaneous Provisions,"*—Section 129 enacts that "Except as otherwise provided by this Act, all laws in force in Canada, New Brunswick and Nova Scotia at the Union, and all Courts of Civil and Criminal jurisdiction, and all legal Commissions, powers and authorities, and all officers, judicial, administrative, and ministerial, existing therein at the Union, shall continue in Ontario, Quebec, Nova Scotia and New Brunswick respectively, as if the Union had not been made; subject nevertheless, (except with respect to such as are enacted by or exist under Acts of the Parliament of Great Britain or of the Parliament of the United Kingdom of Great Britain and Ireland) to be repealed, abolished or altered by the Parliament of Canada, or by the Legislature of the respective Province, according to the authority of the Parliament or of that Legislature under this Act."

p. 3   Section 133, after providing that either the English or French language may be used in debates of the House of Parliament of Canada, and of the Houses of the Legislature of Quebec, and that both should be used in the respective Records and Journals of those Houses, enacts that *"either of those languages may be used by any person, or in any pleading or process in, or issuing from* ANY COURT OF CANADA ESTABLISHED UNDER THIS ACT, and in or from all or any of the Courts of Quebec."

There are no other clauses or provisions that appear to me to bear in any way on this matter.

With respect then to an Appellate Court,—this, without doubt, the Parliament of Canada has full power to establish. But I cannot help thinking that it would have simplified matters, if the organization of a general Court of Appeal had been dealt with in an Act by itself. This, it appears to me, section 101 seems to contemplate, leaving the establishment of "Additional Courts," if found necessary "for the better administration of the Laws of Canada," for separate legislation; even though such Courts should be placed under the administration of the Judges of the Appellate Court.

But this is a small matter compared with other questions which seem to me to present themselves on the whole Bill as worthy of consideration.

An efficient appellate tribunal as a Court of *dernier ressort,* and whose precedents would be a rule of decision for the Courts of all the Provinces, is without doubt much required. It should, I think, be so constituted as to secure its being at all times presided over by Judges in whose learning and character the Profession and Public have, from experience, confidence. It should be easy of access—speedy in its action—and, with a view to dispatch and cheapness, simple in its procedure. It should deal only with cases of sufficient magnitude, either in the amount or principle involved, to warrant further investigation and expense; and then, with the substance of the matter in controversy on broad principles of law and justice, to the discouragement of mere formal or technical objections which do not affect its merits.

Deficient in these particulars, it is more likely to become a burthen than a blessing.

If the Court is composed of those whose legal standing or experience is inferior to the Judges of the Court whose decision is appealed from, and a decision should be reversed by such a tribunal, possibly by fewer Judges in number than originally decided the case, the administration of justice must necessarily be depreciated, rather than elevated in public estimation. And if parties are delayed by being compelled to go to a great distance, and have to employ fresh counsel to obtain relief from decisions against, or to maintain decrees in their favor; or the merits of the case and substantial justice have to give way to technical objections, or objections on the ground of mere formal defects in procedure, or objections which were not raised in the Court below; or the expenses from these or other causes are made too costly; the Court in many cases, instead of rectifying errors, will only afford the litigious or the wealthy, facilities for defeating the ends of justice, by embarrassing and frustrating proceedings, and impoverishing parties, so as to render a final victory worse than submitting to an original defeat.

While the large strides made in legal reform within the last few years, and those which are now in progress, warn us not to adhere too rigidly to ancient modes of proceeding, still we must remember few changes have been made in the great fundamental principles of law, and the wisdom and learning of the ancient Sages of the law still remain as safe guides and beacons; and we should, I think, without unnecessarily departing from established institutions, endeavour to mould them to the altered state of society and the new phases presented by enlarged intercourse, new discoveries, and consequently more novel and intricate relations; and try to discover whether we have not within the system of

p. 4

343

jurisprudence of Great Britain and her Colonies, materials from which a tribunal adapted to our necessities, may be modelled, before attempting to experimentalize, or without looking to the neighbouring Republic; evidence of both, I think, is to be found in this Bill.

No doubt in framing the appellate portion, the Judicial Committee of the Privy Council and the Court of Exchequer Chamber were in the draughtman's mind; and I also would adopt these two Courts as the basis: only adhering much more closely to their constitutions than I think has been done.

The Exchequer Chamber, we all know, is a Court of Error for revising the judgments of the three Superior Courts of Law in matters of law, and is holden before the Judges of the two Courts not concerned in the judgment impeached.

The Judicial Committee was constituted by the Imperial Act 3 & 4 Wm. 4, c.41, the Court of Appeal from the Court of Admiralty in cases of Prize, and from Colonies; leaving however the Royal prerogative untouched. It is thus composed of the President for the time being, of Her Majesty's Privy Council, the Lord High Chancellor of Great Britain, and such of the members of the Privy Council as shall from time to time hold any of the offices following, that is to say—the office of Lord Keeper or First Lord Commissioner of the Great Seal of Great Britain, Lord Chief Justice or Judge of the Court of Queen's Bench, Master of the Rolls, Vice-Chancellor of England, Lord Chief Justice or Judge of the Court of Common Pleas, Lord Chief Baron or Baron of the Court of Exchequer, Judge of the Prerogative Court of the Lord Archbishop of Canterbury, Judge of the High Court of Admiralty, and Chief Judge of the Court in Bankruptcy, and also all persons, members of the Privy Council who shall have been President thereof, or held the office of Lord Chancellor of Great Britain, or shall have held any of the other offices hereinbefore mentioned; with a proviso that the Crown might appoint any two other persons, being Privy Councillors, to be members of the said Committee.

Thus, we see the first of these Courts is composed wholly of Judges in the daily active discharge of judicial duties—and the latter, almost exclusively of Judges similarly situate, or such with others who have held similar offices.

To assimilate the proposed Court to either of these, in this most important feature of its constitution, section 4, relating to the qualification of Chief Justice and Judges, will have to be materially altered.

Unless the attendance of Judges from the different Superior Courts in the Provinces respectively, is secured, and thereby, as may perhaps be reasonably anticipated, greater legal experience and more diversified legal knowledge and talent obtained, a very dissimilar tribunal will be created.

There is no provision that the Chief Justice, or any one of the Judges who are to form this Court, shall have ever exercised judicial functions, or had a day's judicial experience; but may be selected—the Chief Justice, from Barristers of fifteen years, and the Judges from Barristers of ten years standing; and that too, if the Government should so choose, from any one Province.

This startling departure from the models of the two leading appellate tribunals referred to, as also from the general principle prevailing more or less practically in all the appellate tribunals known to the English Law, including the last and highest Court of the nation, the House of Lords, where law Lords, all of whom have held the highest judicial situations alone decide, and who command the services of the Judges whenever required, presents itself more forcibly, when the value and importance *p. 5* attached by eminent Jurists and Statesmen to this ingredient in the constitution of appellate tribunals is borne in mind.

I shall only select the testimony of two; but two alike experienced and learned as Jurists, and eminent as Statesmen—shining lights in Law and Politics, and whose testimony is not the less valuable, because through the greater portions of their lives politically opposed.

I refer to Lords Lyndhurst and Brougham. On the debate on Lord Campbell's Bill for transferring the Admiralty, Ecclesiastical and Colonial Appeals from the Judicial Committee to the House of Lords, the former, when Lord Chancellor, speaking of the Judicial Committee, said—

> "He thought it was a tribunal admirably adapted for the business which came before it, and *for this reason*, there were various kinds of law agitated, discussed, and settled before it; there were questions of Civil and Ecclesiastical Law: and there were Judges who had been brought up in discussing and administering Civil and Ecclesiastical Law; and when questions of that nature arose their attendance was always required. Again, when questions of Equity arose, there were Judges from the Equity Courts, members of that tribunal; and when such questions were discussed their attendance was requested, and they formed part of the Court. There were questions of Common Law discussed, and there were members of the Court who were also Judges of Common Law, and they attended on these occasions to give sentences and decide. There were questions of Hindoo and Mahomedan Law discussed in cases, the results of which were often of the utmost importance to the parties concerned: and in cases of this nature the Court had the assistance of parties familiar with these laws, and who had acted as Judges in India. He asked the House if, considering what the nature of the questions which came before the tribunal in question, often was—he asked if whether he had not fully established the fact that the tribunal was

admirably adapted to the performance of the duties it had to go through."

And Lord Brougham, when Lord Chancellor, on laying a Bill on the Table of the House of Lords, relative to the appellate jurisdiction of that House, in alluding to the difficulties which had to be overcome in effecting modifications of the existing Law, is thus reported—

"The first was the repugnance which he had naturally felt to alter the jurisdiction of their Lordships, and the next was the small number of Judges from whom he could select a certain number to hear appeals: for he held it to be indispensable that Appeals should be decided by Judges taken from other Courts, and not by Judges appointed for the express purpose of deciding such cases, and forming a separate and exclusive tribunal. The example of France, where there were two Courts exclusively for hearing Appeals, namely the *Cour Royal* and the *Cour de Cassation*, proved nothing, for there were such a vast number of inferior Judges, (fourteen or fifteen hundred), and they were of such an inferior class, that it would be most injudicious to call upon them to sit in Appeal. He thought that Judges who were only Judges of Appeal, would not be fit for any thing. What would the Lord Chancellor be worth as a Judge, if he sat forty or fifty days in the year to hear Appeals only, without being accustomed to the forensic *strepitus,* as it were, and without having heard the business done in the first instance, which afterwards became the subject of appeal? There never would be a Court of Appeal worth any thing, unless the Judges composing it sat also in the Courts below. On the one hand, it was necessary that the Judges of the Court of Appeal should not be those whose decisions were appealed against, and on the other, that they should be accustomed to preside in the Courts below. There was but one middle course to take, and that was judiciously to compose a due admixture of the various Judges with those whose decisions were appealed against—thus proceeding on the principle of analogy to the Courts of Common Law. When the Court of King's Bench, or the Court of Exchequer, or the Court of Common Pleas, went wrong, an appeal was made to the Common Law Judges; and so when all these Judges went wrong, an appeal took place to the House of Lords, which sent for the Judges, who intermixed with the Equity Judges, and applied their minds to the subject. It was upon this principle that the Judicial Committee of the Privy Council was constructed;"—

And it is the principle, I think, with slight modifications, admirably adapted to the Dominion.

Assuming, however, the contemplated Court, in its organization, correct in principle, I would venture to point out some difficulties which may arise in its practical working.

1st. The Bill does not seem to me to define with sufficient precision, from what Judgments, Rules, and Orders, parties may appeal.

2ndly. It allows Appeals in cases irrespective of the amount or principle involved.

p. 6　　3rdly. It gives too long time for Appeals.

4thly. It places the Appeal too far away for ordinary cases; entailing too much delay and expense; and

5thly. By retaining the present Appeal to the Judicial Committee of the Privy Council to its full extent, it unnecessarily multiplies Appeals, and those too of the most expensive character.

As to the first—Section 13 states, generally, that "Appeal shall lie to the Supreme Court, from *all judgments*" of certain Provincial Courts therein named; and

Section 15 allows a writ of Error to be brought in the said Court from the judgment in any civil action or criminal proceeding of any of said Provincial Courts, in any case in which the proceedings have been according to the course of the common Law of England.

Section 23 then directs, that proceedings in Appeals from *Decrees, Judgments or Orders* in Equity and Admiralty, shall, when not otherwise provided for, be as nearly as possible in conformity with the present practice of the Judicial Committee.

Now, taking these clauses together, what is intended? Are the Decrees, Judgments or Orders to be in the nature of a final sentence, or may any interlocutory proceedings be appealed from?

Section 13, that gives the Appeal, only mentions Judgments. Section 23 directs how proceedings from Decrees, Judgments and Orders shall be conducted; and Section 28 enacts that no appeal shall be allowed from any final Judgment, Decree, or Decretal Order, unless the same be brought within two years from the signing or pronouncing thereof, and that no Appeal shall lie from any interlocutory *Order* or *Rule*, unless the same be brought within six months from the making or granting thereof.

The inference from all this certainly is, that in the Courts of Equity and Admiralty, the Appeal is to be from Orders of Rules of an interlocutory character. Would it not be wise to define exactly what description of Rules and Orders may be appealed from?

It is said, with reference to the Judicial Committee, that "great difference prevails as to the nature of the Judgments from which Appeals should be admitted from the Courts in the Colonies. In the earliest Order of Council which is known on the subject, that of 13th May, 1572, relating to appeals from the Island of Jersey, it was directed that no appeal in any matter, great or small, be permitted or allowed before the same matter be fully examined and ended by definitive sentence; and the constant practice has since been in causes from that Island, to reserve the appeals from all orders in the suit *"en fin de cause."* In the West Indies and American Colonies where the English Law prevails, the practice has always been to admit appeals from all interlocutory orders in Chancery, but not from those at Common Law.

As the jurisdiction of this Court will be purely statutory, we must bear in mind the unbending nature of a statute, and the necessity therefore of defining with precision and accuracy its jurisdiction and powers. It will be destitute of any aid from the "nursing" principles of the Common Law, or the inherent power of the House of Lords, or the general jurisdiction and large discretion which pertains to the exercise of the Royal Prerogative in appeals to the Queen in Council as the fountain of justice, whereby appeals are allowed or disallowed, or terms imposed, as the special circumstances of the particular case demand, or as may be from time to time directed by general regulations.

In this case, as the Statute is written, so it must be interpreted: *jus dicere et non jus dare,* is the maxim of Judges.

p. 7   While it may be inexpedient to prescribe rules of practice by statute, nothing relating to the jurisdiction should however be left in doubt or to inference.

By Section 23, proceedings in appeals from Decrees, Judgments or Orders in Equity and Admiralty, &c., shall, when not otherwise provided for, be as nearly as possible in conformity with the present practice of the Judicial Committee. I can discover nothing with reference to proceedings on appeals from the other Courts. The inference, I presume, would be that some difference was contemplated. If proceedings on appeals from the Equity and Admiralty Courts are to be according to the practice of the Judicial Committee, why should not the same practice prevail with respect to appeals from the other Courts? While a distinction is apparent, I cannot perceive that any other practice is substituted in lieu thereof.

As to the second point—Considering that there is in this Province an appeal to the Supreme Court from the Equity Court, the Court of Marriage and Divorce, Probate Courts, County Courts, and a general supervision over the proceedings of all inferior tribunals, not expressly taken away by Statute, where matters as well of the greatest magnitude as of very small amount, and involving no important principle, are constantly in controversy, to allow a suitor, in a case of the latter character, to drag his opponent to Ottawa on appeal from a judgment in which the whole matter in controversy might only range from £5 to £50, would only be affording means of gratifying a litigious spirit, or wearing out an adversary, and, in my opinion, conferring on all parties a curse rather than a blessing. By way of illustration, take the case of a cause tried in a County Court in which there is a verdict. The party against whom it is rendered applies in that Court for a new trial, it is refused; he appeals to the Supreme Court at Fredericton; the appeal is dismissed and judgment of County Court affirmed: surely in a matter ranging from £5 to £50, this is law enough; but under this Bill the party might of right appeal to Ottawa.

As to the third point—I cannot understand why periods so long should be allowed for appealing, either in cases of final judgments or interlocutory orders.

If, as provided by Section 36, no appeal shall be allowed upon special cases, or on points reserved, or in cases of new trials, unless notice in writing be given to the opposite party within twenty days after the decision complained of, or within such further time as the Court appealed from or a Judge thereof may allow, why might not the same rule apply to all other cases?

In addition to this, it seems to me that there should be stringent provisions that the Appeal shall be promptly proceeded with. After a party has the judgment of a competent Court in his favor, and perhaps realized his judgment, why should he be kept in uncertainty and doubt as to his right for two years? Surely he ought to have the right to say to his opponent, "The Court has given judgment in my favor; if you are not satisfied give me immediate notice, and proceed at once to have the judgment reviewed on appeal. Don't keep me in suspense and jeopardy for two years."

This applies with even more force to Interlocutory Orders or Rules. The Bill gives six months in such cases. In the meantime large expenses may be incurred and a final judgment obtained; while all this is going on, it would seem by this Bill a party may lie by till the six months are about expiring, and then, by appealing against some Interlocutory Order or Rule, possibly overturn all the subsequent proceedings.

In New Brunswick, Appeals from decisions in Equity must be made within twenty days. Appeals from Courts of Marriage and Divorce must be entered in the Supreme Court on or before the first day of the term next after decision. Probate Appeals must be made within thirty days after decision. And even in Appeals to the Judicial Committee, by order of Privy Council of 27th November, 1852, a party desiring to appeal must, within fourteen days after decree or judgment has been pronounced, apply for leave to appeal, and if leave granted, security is to be completed within twenty eight days thereafter; and by orders of the Privy Council of 13th June, 1853, the appellant is required to prosecute his Appeal within three months after receipt at the Privy Council Office of the transcript of proceedings, or the Appeal stands dismissed without further order. *p. 8*

As to the fourth point—So far as litigants generally in New Brunswick are concerned, an Appeal to Ottawa is really almost practically as remote as an Appeal to London, and will burthen ordinary litigation with expenses very much disproportioned to the means of the ordinary run of suitors, and to the amounts generally in litigation. There must be in all cases, the Appeal, first to the Supreme Court at Fredericton, because it is a Common Law rule, that if there be a fixed ascending scale of inferiority affecting several Courts, an error in the judgment of the inferior Court, must in general be examined and determined in the Court next in order in such ascending scale, and will not lie *per saltum* to the highest tribunal. It now constantly happens, that in causes tried in the out Counties by members of the local Bar, fresh Counsel have to be retained at Fredericton to move or show cause—for the simple reason that the local practitioner, unless he has several cases to attend to at Fredericton, cannot afford (or rather his client cannot afford to pay sufficient to enable him) to visit Fredericton, and wait his chance of a hearing. If, after incurring this fresh expense, a suitor has to send his counsel, or to retain fresh counsel at Ottawa, to pursue or resist an Appeal, the amount at stake will require to be large to stand such an accumulation of counsel fees and expenses. But if after all this, he is liable to be dragged from the General Appeal Court at Ottawa to the Judicial Committee of the Privy Council in London, and there compelled to begin expenditure afresh, by not only retaining a new junior and leading counsel, but employing agents to employ Solicitors, and Solicitors to retain such counsel, what with the delays and expenses, I am afraid the unfortunate suitor will stand a chance of being a gray headed man with empty pockets, before he gets through.

Lastly, as to the Appeal to the Privy Council, while it cannot be disputed that the Judicial Committee is a most valuable and efficient Court, its constitution receiving the services of learned men of diversified legal attainments, in whose combined judgments there is every guarantee that sound decisions will be pronounced, and there may reasonably be a reluctance to give up such a tribunal, I think resort should only be had to it in very exceptional cases, in which questions of a national character are involved. Does it not sound very like a reproach to our Dominion to say that there is not sufficient legal talent within its boundaries to decide finally the legal rights of the parties in all ordinary suits? Does it not ignore the principle so largely conceded, that we are fit for Local self Government?

To say we are competent to legislate on all matters affecting the interests of the people of the Dominion, and yet incompetent to decide what those Laws are, and what are the rights of the people thereunder, seems to involve a contradiction not easy to be reconciled. Apart, however, from this, the delay, expense and inconvenience attending the practical working of such an Appeal, seem to be sufficient objections to justify

its discontinuance. No doubt it will be said that this would be an interference with the Royal prerogative. But I should think there could be no
doubt, that if it was for the interest of the Dominion that appeals to the   *p. 9*
Privy Council should be abolished or limited, the principle, as it has been
heretofore, would be readily conceded. And now that an Appellate
tribunal is about being established within our immediate borders, the
necessity for its continuance not only ceases, but its retention would
subject our system to the imputation of encouraging a multiplicity of
appeals, which is directly opposed to the policy of the law; for as said by
Sir J. Nicholl, "although the law favors *the right of appeal,* yet it does not
favor the multiplicity of appeals."

As to the Appeal in Criminal Cases—Section 41 says, "A person
convicted of treason, felony, or misdemeanour, before the Court of
Queen's Bench or Common Pleas, in the Province of Ontario, or before
the Court of Queen's Bench in the Province of Quebec, or before the
Supreme Court in either of the said Provinces of Nova Scotia or New
Brunswick, or who has been convicted as aforesaid before any Court of
Oyer and Terminer, or gaol delivery, and whose conviction has been
affirmed by any of the hereinbefore mentioned Provincial Courts, *may
appeal against the conviction or affirmation;* and the Supreme Court shall
make such rule or order therein, either in affirmance of the conviction or
for granting a new trial, or otherwise, as the justice of the case requires;
and shall make all other necessary rules and orders for carrying such rule
or order into effect; but no such Appeal shall be made unless allowed by
the Superior Court appealed from, or by two of the Judges thereof, in
term or vacation, nor unless such allowance has been granted, and the
appeal has been (*quoere* can be) heard within six months after the conviction was affirmed, unless otherwise ordered by the said Supreme Court;
and any rule or order of the said Supreme Court shall be final."

In New Brunswick, the only jurisdiction, (independent of writ of
Error), in the nature of appeal or review in criminal cases, is under the
22nd, 23rd, and 24th sections of Cap. 159 of the Revised Statutes, which
have not been repealed by the Dominion Act 32 & 33 Vict. Cap. 36,—by
which the Judge presiding at any Assizes (and the same power is given
to a County Court Judge by 31 Vict. Cap. 13,) may reserve any question
of Law which may have arisen during the trial, for the consideration of
the Supreme Court, and shall, in a case stated by him, state the question
of Law reserved, with the special circumstances, and transmit the same
to the Supreme Court, which shall hear and finally determine such question, and reverse, affirm or amend any judgment given, or avoid such
judgment, and order entry thereof to be made on the record, or arrest the
judgment, or order judgment to be given thereon at some other Assizes,
or make such other order as justice may require. This provision is taken

from the Imperial Act 11 Vict. Cap. 78, of which statute Mr. Archbold, in his excellent book on Criminal Practice and Pleading, speaks as "the greatest improvement which has ever been made in the administration of our Criminal Law, so far as relates to indictable offences. It gives the defendant the full effect of a writ of Error, speedily, and with little expense to either party, and the doubt or difficulty being pointed out by the Judge who tried the case, affords the Judges of the Appeal Court the best assurance they can have that no frivolous objections will be submitted to them."

It is an established rule that no bill of exceptions will lie in criminal cases; and recent cases clearly establish that no *new trial* can be granted in felonies. In the latest case decided by the Judicial Committee, where an order for a new trial was reversed, the Court said, "If irregularity occurs in the conduct of a trial, not constituting a ground for treating the verdict as a nullity, the remedy to prevent a failure of justice is by application to the authority with whom rests the discretion either of executing

p. 10 the law, or commuting the sentence." Reg. *vs.* Murphy, Law Reports, 2 P.C. 535.— And though it is well established, that by inherent prerogative right, there is an appeal to the Queen in Council in all cases, criminal as well as civil, arising in the Colonies, the exercise of this branch of the prerogative in criminal cases will only be granted where a case raises questions of great and general importance in the administration of justice, and likely to occur often, and also where, if true, it shews the due and orderly administration of the Law interpreted or diverted into a new course, which might create a precedent for the future, and also where there is no other means of preventing these consequences. And so far have the Judicial Committee acted on these principles, that appeals have been refused though the Court were satisfied individual injustice had been done—leaving the party aggrieved to the clemency of the Crown. Thus—In Reg. *vs.* Mookerjee, 1 Moore's P.C. Cases, N.S. 295, Dr. Lushington, in delivering the judgment of the Court, says—

> "With reference to the existence of the prerogative of the Crown, their Lordships are desirous that no expression should fall from them which in the slightest degree would throw doubt on the existence of that prerogative, not only under the existing circumstances, but in others which might arise with reference to the other Dominions of the Queen which may have been acquired by conquest. They do not think it necessary that they should, on the present occasion, enter minutely into the considerations upon which the prerogative of the Crown is founded. They think it will suffice for the purpose of this case to assume that it does exist, and consequently that it is in the power of the Judicial Committee of the Privy Council exercising that prerogative right under the Crown, so to advise Her Majesty if they should think an appeal ought to be allowed on the present occasion. With regard to the merits of the case itself, their Lordships certainly are inclined to come to the conclusion, that justice has not been very well administered in the present case;

and supposing it to have been a civil and not a criminal case, they would have had no hesitation whatever in recommending to Her Majesty to allow an appeal, for the purpose of considering these proceedings and of doing justice to the party complaining.

"But this is a criminal case, and subject to very different considerations. Admitting therefore two things—admitting the existence of the prerogative of the Crown, and admitting that this, prima facie and presumptively, is a case of great grievance—their Lordships have now to determine whether, looking at all the circumstances attending the granting of appeals in criminal cases, it would be their duty to advise Her Majesty to grant this appeal or to withhold it.

"We must recollect in the first place *that by granting an appeal* is meant an examination of the whole of the proceedings which have taken place. It is not simply for the investigation of any legal question which might have arisen; it is for the purpose of examining *the whole of the evidence, and the whole course of the proceedings upon the trial, to enable us to come to a conclusion upon the merits.*

"Now it is of no small importance to bear in mind, that notwithstanding the numberless instances in which an application of this kind might have been made to the Queen in Council from all the various dominions subject to Her Majesty, that in no instance whatever of any grievance however great, at any time has any attempt ever been made to apply to Her Majesty for leave to appeal in a criminal case.

"We can easily call to memory very many instances which have occurred in the Colonies, in which it has been alleged that gross injustice has been done, and even lives sacrificed where they ought not to have been exposed to any danger; but no precedent of an Appeal of this nature has existed; and we think it is obvious on the least consideration of the consequences, how it is that no such precedent has existed, and how it is that no such precedent would have been created even if an attempt had been made to call into force the power of the Crown. It may be true that on some occasions it is not very desirable to argue simply from consequences alone; but the consequences of granting an Appeal in cases of this description, are so exceedingly strong, they are so entirely destructive of the administration of all criminal jurisprudence, that we cannot for a single moment doubt that they are of the greatest importance in guiding us to form a judgment. Now, if we were to advise Her Majesty to grant an Appeal on this Petition, how would the case stand? It is simply the case of an individual having been convicted of causing documents to be forged. Would not the same right apply to capital cases? What could be done in a capital case? Is there any distinction which can be drawn? If the prerogative of Her Majesty gives this individual the right of Appeal, could any rules or regulations be imposed whereby that right of Appeal could be governed or could be restricted? So you would go through the whole catalogue of cases, and there is no doubt whatever that whenever punishment was likely to ensue, there would follow an Appeal to Her Majesty in Council, and consequently not only would the course of justice be maimed, but in very many instances it would be entirely prostrated."

This case has been since acted on by the Judicial Committee, and the principles therein enunciated entirely assented to.

p. 11 Now if, as Dr. Lushington puts forward as the judgment of the Judicial Committee, that the legal signification of granting an Appeal is not simply an investigation of any legal questions that might have arisen, but involves an examination of the evidence, and the whole course of the proceedings on the trial—is this intended by the 41st Section? The express power given to the Court to grant *new trials*, would seem to imply an exercise of discretion, as on an investigation of the merits and dissatisfaction therewith, or on the ground that the conviction was unsatisfactory by reason of some irregularity in the conduct of the trial. If the whole proceedings are open to re-examination, can it be doubted that Appeals will be encouraged? And will not the Court appealed from be slow to refuse Appeals? If such an Appeal was not contemplated, should not the section be more carefully worded? If it is intended, is it not worthy of consideration that the present mode of proceeding is plain and simple; and judging from experience, has produced no inconvenience or injustice, and has never (that I am aware of) called forth in this Province, any individual or public complaint of a failure of justice in the improper conviction of a prisoner? If such a case should arise, there is always ready the prerogative of the Crown to interfere. This, in a proper case, I feel assured, never has been, and never will be invoked in vain.

It cannot be denied that it is an anomaly, that in a civil suit involving no great principle, and of comparatively trifling amount, a new trial can be obtained, when the same is denied in cases involving liberty, reputation, life and death. Theory is clearly with the appeal. The question is, are there practical difficulties of an insuperable character in the way. If so, there is overwhelming force in the observation, that "If the thing is impracticable, and can be obtained only with such injury to the administration of justice as to outweigh all the advantages which can be anticipated, we must put up with anomalies, and be content with that which in theory is imperfect and unsatisfactory, but which in practice works well."

In 1860, when the subject of establishing a Court of Appeal in criminal cases was before the House of Commons, Sir George C. Lewis presented the difficulties in the way of establishing a Court of Appeal in criminal cases, with much force and ability, and shewed that the opinions of a majority of the Judges were opposed to it, and that the practice of the civilized world went generally against it. From this speech I take the liberty of extracting some of these opinions. He says—

"Before the Committee of 1848 Lord Denman said— 'What I would state in one word, as my objections to the general power, is, that there would be no

antagonism; there are no adverse parties as in civil cases;' and that principle is explained somewhat more fully in the letter of Mr. Baron Rolfe, now Lord Cranworth:— 'With respect to the inexpediency of any right of appeal in criminal cases, I beg leave to add, in addition to what has been stated by Baron Parke, that a new trial would very rarely indeed be practicable. In civil cases the plaintiff has a direct personal interest in the result of his cause, and when a verdict obtained by him is set aside, and a new trial is ordered, he is obliged, in order to gain his suit, and save himself from the obligation of paying the defendant his costs, to take proper steps for bringing all necessary witnesses to a second trial. But this is not the case in criminal prosecutions; a large proportion of prosecutors come forward only because they are bound to do so; the whole proceeding is rather a burthen imposed on the prosecutor, than a measure which he voluntarily adopts, for the sake of personal redress, and I conceive that in nine cases out of ten, when a new trial is ordered, there would be so much difficulty in getting the prosecutor and witnesses together that no second trial could efficiently take place.'

Sir George then says— "It may be urged, however, that while there is some ground for the distinction between the two classes of cases, there is still a great practical grievance to be remedied. Will any gentleman present take upon himself to affirm the frequency of wrong convictions by juries in criminal cases? If not, the whole groundwork of the proposed measures fails. I will quote (he says) the views of one or two eminent legal authorities on this point.

"Baron Parke, now Lord Wensleydale, when examined before the committee, said— 'I think that the complaints of the present mode of administering the Criminal Law have little foundation, for the cases in which the innocent are improperly convicted, are extremely rare. Some no doubt there are, and I consider p. 12 *it is impossible in any human system of administering justice to avoid such misfortunes occasionally. There are many cases in which the guilty escape, but very few in which the innocent are punished; and having now had more experience upon the Bench in the administration of criminal justice than any other Judge, I can say for myself, that I can hardly call to my recollection any case with which I am personally acquainted, in which I think that a person really innocent has been convicted by the Jury.'*

"Lord Denman expressed a similar opinion—'Juries are extremely unwilling to fall into the error of wrongly convicting. I believe there are a great many very wrong acquittals, and even conscientiously sometimes, from good motives and very respectable feelings, but unfortunately contradicting the truth, and bringing the administration of justice into some contempt, and giving impunity to great offenders.'

"Lord Brougham coincides in that view—'My impression and belief (he said) most undoubtedly is, that there are very rare occasions indeed on which there are wrong convictions.'

"Justice Wightman said—'As far as my experience goes, I entirely concur with Baron Parke in thinking that the conviction of a really innocent person is so rare that there is practically no sufficient necessity for applying a remedy which would be attended with such obvious impediments to the due course of criminal justice.'

"The weight of evidence is, therefore, in favor of the belief that wrong verdicts in criminal cases, at least when they are against the prisoner, are of rare occurrence. But if a wrong verdict is given, and the judge is dissatisfied with it, what is the almost universal result? It is, that the Judge communicates his dissatisfaction to the Home Secretary; and I find it stated by Baron Parke, and assented to by Lord Lyndhurst and Lord Brougham, that such a report is universally acted upon. I maintain, therefore, that no proof of any practical and substantial grievance has been brought before the House, and that none really exists."

Again Sir George says—"I wish now to shew some of the probable consequences with which the Bill is pregnant, in the event of its being passed. These are, first the delay and uncertainty which it would import into the administration of Criminal Law. It is a maxim laid down by all writers on criminal jurisprudence, that punishment is effectual in proportion as it is speedy and certain, and the result of the proposed measure would therefore be to deprive the administration of the Criminal Law of much of its effect.

"Upon this point Lord Brougham said before the Committee of 1848—'The Crimial Law depends for the effect, more or less, which it has in delivering from crime by example of punishment, upon the speediness with which execution of the sentence follows trial. But in this case you would have a prisoner found guilty at York in the first fortnight in July, but no sentence, even in the most flagrant case of murder, ever could be executed till the middle of November following. For certainly in every case of capital conviction, and I believe in every serious case, the moving for a new trial would be a matter of course.' Another important feature in the question, is the expense which the multiplication of trials, and the necessary addition to the number of Judges, would cause. Lord Brougham gave the following opinion as to the probable additions to the Bench, that would be required in the event of Criminal Appeal being established:— 'Another thing is this, for the present number of Judges to do it would be utterly impossible, and then you come to the great difficulty of materially increasing the number of the Judges. Supposing the Bar could furnish the increased number, which is perhaps doubtful, but supposing it could furnish six more Judges to be added to the present fifteen, I beg to know how those Judges could be kept up to the mark for their business?" I do not suppose, of course, that the Hon. and learned gentleman, or any member of this House, would be influenced by the prospect of business at the Bar being increased by the adoption of Appeals, but no less competent an authority than Lord Denman suggested that as a reason for the popularity of the proposal. His Lordship said—'I think there is another *reason for the outcry, which is a great desire, I think, on the part of many active and able persons attached to the law, to see a new Court, and a new course of practice which would be popular and striking, and give a new scope for the display of their talents.'*

"And again Lord Denman said—'I think there are grave objections to any thing which will give countenance to the opinion, that wrong convictions are of frequent occurrence, and that a new Court ought to be erected, or the present Courts empowered to correct them by motions for a second trial. One consequence of such a power might be, a degree of laxity of juries in considering their verdict, and less reluctance to convict on doubtful evidence, because the new trial might correct their mistake. And after all the second trial could not guarantee the security of the truth,—the second Jury is not more infallible than the first.'*

"Lord Brougham said—'Most undoubtedly, if it were thought that you might set an error right by moving for a new trial, there would be a good deal less of that sort of awful feeling of responsibility, under which both Judge, prosecutor's and prisoner's Counsel, and Jury act; whereas at present they feel that what they are doing is remediless, if any error committed. I am quite sure upon Jurors it would have an effect, and this is a question about Jurors rather than about Judges.'*

And Sir George concludes thus—"There is a rule in English Law, which is never departed from—that a penal Statute must be construed strictly. If there is any doubt as to the verbal construction, that doubt always avails in favor of the prisoner. What would be the position of the prisoner if the rules of law, which the honourable gentleman seeks to establish, were substituted for the present law? The Counsel for the prosecution would be able to say with truth, 'Gentlemen of the Jury, if your verdict against the prisoner be wrong, he has an appeal, and it can be set aside, but if you acquit him, your verdict is irreversible, therefore pray incline to the side of severity, and not to that of mercy. If you are wrong, there is an appeal for the prisoner at present at his own expense, though we hope* **p. 13** *soon it will be at the public expense, but if he is acquitted, the Crown and the prosecutor are precluded by your verdict, and the decision is unchangeable. The whole feeling of the Court, which every one familiar with the proceedings of a Criminal Court, knows is tender and merciful towards the prisoner, would be reversed, and there would be found not only a sentiment, but a rational ground for giving the advantage to the prosecutor against the prisoner.'"*

(N.B.: All punctuation markings are reproduced here as in the original document.)

As to the two last jurisdictions proposed to be established by this Bill, are they not *ultra vires* of the Parliament of Canada, and a direct invasion of rights secured to the individual Provinces by the Union Act?

I scarcely know how to discuss the subject, without apparently committing myself to the expression of opinions that may seem to militate against free judicial action hereafter; because I think I can foresee, if the Bill passes in its present shape, many questions of conflict of jurisdiction as likely to arise, on which the Supreme Court of New Brunswick will have to express opinions and pass judgment.

Alive to the caution a Judge should exercise, in confining any opinion he may publicly express to the legal construction of existing Acts rather than on prospective questions, I feel great delicacy in saying any thing that might be construed into a settled judicial opinion on the construction of this Bill, and therefore what I now say I desire may be considered as merely suggestive, and not as a deliberately formed opinion to be held of judicial weight, should the measure become a law; in which event I shall of course hold myself open to decide as I may consider right on a full judicial hearing and consideration of any matter submitted for adjudication. I assume the Parliament of Canada has no power to confer original jurisdiction other than is provided for in 'The British North America Act, 1867.'

By that Act the power of the Dominion Parliament to establish Courts is, as to appellate jurisdiction, apparently full and complete; as to original jurisdiction, limited and restricted. It is by virtue of the Imperial Statute alone that the Parliament of Canada obtains its legislative powers; and the Dominion Parliament and Local Legislatures are alike bound to confine their legislation within the limits therein prescribed. A grave objection then to this Bill would seem to be, that in many particulars it exceeds those limits.

And even if Parliament had the power, the establishment of the proposed Court of Original Jurisdiction would, I fear, be injurious to the interests of New Brunswick; and I wish to be understood in any remarks I have or shall make, as speaking only from a New Brunswick standpoint, leaving those interested in the subject in the other Provinces to deal with the matter in the way that seems to them best.

The effect of the Bill will be, I fear, to weaken and enfeeble the Supreme Court, by depriving it of many of its present powers, and rendering it substantially an inferior Court of comparatively limited jurisdiction; thereby crippling its usefulness, destroying its prestige, and necessarily lowering it in the estimation of the public; and, I fear, not substituting in its place a Court calculated to meet the necessities of the people, or to give that satisfaction which has hitherto been experienced from our present judicial system—a system which has been in operation since the foundation of the Province; which is a counterpart, as near as may be, of that of the mother country, which is well understood through the country; which has worked well, and against which I am not aware that there are any complaints; or if there are, none that the Local Legislature cannot redress. The Courts are accessible at comparatively trifling expense, being held in every County in the Province; and therefore the causes of suitors generally tried in the Counties in which they reside, and the proceedings open to revision before all the Judges, and all conducted and judgment pronounced in a language they can understand. *p. 14*

The case will be very different in the proposed Court—a Court, we shall see, of very extensive original jurisdiction.

The cause—no matter what the amount, however great or however small—no matter in what part of the Province the cause of action arises, however near or however remote—must be tried at Fredericton, whither the suitors and their witnesses must repair.

Then the case will be tried by one Judge, the proceedings before whom will be open to revision within the Province, by two Judges only, the Judge who tried the cause being perhaps one of them—for there is no provision to the contrary—instead of five as the people have heretofore been accustomed to. If further redress is required they must go to Ottawa.

The pleading or process in the suit may be in, to the suitors, a foreign language, and the cause may be discussed at Fredericton, or in Ottawa, and judgment delivered in, what is to the large majority of the people of this Province, a foreign tongue; for we have seen that by section 133 of 'The British North America Act,1867,' it is to be permitted to any person who may choose, to use either the English or French language in any Court of Canada established under the Act—which this Court most certainly is.

If the Courts of the Provinces, as established, have been recreant to their duty, if they have forfeited the confidence of the public, if it is necessary to substitute a new tribunal in their place, and if the Court proposed by this Bill, is the best that can be provided, the case is clear enough, and whatever inconveniences may arise, the public must, from necessity, submit to the change. But as I cannot conceive, at any rate as I hope, that any such case can be presented to Parliament, I humbly think that what is working well, and to which the public is accustomed, and with which they are satisfied, and against which no just complaints (that I have ever heard) have or (as I think) can be truthfully urged, had better be left untouched; believing, as I do, that it is time enough to administer medicine, or apply a remedy, when it is discovered, or there are reasonable grounds for believing that disease exists.

The administration of justice is a delicate subject, and will not stand much experimenting. Palpable evils should be guarded against, and practical grievances remedied. But is there not much truth in the words of Lord Campbell in the House of Lords—"If the present system works well, we are not, with a view to theoretical perfection, to resort to 'the lottery of legislation.'"

But coming to particular provisions—By Section 50, the Governor General, by and with the consent of the Privy Council, may direct a special case to be laid before said Court sitting in general Term, (that is at Ottawa), in which case there may be set forth any Act passed by the Legislature of any Province of the Dominion, and there may be stated for the opinion of such Court such questions as to the constitutionality of said Act, or of any provision or provisions thereof, as the Governor General in Council may order; and by section 51, "said Court shall, after hearing counsel for the Dominion of Canada and for the Province whose Act shall be in question, (if the respective Governments of the Dominion and the Province shall think fit to appear), and also after hearing counsel for such person or persons whose interests may be affected by the said Act, who may desire to be heard touching the questions submitted for the opinion of the said Court, and who shall have obtained leave to appear, and be so heard on application to a Judge of the said Court in Chambers, certify their opinions upon the said special case to the Governor General in Council."

p. 15   Two questions naturally arise—First, by what authority can Parliament establish such a tribunal as this? And secondly, what is to be the effect of this certificate? Is it to have the force of law, and to be from thenceforth binding and conclusive on the Dominion, the Province, and persons interested; or if pronounced *ex parte* at the instance of the Governor General, are all parties, whether cognizant or not of the proceedings, but who may claim to have rights under such laws, to be estopped by such decision, and debarred from any opportunity of asserting their rights, and being heard face to face with their opponents; or is the certificate only for the purpose of advising the Governor General, the better to enable him to exercise his discretion in any given case? But I pass on to the

ORIGINAL JURISDICTION,

which, to my mind, is a very objectionable branch of the Bill.

Section 53 provides that—"The said Supreme Court shall have and possess exclusive original jurisdiction in the Dominion of Canada, in all causes at Law and Equity in the Provinces of Ontario, Nova Scotia, and New Brunswick, and in civil causes in the Province of Quebec, as follows:"—* *

Before proceeding to the list of matters over which exclusive jurisdiction is proposed to be thus given, let us read this section by the light of the Imperial Statute, and see whether we are not approaching a conflict of law, and a clashing of jurisdiction—a state of things of which Lord Campbell in the House of Lords thus spoke—"Surely there cannot be a greater evil than the clashing of jurisdictions in the same State."

We have seen that by the Imperial Statute—Of the exclusive powers of Provincial Legislature—"In each Province the Legislature may exclusively make Laws," coming within the subjects of—

13. "Property and civil rights in the Province."

14. "The administration of justice in the Province, including the constitution, maintenance, and organization of Provincial Courts, both of civil and criminal jurisdiction, and including procedure in civil matters in those Courts."

We have also seen that by the same Statute, the Parliament of Canada, independent of "a General Court of Appeal for Canada," is only empowered to provide "for the establishment of any additional Courts for the *better administration of the Laws of Canada.*"

By what authority then does this Act give exclusive original jurisdiction in causes at Law and in Equity, in matters touching the local laws of the Provinces respectively, as distinguished from the Dominion Laws, or "the Laws of Canada?" Or, touching property or civil rights in the Provinces? Or, by what authority does it interfere with the administration of Justice in the Province, including as before set forth?

Let us now look to the list of subjects, eight in number, and other matters in subsequent sections, exclusively confided to this proposed Court.

No. 1. In all cases in which the constitutionality of any Act of the Legislature of any Province of the Dominion shall come in question.

Is it not obvious, that if exclusive jurisdiction to determine questions, no matter what their nature may be, is vested in this Court, and so taken from the present local Courts, the exclusive rights professed to be secured to the Local Legislatures, are virtually and practically taken away? If so much of the jurisdiction of these Courts can be thus destroyed, why not the balance?

And is this principle not acted on throughout this portion of the Bill? We shall see. *p. 16*

No. 2. In all cases in which it shall be sought to enforce any law of the Dominion of Canada relating to the revenue.

This would seem to come within the power of Parliament, because it relates "to the Laws of Canada." But it practically and substantially sweeps away the Exchequer jurisdiction of the Supreme Court.

No. 3. In all cases in which the Crown, as representing the Government of Great Britain and Ireland, or the government of any British Colony, or the government of any Province of the Dominion, shall be a party, plaintiff or defendant.

This also denudes the Supreme Court of a large jurisdiction; and does it not affect "civil rights" and "the administration of justice, &c.?" If it is the right of Provincialists now to sue or be sued in such cases in local Courts—and have they not such a right—is it not a civil right? If so, where does the Dominion Parliament get authority to interfere with it?

The number of cases to which it may be presumed this paragraph will apply are many, including all bonds given to, or contracts entered into with the Government; all matters affecting the Crown Lands, Mining Leases, &c. &c.; all recognizances with which the Supreme Court has now special statutory power to deal under 33 Hen. 8, c.39, as long since decided in this Province and constantly acted on.

No. 5. In all cases in which any Foreign State or Government shall be a party plaintiff.

It is not likely that many cases of this kind will arise. But the same objections present themselves.

No. 6. In all cases in which any Consul of a Foreign State shall be a party.

The same objections here apply. As matters are in this Province, may it not be fairly asked, why should parties, because they happen to hold the office of Consul, be limited to this new Court, or parties having dealings with them to any extent, however trifling or large, be prevented from asserting their legal civil rights, and from seeking redress in the ordinary and regular tribunals of the country?

In this Province there are, I think, some eight Consuls of Foreign States, besides a number of Consular Agents, all of whom, if I am rightly informed, except one, are permanent residents of the Province, and British subjects, and most, if not all of them, actively engaged in large mercantile and other business operations.

If it is intended to confine "all cases" to suits brought by or against them for acts done in their official capacity, is it so expressed? Is not the plain wording of the section and its grammatical construction, to the contrary; and if so, why should they, or those dealing with them in the ordinary business transactions of life, be placed in a better or worse position than their neighbors and fellow subjects?

No. 7. would seem to be strictly within the power of Parliament.

No. 8. In all cases in which any question shall arise under any Statute or Act of the Parliament of Canada hereafter to be passed, and by which exclusive original jurisdiction shall be conferred on the said Supreme Court.

Under this section, are not conflicts of jurisdiction almost unavoidable?

[NO PAGE 17 — MISTAKE IN ORIGINAL PAGINATION]

If the Parliament of Canada has only a limited authority to constitute *p. 18* Courts of original jurisdiction, can it have power, or can any such clause as this give the Courts it may establish, exclusive jurisdiction to say whether Parliament has or has not exceeded its powers?

Is it not as well the right, as the solemn duty of every Court in the Dominion, to pronounce what the Law is as declared by the Imperial Statute; and if the civil rights of the inhabitants, or the administration of justice in any Province, are interfered with, save by the Imperial Parliament, as possessing transcendent power, or the Local Legislature, to whom within the Dominion they are exclusively confided, will it not be the duty of the Provincial Courts to protect and enforce those rights, even at the risk of a conflict with a Court established regardless of the Union Act, and attempted to be supported by such a clause as this?

By section 57, exclusive original jurisdiction is given to the Supreme Court and the Judges thereof, to issue the writ of *habeas corpus ad subjiciendum* in cases of extradition.

This of course takes from the Supreme Court of this Province, and its Judges, the power they now possess. Unless some of the Judges of the new Court reside in the Maritime Provinces, for which no provision is made, delay and inconvenience must, I should think, ensue, if many cases of this description should arise. Hitherto, however, they have been very rare in this Province.

Section 58 provides—"That the said Supreme Court shall have and possess exclusive jurisdiction in Admiralty in cases of contract and tort, and in proceedings *in rem*, and *in personam*, arising on or in respect of the navigation of, and commerce upon the inland navigable waters of the Dominion, above tide-water, and beyond the jurisdiction of any now existing Court of Vice-Admiralty." This sweeps away a large jurisdiction from the Supreme, the County, and the Magistrates' Courts of the Province, and, unless I am much mistaken, will, before it is very long in operation, astonish not a little some of the merchants, traders, millmen, lumbermen, stream-drivers, steamboat, tugboat, woodboat, and raftsmen, and those dealing with them or suffering from torts committed by them, arising on or in respect of the navigation and commerce upon the inland navigable waters, &c. within this Province, when they discover, that for contract however small, or tort however trifling, and whether committed on or connected with waters in the neighborhood of Fredericton, or waters in the most remote parts of the Province, redress can only be had in this new Court at Fredericton, with an almost certain prospect of revision at Ottawa.

In addition to this exclusive jurisdiction, certain concurrent jurisdiction is likewise given; thus section 56 provides that "the said Supreme Court shall have in the several Provinces of Ontario, Nova Scotia, and New Brunswick, in causes at Law and in Equity, and in the Province of Quebec in civil causes, concurrent and original jurisdiction with the Provincial Courts in the following cases:—

"1. Where the plaintiff and defendant, or one of several plaintiffs, and one of several defendants, are domiciled in different Provinces of the Dominion."

"2. Where either the plaintiff or defendant, or one or more of several plaintiffs, or one or more of several defendants, are domiciled without the Dominion."

This is in no way limited or restricted as to Court or amount; so that for the smallest amount or matter cognizable in a Magistrate's Court, up to the highest cause of action justiciable in the Supreme Court in any of

p. 19   the above cases, a party plaintiff may drag the defendant to Fredericton regardless of the amount in issue, or of expense, or distance. Here again arises the question of civil rights, &c.

Considering the great number of cases that are constantly before our Courts, where some or one of the parties are non-residents, the privilege here given the plaintiff (for the defendant has nothing to say as to the Court in which the plaintiff shall sue) of compelling a defendant, possibly residing in a most distant section of the Province, to defend himself at Fredericton and Ottawa, will entail great inconvenience and expense, and give plaintiffs a power and advantage over their adversary that will, I fear, in many cases, work great hardship, if not injustice. The case would be bad enough if the concurrent jurisdiction was confined to the jurisdiction of the Supreme Court; but when it is to be with the "Provincial Courts," without distinction or limit, the result and consequences will, I fear, be very unsatisfactory. As against this, I can discover no corresponding benefit.

An additional advantage is also given to plaintiffs in such cases, to which I can hardly think they are entitled, and which will in all probability cause the new Court to be often selected, viz: that by section 74, it is provided "That the process of the said Court shall run throughout the Dominion of Canada." This, under many circumstances, may clearly place a plaintiff in a better, and a defendant in a worse position, than those who have to sue and be sued in a Provincial Court, whose process only runs within its own Province.

By section 65 it is declared—"That the rule of decision in all civil actions (except causes in Admiralty) which may be brought in the Province of Quebec, shall be the law of the said Province, and the procedure in such suits shall be regulated by the Code of Procedure of the said Province."

And by section 66, that "the rule of decision in all actions at law, and suits in Equity brought or instituted in the said Court, in any of the Provinces of Ontario, Nova Scotia, and New Brunswick, shall be the law of England."

The first of these sections seems intelligible and reasonable, but section 66 has puzzled me not a little; and I must confess I am still at a loss to understand what is really intended, for I cannot think the only legitimate construction its language seems to bear, could have been contemplated. The rule of decision in Quebec is to be "the law of the said Province." But in Ontario, Nova Scotia, and New Brunswick, the rule of decision is to be the law of England. "*Expressio unius est exclusio alterius.*" Therefore while the law of the Province of Quebec is to prevail in Quebec to the exclusion of any other law; in Ontario, Nova Scotia, and New Brunswick, the law of England is to prevail—necessarily to the like exclusion.

In New Brunswick, why should the laws of New Brunswick, and the laws of the Dominion so far as applicable to New Brunswick, not be the rule of decision? And so in the other Provinces respectively.

Where does the Parliament of Canada get the power thus summarily to wipe away, in the mass of cases over which exclusive original jurisdiction is given, the laws of the Provinces? And in cases of concurrent jurisdiction, giving different rules of decision as the action may be brought in one or the other of the Courts, that is to say, if brought in the new Court, the rule of decision will be the law of England; if brought in the Provincial Court, the rule of decision will be the law of the Province.

Is the rule of decision to be the Common Law of England, or the Statute Law, or both combined? Probably the latter, as we find distinctions expressed where either is to be the rule alone. Thus, in section 15, the *p. 20*   proceedings there referred to are to be "according to the course of the Common Law of England." So in section 68, the trial of the issue there provided for, is to be "according to the rules of the Common Law of England." But by section 72, the procedure in actions against the Crown, is to be as nearly as possible "according to the Act of the Imperial Parliament, known as the Petition of Right's Act."

This 66th sect. as it stands, if it bears the construction indicated, is perhaps the most comprehensive, yet brief repealing and enacting clause to be found in the annals of Legislation, and renders, it seems to me, wholly unnecessary any adoption or enactment by the Local Legislatures of a uniform system of Laws; because a simple Act taking away the balance of jurisdiction left to the Provincial Courts, and giving it exclusively to this Court, with an enactment that the rule of decision shall be the law of England, or any other law, effects the object: for if Parliament can fix one rule, why not another?—and uniformity is established.

But that Parliament has any such power, is a question which, with all humility I submit, will, in all probability, in some quarters be sternly denied, and therefore before any step is taken involving consequences not to be desired, all doubt should be removed.

Referring again to section 68, which declares that "issues of fact on the Common Law side of the said Court shall be tried according to the rules of the Common Law of England, by Jury." Read this in connection with section 66. Why should the laws of New Brunswick, and the improvements the Legislature of New Brunswick have made in the Common Law in regard to trials of issues of fact by Juries, be wholly ignored? When such special care has been taken to respect the law and procedure of the Province of Quebec,—(*vide* section 65 and the latter clause of section 89,) why should the system of seven jurors, and a decision (after two hours deliberation) by five, be abolished, and we be brought back in civil cases to the old Common Law system of twelve, and unanimity? I believe all parties connected with the administration of justice in this Province will admit the change has worked to a charm, and I once heard my most respected predecessor, Sir James Carter, speak of it as practically the greatest and best legal reform that had ever come under his observation.

Is this change no interference with civil rights in, and with the exclusive legislative power of the Local legislature of this Province?

Supposing for a moment it was neither; why this retrograde movement? If our Legislators have had the boldness, and I think I may say, the intelligence, to inaugurate an improved system, and it has been found after fifteen years experience to work well, and to answer the most sanguine expectations, and if the people of this Province are entirely content with its operation, why take it away, and introduce the anomaly that

must necessarily follow; that is to say—In one Court of exclusive jurisdiction in civil cases, parties will be compelled to try issues of fact by one
rule and with one description of jury, and in other Courts of the Province,
with no less important issues, a different rule and entirely different jury
must dispose of the question. And in concurrent jurisdictions, if a party
plaintiff chooses to take his opponent into the Court proposed to be
established under this Bill, before such opponent can successfully defend
himself and get a verdict, he must satisfy twelve minds; but if sued in
other Courts of the Province, if he can convince five out of seven jurors
that he is right, no harm can come to him, because he secures his verdict.
Can it be said that "civil rights" are not affected by this operation?

But apart from this, is it not a violation of all correct principle, that
in the same Province there should be, in Courts having the same juris- *p. 21*
diction, two different rules of decision, and two substantially different
modes of proceeding before juries; and that one side should have the
arbitrary privilege, by selecting a particular Court, of choosing which rule
and procedure shall be adopted, and the other side, without the chance
of a hearing, and without appeal, be bound arbitrarily to submit to such
selection.

The only other point on which I shall make any remarks, though it
involves no principle, and is personal to the profession, is still one I feel
of sufficient importance to be worthy of further consideration.—It is as
to sections 87 and 88, by which a serious, and I think an unnecessary
burthen is cast on the Barristers and Attorneys of the Provinces, by the
condition on which they are to be permitted to practice in this Court, viz.
by admission in general term, which is at Ottawa, and "upon paying such
fees" as the said Court shall fix and determine, and upon signing a roll
to be kept in the custody of the Registrar of said Court, who by section
77 is required to reside and keep his Office at the City of Ottawa.

The Act entitles Barristers and Attorneys to admission as of right;
and it seems hard that to avail themselves of this right, they should all
be required to make a journey to Ottawa, simply to pay fees and sign a
roll; whereas a simple declaration in the Act that Barristers and Attorneys
of the Superior Courts of the Provinces, so long as they shall properly
conduct themselves as such, shall be Barristers and Attorneys of said
Court, would seem to accomplish everything. If so, by simple operation
of law, the journey, the roll, and the fees, are rendered alike unnecessary,
and the profession exempt from what otherwise, I am sure, would be
looked upon as a substantial grievance.

I feel I should be open to reproach if, after taking so many exceptions,
I did not attempt to offer some scheme presenting fewer objections.

Without going into minute details, I will take the liberty of suggesting what I conceive would, in its practical working, be found to be an easily accessible, and, at the same time, simple, cheap, expeditious, and efficient appellate jurisdiction.

A Court of Appeal for Canada—pure and simple, without original jurisdiction—to be simply a Court of *dernier ressort*, to correct the errors of inferior tribunals.

In the high appellate Courts in England—the House of Lords—the Judicial Committee of the Privy Council—the Lords' Justices—the Exchequer Chamber—we find no union of appellate and original jurisdiction.

The Court of Appeal to be composed of the Chief Justice and
Senior Judge (or one of the Judges) of the Queen's Bench
of Ontario, ... 2
The Chief Justice and Senior Judge (or one of the Judges) of the
Common Pleas of Ontario, ... 2
The Chancellor of Ontario, ... 1
The Chief Justice and Senior Judge (or one of the Judges) of the
Queen's Bench of Quebec, ... 2
The Chief Justice and Senior Judge (or one of the Judges) of the
Superior Court of Quebec, ... 2
The Chief Justice of the Supreme Court and Judge in Equity in
Nova Scotia, ... 2
The Chief Justice and Senior Judge (or one of the Judges) of the
Supreme Court of New Brunswick, ... <u>2</u>
                                                                                                          13

p. 22   We have various jurisdictions to be appealed from—Common Law, civil and criminal; Equity; Matrimonial; Maritime; Bankruptcy; Probate, &c. &c. Is it not desirable that as many Judges as possible, conversant from daily judicial connection with those matters, should form the Court of Appeal, rather than that untried men who have never had any judicial experience, should reverse or affirm the judgments of men so experienced.

The Court to be divided into

A GENERAL APPEAL COURT,

to sit at Ottawa twice a year, and if necessary, by adjournment, in vacation; to be composed of all the Judges—five to be a quorum; and

CIRCUIT APPEAL COURTS,

to sit in each of the Provinces twice a year, and if necessary, by adjournment, in vacation; to be composed of any three of said Judges, not being members of the Court whose judgment is appealed from, or who shall not have taken part in the judgment appealed from.

JURISDICTION

Appeals to be allowed from all the Inferior Courts of the Provinces of the Dominion, (on complying with the provision herein contained, and on security being given in all cases for costs, and in the discretion of the Court appealed from, for damages,) from any final decree, judgment, or sentence, or against any rule or order made in any civil suit or action having the effect of a final or definitive sentence; but an order which does not put a final end to the case, or which does not establish any principle which will finally affect the merits of the case, nor deprive the party of any benefit which he may have at a final hearing, to be considered interlocutory, from in which no appeal to be allowed. No appeal to be allowed in matters resting the discretion of the Court only; nor for mere technical or formal objections apart from the merits of the case; nor for objections not raised in the Court below, and on which a decision was made or omitted to be made, unless patent on the face of the proceedings, so that the Appellate Court may take judicial notice of the objections. It being the intention that all cases shall be decided on the merits, according to substantial justice, and not on technical objections of form not affecting the substance of the matter in controversy.

No appeal to be allowed under $400, or some other reasonable sum to be determined, unless in causes matrimonial or testamentary; or of Admiralty jurisdiction; or where the title to land is in question; or an important principle of law of general application is involved; or where the validity of an Act of Parliament, or of any of the Local Legislatures, is in question; or where there is an apparent conflict arising under the laws of the Provinces, or between any of those laws and the laws of the Dominion. The appeal in the first instance to be to the Circuit Appeal Court of the Province in which the cause is pending—whose decision shall be final if judgment of the Court below was unanimous, and the judgment of the Circuit Appeal Court thereon is likewise unanimous; unless the Circuit Appeal Court in its discretion shall, with or without imposing special terms, allow an appeal to the General Appeal Court at Ottawa; and except that an appeal to the General Court be allowed of right in all cases in which the Queen, the Dominion, a Foreign State, or public ministers and officers in their official capacity, are interested; and in all cases in which the judgment of the Court below, or the judgment of the Appeal Court is not unanimous, or the judgment of the Court below is reversed. But in all such last cases, where the judgment is not unani- *p. 23* mous, only on giving security for debt and costs, or to abide the final determination, unless in such last cases, under special and exceptional circumstances, the Circuit Appeal Court shall allow an appeal, then upon such terms as such Court shall think just and expedient. A writ of Error to be brought in said Circuit Appeal Courts respectively, from judgments in any civil action of any of the Courts of said Provinces respectively, in any case in which proceedings have been according to the course of the Common law, and appeals thereon shall be allowed from Circuit Appeal Courts in like manner and on like terms as are provided for appeals therefrom in ordinary cases; and such proceedings to be, as nearly as possible, in conformity with the practice of the Exchequer Chamber in England.

No appeal to be allowed in any case unless a notice of intention to appeal, containing the grounds of appeal, be given to the opposite side, and a copy thereof filed in the office of the Clerk of the Court appealed from within thirty days.

The appellant to comply with terms of appeal, and transmit to the Appeal Court within three months copies of all proceedings, with the decision appealed from, and the reasons therefor. Parties agreeing thereto, to be allowed to present their case to either Appellate Court by printed instead of oral arguments, the appellant stating his case, and furnishing a copy thereof to the opposite side, who shall, if he chooses, answer the same, furnishing the appellant with a copy thereof; the appellant to have the right of reply: copies of all of which to be filed in the Court below, and furnished to the Judges of the Appellate Court, who may give judgment thereon in like manner as if the case was argued orally before such Court.

Barristers and Attorneys of the Superior Courts of the Provinces to be Barristers and Attorneys of the Appeal Court.

The decision of the General Appeal Court to be final and conclusive, unless in cases involving questions of a national and perhaps a constitutional character, where the appeal to the Judicial Committee to be retained.

By this scheme, all matters of trifling value, involving no important principle, are left to the final decision of the local tribunals.

An appeal in other cases is furnished at the door as it were of the suitors, and is only final when the adjudication is the unanimous decision of the Supreme Court of the Province, and of the Appellate Circuit Court composed of three Judges who have had no connection with the original judgment, and even then, in certain exceptional cases, a further appeal may be had of right, and in others, if the Circuit Appellate Court think the same reasonable.

With reference to the extra duty this would throw on the Judges—with the number named I should think the labor would be comparatively light.

Speaking for New Brunswick, with the Court composed, as it has been for upwards of thirty years, of five Judges, I should think satisfactory arrangements could be made. If, from experience, the work should prove too burthensome, the difficulty could be easily obviated by strengthening the Local Courts.

Such an Appeal Court, with ample power to review all judgments rendered, would, without disturbing existing judicial institutions, and unsettling men's minds, in my opinion, without any additional Court of original jurisdiction, secure to the Dominion that appoints all the Judges of the Superior Courts, not only uniform judgment on the constitutionality and construction of all Dominion and Provincial Statutes, but a proper and uniform administration of all local laws, as well as the consistent execution of its own laws, as distinguished from those of the Province; a power no doubt essential to good order, and the avoidance of contradiction, confusion, and conflict of authority, and at the same time *p. 24* essential to the efficient working of the general Government.

My strong opinion of the grave importance of this measure, must be my apology for my great prolixity. The objections I have suggested are conceived in no captious spirit, but are prompted solely by a desire for the general good.

Whatever legislation Parliament in its wisdom may adopt, I shall, so far as I can, cheerfully and loyally give effect to, in the Court over which I have the honor to preside. I am quite alive to the fact, that in the words of an English Jurist, "my duty is plain—it is to expound and not to make the law, to decide on it as I find it, not as I wish to be."

W. J. RITCHIE,

Fredericton, 1st Feb. 1870.   *Chief Justice.*

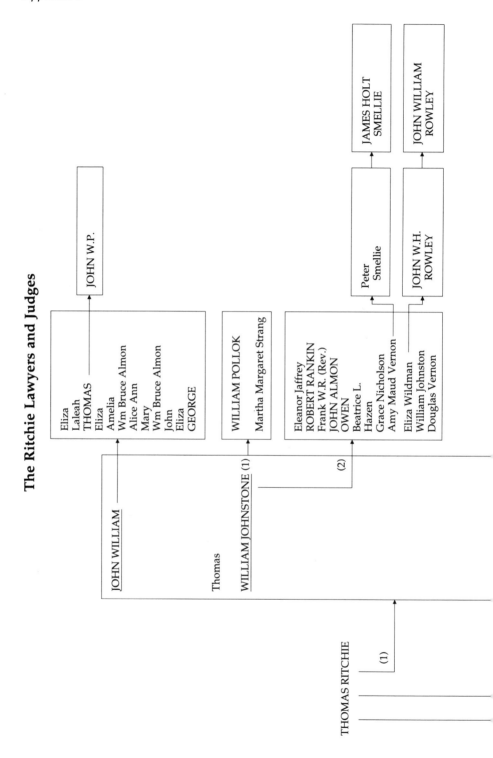

The Ritchie Lawyers and Judges

JOHN W.P.

Eliza
Laleah
THOMAS
Eliza
Amelia
Wm Bruce Almon
Alice Ann
Mary
Wm Bruce Almon
John
Eliza
GEORGE

JOHN WILLIAM

Thomas

WILLIAM JOHNSTONE (1)

WILLIAM POLLOK

Martha Margaret Strang

(2)

Eleanor Jaffrey
ROBERT RANKIN
Frank W.R. (Rev.)
JOHN ALMON
OWEN
Beatrice L.
Hazen
Grace Nicholson
Amy Maud Vernon
Eliza Wildman
William Johnston
Douglas Vernon

Peter
Smellie

JOHN W.H.
ROWLEY

JAMES HOLT
SMELLIE

JOHN WILLIAM
ROWLEY

THOMAS RITCHIE

(1)

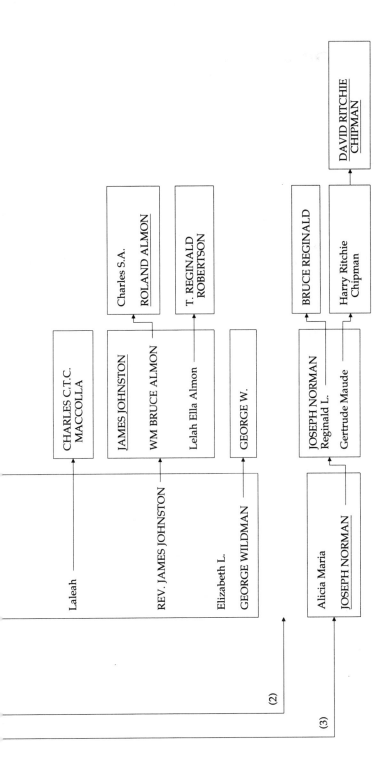

Capitalized Names Indicate Members of the Legal Profession

Underlined Names Indicate Judges of the Superior Courts

* All persons bear the name Ritchie except where a name on a second line appears.

There is a Land

There is a land that we must love,
A land both wide and fair,
A land of pine and maple trees and beauty everywhere,
And there free hearts have found a home,
And space to still be free,
Fronting the morrow confident in her high destiny.
When the leaves are crimson,
When the fields are white,
When the woods are green in spring
Or bathed in summer light,
Be sure we love her dearly,
Her woods, her streams, her flowers,
This sunny pine and mapleland,
This Canada of ours.

And, oh! her skies are bright and blue,
Her waters, bright and pure,
There's balm within her forest shades
All world worn men to cure;
The wholesome sea is at her gates,
Her gates both east and west,
Then is it strange that we should love
This land, our land, the best?
When the hills stand dreaming,
When the winter's here,
When the slumbering earth awakes,
Or summer crowns the year;
Be sure we love her dearly,
Her woods, her streams, her flowers,
This sunny pine and mapleland,
This Canada of ours.

J.A. RITCHIE, K.C.
Ottawa, 1920.

Index